The Art of Attacking Chess

Zenon Franco

Translated by Phil Adams

First published in the UK by Gambit Publications Ltd 2008

ISBN-13: 978-1-904600-97-8
ISBN-10: 1-904600-97-2

DISTRIBUTION:
Worldwide (except USA): Central Books Ltd, 99 Wallis Rd, London E9 5LN, England.
Tel +44 (0)20 8986 4854 Fax +44 (0)20 8533 5821. E-mail: orders@Centralbooks.com

Gambit Publications Ltd, 99 Wallis Rd, London E9 5LN, England.
E-mail: info@gambitbooks.com
Website (regularly updated): www.gambitbooks.com

Edited by Graham Burgess
Typeset by John Nunn
Cover image by Wolff Morrow
Printed in Great Britain by The Cromwell Press, Trowbridge, Wilts.

10 9 8 7 6 5 4 3 2 1

Gambit Publications Ltd
Managing Director: Murray Chandler GM
Chess Director: Dr John Nunn GM
Editorial Director: Graham Burgess FM
German Editor: Petra Nunn WFM
Webmaster: Dr Helen Milligan WFM

Contents

Symbols

+	check
++	double check
#	checkmate
!!	brilliant move
!	good move
!?	interesting move
?!	dubious move
?	bad move
??	blunder
Ch	championship
corr.	correspondence game
1-0	the game ends in a win for White
½-½	the game ends in a draw
0-1	the game ends in a win for Black
(D)	see next diagram

Dedication

To Asunción and Tea

Bibliography

Books

El Ajedrez como yo lo juego, Paul Keres, Editorial Sopena, 1963
Second Piatigorsky Cup, Isaac Kashdan, Dover, 1968
The Life and Games of Mikhail Tal, Mikhail Tal, RHM Press, 1976
El Estilo Posicional, Vladimir Simagin, Editorial Aguilera, 1983
Averbakh's Selected Games, Yuri Averbakh, Cadogan, 1998
Super Nezh, Alex Pishkin, Thinkers' Press, 2000
Storming the Barricades, Larry Christiansen, Gambit, 2000
Vishy Anand: My Best Games of Chess (2nd edition), Vishy Anand, Gambit, 2001
I play against pieces (*sic*), Svetozar Gligorić, Batsford, 2002
Smyslov's Best Games, Volumes I & II, Vasily Smyslov, Chess Agency Caissa-90, 2003
Mis geniales predecesores 2-4, Garry Kasparov, Ediciones Meran, 2004-6
School of Chess Excellence, Volumes 1 to 4, Mark Dvoretsky, Edition Olms, 2001-4
Garry Kasparov's Greatest Chess Games Volume 1, Igor Stohl, Gambit, 2005
Secrets of Chess Training, Mark Dvoretsky, Edition Olms, 2006
The Revolution in the 70s, Part 1, Garry Kasparov, Everyman, 2007
San Luis 2005, Alik Gershon & Igor Nor, Quality Chess, 2007

Periodicals and Electronic

Informator 1-99, 1966-2007
New in Chess Magazine, 1984-2007
Mega Database 2008, ChessBase
Chess Today, 2005-7

Engines

Shredder 9
Fritz 10
Deep Junior 10
Rybka 2.3

Introduction

Mikhail Tal once wrote that on the day before the start of the Alekhine Memorial tournament in 1963, at the birthday party of one of his friends, who was a non-chess-player, someone suddenly expressed a wish that the 'Magician from Riga' should sacrifice something in his first game, against the Dutchman Kuijpers.

"Which piece, and on which square would you like it?" asked Tal jokingly. "A knight, on e6" was the reply.

Naturally Tal soon forgot all about this conversation. The next day, the game against Kuijpers proceeded quietly but then became complicated until, in serious time-pressure, the following position arose:

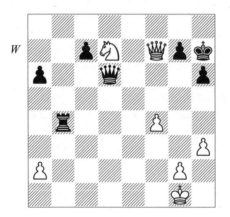

Mikhail Tal – Franciscus Kuijpers
Alekhine memorial, Moscow 1963

The final moves were **36 ♘f8+ ♚h8 37 ♘e6** and faced with unstoppable mate, Black resigned.

On leaving the stage, Tal was surrounded by his friends. "Good lord, did you do it on purpose?" one of them asked. Tal did not understand what he was talking about. "You know, make that last move with your knight to e6", his friend explained.

Only then did Tal remember the conversation of the day before and realize what the fuss was all about. He wrote: "I realized that my chess prestige in these circles had risen sharply, and so as to maintain this, I pompously asked: What would you like me to sacrifice tomorrow, and where?"

This amusing anecdote from one of the greatest attacking virtuosos in history shows the extent to which the course of the game depends less on one's own wishes than on the aspect that the game is taking on, which in turn depends on a host of factors.

Not even someone like Tal can go to play a game, take a deep breath and with a fierce gaze towards the infinite and a resolute expression, simply say to himself: "Today I'm going to attack!".

An attack requires factors that make it advisable and, according to Steinitz, even obligatory, since, as the first World Champion said: "The side that has the advantage is obliged to attack, or lose the advantage."

This dictum is also applicable to balanced positions where there is an advantage on one wing, which generally implies that the opponent has the advantage on the other wing, so that if one side fails to pursue his own attack, this is equivalent to surrendering the initiative to the other side.

There are certain set-ups which clearly force you to attack; a familiar one is where the kings are castled on opposite wings, when victory often goes to the side who wins the attacking race.

Another obvious example is when one side has the bishop-pair aimed along open diagonals at the enemy's castled position, or similarly an open file facing the enemy's castled position, etc., when of course the first idea that springs to mind, and possibly the right one, is to attack the enemy king.

There are attacking players *par excellence* – among others, Adolf Anderssen, Mikhail Tal, the young Paul Keres, Garry Kasparov, and at present Veselin Topalov all immediately spring to mind – but in modern chess we are seeing more players whose style is many-sided, players capable of playing all types of position with equal skill.

This is the so-called 'universal style', the main exponent of which used to be Boris Spassky; in this category we can now include Vishy Anand, Boris Gelfand, Vasily Ivanchuk, and many others.

Perhaps we should qualify this with regard to some games by top-class masters; opening theory now extends well into the middlegame, and chess fashion dictates that some complex lines are played repeatedly, so that sometimes the top players have a greater possibility of knowing whether the game that day will be a complex tactical struggle, with attacks, or a simpler endgame. But this is alien to the majority of chess-players, mere mortals like ourselves, for whom the real struggle on the board begins much earlier.

The attack in chess is of supreme importance, and mastering its secrets is a goal to which we all aspire, but of course the art of attack is not confined to putting a brilliant finishing touch to an advantageous position.

Referring to Alekhine's extraordinary play, Spielmann once wrote "I can comprehend Alekhine's combinations well enough, but where he gets his attacking chances from and how he infuses life into the very opening – that is beyond me." Achieving the positions where combinations are possible is indeed the most difficult task. In this book we shall not only see games with brilliant conclusions but also examine the different stages in the creation of these finishes. For this purpose, within (or supplementary to) each main game we shall frequently examine other complete games which will help us gain a broader view and a better understanding.

In choosing the examples, with a few exceptions, I deliberately went for games that are not well known and already widely annotated.

The book consists of seven chapters:

Chapter 1 deals with positions in which at least one of the kings remains in the centre and this plays an important part in the game.

In Chapter 2 we shall examine attacking positions with the kings situated on opposite wings.

Chapter 3 focuses on games where the attack is directed against a king which has castled on the kingside, and certain weaknesses in the castled position are exploited.

Chapter 4 is devoted to positions in which one side brings about or exploits a numerical superiority of attacking forces in the sector where the enemy king is located.

Chapter 5 features a close examination of positions with the so-called 'Horwitz Bishops'[1].

In Chapter 6 we shall survey various strategic themes which are of great importance with respect to the attack.

---

1 Named after Bernhard Horwitz (1808-85), a notable German player and composer.

Before each game there will be a short description of the contest. During the game we shall look at related examples to try to understand better what is happening, and at the end there will be a rather fuller summary of the key moments and lessons of the game. In some cases, one or more relevant supplementary games follow.

After you finish the chapters there are exercises involving themes we have covered; the more the reader is successful, the more pleased the author will be.

I should like to thank IM David Martinez Martin for his comments and suggestions. I want to stress that all the stages in the creation of this book have given me great pleasure, from the moment of initial bewilderment, when one is as if standing before a mountain that seems impossible to climb, to the point when the ideas begin to take shape and the goal of expressing everything one wants to say no longer seems unattainable, then to that moment when one feels that the book is taking on a life of its own, with a certain harmony. All of this has given the author immense pleasure.

1 The King in the Centre

In this first chapter we shall see games in which the king remains temporarily or permanently in the centre.

It is obvious that the king is generally more vulnerable in the centre than on one of the wings, since it has little protection. It is risky not to transfer the king to a place of safety as soon as the pieces are developed.

Generally when a player chooses to leave his king in the centre, there is a specific reason – he is hoping to gain something in return. The most common is to gain a material advantage, when the player hopes that the king's exposure will prove a temporary issue. Castling may also be delayed in order to seek long-term strategic advantages, such as better structure, bishop-pair, etc. Sometimes a player simply judges that the king is safer in the centre than on a wing where all the opponent's pieces are just waiting for him to castle, so that they can launch a dangerous attack. Or that delaying castling makes it harder for the opponent to make a purposeful plan.

If the boundary between an acceptable risk and a rash undertaking is a clear one, the decision is easy, but this is not always the case. The more experience we have in assessing these positions, the better equipped we shall be to make these judgements.

Game 1
Viktor Kupreichik – Spyridon Skembris
European Team Ch, Debrecen 1992
Petroff Defence, 5 c4

Of course, wasting tempi with the black pieces, even for apparently good reasons, can have fatal consequences. On the other hand, if White does this it is generally not so serious, since the advantage of the first move minimizes the defects of wasting a tempo.

The type of position is also important. If the centre is closed, such a loss of time is of less significance, and there is a greater chance that the 'lapse' will escape punishment, and thus might be justified in order to gain some permanent advantage.

In our first game we see an untypical case; White does not want to simplify and, so as not to exchange pieces, he does not hesitate to lose time, relying on regaining the tempi by harassing the opponent's pieces.

We shall also see that in this respect there are limits, although in order to demonstrate this Black had to display great imagination.

1 e4 e5 2 ♘f3 ♘f6 3 ♘xe5 d6 4 ♘f3 ♘xe4 5 c4 ♗e7 6 d4 0-0 7 ♗d3 ♘g5 *(D)*

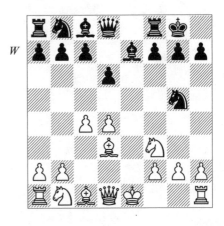

The captures 8 ♘xg5 and 8 ♗xg5 are the most usual moves, but the player of the white pieces, who has a markedly aggressive style, is not looking for a quiet game; he wants to keep as many pieces as possible on the board and so makes an ambitious and non-standard move.

8 ♘fd2?!

White flouts the rules of development and tries to prove that the g5-knight is badly placed; the idea is to gain tempi with f4 and then bring the knight back to f3.

This sort of manoeuvre, delaying natural development in the search for an advantage of some kind – spatial in this case – would be very risky if played by Black, but with White the extra tempo can protect you, so it is an idea worth considering. Even if in the end it proves not to be advantageous, the punishment is generally not serious.

There is only one open file here and Black is not so well developed, so that it looks like an interesting idea. However, the fact that the risk for White appears slight can also reduce his sense of danger.

In a later game Kupreichik played 8 ♘g1, with the same idea as 8 ♘fd2, because the knight is placed very awkwardly on d2, although this is not obvious at this point.

8...♘c6 *(D)*

Black replies in the most natural manner, developing and attacking the centre. It was also possible to prevent f4-f5 with the more radical 8...f5.

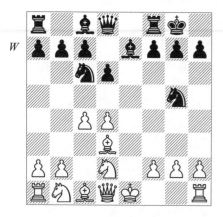

9 ♘b3

Another move with an already-developed piece, but the centre has to be supported. Instead, 9 d5?! is no good because of 9...♘b4, and

the d3-bishop cannot retreat owing to the reply 10...♗f5.

Neither can the main idea of 8 ♘fd2 yet be carried out, since 9 f4? is answered by 9...♘e6 10 d5 ♘xf4!, destroying the white centre.

If White could now complete his development undisturbed with ♘c3, 0-0, etc., retaining his space advantage 'for free', his opening strategy would be justified, and he would gain the advantage. However, Black has more pieces in play, and will try to prevent this.

9...♘b4 *(D)*

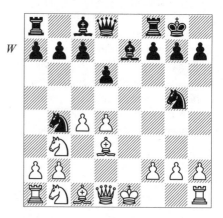

Hunting the more dangerous bishop, which does not have a good retreat-square; if 10 ♗e2 then 10...♗f5, and Black continues to develop his pieces with gain of time.

10 f4?

Now this is definitely playing with fire. The cautious 10 0-0 is preferable, but then obviously his 8th move could not be justified. Black could play quietly 10...♘xd3 11 ♕xd3 and then, among other things, 11...d5, with a good position, or the sharper 10...a5!?, the main idea of which is revealed after 11 f4 ♘h3+! 12 gxh3 a4, regaining the piece having seriously weakened White's castled position. Black's initiative more than compensates for White's material advantage after 13 ♗e4 axb3 14 ♕xb3 d5 15 cxd5 ♗d6 16 ♗d2 ♖e8; White's king is weak and his pawn-structure destroyed.

10...♗g4!

In the last three moves White has moved an already-developed piece and advanced his f-pawn, whereas Black has brought two inactive pieces into play, so it is logical that most tactical confrontations will now be favourable to Black.

11 ♕d2 *(D)*

The white king would not have any decent shelter either after 11 ♕xg4 ♘xd3+ 12 ♔e2 f5 (12...♘e4 is also playable) 13 ♕g3 ♘xc1+ 14 ♖xc1 ♘e4; the move f4 has left a terrible hole at e4.

If 11 ♗e2 then 11...♗f5! follows and after 12 0-0 (not 12 fxg5? ♘c2+ 13 ♔f2 ♘xa1 14 ♘xa1 ♗xb1 winning) 12...♘e6 Black threatens 13...♘c2 and is ready to harass the white centre with ...♗f6 and/or ...d5.

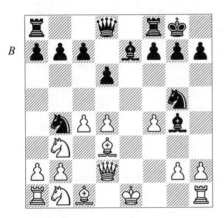

11...♘f3+!!

The most elegant move, and the strongest. It is not possible for Black to continue the policy of introducing more pieces into the battle with 11...♖e8?, since White can finally get his king to safety with 12 0-0, even gaining material after 12...♘xd3 13 ♕xd3 ♘e6 14 h3, followed by g4 and f5.

11...♘xd3+?! 12 ♕xd3 ♘e6 is not convincing either, as White can play 13 h3, once again with the idea of g4 and f5.

12 gxf3 ♗h4+ 13 ♔f1 *(D)*

The most resilient. Instead 13 ♔e2? loses, since it allows another black piece to enter the battle: 13...♖e8+ 14 ♔d1 ♗xf3+ winning. Nor is 13 ♔d1 ♗xf3+ 14 ♗e2 ♗xh1 15 ♕xb4 satisfactory, since Skembris's suggestion 15...a5! is strong. This is the key move in several lines – there are tactics based on the limited mobility of the b3-knight. Then 16 ♕c3 (16 ♘xa5? loses to 16...c5) is met by 16...♖e8, when it is not

possible to develop the queenside with 17 ♘1d2 owing to 17...a4, whilst if 17 a4, Black has many ways to continue, such as 17...♖xe2! 18 ♔xe2 ♕d7, when the white king is very exposed and cannot resist the four black pieces.

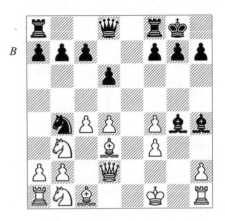

13...♗h3+

Hemming in the white king. This is a logical decision for a human, and a good one, even though the computer shows that 13...♗xf3! 14 ♕xb4 ♖e8! is even better; once the black queen comes into play the white king will be unable to hold out; for example, 15 ♗d2 ♕d7 16 f5 ♗e2+! 17 ♗xe2 ♕xf5+.

However, the fact that the computer is able to come up with something stronger ought not to be a compelling reason for trying to play like a computer – indeed, the computer might well show later that it was actually stronger to play using logic and the human's limited calculating ability after all.

What other lessons can we draw from this example? The most important is that calculation is of prime importance in positions of this type and the general rules are just a guide, not an imperative.

Let us also note the vital importance not only of the absence of the white queen from the defence, but also of the great difficulties that White has in untangling his queenside and helping out the king.

14 ♔e2 *(D)*

Worse is 14 ♔g1? ♘xd3 15 ♕xd3 ♕e8! (threatening 16...♕e1+) 16 ♗d2 f5, with a quick mate.

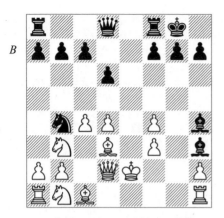

And now? How should Black continue the attack? Once again there are several tempting options. There is 14...罝e8+ bringing the rook into play, although after 15 ♔d1 there is no immediate win.

Even though it involves making another move with an already-developed piece, 14...♗g2 comes into consideration. After 15 罝g1 罝e8+ White cannot now retreat his king to d1, but unfortunately after 16 ♗e4! Black has two pieces under attack, and although he will regain the piece with a later ...f5, White benefits from the simplification.

We can reformulate the earlier question as "which other pieces can come into play?"

14...a5!!

A dual-purpose move, not only defending the b4-knight, and so postponing the capture ...♘xd3 until a more favourable moment, but also leaving the threat of ...a4 hanging over the white position. The unfortunate position of the white knight on b3 makes this move especially tempting. Another advantage is that the black queen can come into play, and the a8-rook might also end up a beneficiary of the complications.

15 ♔d1

White is unable to develop his queenside; if 15 ♘c3? then 15...a4, whilst 15 a3 is met by 15...罝e8+ 16 ♔d1 ♘xd3 17 ♕xd3 ♗f2, followed by ...♗g2 and ...♕h4; Skembris points out the weakness of the h1-rook, the h2-pawn, and of course the white king on d1.

15 d5!? was worth considering, trying to create a good square for the b3-knight. Then if

15...c5 White can insist on securing use of the d4-square with 16 dxc6 (D).

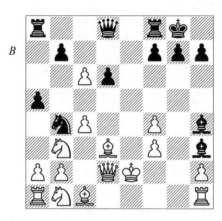

Then 16...bxc6 17 ♘c3 might follow, when Black too could benefit from the opening of lines with 17...♕b6, threatening 18...♕f2+. Then 18 ♔d1 is best. The position is still uncomfortable for White, since his mobility problems persist, but of course there is nothing immediately decisive.

16...♘xc6! is stronger, escaping from the glare of the white queen and thus renewing the threat of 17...a4. If then 17 ♗c2? (to provide the d4-square for the b3-knight), there follows 17...a4 18 ♘d4 ♕b6! (taking advantage of the fact that allowing the queen to invade at f2 would be fatal) 19 罝d1 罝ae8+ winning. 17 ♗e4 looks better, but White's lack of development and poor coordination allow the attack to flare up anew; a possible continuation is 17...罝e8 18 ♔d1 罝xe4! 19 fxe4 ♗g4+ 20 ♔c2 ♗f3, and even with a rook less Black is able to concentrate his forces against the white king after 21 罝f1 ♘b4+ 22 ♔c3 ♗xe4, with a winning advantage. There does not appear to be any defence to the h4-bishop entering play via f6, or the queen after ...d5 or via b6. For example, 23 ♘d4 ♘d5+! 24 cxd5 (24 ♔b3 loses even more quickly, to 24...♕b6+) 24...♕c7+ 25 ♔b3 ♕c5!, with mate in view.

We now return to 15 ♔d1 (D):

15...♕d7

This is partly to be able, depending on circumstances, to capture on d3 and follow up with ...♗f5, and partly to enable the queen to

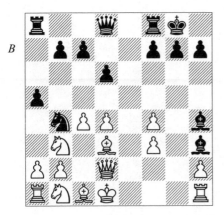

come into play via c6. The main alternative is 15...♖e8!, a move which is almost always useful, and also means that the queen can come into play via b6 after a timely ...c5, as we saw earlier.

16 a3?!

16 d5! is better, as then 16...c5 17 dxc6 bxc6 18 ♘c3 is slightly better for White than in the note to White's 15th move, since there is no ...♕b6.

16...♘xd3 17 ♕xd3 ♗f5!

White has managed to exchange a piece but this does not relieve his position much since, as well as still having more forces in play, Black now also has control of the light squares, in particular the b1-h7 diagonal, and this deprives the white king of this possible escape-route.

18 ♕c3 (D)

Forced; 18 ♕d2? deprives the b3-knight of its retreat-square, and so 18...a4 follows, while 18 ♕f1 ♕a4 19 ♘1d2 ♖fe8 leaves White paralysed; the threat is 20...♖e3.

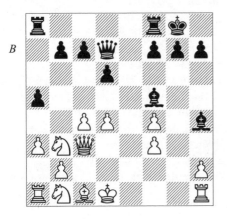

18...a4 19 ♘3d2

The bottled-up white queenside means that Black has several tempi to look for a way to infiltrate.

19...♖fe8!

With the idea of continuing 20...♕e7, threatening 21...♕e1+ and mate, as well as preventing 20 ♘e4 owing to 20...♗xe4 21 fxe4, when the queen comes decisively into play with 21...♕g4+ 22 ♔c2 ♕g2+.

20 ♘f1

The idea of blocking the file with a timely ♘e4 fails; e.g., 20 ♘f1 ♕e6 21 ♘e4 c6, with the deadly threat of ...d5.

20...♖e1+

Winning the queen. Materially White has enough pieces in compensation, but this is not yet sufficient, since the white forces are still uncoordinated. Now Black's task is to increase his threats before White develops his pieces and improves his coordination.

21 ♕xe1

Of course if 21 ♔d2 then 21...♖ae8.

21...♗xe1 22 ♔xe1 (D)

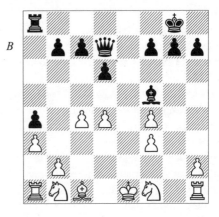

Now Black must hurry, since White threatens to bring his pieces into play quickly with ♘c3, ♗e3, etc., and even perhaps to gain a tempo with ♘g3, threatening ♘xf5, since in general any simplification favours the side with problems.

How should Black try to infiltrate? Does he need to bring the inactive a8-rook into play?

22...♗xb1!

Admittedly this exchanges a piece, but there are compelling reasons. It is the quickest way to bring the queen into play; on the other hand, playing according to general principles and bringing the a8-rook into play with 22...♖e8+?! is a mistake in view of 23 ♗e3.

23 ♖xb1 ♕f5

Activating the queen with a gain of time; in contrast, if 22...♖e8+ 23 ♗e3 had been played, the rook would not be forced to shut itself away on a1.

24 ♖a1 ♖e8+ (D)

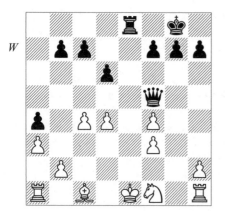

25 ♘e3

It is rather better, but equally miserable, to play 25 ♔f2 ♕c2+ 26 ♘d2 ♕d3.

25...♕xf4 26 ♔f2 ♕xd4 27 ♖d1 ♕h4+ 28 ♔g1 ♖e6

So White has finally managed to get his king out of the centre, but the inclusion of this rook in the attack shows that it is not secure on the kingside either.

29 ♘g2 ♖g6 30 ♗e3 ♕h3 31 ♖d2 ♕xf3

Black now has a material advantage and the initiative, while White does not have any way of creating counterplay.

32 ♖e1 (D)

32...h5!

The best way to make *luft*; this pawn will also come in useful as a battering-ram against the white king. The other kingside pawns, especially the f-pawn, can also help later on.

33 ♗d4

After 33 h4 this pawn is exposed; for example, 33...♕e4 is strong then, targeting both c- and h-pawns.

33...h4 34 ♖e8+ ♔h7 35 h3

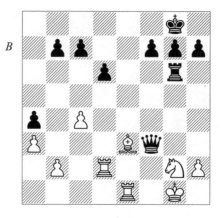

If 35 ♖e3 then, amongst other things, there is a win with 35...♖xg2+ 36 ♖xg2 ♕d1+ 37 ♔f2 ♕xd4; this could also have been the answer to 35 h3, but the move in the game wins another pawn. The result is not in doubt in any case.

35...♕xh3 36 ♖e3 ♕f5 (D)

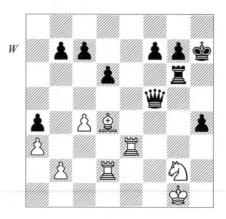

Threatening 37...h3.

37 ♔h2 ♖g3! 38 ♖xg3?!

If 38 ♖ee2 then 38...♕h3+ 39 ♔g1 ♕g4 40 ♔h2 c5! 41 ♗c3 h3 could follow.

38...hxg3+ 39 ♔h1

Here both 39 ♔g1 ♕b1+ and 39 ♔xg3 ♕g5+ would lose immediately.

39...c5 40 ♗e3 ♕f1+ 41 ♗g1 f5!

With the help of this fresh combatant, the struggle comes to an end.

42 ♖xd6 ♕xc4 43 ♖b6 ♕g4

With the threat of 44...♕h5+ followed by ...♕d1+.

0-1

White was convincingly punished for his delay in development, but exceptional energy was required, and some very elegant moves such as 10...♗g4! and 11...♘f3+!!.

The importance of piece coordination was very clear. The maxim "if one piece is bad, the whole position is bad" can be valid even with an advantage in material; the bad position of the white king was perhaps the most important factor, but the extreme clumsiness of the b3-knight also had a great influence on the course of the game, motivating 14...a5!!, which gave Black a lasting initiative.

When one has a dynamic advantage, and the natural methods fail to make progress, it is necessary to seek unconventional solutions, such as the exchange of a developed piece for one that has not moved. Thus with 22...♗xb1! mere control of light squares was transformed into a rapid invasion.

Game 2

Efim Geller – Alexei Dreev

New York Open 1990
French Defence, Tarrasch Variation

In the previous game White changed the semi-closed character of the position by advancing a vital defender, his f2-pawn, which brought a violent storm down on his king.

In this game Black did nothing like this. He delayed his development in order to gain space on the queenside; the position was even more closed than in the preceding game, so that consuming these tempi did not seem to entail any great risk. White could not exploit Black's imprudence by normal developing moves alone, but by taking extraordinary measures he managed to punish Black for his excessive boldness.

1 e4 e6 2 d4 d5 3 ♘d2

The Tarrasch Variation is not in principle the most violent way to confront the French Defence; there is not much contact between the two sides, and the struggle is generally transferred to the middlegame.

3...a6

This apparently modest move is in reality an ambitious one. Before playing ...c5 Black rules out ♗b5+, after which White would develop smoothly, and seeks a more complicated middlegame, admittedly in return for making a move that is generally not very useful.

4 ♘gf3 c5 5 exd5 exd5 6 ♗e2 c4

Another pawn move, to avoid being left with an isolated pawn on d5 and to gain space on the queenside. Black is relying on the position remaining closed.

7 0-0 ♗d6 *(D)*

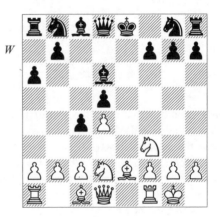

If Black could complete his development undisturbed, his position would be very good, but White will try to show that the pawn advances are not developing moves and are flawed; to do so, it is essential to open the game.

8 b3!

Playing 8...cxb3 9 axb3 ♘e7 now would be a concession of sorts, since the proud advanced pawn on c4 is exchanged for the a2-pawn. However, this position is playable for Black, which indicates that the white centre has weak points, as Mikhail Gurevich has demonstrated on various occasions, although possibly Geller did not share that view.

8...b5

This is rather risky, but consistent with his previous play. It should be noted that Black has already made three pawn moves on the queenside, and his king remains in the centre.

9 a4!

If now 9...c3 White is prepared to give up a piece with 10 axb5 (not, of course, 10 ♘b1? b4) 10...cxd2 11 ♗xd2 ♘e7 12 c4, as Geller himself played with success; White's strong centre provides sufficient compensation for the piece.

9...♗b7 *(D)*

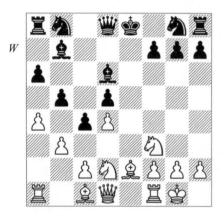

How should White open the game? Black has not 'collaborated' with this endeavour and has kept the position closed.

It is not enough to have a good idea; it is necessary to discover the best way of achieving it, with precise calculation, since general rules are inadequate on their own.

In an earlier game White tried to open the position with the sacrifice 10 ♖e1 ♘e7 11 bxc4 bxc4 12 ♗xc4 dxc4 13 ♘xc4, which looks promising, but Black found a good antidote in 13...♗b4! 14 c3 ♗d5! 15 cxb4 ♗xc4, and White's compensation was insufficient. Black managed to castle and there was no strong white centre as occurred after 9...c3.

10 bxc4!

This is the correct move-order.

10...bxc4 11 ♗xc4!!

The difference between this and the position in the note above is that the inclusion of the apparently useful move 10 ♖e1, which could certainly be made later, was less useful than that of 10...♘e7, since Black was able to

castle quickly, without the e1-rook contributing very much and in fact being subject to attack by 13...♗b4!.

Let us note that after the piece sacrifice, in addition to capturing two pawns, White gains access to two open files – the b-file has been opened and the e-file has also been cleared, so that ♖e1 will have more force.

11...dxc4 12 ♘xc4 *(D)*

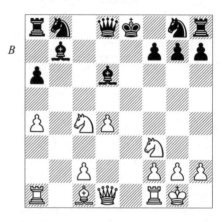

12...♗e7

The priority for Black is to speed up castling, but if 12...♘e7? then 13 ♘xd6+ ♔xd6 14 ♗a3 ♕c7 follows, and then after the natural 15 ♖e1!? ♘c6 16 d5, in order to avoid immediate loss Black has to play 16...0-0-0, when among other things White can play 17 c4 and then continue preparing the advance of his pawns. But 15 d5! is even stronger, threatening 16 d6 and 16 ♖e1 with greater force since Black does not have ...♘bc6.

Black is now trying to play 13...♘f6 followed by castling.

13 ♖e1!

Occupying the e-file at the right moment; the pressure along this file is very strong, and 13...♘f6? is now prevented not only because of 14 ♗a3 but also due to the more spectacular 14 ♖xe7+!, followed by 15 ♗a3 and 16 ♘d6(+), with a winning attack. The black king will have to take a walk during which it will be hounded by the f3-knight and the queen, and will be unable to defend itself. The exposed position of the b7-bishop after ♘d6 will also be a factor.

13...♕c7 *(D)*

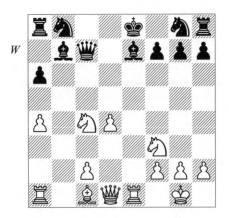

W

Threatening the c4-knight and trying to find refuge on the queenside with 14...♘d7 and ...0-0-0.

14 ♖b1!

Another piece comes into play, taking advantage of the opening of the b-file, not only with the threat of 15 ♖xb7 but also with some less immediate but equally strong longer-term threats, such as 15 ♘b6 followed by c4.

14...♕xc4 15 ♖xb7

A rook on the seventh rank is always strong; here it prevents 15...♘d7? in view of 16 ♖xd7!. Expelling the rook with 15...♕c6 is not of much help after 16 ♖b3, when once again 16...♘d7? is prevented, this time because of 17 d5 ♕d6 18 ♗a3 ♘c5 19 ♖c3. The various pins to which Black is subjected are deadly.

15...♘c6 *(D)*

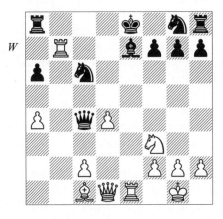

W

How should White continue now? The natural 16 ♗a3? allows the resource 16...0-0-0!, and

Black gains the advantage after 17 ♗xe7 ♘gxe7 18 ♖bxe7? (better, although not advantageous either, is 18 ♕b1) 18...♘xe7 19 ♖xe7 ♖he8.

16 ♘d2!?

White does not hesitate to sacrifice the d-pawn in order to bring the c1-bishop into play.

Another interesting idea was 16 ♖c7!, threatening 17 d5 and 17 ♘e5, lending more force to 17 ♗a3 and preventing Black from castling.

16...♕xd4

After 16...♕d5, 17 c4 could follow, while if 16...♕xa4 the advance 17 d5 is very strong.

17 ♗b2 ♕xa4

If 17...♕f4 putting pressure on the d2-knight, White could play 18 g3!, making useful *luft* (not 18 ♗xg7?! 0-0-0!). Then if the queen defends g7 with 18...♕h6, White dominates the whole board with 19 ♘c4 ♖d8 20 ♕f3, and there is no good defence against 21 ♖b6, while if 18...♕d6, among other continuations, it is possible to bring the queen into the attack with 19 ♕f3, renewing the threat of ♖b6.

18 ♖e4? *(D)*

Another gain of time on the queen, but as before, the tactical element predominates in this position and this indicates that it was time to play more prosaically with 18 ♗xg7!; then after 18...0-0-0 19 ♖b6 ♗c5 20 ♖xc6+ ♕xc6 21 ♗xh8, the black king remains very exposed, and White's advantage is clear.

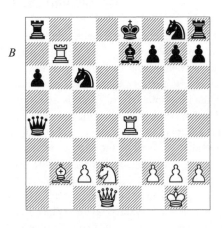

B

18...♕a2?

Missing his great opportunity; 18...♕a5! is better, taking aim at d2; the idea is that then 19 ♗xg7 is strongly met by 19...0-0-0!.

19 ♗xg7 0-0-0 20 ♖b3

Now White regains the sacrificed material, and the bad position of the black king is decisive.

20...♗f6 21 ♕g4+

Amply justifying the retreat 16 ♘d2.

21...♔c7 22 ♕f4+ ♔c8

If 22...♖d6 then the further pin 23 ♖d3 is decisive.

23 ♗xf6 ♘xf6 24 ♕xf6 ♕xc2 *(D)*

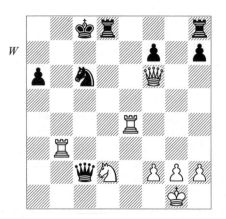

25 ♕f5+!

Winning the black queen.

1-0

White sacrificed a piece for only two pawns, but a king in the centre can justify the investment of even large amounts of material. Of course, subsequently it is vital to activate the attacking pieces to the maximum and prevent the king from reaching safety. This was achieved by occupying the open files with 13 ♖e1! and 14 ♖b1!, which was not difficult to see, although White also employed some less obvious measures, such as the 16 ♘d2!? retreat that allowed other pieces to come into play, such as the e1-rook, the queen, and after the capture of the d4-pawn, the c1-bishop.

Let us note once again that the tactical element is essential to add the finishing touches to a good concept; here it involved finding the correct move-order 10 bxc4! and 11 ♗xc4!!, and it could also have spoiled everything with a tempting move such as 18 ♖e4? instead of 18 ♗xg7.

Game 3

Daniel Rivera – Ehsan Ghaem Maghami

Calvia open 2006

Sicilian Defence, Kan Variation

In the Sicilian Defence, the black king is an important target. Sometimes Black delays castling, sheltering behind his central pawn-majority, watching out for the appropriate moment to bring his king into safety. There is an obvious risk involved in seeking strategic benefits while the king lingers in the centre – and it is these dangers that we shall be focusing upon here.

It is noteworthy that sometimes White starts the battle on the queenside, where Black has made progress and is superior, but this opening of lines can subsequently favour White in the struggle that he desires in the centre and on the kingside.

The main game and the illustrative fragment that we examine provide model examples of these themes.

1 e4 c5 2 ♘f3 e6 3 d4 cxd4 4 ♘xd4 a6 5 ♘c3 b5 6 ♗d3 ♗b7 7 0-0 ♕c7 8 ♕e2 *(D)*

Korchnoi, from personal experience, considers Black's move-order here to be dubious, since the kingside is undeveloped and the king will have to stay in the centre for some moves to come.

The white queen is posted on the e-file, in order to create the possibility of ♘d5. 8 ♖e1 is also playable, with the same idea.

8...♗e7

Closing the e-file and thus restraining the tactical ideas, typical of the Sicilian, based on the knight jump ♘d5. Krogius-Korchnoi, USSR Ch, Riga 1958 continued 8...♘c6 9 ♘xc6 dxc6 10 a4 b4 11 ♘d1 c5 12 ♘e3 ♘e7 and here Korchnoi, in his best games collection, suggests

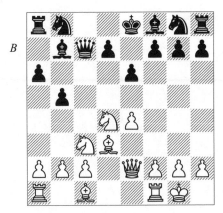

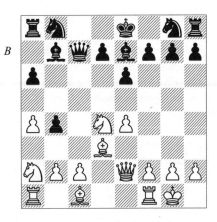

13 ♘c4 ♘c6 14 c3 ♗e7 15 e5, or 15 g3, followed by ♗f4, with advantage to White, since the c6-knight is restricted.

Recapturing on c6 with a piece would fully justify 8 ♕e2, because then would come the thematic manoeuvre 10 a4 b4 11 ♘d5!. In this case the knight jump is not a piece sacrifice, but a way of opening the game so that the bad position of the black king can become a decisive factor. The insertion of a4 weakens Black's structure and allows the c-file to be opened with c3 at an appropriate moment, so that the black king will not be safe on the queenside either.

A more recent, and very instructive, game continued 8...♘e7? – see Supplementary Game 3.1.

The most popular reply is 8...♘f6.

9 a4!?

The quiet 9 ♗d2 is playable, lending more force to a4, but it is more energetic to strike immediately on the queenside, taking advantage of the fact that Black still has to worry about completing his development.

9...b4

9...bxa4 10 ♖xa4 leaves the a6-pawn very weak and helps activate the white rook.

10 ♘a2 (D)

10...♘f6?!

This very natural move is questionable. Instead 10...♘c6 could be tried, when, in contrast to the game, Black is not obliged to open lines with his king in the centre. 11 ♘xc6 dxc6 12 ♗d2 might follow, but then Black can support his b4-pawn with 12...c5. However, after 13 e5!

Black's mobility problems persist and White can follow up with c3.

11 ♗d2

Now White is indeed able to take advantage of the ...b4 advance to open the c-file and gain tempi on the black queen, or else to try to exploit the position of the black king in the centre.

11...d5 (D)

"In for a penny, in for a pound." If it were possible, it would be better to support b4, but that is not appropriate here; defending with 11...a5?! is not a solution, since c3 will come in any case, and the hole at b5 for a white knight might become important.

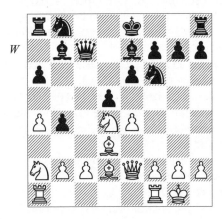

12 e5 ♘e4 13 ♗xb4 ♗xb4 14 ♘xb4 ♕xe5

It is generally beneficial to give up a wing pawn in exchange for a centre pawn, and if Black were castled, this would be an excellent transaction for him. However, in this case the black king still remains in the centre. We already know from the previous games that an open c-file can cause serious headaches. A half-open file is also important and, as in the other examples, the lack of coordination within the black camp, where all his queenside pieces are out of play, is of prime importance.

15 c3 *(D)*

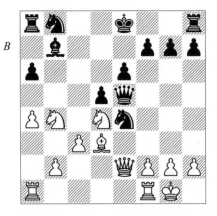

The threat of 16 f3 forces Black to defend his queen or remove it from e5.

15...♕d6

In reply to 15...♕f4 there are various attractive continuations. 16 a5, fixing the weakness at a6, is Rivera's suggestion, although 16 ♗b5+ is also tempting: 16...♔f8 (after 16...axb5 17 ♕xb5+ Black loses a pawn without compensation) 17 ♗d3, and White has prevented Black from castling.

Against 15...♕c7 Rivera had prepared the following blow: 16 ♘xd5! exd5 17 f3 0-0 18 fxe4 ♖e8 19 ♘f5 dxe4 20 ♗c4, and there is a lot of pressure on Black's castled position, while his queenside remains undeveloped.

16 ♖fd1

Developing another piece, with indirect pressure on the black queen.

16...♕e7? *(D)*

It was essential to bring the king to safety right away with 16...0-0!. After 17 ♗xe4 dxe4 18 ♘b5 ♕e5 19 ♘d6 ♗d5 20 ♘c4 ♗xc4 21 ♕xc4, Black still has to develop his queenside but his disadvantage is not decisive.

After the text-move, it looks as if Black's queen has escaped the influence of the d1-rook, and that all he needs is to castle on the next

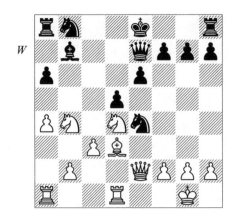

move. However, White now demonstrates that one tempo is an eternity in this position.

17 ♘xd5!!

The apparently solid central black structure is smashed to smithereens.

17...exd5

If 17...♗xd5 18 ♗xe4 ♗xe4 19 ♕xe4 ♖a7 20 ♘c6, White has an extra pawn and an attack on the black king, which is still stuck in the centre.

18 ♘f5 *(D)*

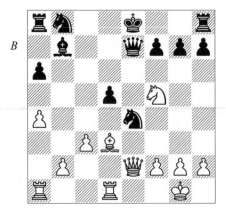

18...♕c7

Defending the b7-bishop against ♘d6+. Instead, 18...♕e5 is met by 19 ♗xe4 dxe4 (19...0-0 20 ♕g4 is awkward; for example, 20...g6 {or 20...dxe4? 21 ♘h6+ ♔h8 22 ♘xf7+ winning} 21 ♗xd5 ♗xd5 22 ♖xd5) 20 ♘d6+ ♔e7 21 ♘xb7. Alternatively, 18...♕f6 leaves Black two pawns down after 19 ♗xe4 0-0 20 ♗xd5.

19 ♗xe4!

Better than 19 f3, which recovers the piece with advantage, but White does not want to allow Black to castle.

19...dxe4

19...0-0 is met by 20 ♘e7+, when the knight is taboo: 20...♕xe7? 21 ♗xh7+.

20 ♘d6+ ♚e7

Or 20...♚f8 21 ♘xb7 ♘d7 (21...♕xb7? 22 ♖d8+) 22 ♕xe4, when White has a material advantage and the black king is badly placed.

21 ♕h5

The double threat of 22 ♕xf7+ and 22 ♕e5+ is decisive.

21...♘d7 22 ♕xf7+ ♚d8 23 ♕xg7 ♖e8 24 ♕g5+! 1-0

If 24...♖e7 then 25 ♕g8+ forcing mate in a few moves.

We shall draw some conclusions after we have examined the following example.

Supplementary Game 3.1
Magnus Carlsen – Gata Kamsky
FIDE World Cup, Khanty-Mansiisk 2005
Sicilian Defence, Kan Variation

1 e4 c5 2 ♘f3 e6 3 d4 cxd4 4 ♘xd4 a6 5 ♘c3 ♕c7 6 ♗d3 b5 7 0-0 ♗b7 8 ♕e2 ♘e7? *(D)*

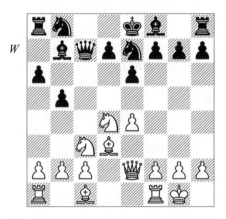

9 ♖e1?!

With the idea of answering 9...♘g6 with 10 ♘d5!.

But is there a better continuation for White? Can you find it?

The uncomfortable position of the black king allows the sacrifice 9 ♗xb5! and if 9...axb5, then 10 ♘cxb5! (preventing ...♕c6) 10...♕b6 11 ♗e3 ♗a6 12 ♘xe6! leads to mate after 12...♗xb5 13 ♗xb6 ♗xe2 14 ♘c7+ ♚d8 15 ♘b5+ ♚c8 16 ♘d6#. Carlsen indicates that interpolating 9...e5 does not help in view of 10 ♘f3!, hitting e5, and after 10...axb5 11 ♘xb5

♕c6 12 ♘xe5 ♕c5 (12...♕f6 loses to 13 ♘c7+ ♚d8 14 ♘g4) 13 ♗f4 ♗a6 14 c4 ♗xb5 15 cxb5, he gives the evaluation that "White has a very strong initiative, without inferiority in material". This is confirmed by the analysis engines, which give an overwhelming advantage to White; Black is undeveloped and his king is stuck in the centre.

9...♘bc6 10 ♘xc6 ♘xc6 *(D)*

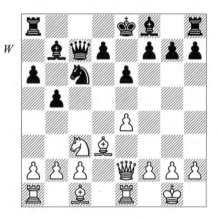

Now ♘d5 would be a real sacrifice. But nevertheless...

11 ♘d5! exd5 12 exd5+ ♘e7 13 c4

White has only one pawn for the piece, but Black has serious development and mobility problems.

13...b4

Black wishes to bring his king to safety on the queenside without opening any files there, but this comes at the cost of leaving the b7-bishop a 'dead' piece.

After 13...bxc4 14 ♗xc4, followed by developing the c1-bishop to b2, g5 or f4, as appropriate, and ♖ac1 or ♖ad1, it is not easy to find a move for Black; while if 13...0-0-0 White has 14 ♗g5, threatening 15 cxb5 and ♖c1.

14 ♗g5 f6 (D)

Forced. 14...d6 can be met by 15 ♗c2 (or 15 ♕h5) 15...h6 16 ♗a4+ ♔d8 17 ♕h5 ♔c8 18 ♗d2, winning a second pawn, and leaving the black pieces uncoordinated.

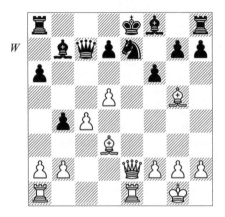

15 ♕h5+ g6

If 15...♔d8?!, after any retreat of the g5-bishop all the black pieces are left badly placed, and there is still the problem of the king stuck in the centre, hindering communications.

16 ♕f3! fxg5

After 16...♗g7 17 ♗f4 (but not 17 ♗xf6?! 0-0! 18 ♖xe7 ♖xf6 19 ♕h3 ♖af8 20 ♖xd7 ♕f4) 17...d6 18 ♖e6 0-0-0 19 ♖ae1 White can be very optimistic about his position.

17 ♕f6 0-0-0

Not 17...♖g8? 18 d6! ♕d8 (18...♕c6?! 19 ♖xe7+) 19 ♖xe7+! ♗xe7 20 ♖e1 mating.

18 ♕xh8

Although Black retains a slight material advantage, his kingside is weak and the b7-bishop lacks prospects. Therefore White has the advantage, which he exploited after a long struggle.

Black was behind in development, both in the main game and in the Carlsen example, where we saw the thematic Sicilian sacrifice ♘d5. This was in a semi-closed position, which we already know is no guarantee of safety for a king if the opponent is better developed and his own pieces are uncoordinated, as was indeed the case here.

Note also the punishment that could have been meted out to 8...♘e7? with another typical Sicilian sacrifice, 9 ♗xb5!, in this case making use of the almost 'smothered' position of the black king.

In the main game, delaying castling for one move too many was sufficient for the apparently solid central barrier to be demolished with the blow 17 ♘xd5!!, showing once again that a lack of coordination and development are not good company for an uncastled king.

Game 4

Veselin Topalov – Vasily Ivanchuk

Linares 1999

English Opening, Symmetrical Variation

In the previous three games, the shortcomings of the king in the centre were made even worse because the e-file was open, or half-open. In the game that we are going to see now, this file is closed. However, this factor did not change the overall scene; White lagged behind in development somewhat and his b5-knight became a weakness rather than an attacking force, which meant that he had to consume more tempi. White had the bishop-pair but this was of little use once Black, in brilliant fashion, was able to open up the white king's position and exploit both his own superior development and White's lack of coordination.

1 ♘f3 c5 2 c4 ♘c6 3 d4 cxd4 4 ♘xd4 e6 5 g3 ♗b4+ 6 ♘c3 ♕a5

Black deviates from the more normal line that is reached after 6...♘f6.

7 ♘b5 (D)

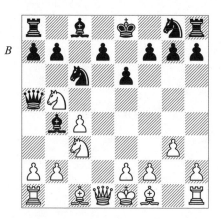

7...d5!

Black takes advantage of the unusual move-order to play more ambitiously than is usual in this line; he prevents ♘d6+ and threatens both 8...d4 and 8...a6.

White has moved his king's knight several times, and has no lead in development, which encourages Black to create threats and provoke complications, delaying his own development for the moment.

8 a3 ♗xc3+ 9 bxc3?!

Topalov thought for a long time before deciding on this capture, which spoils his structure. He was not convinced by 9 ♘xc3 d4, when he is practically forced to give up material with 10 b4 ♘xb4 11 axb4 ♕xa1 12 ♘b5, and here 12...♘f6 13 ♘c7+ ♔e7 14 ♘xa8 ♗d7 15 ♗g2 ♖xa8 16 0-0 had already been played (in Lerner-Khuzman, Kuibyshev 1986), and seems favourable to White. Nevertheless, the analysis engines offer 12...♔f8!? as an interesting alternative, which is possibly what Topalov feared. Black retains his material advantage and it is not easy to prove compensation.

9...♘f6 (D)

10 ♗g2

The b5-knight is rather out on a limb, but it is inadvisable for White to exchange his only

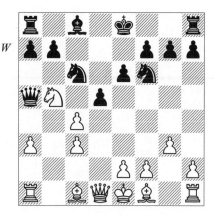

developed piece with 10 ♘d6+ ♔e7 11 cxd5 (worse is 11 ♘xc8+ ♖axc8 12 cxd5 ♘xd5 13 ♗d2? ♘xc3 14 ♕c1 ♘d4) and with 11...♖d8 Black develops quickly; then if 12 dxc6 ♖xd6 13 ♕c2 ♖xc6 14 ♗d2 ♕d5!, followed by 15...e5, White still has problems bringing his kingside pieces into play.

10...0-0 11 ♕b3

It is essential to defend c3 against the threat of 11...a6 and 12...♕xc3+, but this is only a 'semi-developing' move. Admittedly the queen is activated, and is fulfilling the task of defending both c3 and b5, thus allowing White to take on d5 whilst having the knight defended, but the queen is exposed to attack with gain of tempo.

Ivanchuk indicates that in the event of 11 cxd5 ♘xd5 12 ♕b3 (or 12 ♗xd5 exd5 13 ♕d3 ♗h3! and the white king remains very badly placed), 12...a6! is strong. If White is not to lose the c3-pawn for nothing, then he must once again give up his g2-bishop, with the result that many light squares, especially in his castled position, will be weak. After 13 ♗xd5 exd5 14 ♘d6 d4 15 ♘xc8 ♖axc8 we see that the difference in development between the two sides is enormous.

11...dxc4!

The b5-knight loses its best protection, and the d- and c-files are opened, further exposing the white queen.

12 ♕xc4 (D)

White is planning to castle next move; can this be prevented?

12...e5!

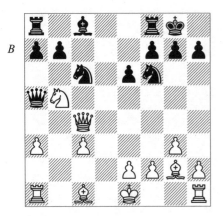

The bishop is ready to gain tempi by attacking the white queen, and the retreat of the b5-knight to d4 is prevented.

There was another tempting move here, pointed out by Ivanchuk, based on the exposed position of the b5-knight, and that was 12...罩d8, preventing ②d6 and threatening to play 13...e5 with greater force. In addition, 13...a6 could be strong in some lines, and we should not forget that 12...罩d8 also brings another piece into play. It simply cannot be good then for White to seek material gain by exchanging his few developed pieces with 13 ③xc6 bxc6 14 ②d4; in terms of a specific reason to reject this, 14...e5! 15 ②xc6 營c7, with a decisive pin, is convincing. If 13 0-0 e5 14 a4 then 14...③e6 and 15...a6 follows, after which the c3-pawn drops. This indicates that there is no easy path to equality for White.

So which move is better, 12...罩d8 or 12...e5? You often get positions like this, where simple calculation cannot provide the answer and exhaustive analysis is required; furthermore the difference, if any, would only be clear after many moves of analysis. From the practical point of view, however, it is not that important; both moves are strong, and the choice cannot be based on 'mathematical' reasons.

Ivanchuk was not sure either, but he opted for 12...e5! because "it is sharper"; it allows the bishop to gain tempo on the queen, and then Black can develop his rooks in the most effective way.

13 ②d6

Moving the knight, with the loss of another tempo, was not what White wanted to do. He would prefer to get on with his development, but Black was threatening to win the knight with 13...③e6 and 14...a6.

Instead, after 13 a4 ③e6 both 14 營h4 a6 and 14 營d3 罩fd8 15 營c2 a6 16 ②a3 ②d4 leave Black with a decisive material advantage.

13...③e6 14 營d3 (D)

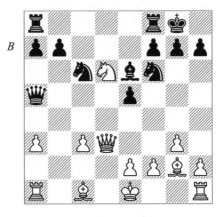

What now? It is not possible to exploit the pin right away with 14...罩ad8? owing to 15 ②xb7! and White can win material at no great risk, since 15...營a4? is no good due to 16 ②xd8 罩xd8 17 ③xc6.

Black has a great advantage in development, but if White manages to castle, or retreat his d6-knight and then castle, his inferiority will not be serious.

14...e4!!

With this pawn sacrifice Black sharpens the struggle; its capture leads to the opening of the vital e-file, and the exchange of White's developed pieces.

15 ②xe4

Leaving the e4-pawn alive means that the g2-bishop stays out of play and 15 營e3 ②g4 16 營d2 罩ad8! 17 ②xb7 營a4 18 ②xd8 罩xd8 does not work for White, since, in contrast to the line mentioned above, he does not have the resource ③xc6.

The retreat 15 營c2 hands over another tempo: 15...②d4!, and after 16 營b2 the overload on the white queen and the king in the centre permits 16...②xe2!.

Staying on the d-file with 15 營d2 is worse, in view of 15...罩ad8, intending 16...營e5.

Capturing with the knight on e4 and keeping the bishop looks better than taking with the bishop, since after 15 ♗xe4 ♘xe4 16 ♘xe4 ♖ad8, followed by 17...♘d4 or 17...♗h3, the white position is full of weaknesses and his king is stuck in the centre, whereas Black only needs to play ...♖fe8 for all his pieces to be in play.

15...♘xe4 16 ♗xe4 ♖ad8 17 ♕c2

If 17 ♕e3 then 17...♖fe8!, and the pin on the e4-bishop is decisive; then 18 ♗xc6 fails to 18...♗b3!, while after 18 0-0 ♗h3, threatening 19...f5, White not only loses the exchange after 19 ♕f3 ♗xf1 20 ♔xf1 but also has to suffer the invasion of his first rank with 20...♖d1+ (even better is 20...♘e5 21 ♕e3 ♘g4 and the queen cannot simultaneously defend the e4-bishop and the c3-pawn).

17...♘d4! 18 ♕b2 (D)

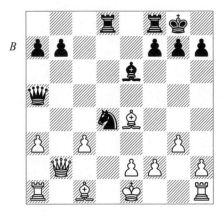

And now? Following the same criterion as before and simply bringing the last piece into play is not sufficient. Ivanchuk pointed out that if 18...♖fe8 White can get out of trouble and even feel optimistic by giving up the exchange with 19 0-0! ♗h3 20 cxd4 ♗xf1 21 ♗f3, when he has adequate compensation, with a good centre and a pawn for the exchange.

18...♗c4 is not decisive either; it wins a pawn but after 19 ♕b4 (19 ♗e3!?) 19...♕e5 (not 19...♕xb4 20 axb4 ♘xe2 21 ♗e3, when having the king in the centre gives White the advantage) 20 cxd4 ♕xe4 21 0-0 ♖xd4, according to Ivanchuk Black has an advantage but not a decisive one. White can continue 22

♕c3!? (but not 22 ♗e3?, which loses after 22...♗d5!).

Of course this is a critical moment; it is necessary to 'go for broke' and calculate deeply, unlike the previous case, where Black simply had to make a choice between two attractive continuations.

18...♘xe2!!

"A splendid combination based on the position of White's uncastled king," commented Ivanchuk. Now the half-open file becomes fully open.

19 ♔xe2 (D)

Here 19 ♕b4 fails to 19...♘xc3!!.

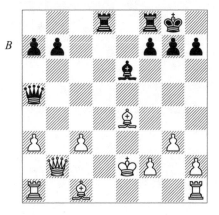

19...♖fe8!!

Finally the last piece actually does come into play, now that the white king cannot escape the crossfire of all the black pieces. "A quiet move, in the spirit of the position, preparing the execution of the white king," commented Ivanchuk.

It was tempting to make the white king continue his walk with 19...♗c4+ 20 ♔f3, and now 20...f5, but surprisingly there is no win after 21 ♗xb7 ♗d5+ 22 ♔e2 ♗xb7 23 ♕xb7, when Black must play 23...♕xc3 24 ♗e3 ♕c4+ 25 ♔e1 ♕c3+, with perpetual check. There are other possibilities, such as 20...♖fe8, but the move-order that Black chose is the most accurate; here precise calculation certainly was essential.

20 ♕b4 (D)

After 20 f3 comes 20...f5! and if 21 ♗xb7 then the elegant 21...♗c4++ 22 ♔f2 ♕b6+! 23

$\underline{\text{W}}$xb6 (23 $\underline{\text{⌯}}$g2 $\underline{\text{Ξ}}$e2+ costs White his queen) 23...$\underline{\text{Ξ}}$e2+ 24 $\underline{\text{⌯}}$f1 $\underline{\text{Ξ}}$d1#. 21 $\underline{\text{W}}$b4 is no better, since Black remains a pawn up with an attack on the defenceless white king after 21...$\underline{\text{W}}$a6+ 22 $\underline{\text{⌯}}$f2 fxe4 23 $\underline{\text{⌐}}$e3 exf3.

Neither is 20 $\underline{\text{⌐}}$e3 an improvement, in view of 20...$\underline{\text{⌐}}$c4+ 21 $\underline{\text{⌯}}$f3 $\underline{\text{Ξ}}$xe4 22 $\underline{\text{⌯}}$xe4 (22 $\underline{\text{⌯}}$g2 $\underline{\text{W}}$d5 is also hopeless for White) 22...$\underline{\text{W}}$d5+ 23 $\underline{\text{⌯}}$f4 h5!, with various mating threats.

Finally, if 20 $\underline{\text{Ξ}}$e1, trying to shelter the king on f1, Ivanchuk gives 20...$\underline{\text{W}}$h5+! 21 $\underline{\text{⌯}}$f1 $\underline{\text{⌐}}$h3+ 22 $\underline{\text{⌯}}$g1 $\underline{\text{Ξ}}$xe4!, highlighting the weakness of the light squares and mating quickly.

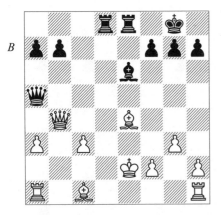

20...$\underline{\text{W}}$h5+!

The queen transfers to the kingside to prevent the white king from finding shelter.

21 f3 f5! 22 g4 *(D)*

Against the pin 22 $\underline{\text{W}}$c5, one winning line is 22...$\underline{\text{⌐}}$d5! 23 $\underline{\text{⌐}}$e3 $\underline{\text{⌐}}$xe4 and there is no defence.

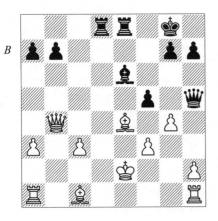

22...$\underline{\text{W}}$h3!

"Accuracy right to the end; inferior was 22...fxg4? 23 $\underline{\text{⌐}}$e3!, with unclear play" – Ivanchuk.

23 gxf5

The opening of lines brings a rapid victory after 23 $\underline{\text{⌯}}$f2 fxe4! 24 $\underline{\text{W}}$xe4 $\underline{\text{⌐}}$d5 25 $\underline{\text{W}}$d3 $\underline{\text{Ξ}}$f8.

23...$\underline{\text{⌐}}$xf5!

Pursuing the attack on White's king is even quicker than gaining material with 23...$\underline{\text{W}}$g2+ 24 $\underline{\text{⌐}}$e3 $\underline{\text{W}}$xh1 25 fxe6 $\underline{\text{Ξ}}$d1, when 26 e7 prolongs the struggle.

24 $\underline{\text{W}}$c4+ $\underline{\text{⌯}}$h8 25 $\underline{\text{Ξ}}$e1 *(D)*

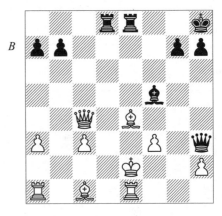

25...$\underline{\text{Ξ}}$xe4+! 0-1

Black's attack leads to a forced mate after 26 fxe4 $\underline{\text{⌐}}$g4+ 27 $\underline{\text{⌯}}$f2 $\underline{\text{W}}$xh2+ 28 $\underline{\text{⌯}}$e3 (or 28 $\underline{\text{⌯}}$f1 $\underline{\text{⌐}}$h3#) 28...$\underline{\text{W}}$g3#.

Between moves 10 and 19 White just needed one tempo to be able to castle but, with the e-file closed, his king did not appear to be in real danger. However, the bad position of the b5-knight compelled White to concede a development advantage to Black. The brilliant pawn sacrifice 14...e4!! to make the e-file half-open was the prelude to a larger sacrifice, 18...$\underline{\text{⌒}}$xe2!!, opening the e-file completely. After 19...$\underline{\text{Ξ}}$fe8!!, with Black's two rooks and queen all in play and hounding White's king, while the white rooks still remained on their original squares, the outcome was not difficult to predict. We should also note the force of the manoeuvre 20...$\underline{\text{W}}$h5+! and 22...$\underline{\text{W}}$h3!, allowing the enemy king no respite.

Ivanchuk's spectacular win was deservedly awarded the brilliancy prize of the Linares tournament.

On another note, it is remarkable that many of the lines that I have given in the notes to this game were indicated by Ivanchuk in *Informator 75* and in *New in Chess Magazine 1999/3*; more than eight years later, the engines did not reveal any clear improvements on Ivanchuk's complicated analysis.

Game 5
Tiger Hillarp Persson – Emil Sutovsky
Turin Olympiad 2006
Grünfeld Defence, Taimanov Variation

In the final game of this chapter we shall see an example where neither king is strictly forced to remain in the centre, but they both stay there for a considerable time, since neither has any pressing need to castle and the best location is in any case not clear.

It is worth noting how Black makes White's kingside inhospitable by inducing weaknesses, so that it will no longer provide a safe residence.

1 d4 ♘f6 2 c4 g6 3 ♘c3 d5 4 ♗g5 ♘e4 5 ♗h4

The Taimanov Variation, with which its creator had considerable success initially.

5...♘xc3 6 bxc3 dxc4 7 e3 ♗e6 *(D)*

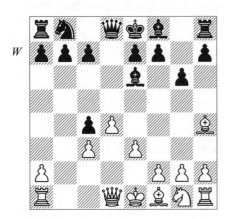

8 ♖b1

The alternative in this line, once again in fashion, is 8 ♕b1.

8...♘d7

Fischer played 8...b6 against Taimanov in the early days of this line, in the 5th game of their Candidates match in Vancouver 1971.

9 ♘f3

The capture 9 ♖xb7 leaves the rook perilously placed after 9...♘b6, threatening 10...♗d5 or 10...♕c8. Following 10 ♗g3 c5 11 ♖c7 (not 11 dxc5?? ♕xd1+ 12 ♔xd1 0-0-0+!, nor 11 ♗e5? f6 12 ♗g3 ♗d5 13 ♖c7 e5) 11...cxd4 12 ♕xd4 ♕xd4 13 cxd4 ♗g7 14 ♘f3 0-0, with the idea of ...♖fc8, the passed pawn on c4 is very dangerous.

9...♘b6 10 a4 a5 *(D)*

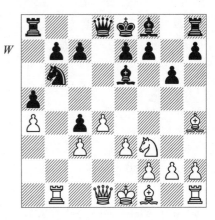

11 ♘g5

White seeks to sharpen the struggle. Sutovsky pointed out that White does not have enough compensation for the pawn after 11 ♗e2 ♗g7 12 0-0 0-0.

11...♗d5 12 e4 h6

This counter-attack is typical of the Grünfeld.

13 exd5 hxg5 14 ♗xg5 *(D)*

The exchange sacrifice 14 ♖xb6 cxb6 15 ♗xc4 leads to nothing special. Admittedly after

15...♗h6 16 ♗g3 White has compensation thanks to his strong centre, and as soon as he manages to castle, his rook will join in the struggle. However, 15...♕c7! is better and, although the black king remains in the centre after 16 ♗b5+ ♔d8, there are no white pieces to trouble it after 17 ♗xg5 ♕xc3+ 18 ♗d2 (exchanging queens with 18 ♕d2 brings about an unpleasant endgame) 18...♕xd4. Here, now that the d4-pawn has disappeared, paradoxically the engines think that the best move is 19 ♗e3, trying to exploit the uncomfortable position of the black king; Black remains better though. On the other hand 19 0-0?! is a mistake in view of the pretty sequence 19...♗h6! 20 ♗xa5 ♗f4! 21 g3 (if 21 ♕xd4 then 21...♗xh2+ followed by 22...♗e5+) 21...♕xd1 22 ♗xb6+ ♗c7 (the king's bishop manages to come to the defence of the black king) 23 ♗xc7+ ♔xc7 24 ♖xd1 ♔d6 and the advantage of the exchange must count.

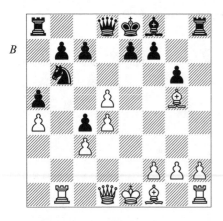

Black has several options, and according to Sutovsky's notes in *Informator 97*, he can fight for the advantage.

14...♗h6!

We shall see that the exchange of these bishops favours Black, since there are various key dark squares in White's camp that will be left unprotected.

Another continuation that deserves consideration is 14...♕xd5!? 15 ♖b5. Then Sutovsky indicates that the passive 15...♕d6 can be answered by 16 ♕f3!, with compensation, and instead he recommends 15...♕e6+ 16 ♗e2 ♘d5

17 ♗d2 ♗h6 18 ♖xb7 ♕e4! 19 f3 ♕e6 with a good position, reaching an equal ending after 20 ♗xh6 ♘xc3 (not 20...♖xh6? 21 ♕d2!) 21 ♕d2 ♘xe2 22 ♕xe2 ♕xe2+ 23 ♔xe2 0-0-0 24 ♖b5 ♖xh6 25 ♔e3. 15...♕e4+ is also interesting. What is clear is that Black already has a good position and with the text-move he seeks more.

15 ♗xh6 ♖xh6 16 ♕f3 (*D*)

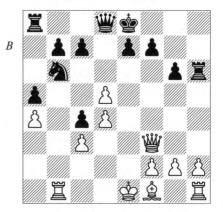

Black can play 16...♕xd5 without risk, but also without ambition, since in the endgame after 17 ♕xd5 ♘xd5 18 ♖xb7 the white bishop is strong enough to hold the position.

Another plan is to postpone the capture of the d5-pawn in favour of strengthening the position. However, after a 'normal' move such as 16...♕d6, followed by ...0-0-0, White can reach a position with good prospects with 17 g3 followed by ♗g2 and 0-0, with strong pressure on the long diagonal. After a timely ♖b5 followed by bringing the other rook into action, the white position will be full of vitality.

Can you think of another plan? It is of great help to ask yourself "what does my opponent want to do?"

16...♖h5!! 17 g4

Expelling the rook, but not without cost; now if White castles kingside, his king will be less secure.

17 g3? is not playable, since the queen is tied to the defence of the c3-pawn, and after 17...♖f5! 18 ♕e4 ♘xa4 Black gains a decisive material advantage.

17 d6 ♕xd6 is equally unpromising for White, who in the future will have to reckon

with penetration by ...♕a3. If 18 ♕xb7 Black plays 18...♖d8, with the aforementioned threat of ...♕a3, as well as hitting the h2-pawn, and with the simple plan of castling 'by hand' with ...♔f8-g7.

17 ♗e2 is possible, but then the bishop is less powerful than on the long diagonal, and Black can return to his original plan with 17...♕d6!.

17...♖h7!

The complement to his previous move; after weakening the white position, the rook stays on the h-file and defends f7, allowing the possibility of queenside castling.

In contrast, 17...♖xd5 does not achieve any advantage after 18 ♖xb6! cxb6 19 ♗xc4, with an endgame in which White is not worse after 19...e6 20 ♗xd5 ♕xd5 21 ♕xd5 exd5 22 ♔d2.

18 ♗g2 ♕d6 (D)

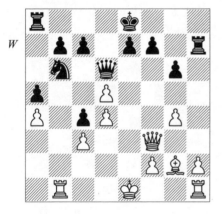

19 ♕g3

The exchange of queens is not something that Black fears or that White would have wanted, but it is not easy to suggest anything better.

It is not appropriate to advance the kingside pawns with 19 h4 0-0-0 20 h5, since after 20...♖dh8 we see that Black has deployed all his pieces harmoniously, whereas the centralized white king has no good shelter anywhere and prevents the connection of the rooks.

Playing more modestly with 19 h3 means that the h-pawn will not be dangerous, so Black can change plan and play 19...♘xa4 20 ♖xb7 ♘b6 21 0-0 a4. In this position the kings have swapped roles: the white king is secure and it is

the black king that is in the centre, but as well as there being a passed pawn on a4, in contrast to the line given in an earlier note, the black king does not have any problems here, and can even go to attack the b7-rook, winning the exchange.

19...0-0-0! (D)

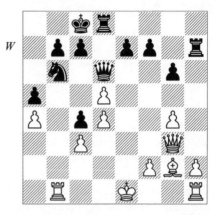

Abandoning the possibility of having the queen's rook behind the passed pawn in an ending, but now this rook will also come into play in the event of an exchange of queens on the d-file.

20 ♖b5

20 ♕xd6 ♖xd6 will transpose to the next note.

20...♘xa4 21 ♖xa5 (D)

After 21 ♕xd6 ♖xd6 22 ♖xa5 ♘xc3 23 ♔d2 b6! 24 ♖a8+ ♔b7 25 ♖e8 (here 25 ♖ha1 is not to be feared on account of 25...♘xd5, providing the escape-square c6 for the king, and with two extra pawns for the moment) 25...♘xd5 26 ♖xe7 and now Sutovsky recommends 26...b5, with two connected passed pawns on the queenside. *Fritz 10* agrees with this whole line, but prefers 26...♔c6, with the idea of playing 27...♖f6 and 28...♔d6; both moves are strong.

But what should Black do after the text-move? The exchange of a4- and a5-pawns doesn't help Black in the ending after 21...♕xg3 22 fxg3. Then, of course, 22...♘xc3? is not playable since the piece is lost after 23 ♔d2. If 22...♘b6 then 23 h4, with an excellent position; the king is very well placed in the centre, there is a passed pawn on the h-file, and Black is passive.

The immediate 21...♘b6 is no better, since 22 h4 follows.

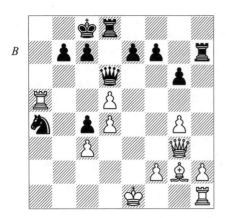

21...♕b6!!

Finally the position of the white king in the centre is the decisive factor.

22 ♖a8+

If 22 ♖xa4 then 22...♕b1+ 23 ♔d2 ♕b2+ 24 ♔e3 (the king has to escape the light-square checks such as 24 ♔d1 ♕b3+, but of course going forward with the king cannot have a good outcome) 24...♕xc3+ 25 ♔f4 ♕xd4+ 26 ♗e4 (26 ♔f3 ♕xd5+ 27 ♔e2 ♕d2+ leads to a quick mate) 26...♕f6+ 27 ♔e3, and now the artistic 27...♖h3! wins the queen.

22...♔d7 23 ♖xd8+

Now 23 ♖xa4 loses to 23...♕b1+ 24 ♔d2 ♕b2+ 25 ♔e3 ♕xc3+ 26 ♔f4 ♕xd4+ 27 ♗e4 f5.

23...♔xd8 24 0-0 *(D)*

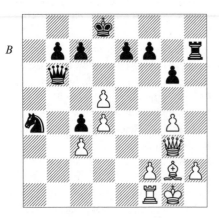

The white king is finally safe, but the price will be very high: the creation of another passed pawn.

24...♕b2 25 ♖e1 ♕xc3!

Gaining a tempo on the white queen. In contrast, 25...♘xc3? leaves the black queen tied up, and as pointed out by Sutovsky, White's initiative is strong after 26 ♕e3! ♕b4? 27 d6!, and White wins material: 27...e6 (27...♕xd6 28 ♕xc3 ♕xh2+ 29 ♔f1 gets Black nowhere) 28 ♕g5+ ♔c8 29 ♖a1 ♘a4 (the answer to 29...♘a2 is likewise 30 ♕e7) 30 ♕e7 cxd6 31 ♕e8+, winning the a4-knight.

We see once again that the safety of a king in the centre demands the utmost care; all the more so here, when the h7-rook is no help in this respect.

26 ♕e5 ♕b4 27 d6

It's now or never – Black was threatening 27...♕d6.

27...♕xd6 28 ♗xb7 ♘b6

A useful regrouping; the knight has already accomplished its task, and can go to d7.

29 ♔g2 *(D)*

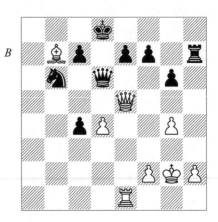

29...♔d7!

29...♘d7 is also possible, forcing the exchange of queens, but the move played, which might appear risky, is the result of a good assessment, and threatens 30...c6.

30 ♕b5+?

It is better to retreat the bishop, although Black has the advantage after, for example, 30 ♗e4 e6 31 f4 ♘d5.

30...c6!

It is not the centralized black king that will be mated, but the castled white king.

31 ♕xb6? ♕xh2+ 32 ♔f1

32 ♔f3 also leads to mate, but in more moves: 32...♕h3+ 33 ♔e4 (if 33 ♔f4 then 33...g5+! 34 ♔xg5 ♖g7+, and mate in two moves) 33...♕xg4+ 34 ♔e3 ♖h3+ 35 ♔d2 ♕f4+ 36 ♔d1 ♖d3+ 37 ♔c2 ♕d2+.

32...♕h3+ 0-1

In Games 1 to 4, after a certain point there was practically no choice but to keep the king in the centre. However, as in Game 5, this is generally not the case, and the decision regarding the best location for the king is a matter of judgement and preference.

In my book *Winning Chess Explained*, there is a section (2.5) devoted to this question, to which I suggest that the reader refers if he wishes to study this topic further. To close this chapter, let us look briefly at a further example where the position of the king in the centre constitutes an advantage.

Supplementary Game 5.1
Yasser Seirawan – Alexander Beliavsky
World Cup, Brussels 1988
Slav Defence, Exchange Variation

1 d4 d5 2 c4 c6 3 ♘c3 ♘f6 4 cxd5 cxd5 5 ♗f4 ♘c6 6 e3 ♗f5 7 ♘f3 e6 8 ♗b5 ♘d7 9 0-0 ♗e7 10 ♗xc6 bxc6 11 ♖c1 ♖c8 *(D)*

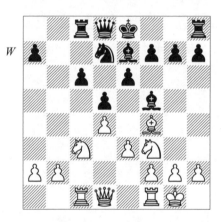

White has created a weakness on c6, which will be eliminated if Black manages to play ...c5. This explains the following move.

12 ♘a4?

The knight strays from the centre, which in a 'normal' position would not be a mistake, since the priority, if White wants to gain the advantage here, is to prevent Black from getting rid of his weakness. Mikhalchishin indicated that it was better to play 12 ♘e5 ♘xe5 13 ♗xe5 f6 14 ♗g3 c5, with equality, although of course this was not White's intention when he played 10 ♗xc6.

We can say that White has played as if the position were 'normal', i.e. as if Black had already castled.

An optimist might think that this is even worse for Black, because although the black king is not beset by the dangers that we saw in the previous games, he still needs a tempo to complete his development. However, this shortcoming is transformed into a virtue here.

12...g5!!

Initiating a violent offensive against White's castled position. The accessibility of the g- and h-files (through not having castled) is what allows this advance to be so strong.

13 ♗g3 h5 *(D)*

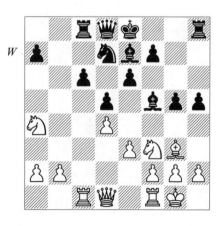

14 h3?

14 ♘c5 is better, and leaves White only a little worse. The text-move creates a 'contact-point', and Black's attack develops with great speed.

14...g4 15 hxg4 hxg4 16 ♘e5 ♘xe5 17 ♗xe5 f6 (D)

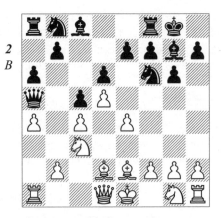

Consider the moves 9...e6 and 9...e5, and select an answer:

a) 9...e6 is better.

b) 9...e5 is better.

c) The two moves lead to different types of structure, but are of equal worth.

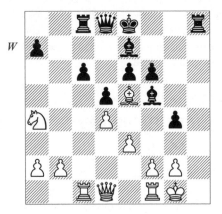

The king will go to f7, where it will not be in the way of the major pieces.

18 ♗g3 ♔f7 19 ♖e1 ♖h5 20 ♕d2 ♗e4! 21 ♔f1 ♗f3!! 0-1

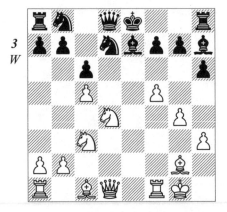

Exercises

Unless otherwise stated, your task is to decide how you would continue as the player to move.

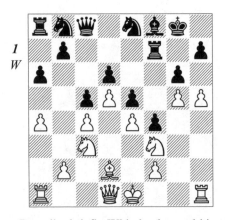

Describe briefly White's plan and his most important moves.

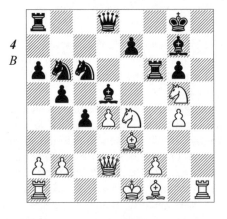

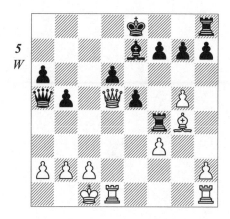

5
W

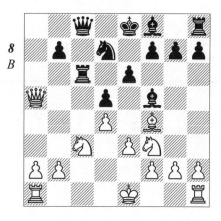

8
B

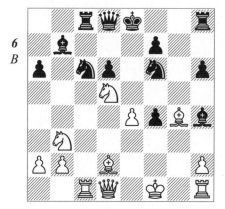

6
B

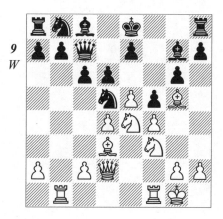

9
W

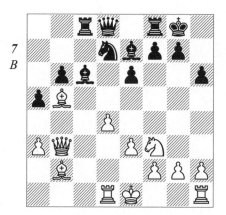

7
B

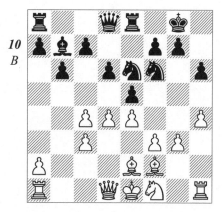

10
B

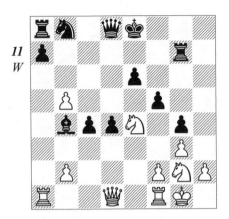

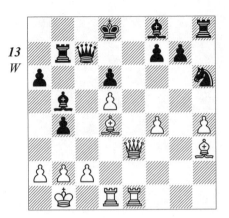

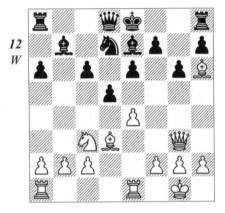

2 Opposite-Side Castling

When the kings are situated on opposite wings, there is a stronger case for sending the pawns forward into the attack, and moving all the pieces towards the opposite wing to the one where our own king is located. Indeed, this strategy becomes not only advisable but even sometimes essential.

We are familiar with the scenario where both sides are attacking with all their might and, as in a race, the first past the post claims victory. The winning-post is reached when the enemy king's defences are overwhelmed, concluding in mate or a decisive advantage. The outcome is often uncertain almost until the end of the struggle.

The outcome is clearer when the contest is of a different sort, where one side attacks while the other only defends. Since it is possible that the defending side might not be able to use all his forces in the defence, the outcome is usually a bad one for him.

There is a third scenario, which consists of combining the attack with prophylactic measures on the wing where one's own king is located, in order to hinder, slow down, or even completely halt the opponent's progress; this type of struggle is more common in today's chess.

Game 6

Andras Adorjan – Zoltan Ribli
Candidates playoff match (game 4), Budapest 1979
Sicilian Defence, Najdorf Variation

In this game White's attack does not encounter any serious opposition and is carried out in a straightforward and effective manner.

1 e4 c5 2 ♘f3 d6 3 d4 cxd4 4 ♘xd4 ♘f6 5 ♘c3 a6 6 ♗e3

This move was a rare guest in the 1970s. Its popularity began to grow in the following decade with the rise of the 'English Attack' and at present it is the main line against the Najdorf Sicilian.

6...e5 7 ♘b3 ♗e6 8 ♕d2 ♘bd7 9 f3 *(D)*

White has shown his cards; his main plan is queenside castling, followed by the advance g4. At present there is a great deal of theory on this position. Black frequently plays with his king in the centre, delaying a decision as to its long-term future, so as not to offer a clear target.

9...♖c8

Black decides to continue playing 'normal' moves on the queenside, postponing any decision about what to do on the kingside. In the

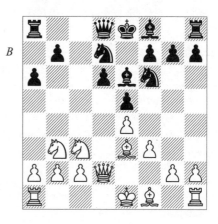

same spirit, it is possible to play 9...b5, which we discuss in the context of Supplementary Games 6.1 and 6.2, both of them much more modern examples.

10 g4 ♗e7

Continuing his development. Another idea is to play ...h6 (now or later), which is the modern treatment of the line. Black hinders White's attack by keeping the f6-knight on its natural square, although of course it provides a contact-point on g5 for the future.

11 0-0-0 ♘b6 12 h4 (D)

In this and many similar positions it is possible (but not always better) to dislodge the f6-knight with 12 g5, since after 12...♘h5, although the knight moves away from the centre, it also makes it harder for White to open lines on the kingside. White tries to prevent this possibility by bringing a pawn to h5 before playing g5. This plan is a slow one, and normally Black can make constructive use of these two tempi, although that was not the case in this game.

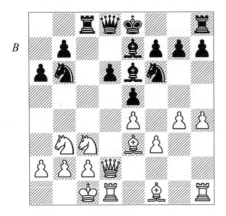

12...0-0?!

Very risky, since it provides White with an obvious target without having any clear idea of where his counterplay will come from; it does not seem possible to counter-attack against the white king, so Black will need to come up with something special.

With the same ideas as in the game, it was possible to play 12...♘c4, keeping the king in the centre, and after 13 ♗xc4 ♖xc4 14 h5, there is the 'modern' resource 14...h6.

13 h5 ♘c4?

This is the decisive error. Instead, 13...d5 was to be considered, although White is slightly better after 14 g5!, when best seems 14...♘xe4 15 fxe4 d4 16 ♘xd4 exd4 17 ♕xd4 (not 17 ♕g2 ♖xc3! 18 bxc3 ♗a3+ 19 ♔b1 ♘a4, winning) 17...♗xg5 18 ♗xg5 ♕xg5+ 19 ♔b1, although of course the position remains complicated.

On the other hand 14 ♗xb6?! ♕xb6 15 g5 is not as good as it looks, since after 15...d4 16 ♘a4 ♕c6 17 gxf6 Black does not play 17...gxf6? since he would mated with 18 ♘ac5! ♗xc5 19 ♖g1+ ♔h8 20 ♕h6. 17...♗xf6! is playable, and Black's limited threats on the c-file prove far from harmless after 18 ♘ac5 ♗xb3! 19 ♘xb3 ♗g5, when it is Black who wins.

Another idea is 13...♘fd7!, not waiting passively for 14 g5 but seeking complications with the defensive resource 14...f5!, as played in Iordachescu-Neverov, Dubai open 2005.

14 ♗xc4 ♖xc4 15 g5 ♘d7 (D)

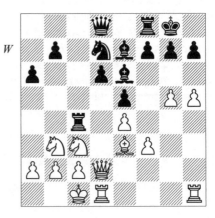

What should White do now? If the position were a 'normal' one (i.e. if each tempo were of the utmost value, since normally the first to open lines against the enemy king gains the advantage), then the first idea that should be considered is the thematic sacrifice 16 g6, which is good, but here White is in no hurry and can attack with maximum force without sacrificing anything.

16 ♖dg1!

The g6 break, opening lines, cannot be prevented, and this move is not a waste of time, since the rook will be very useful on the g-file.

16...♕c7 17 g6 ♖c8

Black's castled position is demolished after 17...♘f6 18 ♗h6! ♘e8 19 ♗xg7! ♔xg7 (or 19...♘xg7 20 ♕h6) 20 h6+ ♔g8 21 g7, with a material advantage and an attack.

17...♗f6 will probably transpose into the game.

18 ♗h6!! ♗f6 19 gxh7+ ♔xh7 (D)

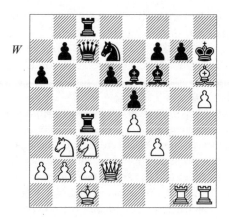

20 ♗xg7!

Opening up Black's castled position is worth more than the piece. This sacrifice is based on concrete calculation, which is possible in this position.

20...♔xg7 21 h6!

This is the right way. White should not get carried away with 21 ♖xg7+? since, as Adorjan indicates, after 21...♔xg7 22 ♕g5+ ♔f8 23 h6 Black does not play 23...♖xc3? 24 h7 ♖xc2+ 25 ♔b1 ♖xb2+ 26 ♔xb2 ♕c3+ 27 ♔a3, after which he is mated, but instead defends with 23...♕d8! and retains a decisive material advantage.

21...♗f6

The other bishop moves also lead to mate: after 21...♗h8, 22 ♕g5 wins, while if 21...♗f8 White wins with 22 ♕g5 f6 23 ♕g6+ ♔h8 24 h7.

22 ♕g2!

With the unstoppable threat of 23 ♕g7+!, followed by mate.

1-0

The success of White's attack is unquestionable, although in the 21st century we rarely see so 'cooperative' a defence in a game between two world championship candidates, which the two Hungarian grandmasters were when this game was played.

Black was unable to halt the attack on his king or create serious threats against the enemy king. Of course, some major defensive ideas on the kingside were unknown or underestimated at the time: ...h5 by Black to prevent or delay White's g4, or else, after g4, playing ...h6, to prevent the f6-knight from being dislodged, or the ...f5 resource mentioned in the note to move 13.

So let us now, as promised, consider two more modern encounters in this same opening line.

Supplementary Game 6.1
Viswanathan Anand – Boris Gelfand
Wijk aan Zee 2006
Sicilian Defence, Najdorf Variation

1 e4 c5 2 ♘f3 d6 3 d4 cxd4 4 ♘xd4 ♘f6 5 ♘c3 a6 6 f3 e5 7 ♘b3 ♗e6 8 ♗e3 ♘bd7 9 ♕d2 b5 10 0-0-0 ♘b6 11 ♕f2 (D)

11...♘c4

If 11...♘fd7 White can change plan and play 12 f4, taking advantage of the absence of the f6-knight. Thus the text-move is more fashionable.

12 ♗xc4 bxc4 13 ♘a5

This 'spectacular' move has replaced 13 ♘c5.

13...♕d7

The knight is immune since 13...♕xa5? runs into 14 ♗b6 ♕b4 15 a3, winning the queen.

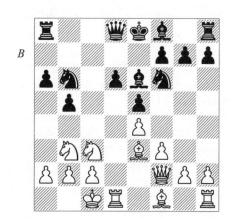

14 ♖d2 ♗e7 15 ♖hd1 ♖b8?

Black wants to continue delaying castling with a useful move on the queenside, but surprisingly the rook becomes a tactical weakness.

16 ♗c5! ♕c7 (D)

No better is 16...0-0 17 ♗xd6 ♗xd6 18 ♖xd6 ♕c7 19 ♘c6, winning.

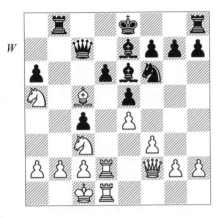

17 ♖xd6!

This sacrifice deals a heavy blow to the black king in the centre.

17...♕xa5

If 17...0-0 White has 18 ♖c6!, winning even more material.

18 ♖xe6 fxe6 19 ♗xe7 ♖b7

19...♔xe7? fails to 20 ♕a7+!, winning immediately (here we can see one of the unexpected

drawbacks of 15...♖b8?) and 19...♔f7 is no good either, since White wins material with 20 ♗xf6 gxf6 21 ♖d7+ ♔e8 22 ♕a7 ♕b4 23 a3! ♕xb2+ 24 ♔d2 ♕xa3 25 ♕xb8+ ♔xd7 26 ♕xh8.

20 ♗d6

White has more than adequate compensation for the exchange; he is a pawn up, the black structure is weak, and furthermore the black king has no secure refuge. If now 20...♔f7?! then 21 f4! exf4 22 e5 opens more lines, with a winning attack. To avoid something worse, Black opted to enter an endgame that was better for White, where the weakness of the black pawns was a decisive factor and they fell one after the other.

A completely different idea for Black is to play ...h5 before White plays g4, rendering it substantially more difficult to achieve this advance. However, the snag is obvious: if Black ever castles kingside, his position will never be as safe as if the pawn were still on h7. Although the black king can stay in the centre for a while in relative safety, this has longer-term risks, as we know.

The manoeuvre ...h5 by Black has been employed with satisfactory results by several of the strongest defenders of the Najdorf Variation. Here is an example between two of the superstars of modern chess.

Supplementary Game 6.2

Vladimir Kramnik – Veselin Topalov

Linares 2004

Sicilian Defence, Najdorf Variation

1 e4 c5 2 ♘f3 d6 3 d4 cxd4 4 ♘xd4 ♘f6 5 ♘c3 a6 6 ♗e3 e5 7 ♘b3 ♗e6 8 f3 ♘bd7 9 ♕d2 b5 10 0-0-0 h5 11 ♘d5!? (D)

This leap is one of White's most important ideas. The presence of the d5-knight can hardly be tolerated, as the idea of meeting ...♗e7 with ♘xe7 would sometimes win the d6-pawn, plus the knight controls b6, etc. However, after an exchange on d5 White gains an outpost on c6, which the b3-knight is ideally placed to exploit.

The ♘d5 idea is interesting even when Black can play a later ...♘b6 and capture the d5-pawn, because the opening of lines can highlight the insecurity of the black king.

11...♗xd5

Since White has not played g4, capturing with the knight was to be considered. After 11...♘xd5 12 exd5 ♗f5 13 ♗d3 ♗xd3 14 ♕xd3 White is slightly better, as indicated by Kramnik, since after the necessary preparations

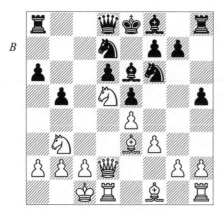

White can select the most suitable pawn-break, either on the queenside with c4 or on the kingside with f4.

12 exd5 g6 13 ♔b1 ♘b6? *(D)*

With this ambitious move, Black takes an unreasonable risk, embarking on complications when behind in development and with his king in the centre. Kramnik's brilliant play shows that this was an error, as he carries out the plan of occupying c6 to perfection.

Kramnik suggested instead 13...♗g7 14 ♘a5 ♘b6 15 c4 bxc4 16 ♘c6 ♕c7 17 ♗xb6 ♕xb6 18 ♗xc4 when, despite the well-placed knight on c6, White can only claim a slight advantage.

14 ♕c3! ♗e7

The d5-pawn is taboo in view of 15 ♖xd5 followed by 16 ♕c6+, while in the event of 14...♖b8, defending the b6-square in advance, White can try to exploit Black's lack of development with 15 f4!, when even going into an ending with 15...♕c8 16 ♕xc8+ ♘xc8 17 fxe5 dxe5 18 c4! bxc4 19 ♗xc4 is much better for White, on account of his greater activity, with the rooks close to invading the black camp, helped by the bishop-pair.

15 ♕c6+ ♘bd7 16 ♗b6!

A spectacular way to exploiting the overload on the black queen.

16...♕xb6

Sacrificing the exchange, seeking to exploit the fact that the white queen will be short of squares, since 16...♕c8?! just loses the d6-pawn after 17 ♗c7.

17 ♕xa8+ ♘b8 18 ♘a5 ♘fd7!

More promising than 18...0-0 19 ♕b7 ♕xa5 20 ♕xe7 ♘xd5 21 ♕g5, when the white queen easily escapes.

19 ♘c6 ♗g5

Here instead of **20 ♕a7?!**, which allowed Topalov to continue to complicate the game, Kramnik pointed out that the strongest line was 20 h4! ♗e3 21 g4, when it is not possible to take advantage of the white queen's position, since the weak defences of the black king do not allow this. One of White's ideas is to play g5 and bring the light-squared bishop decisively into play via h3.

Game 7

Judit Polgar – Viswanathan Anand
FIDE World Ch, San Luis 2005
Caro-Kann Defence, 4...♘d7

Attacks against kings situated on opposite wings sometimes have a different character, as in the game that we shall see now. To reduce it to its bare essentials, we could say that it is a contest between an open file and contact-points – which is worth more?

1 e4 c6 2 d4 d5 3 ②c3 dxe4 4 ②xe4 ②d7 5 ②d3 ②gf6 (D)

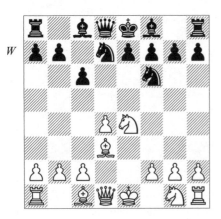

6 ②f3

6 ②g5 is the most incisive move and the one considered to be the most critical. Anand even rates 6 ②f3 as dubious, on the basis that it allows Black to solve his opening problems simply by carrying out the idea of 4...②d7, which is to play ...②f6 and exchange the knights, without having to pay the price of doubled pawns on f6, as happens after 4...②f6.

6...②xe4 7 ②xe4 ②f6 8 ②d3 ②g4

Accomplishing the idea of the Caro-Kann Defence; Black develops his queen's bishop outside the pawn-chain, to a good square.

9 ②e3 (D)

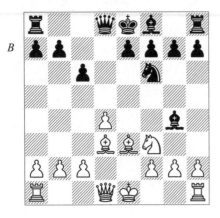

9...e6

It is not possible to extract any further benefit from the pin on the f3-knight; Anand pointed

out that after 9...豐d5 10 ②e2 e6 11 h3 ②h5 12 0-0 ②e7 13 c4, White is slightly better.

10 c3

Now it is necessary to continue development.

10...②d6!

Here the bishop is more active than on e7, and not just on general considerations; from d6 it controls the e5-square, thus interfering with White's plan of shaking off the pin and eliminating the g4-bishop with h3, g4 and ②e5.

11 h3 ②h5 12 豐e2 (D)

Now 12 g4 ②g6 13 ②e5? is not possible, owing to 13...②xe5 14 ②xg6 hxg6 15 dxe5 豐xd1+, followed by 16...②xg4, and simply weakening the kingside with g4, without being able to play ②e5, is not advisable. 12 0-0 is the soundest option.

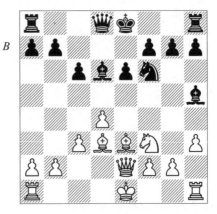

How should Black continue? After completing his kingside development, Black has to decide where to put his king. He could consider preparing queenside castling, although the most natural seems to be simply 12...0-0. However, as Dvoretsky emphasizes in his books, it is important to ask yourself "what is my opponent planning?" and if this plan is favourable for the opponent, try to frustrate or hinder it, preferably with a move that is also useful for your own purposes.

12...豐a5!

White's plan was to castle queenside, which is ruled out now since it would lose the a2-pawn. Admittedly the queen can be dislodged with b4, but that would discourage queenside castling by White, and such advances on the queenside can be weakening, not forgetting that there is a possibility of ...♕d5, putting more pressure on the pinned f3-knight.

13 a4

An awkward move to have to make, but if 13 0-0 then Black plays 13...♕d5!, threatening to double the pawns with ...♗xf3; then if 14 g4 ♗g6, the exchange 15 ♗xg6 would open the h-file in Black's favour, and in any case playing g4 would weaken White's castled position.

Let us note that in this case it is an advantage to Black to have delayed castling, since he could use the h-file or play, depending on the circumstances, ...♗xd3 and ...h5, if White does not play ♗xg6.

13...0-0 *(D)*

Anand plays the soundest move. He pointed out that 13...♕d5 14 g4 ♘xg4 15 ♗c4 ♘xe3 (15...♕e4 16 hxg4 ♗xg4 is strongly met by 17 ♖h4!, solving his problems with the pin) 16 ♗xd5 ♘xd5 17 ♖g1! is not clear.

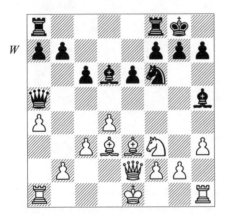

14 ♕c2

While Black makes natural moves and continues to develop his forces, White moves her queen once again, with the idea of defending the a4-pawn and castling queenside. White considers that it is risky for Black to play ...♗xf3, since it opens the g-file onto Black's castled position, added to which there would be the two bishops also aiming in that direction.

The most logical move, now that Black has castled, was to play 14 0-0, although the white

position can aspire to no more than equality after 14...♖fe8, with the idea of ...e5.

14...♗xf3!

Not fearing the opening of the g-file; the weakness of the white structure is permanent, and Black has a plan for counteracting the dangers of the open file.

15 gxf3 ♕h5! *(D)*

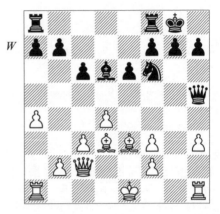

The queen is very useful on the kingside, since defending h7 releases the f6-knight to play ...♘d5. This is the second part of the defensive plan, the importance of which we shall see later. From h5 the queen also eyes the pawns at f3 and h3, but Black's priority is not to capture pawns, opening more lines onto his king, but to defend his castled position adequately. Nevertheless, in the future, with the king well defended, this possibility will become more important.

16 0-0-0

This was the idea, but for the future there is one contact-point on b5 and another on b4.

16...♘d5 17 ♔b1 b5!

Beginning the counter-attack.

18 ♖dg1 *(D)*

White wants to play 19 ♖g5, followed by ♖hg1 or even ♖g4, repeating moves, since the h7-pawn is attacked. How should Black defend?

Not, of course, with 18...♘xe3?, which repairs White's structure and loses the services of the strong knight. 18...h6 is not trustworthy either, since 19 ♖g4 follows, with the powerful threat of 20 ♖hg1. And closing the diagonal with 18...g6, although preventing 19 ♖g5? for

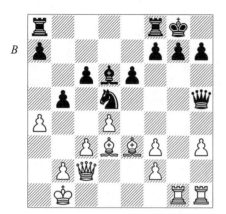

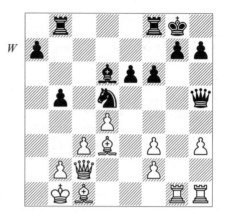

the time being, because 19...♘xe3 gains a decisive advantage in material, just presents White with a contact-point on h5. White would then renew her threat to play ♖g5 with 19 h4!.

18...f6!

This 'ugly' move is the third part of the manoeuvre begun with 14...♗xf3. By 15...♕h5 and 16...♘d5, the two black pieces relieved one another from the defence of h7, in order to make way for the f-pawn to advance. Now, if necessary, it is possible to defend the most important weak point in Black's position, g7, with ...♖f7. Admittedly there is now a weakness on e6, but Black can easily defend this, without any loss of mobility.

19 axb5

Opening lines onto one's own king is not ideal, but otherwise the capture ...bxa4 hangs over White, tying down her queen, which cannot join in the attack. Furthermore, ...bxa4 would open the b-file.

19...cxb5 20 ♗c1 ♖ab8 *(D)*

Preparing the ...b4 break.

21 ♕e2 ♖fe8 22 ♕e4?

The queen hits h7, but this is no great hardship for Black, who can advantageously get rid of this pressure. Anand commented that 22 ♖g4 was better, with the idea of 23 ♖e4. After 22...f5 23 ♖g5 ♕h4! (23...♕f7 would be answered by 24 ♖hg1 g6 25 h4, gaining counter-chances thanks to the h5 break) 24 ♖g2 ♗f4 25 ♗e3, Black has a slight advantage.

22...♔h8!

Black continues unhurriedly to strengthen his position. Now the g7-pawn can additionally

be defended with ...♖g8, and Black avoids the obvious problems that can arise from having his king on a half-open file on which the opponent will soon double rooks.

23 h4 *(D)*

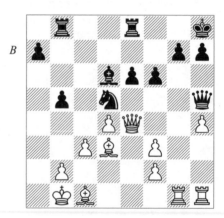

Black's preparatory moves are complete, everything is adequately defended, and it is time to think about attacking the white king. What is required?

23...f5!

First Black nullifies the pressure on h7, leaving the d3-bishop 'dead'.

24 ♕e2 ♕f7!

And now, after reinforcing the safety of his king and nullifying White's attack, comes the final defensive manoeuvre, which becomes an offensive one when the most powerful black piece transfers to the queenside to join in the attack on the white king.

25 ♖g2 *(D)*

Of course 25 ♗xb5? looks very bad; a possible continuation is 25...♘xc3+ 26 bxc3 a6 27 c4 and now much stronger than 27...axb5 28 c5 is 27...e5!, completely opening the queenside.

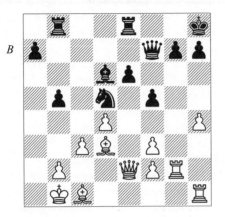

25...♗f4!?

A blockading move, threatening to gain material with 26...♗xc1 and 27...♘f4.

Analysis engines tend to prefer moves like 25...b4 or 25...e5, but it is not the most 'human' decision to enter complications when the natural course of the game brings a clear advantage.

26 ♖hg1 ♖g8

Not 26...♗xc1?! owing to the *zwischenzug* 27 ♖xg7!.

27 ♗e3 ♕d7 28 ♕d2 ♗d6

Of course, there is no need to strengthen the white centre; on d6 the bishop is useful on the queenside.

The engines think that 28...b4 was also very strong, but this is hardly the first move that a strong human player would consider. Anand wishes to have all his pieces deployed optimally before embarking on any complications, which is understandable since White does not have any counterplay, or any satisfactory way to defend.

29 ♗c2 (D)

29...♕b7!

Involving the queen in the attack is stronger than entering complications without it. Nevertheless, as on the previous move, Black's position is so strong that 29...b4 30 c4 ♘c3+ 31 ♔c1 ♘a2+ 32 ♔d1 b3 is also advantageous, as Anand pointed out.

30 ♗g5

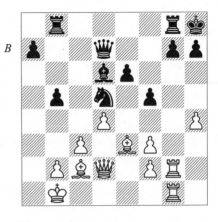

In answer to 30 ♕d3 Black brings the infantry into the attack with 30...a5, and White is defenceless.

30...b4!

This starts a forcing sequence which brings about the destruction of White's king's defences. In contrast, White's greatest achievement, the g-file, has been neutralized. Now Black's pieces infiltrate White's queenside without White being able to do anything to prevent them.

31 c4 b3

The retreat ♗b1, as in the line with 29...b4, is no longer possible.

32 ♗d3 (D)

No better are 32 cxd5 bxc2+ 33 ♕xc2 ♕xd5 and 32 ♗xb3 ♕xb3 33 cxd5 ♗a3.

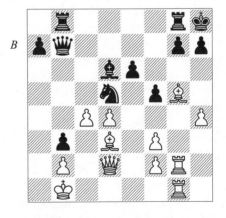

32...♗b4!

The black bishop penetrates White's defences with a gain of time, and supports the coming invasion by his queen.

33 ♕e2 ♕a6 34 ♗h6 ♘c3+!

Black exploits the fact that all White's pieces are on the other side of the board in order to land the final blows. This move was prepared with 32...♗b4.

35 bxc3 ♗xc3 36 ♔c1 ♕a3+

36...b2+ 37 ♔c2 ♕a2 is quicker, but the white king has no defence anyway.

37 ♔d1 ♕a1+ 38 ♗c1 b2 39 ♕e3 ♗xd4 40 ♕d2 bxc1♕+ 41 ♕xc1 ♕a2 0-1

The short reply to the question posed before the game is that the contact-points proved more valuable than the open file, but this was not an effortless victory. Let us summarise the main points and key moments.

The contest between two types of advantage, the contact-points on b5 and b4 (favouring Black), versus the half-open g-file (favouring White), ended in a clear triumph for Black.

Both factors are important, and allow an attack on the enemy king, but the basic difference in this game was that one could be defended and the other could not. Black was able to neutralize the white offensive on the g-file with some very accurate moves, and combine this with the attack, something that White was unable to imitate.

It is worth highlighting Black's manoeuvre 15...♕h5! and 16...♘d5, culminating in 23...f5! and 24...♕f7!, with which the queen was able to transfer to the queenside.

Black's attack starting with 17...b5!, right up to the finish with 29...♕b7!, 32...♗b4! and 34...♘c3+! could not be parried.

White's play could have been improved, but she would still have stood worse, while the clarity with which Black combined defence and attack, as well as being effective, creates a strong aesthetic effect.

Game 8

Alexander Dreev – Sergei Tiviakov

Dos Hermanas 2003

Queen's Indian Defence, Petrosian Variation

Even when the kings are castled on opposite sides, sometimes the attacks on the two kings do not develop in a clear or simple manner. It is not always possible to advance the pawns against the enemy king and open lines, or quickly concentrate enough forces against the opponent's castled position for the attack to be successful. Sometimes, as in the game that we shall examine now, it is necessary to prepare the attack, something that can be done in an unhurried fashion only if the opponent is unable to attack with greater speed.

1 d4 ♘f6 2 c4 e6 3 ♘f3 b6 4 a3

This move introduces the Petrosian Variation, which was revitalized in the 1980s by Garry Kasparov. The main idea of this apparently modest move is to avoid the pin ...♗b4, and thus set up the positional threat of d5.

4...♗b7 5 ♘c3 *(D)*

With the aforementioned threat of 6 d5, nullifying the b7-bishop.

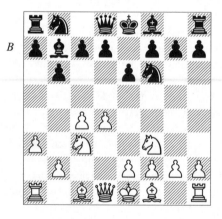

5...d5 6 cxd5 ♘xd5

6...exd5 leads to a different structure and is also fully playable.

7 ♗d2

This is a secondary variation. The main line is to prepare e4 with 7 ♕c2 or 7 e3 followed by ♗d3 and e4; in both continuations White intends to meet ...♘xc3 with bxc3, strengthening his centre.

With the move in the game White intends to assign the c3-square not to the b2-pawn but to the bishop.

7...♘d7 8 ♘xd5 ♗xd5 9 ♕c2

Occupying the centre with e4 remains a fundamental plan for White.

9...c5 10 e4 ♗b7 (D)

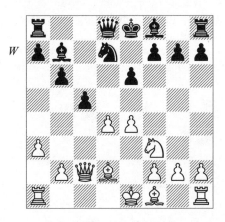

How should White deal with the central tension? The most natural way is to continue with the main idea of ♗d2 and play 11 ♗c3, followed by ♖d1. Another idea is the immediate 11 ♖d1, seeking to put pressure on the d-file and decide later what to do with the d2-bishop.

Against both continuations Black takes on d4 and manages to develop his pieces fairly easily, nullifying the pressure both on the diagonal and on the d-file. Let us, for example, look at the play in Dreev-Leko, Moscow (rapid) 2002, which continued 11 ♖d1 cxd4 12 ♘xd4 a6 (this move is very important to prevent both ♗b5 and ♘b5; the black queen can move off the d-file, where it will feel uncomfortable in the event of White playing ♗c3) 13 ♗e3 ♗e7 14 ♗e2 ♕c8 15 ♕b1 ♘c5 16 f3 0-0 17 0-0 ♕b8, and Black did not have any problems. In R.Bagirov-Palac, European Team Ch, Batumi 1999, 11 ♗c3 was played, but the evaluation was similar; after 11...cxd4 12 ♘xd4 a6 13 ♖d1 ♕c7 14 ♗e2 ♗e7 15 0-0 0-0 Black could deploy his pieces comfortably, occupying the c- and d-files, and with an agile d7-knight.

11 d5!?

An ambitious advance. White gains space, but at the same time isolates his d-pawn, which in the future might become weak, both in the endgame and the middlegame, if White's greater space and activity are neutralized.

11...exd5 12 exd5 (D)

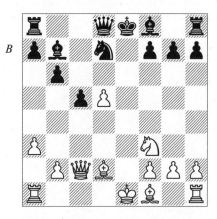

12...♗d6

Black chooses to proceed with his development, preparing kingside castling.

11 d5 was actually a pawn sacrifice, but the capture 12...♗xd5? is very suspect. White gains an advantage in development and an initiative with 13 0-0-0, and the white pieces invade the black camp with 14 ♗g5, 14 ♗c3 or 14 ♗b5 and it is impossible for Black to meet all the threats.

Another idea is to place the king on the queenside with 12...♕e7+ 13 ♗e3 0-0-0. Then:

a) 14 ♕a4 ♔b8 15 0-0-0 f6 and now 16 ♕g4 did not achieve very much in Anand-Almasi, Dortmund 1998, but 16 ♗b5! is more awkward to meet, intending to play 17 ♖he1 and then invade Black's castled position at an appropriate moment. For example, 16...♘e5 17 ♘xe5 fxe5 18 ♗c6 is favourable to White, as the isolated passed pawn becomes a strong supporting force.

b) In Atalik-Almasi, Jahorina 2003, White played 14 0-0-0 and after 14...♘f6 he gained a good game with the sacrifice 15 d6!. Both players analysed the same line during the game, reaching the conclusion that White's initiative gives more than enough compensation; this long variation holds up quite well under the scrutiny of the analysis engines: 15...♖xd6 16

♖xd6 ♕xd6 17 ♘g5 ♕d7 18 ♗c4 ♘d5 19 ♖d1 h6 20 ♕e4! f5 21 ♕f3 hxg5 22 ♗xd5 ♗xd5 23 ♖xd5 g4 24 ♕d1. Almasi delayed capturing the pawn with 15...♕e8 16 ♗c4 ♗xd6 but White had a strong initiative after 17 ♘g5 ♖f8 18 ♖he1! ♗c7, and here Atalik failed to play the strong and complex continuation 19 ♗xc5!, which would have brought him the advantage.

13 0-0-0 0-0 *(D)*

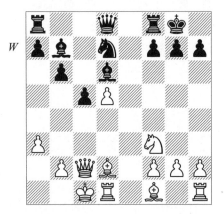

14 ♗b5

White completes his development before taking any other measures; on b5 the bishop is much more useful than on d3, since as well as not getting in the way of the white queen it can come to the defence of the d5-pawn with ♗c6.

However, as the kings have been placed on opposite wings, in principle we should consider whether a quick attack might work. 14 ♘g5?! proved too precipitate in Dreev-Karpov, Cap d'Agde (rapid) 2002; after 14...♘f6, 15 ♗c3 is still not possible owing to 15...♗f4+, so White continued 15 ♔b1 ♗e5 16 ♘f3 ♗d4! 17 ♘xd4 cxd4 18 ♗b4 ♖e8 19 ♗b5 ♖e5 20 ♗c6 ♖c8, and White had overextended; Black had a development advantage and the better position.

14 ♗c3 is worth considering, as it is an 'essential' move – i.e. one that White is likely to need to play at some point. On principle, one should consider moving pieces whose best destination is not yet clear. However, here it is not the most flexible, since it prematurely abandons the c1-h6 diagonal, and Black no longer has to worry about the pin with ♗g5 after ...♘f6.

A routine move such as 14 ♗d3 is not convincing either, since as well as neglecting the d5-pawn, it obstructs the white queen, reducing its mobility and hindering its possible transfer to the kingside to join in the attack.

14...h6 *(D)*

14...♗xd5? fails to 15 ♗g5, winning material.

The text-move enables Black to play ...♘f6 without fearing the pin with ♗g5, although we should keep in mind that it also weakens the castled position somewhat.

14...♕c7 is another possibility, controlling c6 and dodging the possible pin after ...♘f6.

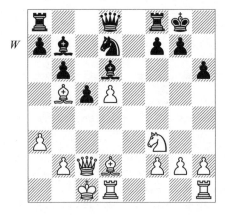

How should White begin the attack against the black king? The first thing that stands out is that, with ...h6 played, the manoeuvre ♕f5 and ♗d3 gains in force, but the immediate 15 ♕f5 is answered by 15...♘f6, and the defence of the d5-pawn is compromised; if necessary, Black then follows up with 16...♗c8 and the queen has to abandon the b1-h7 diagonal.

There is a contact-point on g5, but a pawn attack with g4-g5 is very difficult to carry through; the new weaknesses thus created, combined with the existing weakness of the d5-pawn, prevent it from working. Black can answer 15 g4? with, for example, 15...♘e5 or 15...♕f6, creating problems.

The ♘g5 leap, combined with ♗c3, is a basic weapon for White. After 14...h6 it is no longer possible to play this in a 'normal' manner, but as in some positions of the Queen's Gambit, after Black plays ...♘f6 it becomes possible to 'manufacture' this possibility by playing h4, to be able to recapture on g5 with the pawn, opening the h-file. The first move to consider then would be 15 h4.

15 ♗c3!

It is not enough to have a correct idea; the move-order is very important. 15 h4 is less appropriate because then 15...♘f6 would follow, when White has problems supporting his d-pawn. If then 16 ♗c3, Black could fearlessly play 16...♘xd5, while if 16 ♘g5 Black replies with Karpov's recipe, 16...♗e5.

15...♘f6 16 ♗c6 (D)

Fully vindicating one of the ideas of 14 ♗b5.

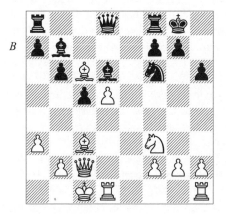

16...♖b8

Black could try to capture the pawn on c6, but the tempo consumed and the opening of the d-file would give White a lot of play after 16...♗xc6 17 dxc6 ♖c8 when even better than Dreev's suggestion of 18 ♕a4 is 18 ♕f5! and after 18...♖xc6 19 ♘e5 ♖c7 20 ♘c4! White seriously weakens Black's castled position, gaining the advantage after 20...♖d7 21 ♗xf6 gxf6. Then both 22 ♘e3 (with the idea of bringing it to f5 or g4, with devastating effect) and 22 ♕f3! (with the threat of 23 ♖xd6 ♖xd6 24 ♕g3+, winning, and meeting 22...♔h8 with 23 ♕e3, regaining the pawn) are strong. In both cases, inflicting such major weaknesses in Black's castled position is worth much more than a pawn.

17 h4

Now this, having completed all the preparations, and in the correct order; the ♘g5 leap is now on the agenda.

17...♘g4!

This 'only' move has many virtues. The white king is badly placed on c1 and White is obliged to waste a tempo; it also hits f2, and an eventual ♘g5 and hxg5 by White will no longer threaten the f6-knight.

If Black seeks counterplay with 17...b5?, White crowns his idea, begun with 15 ♗c3 and 17 h4, by playing 18 ♘g5!, with the threat of 19 ♗xf6, and after 18...hxg5 (if 18...g6 then 19 ♘e6!) 19 hxg5 with a winning attack; for example, 19...♘e4 20 ♕xe4 ♕xg5+ 21 ♖d2 ♕g6 22 ♕h4 f6 23 ♗d7! ♗c8 24 ♗e6+.

18 ♔b1 (D)

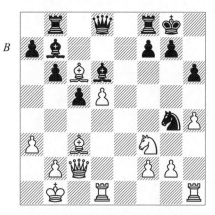

Once again it is Black's turn to defend, waiting for the storm to pass over before thinking about counter-attack.

18...♗c8?

Black tries to prove that the c6-bishop is out of play, and hopes to activate his own bishop with ...g6 and ....♗f5. But if this never comes to pass, then 18...♗c8 will seriously worsen his position, since the black pieces are more uncoordinated than before.

The capture on c6 is still inappropriate: after 18...♗xc6?! 19 dxc6 ♕c7 (if 19...♖c8 then 20 ♘g5 hxg5 21 hxg5 ♘h2 22 g3, followed by 23 ♖xh2, with a winning attack) the modest 20 ♖hf1! is strong, freeing the queen from the defence of f2. Then if 20...♕xc6 White exploits the weakness of Black's castled position with the crushing 21 ♗xg7! and after 21...♔xg7 comes 22 ♘d4, followed by ♘f5+ and ♖xd6, with a winning attack.

The most tenacious defence was 18...♕c7!, pointed out by Dreev, inviting an exchange of bishops with ♗xb7, which would ease the tension but without opening the d-file; another fundamental idea is that if 19 ♘g5, Black has 19...hxg5 20 hxg5 f5 21 gxf6 ♘xf6 22 ♗xf6 ♖xf6 23 ♕h7+ ♔f8 and White has no more than a draw by perpetual check.

19 ♖de1! *(D)*

The e-file is very important; this move lends more force to the ♘g5 leap.

Here the immediate 19 ♘g5 was interesting; after 19...hxg5 20 hxg5 f5 White has an attack but there is nothing decisive after, for instance, 21 gxf6 ♘xf6 22 ♕g6 ♕e7, intending 23...♕f7. But now Black will no longer have this defence.

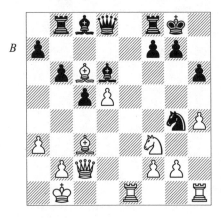

B

19...g6?

The threat of ...♗f5 will be forcefully prevented, and in fact this is the decisive error, since it leaves the castled position more vulnerable, weakens g6 and increases the power of the c3-bishop. White's initiative will be irresistible.

However, Black's position was already very precarious; let us look at a few example lines:

a) 19...b5 is met by a similar idea to the one seen in the game: 20 ♘g5! hxg5 21 hxg5 f5 22 gxf6 ♘xf6 23 ♖e6! (23 ♕g6?! b4 24 axb4 ♖xb4! is unclear). After 23...♗xe6 24 dxe6, White threatens 25 ♗xf6 ♖xf6 26 ♕h7+ ♔f8 27 ♕h8+ ♔e7 28 ♕xg7+ ♔xe6 29 ♕g4+, and 24...♗h2!? 25 ♖xh2 ♕d6 26 ♖h1 ♕xc6 27 ♗xf6 ♕xe6 28 ♗xg7! leads to a good ending for White.

b) The same recipe works against 19...♕c7: 20 ♘g5! hxg5 21 hxg5 f5 22 gxf6 ♘xf6 (or 22...gxf6 23 f3) 23 ♗xf6 gxf6 24 ♖h6, with the plan of doubling rooks, winning.

c) After 19...♗d7 the play is more complicated, but White still wins by means of the same sacrifice, 20 ♘g5!. The main variation then is 20...hxg5 21 hxg5 f5 22 gxf6 ♘xf6 23 ♕g6 ♗xc6 24 dxc6 ♖e8 and here White prevails with the quiet move 25 ♖d1!, pausing for a moment to prevent simplification and persisting with the idea of doubling rooks on the h-file, against which there is no adequate defence. For example, if 25...♗e6 (25...♖f8 meets the same reply) then 26 ♖h7 ♕c7 27 ♖dh1 wins.

In some of these lines we see the serious consequences of 18...♗c8?, interfering with the communication between Black's rooks.

d) There remains therefore the only move that radically prevents 20 ♘g5, namely 19...f6!?, a move to be contemplated only when all else fails. The castled position is further weakened, so that a tough defensive task can be expected. If White tries to prepare the sacrifice with 20 ♕g6, once again enhancing the c3-bishop, Black plays not 20...b5?, because of 21 ♘g5! hxg5 22 hxg5 ♘e5 23 ♕h7+ ♔f7 24 ♖h6, winning, but 20...♕c7!, which prevents 21 ♘g5?, since after 21...fxg5 the g7-square is defended. The position remains difficult for Black, but he still has defensive resources.

We now return to the position after 19...g6? *(D)*:

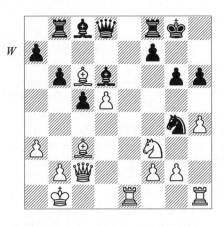

W

20 ♖e6!!

This elegant move creates the threat of 21 ♖xg6+, so the capture of the rook is forced and a powerful new guest arrives on e6.

20...♗xe6

If 20...♔h7 then amongst other moves 21 ♘g5+! wins (21 h5 is also very strong); e.g., 21...hxg5 22 ♖xd6! ♕xd6 23 hxg5+ ♘h2 24 g3.

21 dxe6 f5

If 21...♘f6 then 22 exf7+ ♔xf7 (22...♔g7 meets the same reply) 23 ♘g5+ hxg5 24 hxg5 and White wins.

22 h5! *(D)*

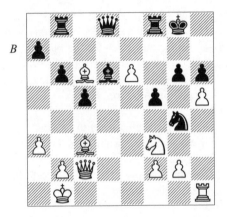

Decisively weakening Black's castled position.

22...gxh5

It is better to close the position with 22...g5, but White clears the diagonals with the thematic sacrifice 23 e7! to open lines. After 23...♗xe7 24 ♖d1 ♕c7 25 ♕b3+ ♖f7 26 ♕e6, faced with the threats of ♖d7 and ♗d5 the black position collapses, while if 23...♕xe7 then 24 ♗d5+ ♔h7 25 ♖e1 ♕c7 26 ♗e6 is decisive.

23 ♖xh5

The h-file becomes yet another attacking front.

23...♕e7 24 ♘h4!

Another piece comes into play, aiming at the weakness on f5, as well as the black king.

24...♕xe6 25 ♘xf5 ♗e5

Here 25...♖f6 would meet the same reply, as would 25...♖f7. If 25...♖xf5 Dreev pointed out the line 26 ♖xf5 ♗e5 27 ♕e4, winning.

26 ♗d5!

Highlighting all Black's weaknesses.

1-0

We see that neither side had an easy attack to start with. White created an isolated pawn on d5, with its strong and weak points, and later gained the initiative, through incisive play that contained a good dose of creativity. Black made a serious error with 18...♗c8?, wrongly thinking that his position was good enough for him to take on White in open combat, but in doing so his position became uncoordinated, which helped White's attack. The last chance for Black to strengthen his position was with 18...♕c7!. After the preparatory move 19 ♖de1! White finished off the game accurately and brilliantly.

Game 9

Alexander Motylev – Peter Svidler

Wijk aan Zee 2007
Grünfeld Defence, 3 f3

In the majority of cases with opposite-side castling, the plan of attack is clear: open lines, occupy weak points, etc. But the attack is not always so obvious. Sometimes the opponent has attacking chances, but we do not; there are no weaknesses for us to attack, no basis for an attack. Then, to maintain the tension, it is possible or even necessary to give up material, to prevent the focus of the struggle from being transferred to the opposite wing, where the opponent has the advantage. That is what occurs, in part, in the following game.

1 d4 ♘f6 2 c4 g6 3 f3 d5 4 cxd5 ♘xd5 5 e4 ♘b6 6 ♘c3 ♗g7 7 ♗e3 0-0 8 ♕d2 *(D)*

We are in a minor line of the Grünfeld which has grown in popularity in recent years, on

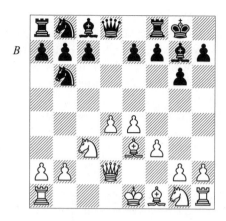

account of the attacking possibilities offered by Black's relatively unprotected castled position, with his king's knight far away on b6.

The position still has some features of the Grünfeld structure, but is also rather similar to the Sämisch King's Indian. White has occupied the centre and thanks to this advantage has deployed his pieces aggressively. The h4-h5 break is an obvious idea, and queenside castling is the most probable destination for the white king.

8...♘c6

Black increases the piece pressure on the centre, before attacking it with pawns.

Black can also attack the centre with pawns immediately, but one of the reasons for the revival of this line is that after 8...e5 9 d5 c6 Black has not yet found a good antidote to White's strong attack after 10 h4 *(D)*.

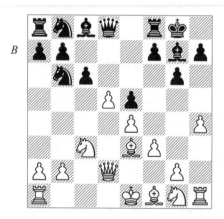

For example, 10...h5 11 g4! (White had secured an advantage with the slower 11 ♗e2 in

Kramnik-Shirov, Match (game 9), Cazorla 1998, but with the immediate break on g4 White manages to weaken the black king before Black can take advantage of White's lag in development) 11...cxd5 (if 11...hxg4 there then logically follows 12 h5) 12 exd5 ♘8d7 (opening lines towards one's own king is always risky; after 12...hxg4 13 h5 gxh5 14 ♖xh5 f5 15 ♗h6 ♕f6 16 ♗xg7 ♔xg7 17 0-0-0 ♘8d7 18 fxg4 Black's castled position does not have the protection of his pawns, and there are multiple invasion points) 13 gxh5 ♘f6 (if 13...gxh5 14 0-0-0 ♘f6 then once again 15 ♗h6, exchanging the best defender of the castled position) 14 hxg6 fxg6 15 ♘h3! ♘fxd5 16 ♘xd5 ♕xd5 17 ♕xd5+ ♘xd5 (the exchange of queens does not make things any safer for the black king) 18 ♗c4 ♗e6 19 ♘g5 ♘xe3 20 ♗xe6+ ♔h8 21 ♔f2 ♘f5 22 h5 with a great advantage to White, Ivanchuk-Åkesson, European Ch, Antalya 2004.

In general, the exchange of the g7-bishop is practically unavoidable, so the castled position loses a very important defender, which combined with the opening of the g- and/or h-files makes Black's defence very difficult.

9 0-0-0 *(D)*

Strengthening the centre and bringing the a1-rook into play. It is strange that no less a player than Alekhine himself advanced his centre, thus weakening it, with 9 d5? ♘e5, threatening to invade on c4. In Alekhine-Bogoljubow, Bled 1931 he was forced to lose a tempo with 10 ♗g5, when the white centre was attacked again with 10...c6 and after 11 ♖d1 cxd5 12 exd5 ♗f5 White already had serious problems. Play continued 13 g4 ♗d7 14 d6 f6 15 ♗h6 ♗c6 16 ♗xg7 ♔xg7 and White's position was in ruins, although the game ended in a draw.

Let us attempt a general summary of the position after the text-move (9 0-0-0). Both kings have weaknesses; Black's is missing the f6-knight, and has a single defender, the g7-bishop, which runs the risk of being exchanged. In White's case, the exchange of the c-pawn leaves his king more exposed.

White is clearly better placed for an attacking race; h4 and h5 will come very quickly, while Black does not find it so easy to generate

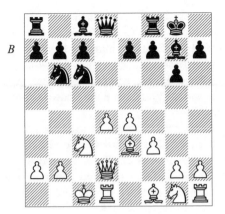

against the white king. Compared with 'normal' positions, Black has an extra piece on the queenside (the b6-knight) that he could potentially use in an attack, but it also obstructs the advance of the b-pawn, and it is not clear how it could actually help the attack. This implies that Black has to be faithful once again to the spirit of the Grünfeld and attack the white centre, so that the struggle is not focused exclusively on the kingside. For a long time the main continuation here was 9...e5, but at the moment the line 10 d5 ♘d4 11 f4 ♗g4 12 ♖e1 c5 13 fxe5 ♗xe5 14 h3 is giving Black a hard time.

9...f5

This is another way to attack the centre, made possible precisely because of the absence of the f6-knight; it definitely weakens the castled position, but in the event of the game opening up it allows more defenders to come to the kingside.

10 e5

Blunting the g7-bishop in exchange for ceding the d5-square; the plan of h4-h5 remains latent in the position.

10 exf5?! is inappropriate, since the black pieces become very active after 10...♗xf5, but 10 h4 fxe4 11 h5 is another line to consider. Black appears to arrive in time to support his castled position after 11...gxh5 12 ♖xh5 ♗f5, when Laznicka-Krasenkow, Ostrava 2007 continued 13 ♖g5 ♗g6 14 ♗e2 e5 15 d5 ♘d4 16 fxe4 c6 17 dxc6 ♘xc6 18 ♖e1 ♕f6 19 ♕g3 ♖ad8 20 ♘f3 ♘d4! and Black had a good position.

10...♘b4

Black aims to control the square that has just been conceded (d5).

11 ♘h3

Here once again 11 h4 should have been considered, but in Av.Bykhovsky-Dub, Tel Aviv 2002, Black managed to repel the assault after 11...♗e6 12 h5 (12 ♔b1!?) 12...♘xa2+ 13 ♘xa2 ♗xa2 14 hxg6 hxg6 15 ♗h6 ♕e8!, propping up his castled position.

11...♗e6 12 ♔b1 *(D)*

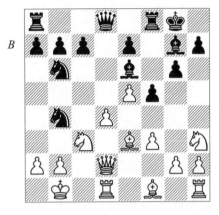

12...♕d7

Black brings more pieces into the fight; a rook will come to d8, applying more pressure to the d4-pawn.

Black had various other possible moves; the most obvious is to occupy d5 with 12...♘4d5, but after 13 ♘f4 ♘xc3+ 14 ♕xc3 ♘d5 15 ♕c1, the problem of the g7-bishop is highlighted, while Black's control of the d5-square is not very important.

12...♘c4?! is even less convincing; Black eliminates one of White's bishops but is left with a passive position and less space after 13 ♗xc4! ♗xc4 14 b3 ♗f7 15 ♗h6.

13 ♘f4

Svidler indicates an interesting move here: 13 ♘g5!?, which is possibly slightly better than the move played. In the event of 13...♘c4?!, White does not play 14 ♗xc4 ♗xc4 15 b3, since after 15...♗d3+ 16 ♔b2 f4 17 ♗f2 ♗a6, the f2-bishop is passive and the absence of the light-squared bishop is felt. The correct move is 14 ♕c1!, giving up the dark-squared bishop; after 14...♘xe3 15 ♕xe3 the g7-bishop remains shut out of play, and White need not fear 15...f4 16 ♕c1 ♗f5+ 17 ♘ge4.

13...♗f7 14 a3 *(D)*

White brings about a crisis on the queenside, forcing Black to make a decision.

14 h4 is playable, and after 14...♖fd8 the game is balanced; both attacks lack a clear way forward.

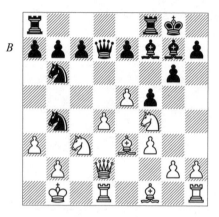

Now Black must make a decision; the most obvious move is 14...♘4d5 but after 15 ♘fxd5 ♘xd5 16 ♗c4 White is slightly better; the phrase "if one piece is bad, the whole position is bad" is applicable to the g7-bishop. Black's position is passive, although his inferiority is not decisive, but if there is an alternative, and an exciting one at that, it is understandable that Black should prefer it.

14...a5!

As if it were a game of tennis, the ball crosses the net and now it is White who has to make a critical decision.

The capture of the b4-knight would lead to the opening of the a-file, guaranteeing attacking chances, although it remains to be seen whether this sufficiently compensates for the sacrificed piece. The character of Black's sacrifice is that its acceptance is not forced. The b4-knight is annoying but it has not captured any material or set up any serious threats, so that it is necessary to analyse whether it is important to capture it right away or later; in this position calculation is essential.

The fact that White's king's rook is out of play allows Black to be optimistic about this sacrifice.

15 d5

Now it was not so attractive to go back to the plan of attack with 15 h4, because 14 a3 has weakened the b3-square, allowing Black to play 15...♗b3! 16 ♖c1 ♖fd8, and now the b4-knight cannot be captured; Black can go back with ...♘c6, and the pressure on the centre becomes intolerable.

The immediate capture 15 axb4? is not advisable either; after 15...axb4 the knight cannot retreat since 16 ♘ce2? allows a brutal forced mate by 16...♖a1+ or the pretty winning line 16...♗a2+ 17 ♔c1 ♕c6+ 18 ♕c2 ♗b3! 19 ♕xc6 ♖a1+ 20 ♔d2 ♖xd1#.

15 ♗b5!? is very complicated; the black queen remains shut out of the attack in the event of 15...♕c8? 16 axb4 axb4 17 ♘ce2 c6 18 ♗d3 White does not have the problems that we saw before. The correct response is 15...c6!, when Svidler thinks that after 16 d5! Black is also forced to sacrifice a piece with 16...♗xe5! 17 ♗xb6 cxb5, when after 18 axb4?! axb4 19 ♘ce2 ♕d6 20 ♗d4 b3!, with the threat of ...♖a1+, Black is on top; for example, 21 ♕c3 ♖fc8! 22 ♕xb3 ♗xf4. Naturally White can, and possibly should, reject the sacrifice of the b4-knight, for example with 18 ♖he1, and the struggle continues.

We now return to the position after 15 d5 *(D)*:

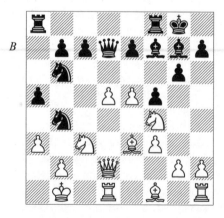

15...♗xe5

Black threatens to capture the d5-pawn with 16...♗xc3 17 ♕xc3 ♘4xd5, so that White has another important decision to make.

16 axb4

White accepts the sacrifice, relying on his defensive resources.

The alternative was 16 &d4!?, when Black, with his king so weak, must not leave the d4-bishop alive in exchange for winning another pawn with 16...&xf4? 17 ♕xf4, when White wins a piece after both 17...♘4xd5 18 ♕e5 ♘f6 19 &xb6 and 17...♘6xd5 18 ♕e5 ♘f6 19 axb4 axb4 20 &c5!. The correct reply is 16...&xd4 17 ♕xd4 g5!, when Svidler indicates that the balance is maintained after 18 &b5 ♕d6 19 ♘e6 &xe6 20 dxe6 ♕xd4 21 ♖xd4 ♘a6 22 &xa6 ♖xa6 23 h4, as White has clear compensation for the pawn.

16...axb4 17 ♘b5 (D)

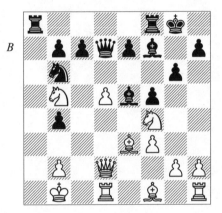

Now it is necessary to decide whether to capture another pawn or to double rooks on the a-file; in the latter case, which move is better? With 17...♖a4 the b4-pawn is defended, and with 17...♖a5 the b5-knight is attacked.

It is inconsistent now to abandon the idea of the attack with 17...&xf4?! 18 &xf4 &xd5; after 19 b3! the three pawns for the piece are not worth much and the white king can easily be defended, since White now controls the dark squares. Thus 17...&xf4?! can be ruled out, and the other dilemma must be faced.

17...♖a5

In this case there is no clear answer; in the event of 17...♖a4 18 &xb6 (White cannot play 18 &d4? now since the black queen and the f7-bishop help all the other pieces after 18...&xf4 19 ♕xf4 ♕xd5 20 &d3 c5!, regaining the piece with a decisive attack) 18...cxb6 19 ♕e3 &xf4

20 ♕xf4 ♖fa8, Black has sufficient compensation; the lack of play for the h1-rook prevents the extra piece from being effective. Svidler indicates that 21 ♕e5 is then forced, when after 21...♖a1+ 22 ♔c2 ♖c8+ 23 ♔d2 ♖xd1+ 24 ♔xd1 &xd5 25 ♔e1 ♖c5! 26 ♕b8+ ♖c8 Black has at least a draw.

18 &xb6

The snag with this simplification is that it hands over the dark squares to the opponent and the f4-knight is in danger. However, White has little choice; if 18 ♕xb4? ♖fa8 19 ♘a3 then 19...&d6 is very strong, and Black can now capture on a3, with a very strong attack. Svidler pointed out that if 20 ♕d4 then 20...♖a4 is also strong, since 21 &b5 fails to 21...♖xd4 22 &xd7 ♖xd1+ 23 ♖xd1 ♘xd7 with a winning ending, while 21 ♘c4 fails to 21...&xf4 22 &xf4 ♖a1+ 23 ♔c2 ♕a4+, with a decisive attack.

Just as after 17...♖a4, there was no time to exchange bishops with 18 &d4?, owing to 18...&xf4 19 ♕xf4 ♕xd5, with the threats of 20...♖a1+ and 20...c5.

18...cxb6 (D)

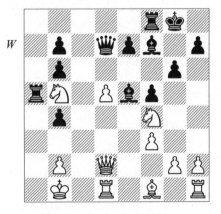

Black is going to play 19...♖fa8, and also has the threat of 19...♖xb5, which would follow any developing move, such as 19 &c4; Black will then only be the exchange down and have a strong attack, thanks to the open lines and the strong dark-squared bishop.

It is not possible to retreat the b5-knight; if 19 ♘d4? then 19...♕a4, with an irresistible attack.

19 ♕xb4?

This solves all the immediate problems but is in fact the decisive error, since after Black's reply the defence will become even more difficult.

The best course was to try to deflect the attack by harassing the e5-bishop with 19 ♕e3!; after 19...♗xf4 20 ♕xf4 ♖xb5 21 ♗xb5 ♕xb5 22 ♕e5!, Black is fine, but White can say the same. Svidler mentions the possibility of 19...♗f6, giving up a second exchange after 20 ♘e6! ♖fa8 21 ♗c4! ♖xb5 22 ♗xb5 ♕xb5 23 ♘c7 ♕a4 24 ♘xa8 b3! 25 ♔c1 f4 26 ♕e4 ♕a1+ 27 ♕b1 ♕xa8, with a complex position.

19...♖fa8 *(D)*

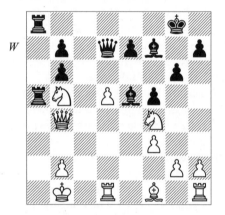

Now the attack cannot be parried; the main threats are 20...♖a4, 20...♖a2 and 20...♖a1+.

20 ♖d4

Trying to neutralize the pressure of the black bishop, but it is a desperate measure that will not succeed.

If 20 ♘c3 then 20...♗xc3! 21 bxc3 ♖a4; neither is it possible to close the a-file with 20 ♘a3, since the f4-knight drops after 20...♖a4 21 ♕b5 (no better is 21 ♕e1, when there are various favourable possibilities, including 21...♗xb2!, with a winning attack) 21...♕xb5 22 ♗xb5 ♖xf4 23 ♘c4 ♗f6.

Retreating the loose piece with 20 ♘h3 does not look very good; this gives Black time to continue his offensive with 20...♖a2. After 21 ♘c3 ♗xc3 22 ♕xc3 ♕a4, there is no defence; the threat of capturing on b2 is strong. If 21 ♕b3 Svidler indicates the continuation 21...♖xb2+ 22 ♕xb2 ♗xb2 23 ♔xb2 and the queen comes into play with 23...♕c8! followed by ...♕c5.

Finally, defending the f4-knight with 20 g3 does not stop the attack; Svidler's pretty main line is 20...♖a4 21 ♕e1 ♖a1+ 22 ♔c2 ♖c8+ 23 ♔d2 ♗xf4+ 24 gxf4 ♖xd5+ 25 ♗d3 ♖d8! 26 ♔e2 (if 26 ♕e2 there is a simple win with 26...♖xd1+ 27 ♖xd1 ♕xb5) and now the spectacular 26...♕xd3+! 27 ♖xd3 ♖xe1+ 28 ♖xe1 ♗c4 wins.

20...♗xd4 21 ♕xd4 ♖a1+ 22 ♔c2 ♖xf1!

The simplest and most practical; after regaining the sacrificed material, Black is left with just a slight material advantage but has a strong attack.

23 ♖xf1 ♕xb5 24 ♖c1! *(D)*

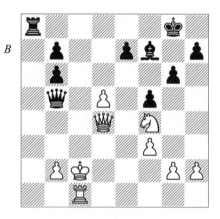

White plays the most stubborn line; several of the favourable endings are not trivial, because the black bishop is passive.

24...♖d8!

Black is in no hurry and since sometimes "the threat is stronger than its execution", he can strengthen his threats. This is a real hammer-blow; the threats of 25...g5 and 25...♗xd5 cannot be parried.

Instead, after 24...♖c8+ 25 ♔b1 ♖xc1+ 26 ♔xc1 g5 27 ♘d3 ♕xd5 28 ♕c3, Black's task is not simple according to Svidler. It should not be forgotten that the black king is weak, so 24...♖a4 fails to 25 ♕e5! ♗c4+? 26 ♔b1 and the advantage evaporates. There remains the active 24...g5, but Black did not like 25 ♘e6 ♗xe6 26 dxe6 ♕e2+ 27 ♔b1 ♕xe6 28 ♖c7, when White's activity allows him to resist.

25 ♕e5 ♗xd5 26 ♘xd5 ♖xd5 27 ♕e6+ ♔f8 28 ♕c8+ ♔f7 0-1

White appeared to have a very straightforward game, with a clear plan: open the h-file with h4-h5. Black had to resort to extreme measures to prevent White's attack from having a free run and without hesitation he decided to sacrifice a piece.

The sacrifice of the b4-knight with 14...a5! was neither forced nor winning, but it offered Black good attacking chances.

From the practical point of view, Black's game was much easier to play. The essential thing was to occupy the open file, while White, who was faced with multiple options, did not find the correct path at every critical point in the game.

"If one piece is bad, the whole position is bad" is a saying that is almost always appropriate. This principle was applicable to the g7-bishop, but then the fact that the h1-rook never got into the game, either by being developed or with h4-h5, was likewise a very important factor.

Game 10

Nigel Short – Jaan Ehlvest

World Cup, Rotterdam 1989

Sicilian Defence, English Attack

When there is an attacking race, there is a risk that a player will rush matters, as happened in this game, and make committal decisions before they are necessary, such as advancing with undue haste, or giving up material before this is wise. Generally such haste is punished by the defending side. If possible, the attack has to be nullified completely, because if it is allowed to continue, even with a material deficit or some other concession, it remains dangerous, since king safety is the most volatile element in the whole of chess.

1 e4 c5 2 ♘f3 d6 3 d4 cxd4 4 ♘xd4 ♘f6 5 ♘c3 a6 6 ♗e3 e6 7 f3 ♘c6 8 g4 ♗e7 9 ♕d2 0-0 10 0-0-0 ♘xd4 11 ♗xd4 ♘d7 12 h4 b5 13 g5 *(D)*

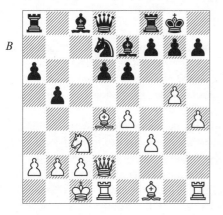

There are many games with this theoretical position from the English Attack. White has just advanced his pawns, although it is still not easy to open lines effectively against Black's castled position, and the chances appear to be balanced.

There are various possible moves here. The greatest connoisseur of this structure, Garry Kasparov, preferred to play 13...♗b7 followed by ...♖c8, keeping the advance ...b4 hanging over White's position.

We examine 13...b4 in the context of a game between two world champions – see Supplementary Game 10.1, Fischer-Spassky, Match (game 25), Sveti Stefan/Belgrade 1992.

In Supplementary Game 10.2, Topalov-Kasparov, Amsterdam 1995, we consider a more consistent treatment by Black after 13...♗b7 14 ♔b1 ♖c8.

13...♖b8?! *(D)*

Not a very popular move. Black prepares the advance ...b4, ...a5, etc., and at the same time guards b6, the importance of which we shall see in the Fischer game. Nevertheless, it is slow and not the most flexible.

14 ♗h3?!

White seeks to put pressure on e6 in order to facilitate the g6 break, opening lines, but this move is not very flexible; it obstructs the h-file and loses control of the c4-square. If the attack

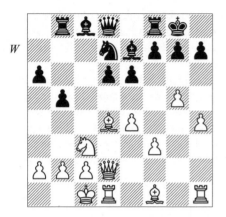

is successful, and White manages to confine the struggle to the kingside, it will be justified, but if not, it can create discoordination among his own forces.

The most usual move here is the prophylactic 14 ♔b1. Here is an example where White manages to carry out all his plans; it is a blindfold game, but is useful as an illustration: 14...♘e5 15 ♕g2! *(D)*.

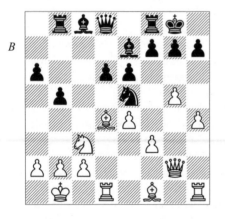

The queen is very useful here, since as well as occupying the vital g-file, it defends f3, controls g4 and evades in advance the attack by an eventual ...♘c4. 15...♗d7 16 f4 ♘c6 17 ♗e3 b4 18 ♘e2 a5 19 h5 a4 20 g6 (White comes first in the race, but the main factor is that he has more pieces attacking on the kingside than Black has on the queenside) 20...b3 21 cxb3 axb3 22 a3 (the standard defensive manoeuvre, to open as few lines as possible) 22...♕c7 23 gxh7+ ♔xh7 24 ♘c3 ♖fc8 25 ♗d3 ♔h8 26 ♖dg1 (there is no

way to resist so much firepower concentrated against such a poorly defended king) 26...♗f6 27 e5 dxe5 28 ♕e4 ♔g8 29 ♗c5 1-0 Anand-Ljubojević, Monte Carlo (Amber blindfold) 2000.

14...♕c7

The queen leaves the d-file and in the future, backed up by a rook, intends to put pressure on the c2-square. The alternative was 14...♘e5.

15 g6

Short marked this thematic sacrifice as dubious, even though it was the idea behind his previous move. But it is not easy to find a direct way to continue the attack; if 15 h5 then 15...b4 forces the retreat 16 ♘b1, since if 16 ♘e2? then 16...♕a5, with a double attack on the g5- and a2-pawns. Here we see the usefulness of the prophylactic ♔b1.

15 ♖dg1 is equally unconvincing: 15...♘e5 16 ♕e3 b4 17 ♘e2 ♗d7, followed by ...♖fc8, and, compared with the preceding examples, Black's attack is much more advanced.

15...hxg6 16 h5 *(D)*

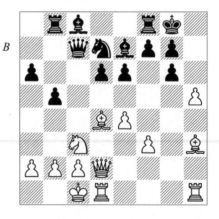

Although objectively White's attack should not work, it must not be underestimated.

16...♘e5!

Blocking the long diagonal, and eyeing the f3-pawn.

Opening the game further with 16...gxh5? is clearly a mistake, since White has the immediate 17 ♗xg7! and if Black captures by 17...♔xg7 he gets mated after 18 ♖dg1+ ♔h7 19 ♗f5+.

Neither is it possible to keep the game closed with 16...g5?; White still manages to open it up with 17 h6 gxh6 18 ♗g4 and Black cannot defend against the attack on the h-file.

And finally, it is not possible to counter-attack with 16...b4?, since then 17 ♘d5! exd5 18 hxg6 follows, threatening 19 ♗xd7, 20 ♖h8+ and 21 ♕h6+. Then 18...fxg6? loses quickly to 19 ♗e6+ ♖f7 20 ♖h8+! ♔xh8 21 ♗xf7 and mate. 18...b3 is more stubborn, although after 19 axb3 ♘c5 20 ♗c3! the attack is unstoppable; in addition to the aforementioned idea of ♖h8+ followed by ♕h6+, which can be prevented for the time being with 20...d4, with the pawn on g6 there is a mating pattern with ♕h7# and White wins with 21 ♗e6! (not 21 ♗xc8?, since this allows the king to escape via f8), with the threat of 22 ♖h8+ followed by 23 ♕h2+, and an irresistible attack.

17 hxg6 fxg6?!

Missing a great opportunity to eliminate some attacking pieces while capturing another pawn; with 17...♘xf3! *(D)* Black could have halted White's attack.

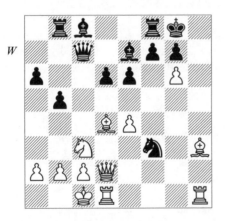

If then 18 ♗xe6? Black has just one saving move, but it is also a winning move. Note first that 18...♘xd2? fails to 19 ♖h7!! ♘b3+ 20 ♔b1 (not 20 axb3? ♗g5+ and ...♗h6, winning) 20...♘xd4 21 ♖dh1 with unavoidable mate. The correct move is 18...♗g5!, when there is no way for White to make progress with the attack: if 19 ♖h7 then 19...♗xd2+ 20 ♔b1 (or 20 ♖xd2 fxe6, and both the g7-pawn and the h2-square are defended) 20...♘xd4 21 ♖dh1 and the fatal file is closed with 21...♗h6, winning.

The move 18 ♕g2 is very dangerous. As we already know, in the event of 18...fxg6? 19 ♕xg6 ♘xd4 White does not have to be content with a draw after 20 ♖xd4 ♖f6 21 ♕e8+ ♖f8 22 ♕g6 ♖f6 (but not 22...♗f6? 23 e5!, when 23...dxe5 24 ♖g4 gives White a strong attack, while 23...♗xe5? loses to 24 ♖h4) but can play 20 ♗g4! instead, creating very serious problems. Then 20...♗f6 loses to 21 ♕h7+ ♔f7 22 ♖hf1 ♔e7 23 ♖xf6! ♖xf6 24 ♗h5! ♖f7 25 ♕g8 and wins. But Black has 18...♘h4! and can solve his most serious problems, although the position remains complicated.

We now return to 17...fxg6?! *(D)*:

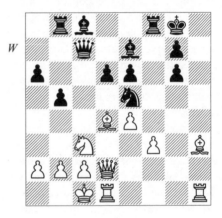

18 ♗g4

White has managed to open the h-file. We should note that 18...♘xf3? now fails to our well-known shot 19 ♖h8+!.

18...b4!

A strong advance, pushing the c3-knight away from the d5-square.

19 ♗xe5

If 19 ♘e2?, Black wins another pawn and attends to the defence with 19...♘xg4 20 fxg4 e5, followed by ...♗xg4-h5. Thus White must give up his dark-squared bishop; this opens the d-file in Black's favour. Black is already a pawn up and can use the d-file to exchange pieces, as well as to divert forces from White's domination of the h-file.

19...dxe5 20 ♘e2 *(D)*

We are in the position mentioned in the introduction. White's attack has ground to a halt, the h-file is no longer frightening, and with the

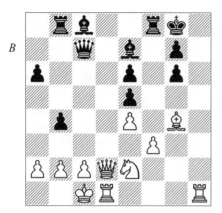

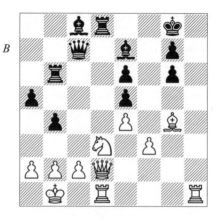

disappearance of the d4-bishop there are no longer any threats against g7. White has nothing immediate, but this does not mean that the position is completely safe for Black; his castled position is exposed, the h-file is still open, and if the white queen can link up with the attack, Black could be in trouble.

20...罩b6?!

A very timid move, defending e6, but it is hard to see what the idea is. The most ambitious move was 20...a5, with the idea of a timely ...a4. It was also possible to preface this with 20...罩d8 and only after the exchange of rooks with 21 豐e3 罩xd1+ 22 罩xd1 play 22...a5, in both cases with good prospects.

21 含b1 a5?

This move, which was good previously, is now a mistake. You should not forget to ask yourself what the opponent wants to do. There was still time to reach a good position with 21...罩d8 22 豐e3 罩xd1+ 23 罩xd1 a5.

22 ②c1!

A multi-purpose move, allowing the queen to go to h2 and making it harder for Black to exchange rooks by going to d3, from where it will also hit the e5-pawn.

22...罩d8 23 ②d3 (D)

The position has changed; White's activity already inspires respect, although Black also has his chances on the queenside. How should Black continue?

23...a4?!

There will be no contest between attacks. White will be able to concentrate more pieces against the black king, and will get there first.

It was best to eliminate the annoying d3-knight and also open the game against the white king by means of 23...盦a6! 24 豐h2 b3 25 axb3 盦xd3 26 cxd3 含f7, with a playable position for Black.

24 豐h2 盦f6 (D)

If 24...b3 25 cxb3 axb3 26 罩c1 豐a7 27 a3 罩xd3 White can win in various ways, the most elegant being 28 豐h7+ 含f7 29 盦h5! gxh5 30 豐xh5+ 含f8 31 罩xc8+ 盦d8 (if 31...罩d8 then 32 豐g6!) 32 豐h8+ 含f7 33 罩g1 and wins. In this line we see that the numerical superiority of the white attacking pieces is overwhelming.

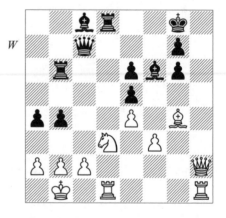

25 f4!

Opening up the kingside even more. We can see that the d3-knight fulfils an important role, unlike the c8-bishop.

25...exf4

Short indicates that the endgame after 25...b3 26 cxb3 axb3 27 fxe5 豐c2+ 28 豐xc2 bxc2+ 29

♔xc2 is very difficult for Black, since White has two connected passed pawns.

26 e5 ♗g5

26...♖xd3 27 exf6 ♖xd1+ 28 ♗xd1 leads to mate.

27 ♕h7+ ♔f7 *(D)*

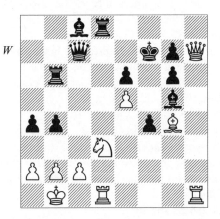

Black is ready to continue with ...b3, creating confusion, but Short has foreseen a winning shot.

28 ♗h5!

Each tempo counts; the capture is forced, and the g-file is opened.

28...gxh5 29 ♕xh5+ ♔g8 30 ♖dg1!

Much better than 30 ♕xg5 ♗b7! 31 ♖h2 b3!, complicating the game unnecessarily. Just as before, the time factor is the most important one. Now another piece comes into play, exploiting the opening of the g-file.

30...♗b7

30...b3 changes nothing: 31 ♖xg5! ♕xc2+ 32 ♔a1 and there is no defence.

31 ♕h7+ ♔f8 32 ♖xg5 ♕f7

Of course, 32...♗xh1? leads to mate in two after 33 ♕h8+.

33 ♖h4 ♖d4 34 ♖hg4 g6 35 ♕h8+ ♕g8 36 ♕h4 *(D)*

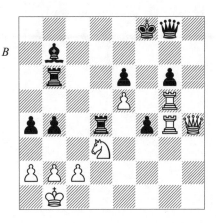

All the white pieces are working together, while Black's attack remains dormant, with the b6-rook and the b7-bishop a long way away from the defence. There is no reasonable way to defend the g6-pawn.

36...b3

If 36...♔f7 then 37 ♕f2 and 37 ♖h5 both win.

37 ♖xg6 bxc2+ 38 ♔c1 1-0

The art of attack might well be imperfect, but even when an attack is parried, if the king's defences are weakened there can be no room for carelessness, since the attack might flare up again, based on the weaknesses already created.

In this game Black neglected the tactical shot 17...♘xf3!, missed the opportunity to accelerate his own attack with 20...a5 and failed to nullify White's possible attack by exchanging pieces with 20...♖d8 or 21...♖d8. Finally, Black missed his last opportunity, 23...♗a6!.

Supplementary Game 10.1
Bobby Fischer – Boris Spassky
Match (game 25), Sveti Stefan/Belgrade 1992
Sicilian Defence, English Attack

1 e4 c5 2 ♘c3 ♘c6 3 ♘ge2 d6 4 d4 cxd4 5 ♘xd4 e6 6 ♗e3 ♘f6 7 ♕d2 ♗e7 8 f3 a6 9 0-0-0 0-0 10 g4! ♘xd4 11 ♗xd4 b5 12 g5 ♘d7 13 h4 b4 14 ♘a4 *(D)*

14 ♘e2 is slightly more popular.

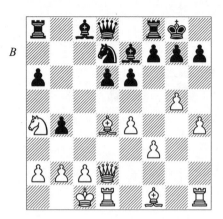

14...♗b7?

This very natural move is an error; 14...♕a5 is preferable.

15 ♘b6!

Not 15 ♕xb4?! ♗c6! and the white pieces are awkwardly placed to deal with the threats of 16...d5 and 16...♖b8.

15...♖b8

After 15...♘xb6 16 ♕xb4 Black loses a pawn without enough compensation.

16 ♘xd7 ♕xd7 17 ♔b1 ♕c7 (D)

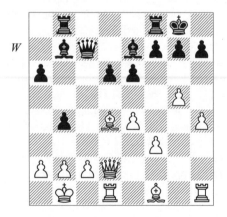

What has changed since move 13? Nothing startling seems to have happened; the somewhat uncomfortably placed a4-knight has been exchanged for the harmless d7-knight. This does not seem to be any big deal, and yet White is now clearly better, since in a way the position, to use Capablanca's phrase, "has been cleared

of the dead leaves", and now White has a clear plan of attack against the enemy king, whereas Black does not.

18 ♗d3

Making way for the d1-rook to support the advancing pawns; the numerical superiority of the white forces aiming at Black's castled position makes the opening of files imminent.

18...♗c8?!

This manoeuvre to transfer the bishop to e6 was criticized and instead the standard manoeuvre 18...♖fe8 was suggested, in order to answer 19 h5 with 19...♗f8.

19 h5 e5 20 ♗e3 ♗e6 21 ♖dg1

White's moves are natural and now he is ready to open lines against the king. In contrast, Black has to go into contortions to try to create something on the queenside, as well as to defend himself.

21...a5 22 g6 (D)

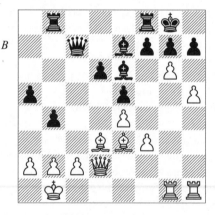

In many cases, when the attacking race can depend on a single tempo, this move to open Black's castled position is played as a sacrifice, but in this case White is so far ahead in the race that it is not at all necessary to give up material to have the same effect.

22...♗f6

Here 22...fxg6 23 hxg6 h6 fails to the sacrifice 24 ♗xh6, winning easily; opening the h-file is also losing, as can easily be seen.

23 gxh7+ ♔h8

Black seeks to make an ally of the h7-pawn, keeping the kingside lines closed; in the event of 23...♔xh7, 24 f4 would follow.

24 ♗g5!

Eliminating the defender of the most vulnerable point, g7.

24...♕e7 25 ♖g3

Now with the doubling of the rooks, we can see that Black is powerless to withstand such pressure.

25...♗xg5 26 ♖xg5 ♕f6 27 ♖hg1

It only remains to play ♕g2.

27...♕xf3

This is equivalent to throwing in the towel but if 27...♔xh7, to defend with ...♖g8, then 28 ♕g2 ♖g8 29 ♖g6! wins.

28 ♖xg7 (D)

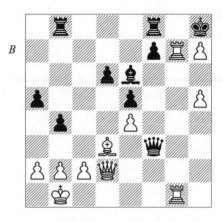

28...♕f6?!

Here 28...♕f4 is more tenacious, to answer 29 ♕g2 with 29...♕h6. Even so, Black is paralysed by the possibility of ♖g8+ and White can win by exchanging the now-vital defender of the light squares with 30 b3! a4 31 ♗c4 ♗xc4 32 bxc4 b3, and then, for example, 33 cxb3

axb3 34 a3 b2 35 ♕g4!, intending 36 ♖g8+ ♔xh7 37 ♕f5+. Here we should note the importance of eliminating the defender of the light squares.

29 h6 a4 30 b3 axb3 31 axb3 ♖fd8 32 ♕g2 ♖f8 33 ♖g8+! ♔xh7 34 ♖g7+ ♔h8 35 h7 1-0

Now ♖g8+ will open the h-file.

Supplementary Game 10.2
Veselin Topalov – Garry Kasparov
Amsterdam 1995
Sicilian Defence, English Attack

1 e4 c5 2 ♘f3 ♘c6 3 d4 cxd4 4 ♘xd4 e6 5 ♘c3 d6 6 ♗e3 ♘f6 7 f3 ♗e7 8 g4 0-0 9 ♕d2 a6 10 0-0-0 ♘xd4 11 ♗xd4 b5 12 ♔b1 ♗b7 13 h4 ♖c8 14 g5 ♘d7 (D)

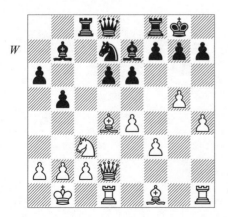

15 ♖g1?

With this natural-looking move, White defends the g5-pawn so as to be able to play h5. However, just as important as preparing one's own attack is restraining that of the opponent, and if one decides to enter a race, it is essential to be sure that one will get there first, which is not the case here. The prophylactic 15 a3! was preferable.

15...b4!

Now Black gains an overwhelming initiative.

16 ♘e2

The set-up with ...♗b7 and ...♖c8 rules out the alternative which is valid in similar positions, 16 ♘a4, owing to 16...♗c6 17 ♕xb4 d5 18 ♕b3 ♖b8, winning material.

16...♘e5! 17 ♖g3

If 17 ♕xb4 then Black guards his b7-bishop and at the same time hits c2 with 17...♕c7. The weakened white structure is falling apart after, for example, 18 ♘c3 ♘xf3 19 ♗b6 d5! 20 ♕b3 ♕f4.

17...♘c4! *(D)*

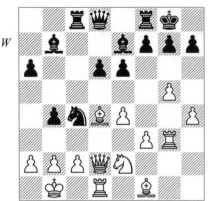

18 ♕c1?

This retreat is a symptom of the difficulty of White's position. Although it appears almost suicidal, because it opens the b-file and exposes the queen to potential attack from the e7-bishop, the best move according to Kasparov was 18 ♕xb4, even though after 18...♕c7 19 ♕c3 e5 20 ♗f2 Black has a strong initiative.

18...e5 19 ♗f2 a5

Kasparov considers that Black's position is already winning; the game lasted just a few more moves.

20 ♗g2?! ♗a6!

Threatening 21...♘xb2.

21 ♖e1 a4 22 ♗h3 ♖c6 23 ♕d1 d5!

Black activates his pieces to the maximum with this thematic break, taking advantage of the lack of coordination between the white pieces.

24 exd5 ♖d6 25 f4 ♖xd5 26 ♖d3 ♘a3+ 27 bxa3 ♗xd3 28 cxd3 ♖xd3 0-1

Exercises

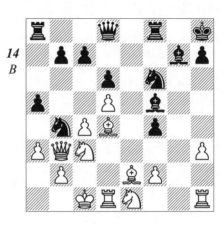

14
B

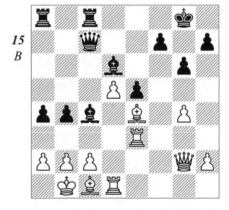

15
B

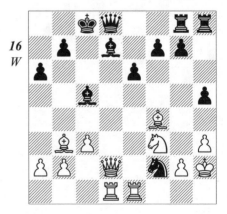

16
W

17
B

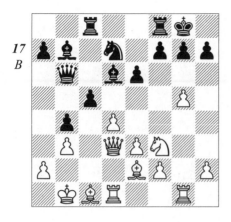

20
W

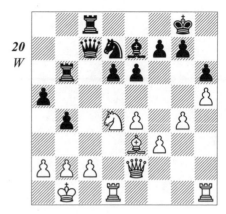

18
W

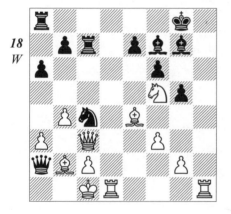

21
W

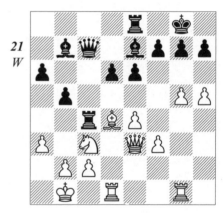

19
W

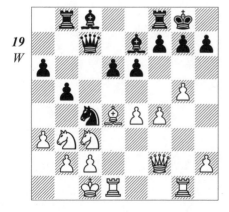

22
B

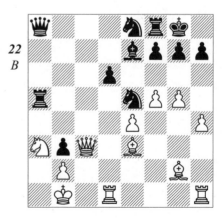

23
B

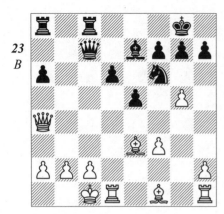

24
W

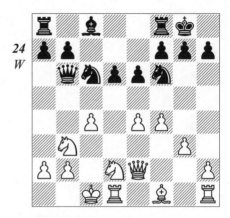

Which move is best?
a) 13 ♔b1
b) 13 g4
c) 13 ♘f3

3 Attacking the Castled King (Same-Side Castling)

To attack the king successfully when both sides are castled on the same wing, it is of course necessary to have greater justification than when the king is in the centre. Generally a castled king is much better defended than a king in the centre or when the kings are castled on opposite wings, in which case attacking is almost compulsory.

There are various factors that can justify an attack. These might be permanent factors, such as an open file, doubled pawns, the disappearance of a vital defender (such as the fianchettoed bishop, or even the f1-rook or f8-rook), leaving f2 and f7 vulnerable, a contact-point, a pawn-majority on the wing where the enemy king is located, etc. There can also be temporary factors, principally a momentary absence of defenders, or a superiority of attacking forces at a particular moment, etc. In these cases, the speed of the offensive is crucial for its success, since a single tempo can be all that is required for the defending forces to regroup and cause the attack to fail.

It cannot be over-emphasized that a game, or the success of an attack, is not decided by a single element but by several, and that good handling of the tactical phase is essential.

In this and the following chapters we shall see games with kings castled on the same wing, with different reasons underpinning the attack's success.

Let us not forget that to attack without sufficient justification can be counterproductive. To cite an extreme case, the Minority Attack in the 'Carlsbad' structure of the Exchange Queen's Gambit basically consists of advancing pawns on a wing where White's forces are outnumbered, in order to try to weaken the enemy pawn-formation. To carry out such an attack when one's own king is located on that wing would be suicidal in normal circumstances. Logically this would change if there were other factors, such as a great superiority in attacking pieces.

The opposite case also holds true, when it is not only possible to attack, but compulsory, since "the side with the advantage is obliged to attack", according to Steinitz's telling phrase.

Game 11
Magnus Carlsen – Vasily Ivanchuk
Morelia/Linares 2007
Grünfeld Defence, Exchange Variation

To start with, we shall look at a simple example, where amazingly, it seems that one of the world's best players loses almost without a fight.

First White weakens Black's castled position and then seizes some vital kingside squares.

The game was actually decided by a tactical motif on the opposite wing, but this does not change the characterization of this game.

1 d4 ♘f6 2 c4 g6 3 ♘c3 d5 4 cxd5 ♘xd5 5 e4 ♘xc3 6 bxc3 ♗g7 7 ♗c4 c5 8 ♘e2 ♘c6 9 ♗e3 0-0 10 0-0 *(D)*

White has chosen the most aggressive system against the Grünfeld Defence. The strong pawn-centre, the pawn-majority in the centre and on the kingside, coupled with the fact that Black's castled position is defended only by the

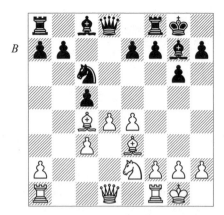

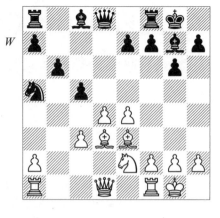

g7-bishop, signify that White can contemplate an eventual offensive against Black's castled position. Black has the queenside majority and pressure on the white centre. The player who makes better use of his own advantages will emerge on top from the following phase.

10...♘a5

In the line 10...♗g4 11 f3 ♘a5 12 ♗d3 cxd4 13 cxd4 ♗e6, David Bronstein popularized the exchange sacrifice 14 d5!?, which has come back into fashion in a big way in recent years. White argues that the removal of the key g7-bishop justifies the surrender of the rook.

Fischer's preference was for Smyslov's idea of increasing the pressure on the d4-pawn with 10...♕c7 followed by ...♖d8. However, this also leaves the castled position – specifically the f7-square – somewhat exposed. One indication of how difficult it is to defend it successfully is that Fischer achieved very good positions against Spassky, when both players were in their prime, but was routed on two occasions.

11 ♗d3 b6 (D)

Black continues his development, postponing pressure on the white centre. Theory regards Black's set-up with suspicion, since it leaves White with a free hand to improve the position of his pieces, without having to sacrifice any material.

12 ♖c1

It is advisable to evade the pressure of the g7-bishop. Another idea is 12 ♕d2, a natural move that meets the 'demands' of the position, since it connects the rooks, vacates d1 for one of them, and prepares a favourable exchange of

bishops with ♗h6 at the appropriate moment. This would weaken Black's castled position. However, in P.H.Nielsen-Ivanchuk, Monaco (Amber blindfold) 2006, the reply was 12...e5! and Black achieved the better position after 13 d5 f5 14 ♗g5 ♕d6 15 ♗h6 f4 16 ♗xg7 ♔xg7 17 f3 c4 18 ♗c2 g5 19 ♔h1 ♗d7. The exchange of bishops helped Black get rid of his 'bad' bishop and gain a space advantage. The sacrifice of Black's c5-pawn is thematic; after 13 dxc5 ♗e6 Black gains control of the c4-square and achieves good play on the c- and a-files after White plays cxb6. A well-known example of this general idea (although actually arising from a Queen's Indian) is Kasparov-Korchnoi, Candidates match (game 1), London 1983.

12...cxd4

The opening of the c-file "does not seem very good after ♖c1, but is part of the black scheme" – Carlsen.

Here, in contrast with 12 ♖c1 instead of 12 ♕d2, 12...e5 is not justified, since after 13 dxc5 (but not 13 d5?! f5 14 f3 c4 15 ♗b1 f4 16 ♗f2 g5 when Black is better, as pointed out by Svidler, on account of the bad position of the e2-knight and the b1-bishop) 13...♗e6 14 c4 bxc5 15 ♗xc5 ♖e8?! (it was later demonstrated that 15...♗h6 is better) 16 ♗e3 Black's compensation for the pawn is insufficient, Topalov-Svidler, Morelia/Linares 2006.

13 cxd4 e6

Before playing ...♗b7, Black prevents the advance d5, but this move further weakens the dark squares.

14 ♕d2 ♗b7 (D)

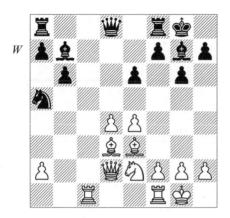

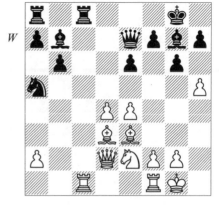

White has the centre well defended and for the time being has a free hand to decide what to do, so he tries to weaken Black's castled position even more.

15 h4!

Taking advantage of the fact that the h-pawn is taboo, since 15...♕xh4? loses to 16 ♗g5 ♕g4 (16...♕h5 is even worse: 17 ♘g3 ♕g4 18 ♗e2) 17 f3 ♕h5 18 ♘g3 ♗xd4+ 19 ♖f2 ♗xf2+ 20 ♔xf2 ♕h2 21 ♖h1.

The equally logical alternative is 15 ♗h6, exchanging the defender of the castled position, an idea that White does not rule out. A great Grünfeld Defence expert, the Czech grandmaster Jan Smejkal, gave up this line in the 1970s on account of this plan.

15...♕e7

A passive or "indifferent" move as Carlsen described it; White is making progress on the kingside and Black has still not initiated any counter-attack.

Carlsen suggested 15...♘c6, bringing the knight back into the struggle, but Ivanchuk disagreed.

16 h5 ♖fc8 *(D)*

The general rule is that exchanging pieces reduces the strength of an attack. Usually this is the case, but it applies less here, since the rooks are not actually participating in the attack.

How should White make progress now?

17 e5!

The dark squares in Black's castled position will be even weaker after this strong advance.

This idea in such Grünfeld positions was discovered by Gligorić several decades ago.

White abandons the d5-square, which is not very important because at the moment Black does not have any piece that can make good use of it. In return, White gains control of the dark squares.

The alternative is 17 ♗g5.

Tracking back, in the event of 15...♘c6 Carlsen was also thinking of playing 16 e5!.

17...♖xc1?

Black continues with his idea of simplifying, but White's attack continues to make progress, with undiminished force.

Here again Carlsen suggested 17...♘c6, giving priority to bringing the knight back into the struggle.

Another idea is 17...♕d8, to be able to play ...♕d5 and try to distract White from his attack. This was suggested by Ivanchuk, who considered that Black's disadvantage was not serious. Let us see an illustrative line: 18 ♗g5 ♕d7 (Ivanchuk was less convinced by 18...♕d5 19 f3 ♘c4 20 ♗xc4 ♖xc4 21 ♖xc4 ♕xc4 22 ♖c1, since White seizes the open file and breaks through to the seventh rank) 19 f3 (now 19 ♗f6? does not work on account of 19...♗xf6 20 exf6 ♕d5, winning a pawn) 19...♖xc1 20 ♖xc1 ♖c8 21 ♖xc8+ ♗xc8 22 ♕f4 ♘c6!, heading for d5 and, in comparison with the game, there is a harmony among the black forces that allows for some optimism.

18 ♖xc1 ♖c8?!

Consistent with the previous move, but once again 18...♕d7 was to be considered, to play ...♖c8 and be able to recapture with the queen. The importance of not leaving any tactical weaknesses will become clear in the course of the game.

19 ℤxc8+ ♗xc8 20 ♗g5 *(D)*

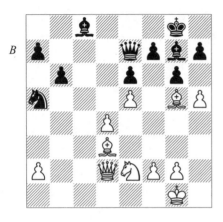

20...♕c7?

The final error, as this move fails tactically. It was better to play 20...♕d7!, even though after 21 ♗f6, exchanging the sole defender of the castled position, Black's position is unpleasant.

20...f6 is also unsatisfactory, since White can now win a pawn with 21 exf6 ♗xf6 22 ♗xf6 ♕xf6 23 hxg6 hxg6 24 ♕c2, but he also can aspire to more by playing 21 ♕c2!? when 21...fxg5?! 22 ♕xc8+ ♔f7 23 hxg6+ hxg6 24 ♗e4 leaves Black paralysed, and 21...♗b7 22 exf6 ♗xf6 23 ♗xf6 ♕xf6 24 ♕c7 ♕f7 25 ♕b8+ ♕f8 26 ♕g3 is not much better.

21 ♗f6

Instead of the usual way, i.e. with ♗h6, White exchanges the defending bishop from f6, or else is left in command of some vital squares if Black retreats the bishop.

21...♘c6

It is already too late for the knight to be of any help, and this move even hastens the defeat. In the event of 21...♗b7, 22 ♕g5 could follow as in the game, with almost irresistible pressure.

22 ♕g5! *(D)*

Threatening 23 ♗xg7, and 24 h6+, mating quickly.

22...h6

This prevents the main threat. There was no salvation in 22...♘b4 23 ♗xg7 ♔xg7 24 ♕f6+ ♔f8, when 25 ♗xg6! (the simple 25 hxg6 also

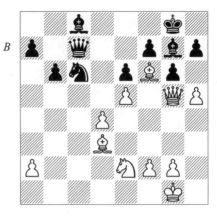

works) 25...hxg6?! 26 h6 wins. But after the text-move, Black's castled position is weakened even more.

23 ♕c1!

With the double threat of capturing the g6-pawn and exploiting the pin. Here we see the drawback of 20...♕c7?, which created a decisive tactical weakness.

23...g5

There was no salvation in 23...♗b7 24 hxg6 fxg6 25 ♗xg6, nor in 23...♕d7 24 hxg6 fxg6 25 ♘f4! ♘xd4 26 ♘xg6 with an attack that is very difficult to resist. For example: 26...♗b7 27 ♘e7+ ♔f7 28 ♗g6+ ♔f8 29 ♕e3! and the black king is very exposed; the threat is 30 ♗h5, covering e2, followed by ♕f4 or ♕g3, and if 29...♘f5 then 30 ♘xf5 exf5 31 ♕a3+ ♔g8 32 ♕g3, threatening 33 e6 and 33 ♗xf5.

24 ♗b5 ♗d7 *(D)*

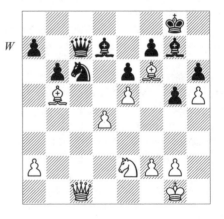

25 d5!

By vacating the d4-square, White wins a piece.

25...exd5 26 ♘d4 ♗xf6 27 exf6 ♕d6 28 ♗xc6 ♕xf6 29 ♗xd7 ♕xd4 30 g3

Black cannot offer any resistance, because there are pawns on both wings, and also because the black structure is not compact.

30...♕c5 31 ♕xc5 bxc5 32 ♗c6 d4 33 ♗b5 ♔f8 34 f4 gxf4 35 gxf4 1-0

Magnus Carlsen commented that he felt very strange after this game, and did not really understand what had happened. It is not every day that someone smashes one of the best players in the world like that, without doing anything spectacular.

Nevertheless, from our point of view the key moments of the attack are very instructive: how White weakened Black's castled position and seized the weak squares with moves such as 15 h4! followed by h5; the move 17 e5!; and the preparation of a favourable exchange of pieces with 20 ♗g5 and ♗f6, eliminating the best defender. It is rare to see such a clear plan, and one carried out so effectively.

Game 12
Darius Zagorskis – Matthew Sadler
Elista Olympiad 1998
English Opening, 1...b6

As we noted in the introduction, just saying to yourself "today I'm going to attack!" does not work. What *is* possible, and in fact advisable, is to keep improving the position of your pieces, so that they are more effective, and sometimes it happens then that a move by the opponent, such as one that momentarily leaves his king unprotected, offers an opportunity, and then we can, and should, say to ourselves "now I'm going to attack!". This is what happens in the brilliant game that follows.

1 c4 b6 2 d4 ♗b7

With this move-order Black avoids the line 2...e6 3 e4 ♗b7 4 ♗d3.

3 ♗g5 (D)

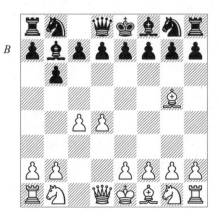

This 'strange' move by White is not the most usual here, but it is played by analogy with the line 1 b3 d5 2 ♗b2 ♗g4, which is considered to be fully playable, so that with the extra tempo c4 it must be OK.

3...♘f6 4 ♗xf6

As in the Trompowsky, White does not squander the opportunity to damage Black's pawn-structure. This comes at the cost of conceding the bishop-pair. The value of this compensation is not absolute; it can range from very significant to almost worthless, depending on the later course of the struggle.

4...exf6

The alternative was to keep the central pawn-structure more compact with 4...gxf6, but Black believes that the half-open e-file is more important.

5 e3 f5 6 ♘f3 g6 7 ♘c3 ♗g7 (D)

Black has changed his pawn-formation so that his pieces will have better prospects. Not only has the diagonal for the g7-bishop been opened, but f6 has also been vacated for the b8-knight.

8 ♗e2

White's better structure is compensated by Black's greater dynamism. One way to neutralize the latter is by exchanging pieces of equal value.

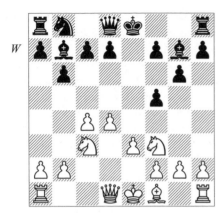

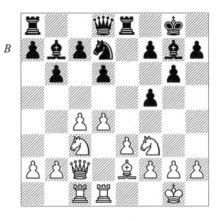

This is the most natural way to develop the f1-bishop, but the course of the game 'suggests' the alternative method of 8 g3 0-0 9 ♗g2, after which it would be simpler to nullify Black's pressure after 0-0 and ♘e1, exchanging the b7-bishop.

8...d6 9 0-0 ♘d7

As we mentioned earlier, the knight has a 'natural' position on the e4-square in the future, after a timely ...♘f6-e4.

10 ♕c2

With the same idea as 8 g3, White could play here 10 ♘d2!?, intending ♗f3.

10...0-0 11 ♖fd1 ♖e8

The most flexible move; the f8-rook does not have any better square than occupying the half-open file. In contrast, the immediate 11...♘f6, heading for e4, would require calculation and evaluation of 12 c5!? dxc5 13 dxc5, so before moving the d7-knight Black makes other useful moves.

12 ♖ac1 *(D)*

If 12 ♘d2?, with the plan of ♗f3, the influence of the e8-rook makes itself felt since now 12...f4! is strong. On the other hand 12 ♘e1 would 'force' Black to continue with his plan by playing 12...♘f6 13 ♗f3 ♘e4.

12...a6!

A difficult move; at first glance, it does not appear to be as useful as 11...♖e8. So why this move, and not 12...♘f6? The reason is that 12...♘f6? would allow our well-known manoeuvre 13 c5!. This is why White played ♕c2 and ♖fd1, so that after 13...dxc5 14 dxc5 ♕e7, White has the unpleasant 15 ♘b5, threatening

to play 16 c6, or else to take on b6 and then occupy squares in the weakened queenside with the b5-knight.

White has a lot of pieces on this wing and it would obviously suit him for the struggle to be concentrated there.

13 b4 ♘f6

Now Black has exhausted all the useful moves and the advance c5 by White is unstoppable, so Black improves his knight.

14 ♘d2?!

We know that the idea of ♘d2 is to exchange bishops with ♗f3 and then try to exploit the weak light squares on the queenside left by the disappearance of the b7-bishop. However, White's castled position is left with suspiciously few defenders, something that White did not believe to be dangerous.

With the same idea, White could have tried 14 ♘e1, which does not allow the game continuation, but this does not control e4 and Black can reply with 14...♘e4; instead 14...♘g4?! does not achieve anything after 15 ♗f3, when the impetuous 15...♕h4? fails to 16 h3, winning material.

Also harmless is 14 c5 ♕e7, and White has not achieved anything.

14...♘g4! *(D)*

With the threat of ...♕h4, when there would already be too many black pieces homing in on White's unprotected castled position.

15 h3?

White does not believe in Black's attack, and forces him to demonstrate the strength of 14...♘g4, but this is not a good decision, at

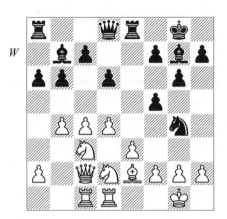

least in practice, because Black's position will be easier to play.

So how should White have played?

It is clear that the panic reaction ♗xg4 (either now or subsequently) would fully justify 14...♘g4, since then the b7-bishop is firing at White's kingside without any opposition.

If White puts the knight back with the miserable 15 ♘f3 then 15...♕e7 is playable, improving the position of the queen and creating combinative possibilities against f2 and e3. The more direct 15...♗h6 is also possible, after which the threat of 16...♘xf2 comes into consideration, since Black would obtain sufficient material for the piece, as well as weakening the white king.

If 15 ♗f3 Black's attack is very strong after 15...♕h4! *(D)*, as we shall see:

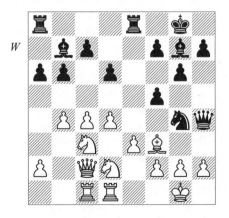

a) 16 ♗xb7 ♕xh2+ 17 ♔f1 ♖xe3! 18 fxe3 (inferior is 18 ♘f3?? ♕h1+ 19 ♘g1 ♘h2#)

18...♘xe3+ 19 ♔e2 ♘xc2 20 ♗xa8 ♘xd4+ 21 ♔d3 and now, for instance, 21...c6, when Black has much the better position at very little cost in material, while White's position is very shaky and his king very weak.

b) 16 ♘f1 is not convincing, since White's castled position is considerably weakened, at no cost to Black, after 16...♗xf3 17 gxf3 ♘f6.

Returning to the original question, 15 ♘d5 seems best and after 15...c6 (not 15...♗xd4? owing to 16 ♗xg4, winning, but 15...♕h4 is a good alternative, forcing 16 ♗xg4 ♕xg4) 16 ♘f4 *(D)* Black faces a major decision:

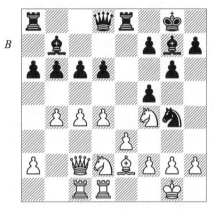

a) After 16...♕h4 17 ♗xg4 fxg4 (and not 17...♕xg4? on account of 18 ♘f3 and 19 h3, trapping the black queen) there could follow, for example, 18 c5, and although White has exchanged the e2-bishop for the g4-knight, given the change in the pawn-structure, and the closure of the h1-a8 diagonal, the b7-bishop is not a worry.

b) However, White's castled position is left with very few defenders, and so Black could consider 16...♘xf2!? 17 ♔xf2 ♕h4+ 18 ♔g1 ♖xe3 19 g3, and now simply 19...♕e7, followed by ...g5 gives Black good compensation for the piece. *Fritz 10* even prefers 19...♖xg3+!? 20 hxg3 ♕xg3+ 21 ♔h1 (forced, since 21 ♘g2? or 21 ♔f1? would lead to mate after 21...♗xd4(+)) 21...♕xf4 22 ♘f3 c5 23 d5 cxb4, with five pawns for the rook; it would only require another piece to join in for the attack to become irresistible, given the exposure of the white king.

15...♘xf2!

It is impossible to calculate everything, but the previous lines show us that the pawns and the initiative provide more than reasonable compensation for the sacrificed piece.

16 ♔xf2 *(D)*

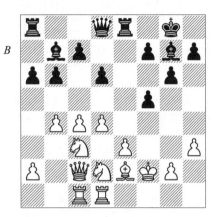

16...♕h4+

Instead, as Sadler pointed out, 16...♕g5? would allow White to regroup satisfactorily with 17 ♘f3 ♕xe3+ 18 ♔f1, with threats of 19 ♕d2 and 19 ♘d5; and the variation 18...♗xf3 19 ♗xf3 ♗xd4 20 ♖xd4 followed by 21 ♗xa8 would simplify the position to White's benefit.

17 ♔f1

There were other defences; for example:

a) Against 17 ♔g1 Black's attack is very strong after the natural 17...♖xe3 (setting up various tactical ideas). 18 ♘f3 is no good, since Black could play 18...♗xf3 19 ♗xf3 ♗xd4 20 ♖xd4 ♕xd4 21 ♔h1 ♖ae8 with a material advantage and the attack. After 18 ♘f1 Black carries out one of his strongest threats with 18...♖xh3!; e.g., 19 gxh3 ♗xd4+ 20 ♖xd4 ♕xd4+ 21 ♘e3 ♕xe3+ 22 ♔f1 and here the attack is winning after 22...♖e8, bringing the rook into the attack with decisive effect, as well as already having more than sufficient pawns for the piece.

b) Another possible defence is 17 g3 ♕xh3 18 ♘f1 (if 18 ♘f3 then 18...♗h6 19 ♖d3 ♗e4!, keeping the initiative and still able to capture more material at an appropriate moment) and now there are many possibilities, of which the strongest seems 18...f4!, opening further breaches in the white king's defences.

17...♖xe3 18 ♘f3 *(D)*

This is the only defence.

If 18 ♘d5 then our by now well-known tactical shot 18...♖xh3! 19 gxh3 ♕xh3+, followed by a timely ...♗xd4(+), will force mate. There are also other ways of finishing off the game.

In reply to 18 ♗f3 the strongest continuation is 18...♗xd4! 19 ♘b3 (not 19 ♗xb7? ♖e1+ and 20...♕f2#) 19...♗xc3 20 ♗xb7 ♖ae8!, and the threat of ...♖e1+ forces White to lose material.

Let us note the ease with which all the black pieces can join in the attack, made possible by the exposure of the white king.

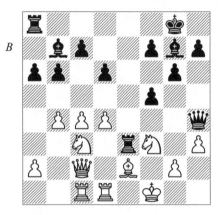

18...♕f4

With the nasty threat 19...g5 and ...g4, which 'keeps White busy', and prevents him from organizing his defence quickly.

The priority is to bring the last piece into the struggle with ...♖ae8. For the future, ...c5 to increase the range of the g7-bishop is to be considered.

19 ♘d5

White opts to nullify the b7-bishop.

Against the attempt to simplify with 19 ♖d3? there are various winning moves, the simplest being 19...♖xd3 20 ♗xd3 ♗xf3, winning more pawns and activating the a8-rook with check.

19...♗xd5 20 cxd5 *(D)*

20...♖ae8!

All the reserves join in the attack. The immediate 20...g5 naturally deserves attention, especially as ...♖ae8 can also be played in the near future. It may not be the most natural thing to rush in this way, but it is always worth

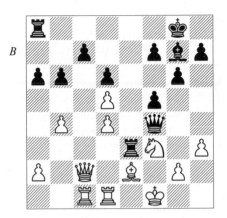

analysing a move that looks like it might win by force. However, 21 罩d3! simplifies just in time, and Black is in fact the one struggling just to stay afloat:

a) 21...g4 22 豐d2 皇h6 23 罩xe3 豐xe3 24 豐xe3 皇xe3 25 罩xc7 gxf3 26 皇xf3 皇xd4 27 皇h5 and even though White is a pawn down, it is he who has winning hopes, since his rook is on the seventh rank and his king is more active.

b) 21...罩ae8!? 22 罩xe3 罩xe3 23 豐xc7 and now 23...g4? fails to 24 豐d8+ 皇f8 25 罩c8!, but 23...皇f8! prepares ...g4, and maintains rough equality (e.g., 24 罩c3 g4 25 罩xe3 豐xe3 and White should avoid 26 豐xb6?! g3), since 24 豐d8? fails to 24...罩xf3+.

21 皇xa6 (D)

Escaping from the threat by capturing material. If 21 罩e1 the odd-looking 21...g5 would now be strong.

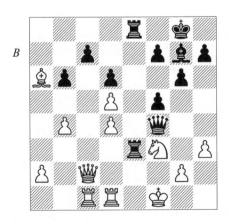

21...罩xf3+!!

Not just attractive but also necessary. The livelier 21...g5? is met by the quiet but strong reply 22 豐f2, after which the queen joins in the defence and causes the black attack to fail.

22 gxf3 罩e3!

Bringing all the pieces into the attack. Black is currently a rook down, so that the involvement of this piece is clearly the priority; in contrast, 22...豐xf3+ 23 含g1 suffices to draw, but no more than that.

23 皇e2 (D)

The logical defence of f3, but one that will be answered forcefully and brilliantly.

23 罩d3 fails to 23...豐xf3+ 24 含g1 (24 豐f2 豐xh3+ followed by 25...罩xd3 wins for Black) 24...豐g3+ 25 含h1 豐xh3+ 26 含g1 罩g3+! 27 罩xg3 皇xd4+ and mate in three moves.

If 23 含g1 there follows 23...罩xf3, when there are two possible defensive tries:

a) 24 皇f1 loses to 24...皇xd4+ 25 罩xd4 豐xd4+ 26 含h1 (if 26 含g2 then 26...豐e3, which wins the queen after 27 含h1 罩f2) 26...豐xd5 27 含g1 (27 含h2 罩a3! gives Black four pawns and the attack for the piece) 27...豐d4+ 28 含h1 c5, once again with four pawns for the bishop, and an attack against the unprotected white king.

b) After 24 豐d2, in addition to spectacular lines, Black can win with the prosaic continuation 24...豐h4 25 皇f1 皇h6 with a winning attack.

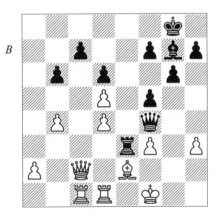

23...豐h2!!

With the 'quiet threat' of 24...皇f6, ...皇h4 and ...豐f2#.

24 豐d2 (D)

If 24 ♖d3 Black wins by force with the surprising continuation 24...♗f6!! 25 ♔e1 (or 25 ♖xe3 ♕h1+ 26 ♔f2 ♗h4#) 25...♗h4+ 26 ♔d1 ♕g1+ 27 ♔d2 ♖xe2+ 28 ♔xe2 ♕f2+ followed by mate.

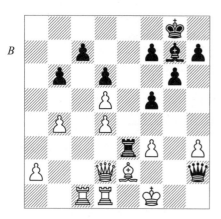

B

24...♗h6?

Continuing the plan, but there is a flaw. 24...♗xd4! is best, since Black achieves perfect coordination of his rook and queen after 25 ♕xd4 ♕xe2+ 26 ♔g1 ♖xf3 27 ♕h4 and now not 27...♕e3+? 28 ♔g2 ♕e2+ 29 ♔g1, when there is no more than a draw by perpetual check, but 27...f4!!, when Black is winning due to the threat of 28...♖g3+; e.g., 28 ♖e1 ♕d3 (again threatening 29...♖g3+) 29 ♔h2 ♕d2+ 30 ♔h1 ♖f2, when 31 ♕xf2 is forced, and Black's extra pawns are decisive.

25 ♕e1?

Returning the favour. 25 ♖c3! holds the draw.

25...♕h1+ 26 ♔f2 ♕h2+ 27 ♔f1 ♕xh3+ *(D)*

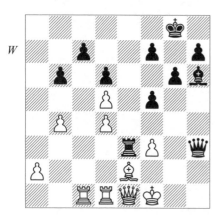

W

28 ♔g1

Black also wins after 28 ♔f2 ♖a3 (threatening 29...♗e3#) 29 ♖c3 ♕h4+, followed by 30...♕xe1 and 31...♖xc3.

28...♖e4!

With the threat of 29...♗e3+. The rook goes to e4, not merely for the sake of making a brilliant move, but to have the possibility of rejoining the attack by occupying the h-file.

29 ♖c3

If 29 fxe4 then 29...♗e3+ 30 ♕f2 ♕g3+! wins.

29...♖h4 30 f4

Equally unavailing was 30 ♕xh4 ♕xh4 31 ♔g2 ♗f4, with a winning attack for Black; e.g., 32 ♖h1 (or 32 ♖g1 ♗g3 33 ♖h1 ♕xd4) 32...♕g3+ 33 ♔f1 ♗d2 winning material.

Now the attack recoups all the sacrificed material.

30...♕h1+ 31 ♔f2 ♖h2+ 32 ♔e3 ♕e4+ 33 ♔d2 ♗xf4+ 0-1

In the opinion of the author, this is one of the most beautiful attacking games in chess history, despite the error on move 24. Once we get over the feeling of euphoria inspired by moves like 21...♖xf3+!!, 23...♕h2!!, 28...♖e4!, etc., we should take note of the preparatory moves and manoeuvres which made it all possible; first of all the modification of the pawn-structure with 5...f5 and 6...g6, to enable the pieces to coordinate better, combined with the deployment of the pieces to their best squares with 9...♘d7, 11...♖e8 and 13...♘f6. The most important factor was that all the pieces were brought into the attack, both the undeveloped ones (20...♖ae8!) and those already attacking (23...♕h2!!, 24...♗h6, 28...♖e4!, etc.).

As for White, it is notable that, as well as having left his castled position weak with 14 ♘d2?! and the provocative 15 h3?, he was unable to achieve anything concrete on the queenside.

No one weakens his own king voluntarily – that much seems obvious – yet sometimes excessive optimism with regard to his own attacking possibilities can lead a player to weaken his kingside. This is what happens in the following game.

Game 13
Isaak Boleslavsky – Igor Bondarevsky
USSR Team Ch, Tbilisi 1951
Ruy Lopez, Chigorin Defence

1 e4 e5 2 ♘f3 ♘c6 3 ♗b5 a6 4 ♗a4 ♘f6 5 0-0 ♗e7 6 ♖e1 b5 7 ♗b3 0-0 8 c3 d6 9 h3 ♘a5 10 ♗c2 c5 11 d4 ♕c7 12 ♘bd2 cxd4 13 cxd4 ♗b7 *(D)*

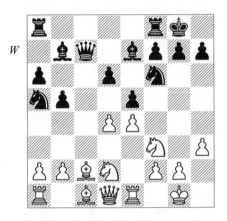

14 d5

Boleslavsky comments that since Black has opened the position somewhat with 12...cxd4, White has the possibility of playing on both wings, albeit in a limited way, because the position remains relatively closed.

For this reason, White's move might appear inconsistent but, as is almost always the case, there is not just one single important factor in the position. With this advance, the b7-bishop is blunted, which is always an idea to consider, and at the same time the mobility of the a5-knight is somewhat restricted.

The alternative was the natural 14 ♘f1.

14...♗c8!

Before taking any other decision, Black solves his most obvious problem.

15 ♘f1

White had other moves. Another factor to consider was, as we indicated above, the position of the a5-knight; 15 ♖b1 and 15 b3 have been played here, based on a similar idea, as we shall see.

In the game Kariakin-Radulski, Calvia Olympiad 2004, White continued 15 b3 ♗d7 16 ♖b1 *(D)*.

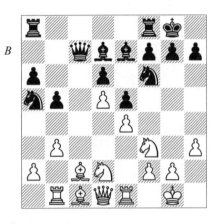

This move is designed to reply to 16...♘b7 with 17 b4, depriving Black of the use of the c5-square, and after 17...a5 it is possible to support the b4-pawn with 18 a3, since now there is no pin on the a-file. The game continued 16...♖fc8 17 ♗d3 g6 18 ♘f1 ♘h5 (the alternative is 18...♘b7; the knight will be unable to go to c5 after 19 b4, but on the other hand it can be recycled via d8-f7, a manoeuvre devised by Akiba Rubinstein) 19 ♗e3 ♕b8 (with his pieces so scattered, the 'active' 19...♘f4 is not appropriate, since after 20 ♖c1 ♕d8 21 ♗xf4! exf4 22 ♕d2 g5 White demonstrates that Black does not have enough control of the centre by playing 23 e5!) 20 g4 ♘g7 21 ♘g3 ♘b7 22 b4 ♘d8 23 ♕e2 f6. Now White tried to take advantage of the fact that many of Black's pieces are away from the queenside by opening the game on that wing with 24 a4 ♘f7 25 ♖a1 ♕b7 26 axb5 axb5 27 ♘d2, heading for a5. Black reacted excellently with a thematic manoeuvre which is important to remember: 27...♗d8! 28 ♘b3 and here, instead of 28...♘e8?!, Black should have completed the manoeuvre to exchange his passive dark-squared bishop with 28...♗b6!.

We now return to 15 ♘f1 *(D)*:

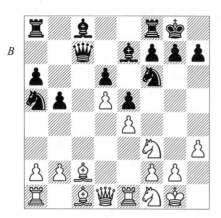

15...♘e8

The start of an optimistic plan; Black prepares to break with ...f5.

At this point it will be clear to us that the best course for Black is to solve the problem of his inactive 'knight on the rim', and send it on its way to its ideal square with 15...♘b7!, followed by ...♘c5; now 16 b4 is not to be feared since Black has the counter-blow 16...a5!.

16 b3

A move clearly motivated by practical considerations, as Boleslavsky explained. White perceives that the idea of ...♘b7-c5 is not a priority for Black, and he prevents the other circuit ...♘c4-b6, which would also be a good solution for the knight.

16...g6 *(D)*

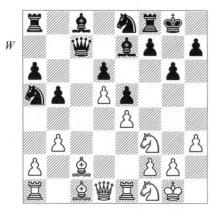

17 ♘e3

Heading for g4. Playing 17 ♗h6 'for free' is tempting, but does not in itself constitute progress for White; it forces the move ...♘g7, which is part of Black's plan in any case and it provokes a typical manoeuvre that we shall mention later. White has another task in mind for the bishop.

17...♘g7 18 ♗d2!

Here we see the reason why White did not play ♗h6, although at first sight it is not so easy to understand. As well as preparing ♖c1, White is creating the positional threat of 19 ♘xe5 dxe5 20 d6, regaining the piece having weakened Black's position, and gaining the strong d5-square for the e3-knight.

18...♘b7

Almost forced; you might say that Black has been compelled to improve his knight, but there are differences from the previous position.

19 ♖c1 ♗d7 *(D)*

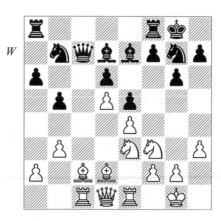

20 b4!

Of course, now the b7-knight will not have the use of c5.

20...♖ac8 21 ♘g4 ♕d8?!

Black continues with his plan of becoming active on the kingside, but this is too optimistic; the white pieces are well prepared, both numerically and in terms of activity, for a tactical duel on the kingside.

It was essential to find a useful post for the b7-knight, which could have been achieved with the manoeuvre that we saw in Kariakin-Radulski, i.e. 21...f6! followed by ...♘d8-f7.

This is the typical manoeuvre mentioned in the note to 17 ♘e3, and which is even better when there is a white bishop on h6. But now the d8-square is occupied and so reverting to that plan would cost more tempi.

22 ♕e2 f5?

This break is thematic, and is the culmination of Black's idea, but here it will be clearly punished, demonstrating that the weaknesses created in the castled position are more important than the activity gained, since then the bad position of the b7-knight will count, on the grounds that "if one piece is bad, the whole position is bad".

Boleslavsky suggested 22...f6 as an improvement, although White's advantage is clear after the illustrative line 23 ♘h6+ ♔h8 24 g4 ♖c4 25 ♗d3 ♖xc1 26 ♖xc1 ♕b8. White has paralysed Black's counterplay on the kingside and now seeks to open the queenside with 27 a4. After 27...bxa4 28 ♗xa6 ♖c8 29 ♗b5 ♖xc1+ 30 ♗xc1 ♕c8 31 ♗b2 White is better on both wings; Black's castled position is weakened and on the queenside White's passed pawn on b4 is worth much more than Black's weak passed pawn on a4.

23 exf5 gxf5 24 ♘h6+ ♔h8 (D)

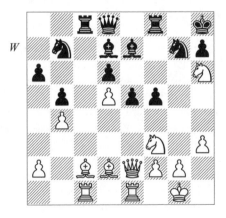

25 g4!

This blow is also very important; Black must not be given time to consolidate on the kingside, where he could definitely go over to the attack once his forces have become better coordinated.

Now both sides' castled positions are exposed, but Black's is in a worse state and in view

of his b7-knight he cannot say, as in the previous game, that 'all the pieces are attacking'.

25...♕e8?!

This will meet with a convincing refutation.

Boleslavsky considered that 25...♖c4 was better. Then 26 ♗b1 ♖xc1 27 ♖xc1 could be considered, when White is better on both wings. The line given by Boleslavsky was 26 ♘xf5 ♘xf5 27 ♗xf5 ♖xc1 28 ♖xc1 ♗xf5 29 gxf5 ♖xf5 30 ♕e4, when White is better on account of his control of the c-file, which is more important than Black's f-file, plus the fact that all the white pieces are better than their black counterparts, handicapped by the eternal problem of the b7-knight. But White still has nothing concrete in either of these variations.

26 gxf5 ♘xf5 (D)

After 26...♕h5 White damps down all counterplay with 27 ♘g5! and after the simplification 27...♗xg5 28 ♕xh5 ♘xh5 29 ♗xg5 ♖g8 30 h4, or 30 ♔h2, White has an extra pawn, and the weaknesses in the black camp are decisive.

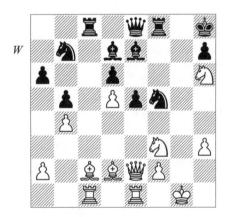

27 ♘xe5!

The whole concentration of forces against Black's castled position crystallizes with this temporary sacrifice, which highlights the weakness of Black's kingside.

A variation on the same theme also works: 27 ♗xf5 ♗xf5 28 ♘xe5! and White wins at least two pawns.

27...♘d4 (D)

Of course if 27...dxe5 then 28 ♕xe5+ ♗f6 29 ♕xe8, followed by the capture of the f5-knight, winning.

Equally unavailing are 27...♘xh6 28 ♘xd7 ♛xd7 29 ♕xe7 ♕xe7 30 ♖xe7 ♖f7 31 ♖ce1! and 27...♖xc2 28 ♖xc2 ♘xh6 29 ♘xd7 ♕g6+ 30 ♔h1 ♕xc2 31 ♕xe7, among other things, with a decisive material advantage in both cases.

These three lines were given by Boleslavsky more than half a century ago, and today's analysis engines agree with all of them.

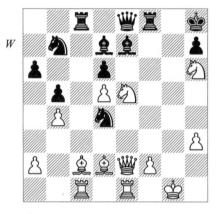

28 ♕e4!

It should not be forgotten that the defences of White's castled position have also been reduced; 28 ♘ef7+?? is a blunder on account of 28...♖xf7 29 ♘xf7+ ♕xf7 30 ♕xe7 ♖g8+! and it is Black who wins; 31 ♗g5 is met by 31...♖xg5+ and a fork on f3.

28 ♘g6+? is also incorrect due to 28...hxg6 29 ♕xe7 ♘f3+, followed by ...♘xe1, and the danger is over.

The move played is the strongest, threatening mate on h7 and staying on the e-file, thus preserving the tactical ideas which do not work at the moment.

28...♘xc2

No better was 28...♖xc2 29 ♕xd4 dxe5 30 ♕xe5+ with a decisive material advantage.

29 ♘xd7 ♘xe1

If 29...♕xd7 then 30 ♕xe7 ♕xh3 31 ♖xc2 ♖g8+ 32 ♗g5 ♕xh6 33 ♖xc8 wins.

30 ♘xf8 ♗xf8 (D)

After 30...♘f3+ 31 ♕xf3 ♖xc1+ 32 ♗xc1 ♗xf8 White wins with 33 ♕f6+ ♗g7 34 ♕e6! and the exchange of queens leads to the promotion of the pawn: 34...♕g6+ 35 ♔h1 ♕xe6 36 dxe6 ♗f6 37 ♗b2 (or 37 e7!).

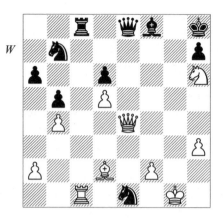

31 ♖xc8

This wins without any difficulties, because 31...♕xe4? 32 ♗c3+ leads to decisive material gain.

It was not the only way to win though; Boleslavsky indicated that 31 ♗c3+ ♗g7 32 ♗xg7+ ♔xg7 33 ♖c7+! also works, and 31 ♕g4! is effective too, with the double threat of taking on c8 and mating on g8; for example, if 31...♘f3+, then 32 ♔g2 ♘h4+ 33 ♔h2 ♘f3+ 34 ♔g3.

31...♕xc8 32 ♕xe1 ♗g7 33 ♕e6 1-0

White wins in a similar way to lines we have already seen after 33...♕xe6 34 dxe6 ♗f6 (or 34...d5 35 e7 ♘d6 36 ♘f7+!) 35 e7 ♗xe7 36 ♗c3+.

The lessons of this game are that thematic breaks are not necessarily good; all the factors have to be evaluated, and king safety is one of fundamental importance.

It should be emphasized that it is not enough for one side to make a mistake; it is necessary to punish this in the most suitable manner, and this sometimes involves creating weaknesses in your own camp, as with 25 g4!. Otherwise there is a risk that the opponent's bad move might go unpunished and thus become justified.

This game is also another example of how tactics are essential to capitalize on the advantage (27 ♘xe5!).

When you sacrifice material, you generally seek clear compensation, and the bigger the sacrifice, naturally the greater (or quicker) you want this compensation to be.

When it is a question of long-term, positional compensation, the sacrifice is usually a lighter one, of a pawn for example, as in the following game, which is included in this chapter because

part of the compensation is that the enemy king remains rather short of protection. Although this cannot be exploited immediately, it can lead to an attack in the medium or long term.

Game 14

Vladimir Kramnik – Lazaro Bruzon Bautista

Turin Olympiad 2006

Queen's Gambit Declined, Cambridge Springs Variation

1 ♘f3 d5 2 d4 ♘f6 3 c4 c6 4 ♘c3 e6 5 ♗g5 ♘bd7 6 e3 ♕a5 7 cxd5 ♘xd5 8 ♕d2 ♗b4 9 ♖c1 h6 10 ♗h4 0-0 *(D)*

A possible alternative here is 10...c5.

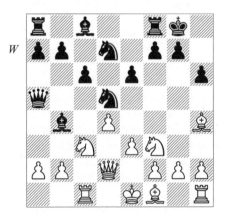

What should White play now? A short description of the position is useful here.

Black has put pressure on the c3-knight, which has enabled him to complete the development of his kingside and to castle, while White has had to defend against this pressure and has not yet completed his own kingside development.

On the other hand, Black has yet to complete the development of his queenside, where the c8-bishop is a particular worry. The way to activate this bishop is with the advance ...e5, opening the c8-h3 diagonal, or else with ...c5, in order then to occupy the long diagonal, or even play it to a6, seeking a favourable exchange of bishops.

The most natural move for White is to continue development with 11 ♗d3, when there

can follow 11...e5 12 0-0 *(D)* (we shall examine 12 a3?! in the next note).

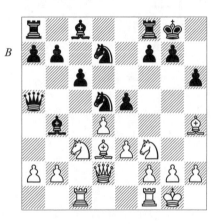

Then 12...♖e8 led to a promising position for Black after 13 e4 ♘f4 14 ♗c4 ♘g6 15 a3 ♘xh4 in Alekhine-Bogoljubow, World Ch match (game 13), Berlin 1929, while after the more modern treatment 12...exd4 13 exd4 ♖e8, White must justify his isolated d-pawn. Here is an example in which Black was successful: 14 ♗b1?! ♘f8 15 ♘e5 ♗e6 (Black has managed to solve his opening problems; all his pieces are developed harmoniously and his king is reasonably safe) 16 ♖fe1 c5! and in Oll-Smagin, Copenhagen 1993 Black had already gained a slight initiative, since 17 dxc5 ♘xc3 18 bxc3 ♗xc5 is not appropriate, on account of Black's better structure. Smagin recommended the modest 17 ♘f3, but the game actually continued 17 ♘c4?! ♕a6 18 ♘e3 ♘xe3 19 fxe3 (the other captures are answered in the same way) 19...♗xa2! 20 ♗xa2 ♕xa2 with a healthy extra pawn for Black. Of course, White

has better continuations, such as 14 ♖fe1, successfully contesting the e-file thanks to his better development.

11 a3

White decides to give up a pawn to prevent Black from completing his development comfortably. As is almost always the case, the idea is not sufficient in itself – the correct move-order for carrying it out is also important. 11 ♗d3 e5 12 a3?! is a closely related idea, but it is not the same. After 12...♗xc3 13 bxc3 *(D)* Black must choose carefully:

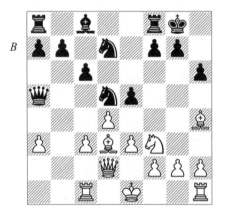

a) The obvious 13...♕xa3? is bad as White plays simply 14 0-0, with good compensation.

b) Nor is it correct to decline the sacrifice with 13...♖e8, although Black achieves a satisfactory position after 14 c4 ♕xd2+ 15 ♘xd2 ♘e7 16 0-0 exd4 17 exd4 ♘f8 18 ♖fe1 ♗f5!, Beliavsky-Oll, Polanica Zdroj 1996.

c) The strongest line is 13...exd4! 14 cxd4 (worse is 14 exd4 ♖e8+) 14...♕xa3 15 0-0 ♖e8 16 e4 and here the preliminary exchange of pawns means that 16...♘f4! is possible, and Black can defend his position. After 17 ♗c2 ♘g6 18 ♖a1 ♕f8 19 ♗g3 ♘f6 20 ♖fe1 ♘h5! 21 ♘e5 ♘xg3 22 ♘xg6 fxg6 23 hxg3 ♗e6 24 f4 ♖ed8 25 ♖a5 ♕d6 26 ♖e5 ♗f7 27 ♖d1 b6 28 ♕c3 a5 29 ♗b3 ♖a7 30 ♗xf7+ ♖xf7 White did not have enough compensation for the pawn in Pelletier-Fridman, Essen 2001.

11...♗xc3 12 bxc3 ♕xa3 13 e4 *(D)*

The alternative is 13 ♗d3.

For the pawn, White has made several gains, such as the bishop-pair and a slight weakening

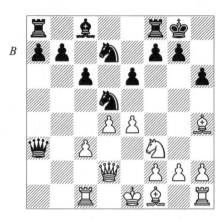

of Black's castled position, while the problem of Black's queenside development persists.

It is also important for White to be able to contain the extra pawn, the one at a7, which is passed, without having to divert any of his pieces.

13...♘e7

13...♘5b6 ensures that the knight is safe from future harassment but makes it harder to mobilize the queenside. Let us see an example: 14 ♗d3 ♖e8 15 0-0 e5 16 ♗g3 exd4 (a sad decision; the white centre now dominates the game) 17 cxd4 ♘f8 18 ♖fe1 ♗e6 19 ♖a1 ♕e7 20 ♕b2 ♗c4 21 ♗c2 ♗a6 22 ♕c3 ♗c4 23 ♖a5 f6 24 ♘h4 and, sheltered by his powerful centre, White was able to manoeuvre as he pleased, preparing a strong attack on Black's castled position, in Kramnik-Lobron, Frankfurt (rapid) 1995.

14 ♗d3 ♘g6 15 ♗g3 e5 *(D)*

Black blocks the e4-pawn, to keep the b1-h7 diagonal closed and avoid having White's e5 advance constantly hanging over him. Here is an example in which Black simply develops: P.H.Nielsen-C.Hansen, Esbjerg 2002 continued 15...b6 16 0-0 ♗b7 17 e5 ♕e7 18 h4 c5 19 h5 ♗xf3 20 gxf3 ♘h4 21 ♕f4 ♘f5 22 ♗xf5 exf5 23 ♕xf5 (once White has recovered the material, the pawn-centre gives him a clear advantage) 23...♕e6 24 ♕e4 f5 25 d5! and after this tactical blow White's advantage became more serious, since 25...fxe4 fails to 26 dxe6 ♘b8 27 fxe4 ♖e8 28 f4 ♖xe6 29 f5 ♖e8 30 e6 with an overwhelming position.

16 0-0

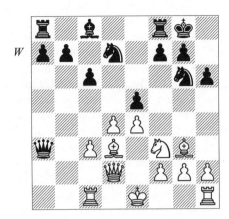

18...豐d8 *(D)*

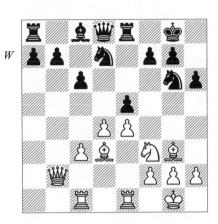

16 h4 has also been played here, which is a move that will always be 'in the air', but the text-move is more flexible, since it is a move White will need to play in any case (an 'essential' move), whereas the same cannot be said for h4, despite its frequent usefulness.

Black is not offering the pawn back for nothing; in the event of 16 dxe5?! 豐e7 or 16 包xe5?! 包dxe5 17 dxe5 罩d8 18 0-0 豐c5!, the tension has been released to Black's advantage and he will be a pawn up again, with no great problems.

16...罩e8 17 罩fe1

Another 'essential' move, bringing the rook into play. You should never forget to ask yourself what your opponent is planning, since if 17 h4?! Black can gain counterplay by attacking the centre with 17...exd4! 18 cxd4 包f6 and now 19 罩fe1 can be answered with 19...盒g4.

17...豐a5

It is less easy for Black to find useful moves. Understandably he does not want give up the centre. He can still not make any use of his passed pawn with 17...a5, since now 18 h4! is good, after which it is difficult to maintain the pawn on e5. After 18...exd4 19 cxd4 包f6 20 罩a1 White regains the a5-pawn; if 20...豐b3 then 21 罩eb1 is better for White, because the e4-pawn is taboo following 21...豐e6 22 罩xa5 罩xa5 23 豐xa5 as 23...包xe4? is answered by 24 盒xe4 豐xe4 25 罩e1, winning.

Given the course of the game, it is easy to suggest 17...豐e7.

18 豐b2

Evading the influence of the black queen and putting pressure on b7.

Black has no threats, so White has freedom of action. But what should he play? The pieces appear to be on their best squares, or else without any clearly better squares. All the pieces, that is, with just one exception...

19 盒b1!

Heading for a2, from where it will not only prevent Black's a-pawn from advancing too far but also aim at the weak f7-square, as well as clearing the d-file so that the c1-rook can have a better role.

19...a5

Kramnik commented that in reply to 19...豐f6 he would not automatically have played 20 盒a2, since Black could then improve his position noticeably with 20...包f4!. Then if 21 豐d2 there is time for 21...g5, with which Black has taken a considerable step forward, and a once-passive piece is well placed. Kramnik intended 20 豐d2!, preventing ...包f4, and if 20...a5 then 21 h4.

20 罩cd1 a4 *(D)*

21 盒a2

White's last two moves were according to plan and clearly the best. In contrast, regaining the pawn at the cost of damaging his pawn-structure with 21 dxe5?! would be punished with 21...豐b6 when, to avoid losing the pawn, White must exchange queens. This is very advantageous for Black, because his passed pawn is worth much more than the doubled pawn on e5.

21...豐e7

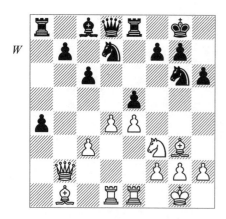

Kramnik indicates that 21...♕a5 was better, keeping the queen more active, although of course Black's mobility problems would persist.

22 ♕c1

Since Black still lacks threats, White continues to strengthen his position; he controls f4 once again, while retaining the idea of h4 followed by h5.

22...♖a5 (D)

If 22...b5 23 h4 exd4 White would not recapture with the pawn, which would give Black two dangerous passed pawns, but with the knight: 24 ♘xd4!, attacking the c6-pawn, and with ideas of ♘f5 and including the f-pawn in the struggle.

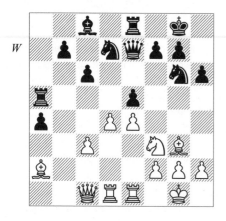

23 ♕d2!

Another piece improvement, with the possibility of advancing with c4, exploiting the fact that the a5-rook is unguarded.

23...exd4?!

If he defends the rook with 23...b6, the black structure, in particular the c6-pawn, will be left rather weak. White could continue with 24 h4, when according to Kramnik it is possible to relieve the pressure by giving up the exchange with 24...♘f6 25 ♘xe5 ♘xe5 26 ♗xe5 ♖xe5 27 dxe5 ♕xe5, although White has the advantage. 24...exd4?! is also unsatisfactory in view of 25 ♘xd4 ♕c5 26 ♘f5, followed by 27 ♘d6, and of course blocking the advance of the pawn with 24...h5 further weakens the kingside: 25 ♘g5 ♖f8 26 dxe5 ♘dxe5 27 f4 ♘g4 and here even 28 ♕d6! is strong, with a double threat against the g6-knight and the c6-pawn.

The best was to take a leaf out of White's book and leave the structure unchanged, by playing 23...♖a6!.

24 ♘xd4 (D)

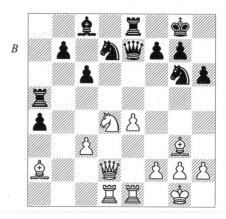

Of course, the f5-square is extremely attractive, and the f2-pawn is ready to advance.

24...♕c5

Closing the diagonal of the g3-bishop by flicking in 24...♕g5 25 f4 ♕c5 is not an improvement, since the bishop comes back into play with 26 ♗f2!, followed by 27 ♘f5.

25 ♗c7!

This is what 24...♕g5 was designed to avoid – the bishop embedding itself in Black's position, threatening the a5-rook, and...

Kramnik pointed out that the natural 25 ♘f5 is not convincing; after 25...♘de5 26 ♘d6 there follows 26...♖d8, creating unnecessary complications.

25...♖a8? (D)

Given the outcome of the game, 25...♞df8 was better, or else 25...♞f6, although the result would not be in doubt.

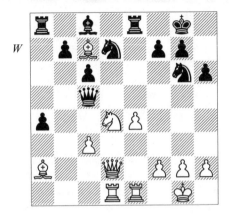

W

26 ♗xf7+!!

The weakness of the black king is finally punished. It is important that all the white pieces are working together in the attack, and the inclusion of 25 ♗c7! is fundamental, as we shall see, showing that mastery of the tactical phase is vital to be able to exploit a positional advantage.

26...♔xf7 27 ♕a2+ ♔f8

The retreat 27...♔e7 fails to 28 ♕e6+ ♔f8 29 ♗d6+, while 27...♔f6 is brilliantly met by 28 ♗d8+!!:

a) 28...♖xd8 29 ♕e6+ ♔g5 30 ♞f3+ ♔f4 31 g3+ ♔xf3 32 ♖d3+ mating.

b) The outcome is the same after 28...♔e5; mate is forced as follows: 29 ♞f3+ ♔f4 30 ♕d2+ ♔g4 31 h3+ ♔h5 32 g4#.

c) Similarly if 28...♞e7 then 29 ♕e6+ ♔g5 30 ♞f3+ ♔f4 31 g3+ ♔xf3 32 ♖d3+ mates.

28 ♞e6+ ♖xe6 29 ♕xe6 ♞e7

If the c7-bishop were on g3, then Black could play 29...♞ge5, shutting out the bishop for the time being, but here the threat of 30 ♗d6+ prevents this.

Black could deal with the threat by playing 29...♕g5, but then 30 ♖e3 wins, and 30 ♖xd7 ♗xd7 31 ♗d6+ ♞e7 32 ♕xd7 seems even stronger, with the idea of 33 ♖e3, and if 32...a3 White wins easily with 33 f4 ♕h4 34 g3 ♕f6 35 e5 ♕f7 36 ♕xb7 ♖e8 37 ♗xa3.

30 ♖e3 ♔e8 31 ♖f3 ♕h5 32 ♗d6 1-0

Black is faced with unavoidable mate after 32...♕g5 33 ♖f7.

As we mentioned in the introduction to this game, White did not gain an immediate attack with his pawn sacrifice, but obtained permanent compensation in the form of the bishop-pair and a strong centre. Thanks to this, he was able to manoeuvre with ease, and improve the position of his pieces until they were all in their optimal positions. In this context we should note moves such as 19 ♗b1! to put the bishop on a2 and occupy the d-file.

Black could have defended better, although the impossibility of developing the c8-bishop hindered the smooth communication of his pieces. 23...exd4?! was a very debatable decision that increased the scope of the f3-knight (heading for f5 and d6), as well as the g3-bishop and the d1-rook.

The move 25 ♗c7! not only improved the position of the bishop, so that it would not be shut out of the game on g3, but also enabled the bishop to collaborate decisively in the finish beginning with 26 ♗xf7+!!.

Let me state once again that the precise handling of tactics is essential to be able to capitalize on a dynamic advantage.

Game 15

Alexei Shirov – Vasily Ivanchuk

Foros 2007

Ruy Lopez, Closed without h3

In the previous four games, the centre was closed or relatively stable, so that the defence could not make use of the principle "The best reply to an attack on the wing is a break in the centre".

In the game that we shall look at now, attack and defence are balanced. White attacks right from the start on the kingside, under cover of his pawn-majority. Black defends himself appropriately, and at a certain moment the attacking side over-reaches and a variation of the above saying comes to pass.

1 e4 e5 2 ♘f3 ♘c6 3 ♗b5 a6 4 ♗a4 ♘f6 5 0-0 b5 6 ♗b3 ♗e7 *(D)*

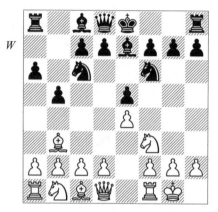

7 d4

The most usual move here is 7 ♖e1. White is trying to exploit Black's unusual move-order, but he will end up playing a popular line that does not form part of his usual practice, which is not a good idea. Decades ago this would have been a great success for Black, but nowadays, when computers have changed preparation so much, his advantage is minimal, since all the top players know 'almost everything'.

7...d6

Ivanchuk rejects 7...exd4 in view of 8 e5 ♘e4 9 ♗d5 and he seeks a transposition to the normal line in which White plays d4 without a previous h3.

8 c3 0-0 9 ♖e1

This position is usually reached by the move-order 5...♗e7 6 ♖e1 b5 7 ♗b3 d6 8 c3 0-0 9 d4.

9...♗g4 10 ♗e3

The alternative is 10 d5 ♘a5 11 ♗c2.

10...exd4 11 cxd4 *(D)*

11...d5

In the famous games Capablanca-Bogoljubow, London 1922 and Fischer-Korchnoi, Curaçao Candidates 1962, the main alternative was

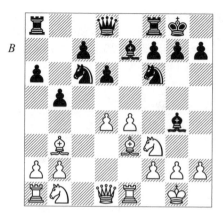

played: 11...♘a5 12 ♗c2 ♘c4 (12...c5 is also popular) 13 ♗c1 c5.

12 e5 ♘e4 13 ♘c3 ♘xc3 14 bxc3 ♕d7

This queen move prepares the tour ...♘d8-e6 at some point, which is typical of this line. This would also allow ...c6, fortifying the centre and the queenside, and sometimes even ...c5, to attack the white centre.

Shirov consumed a lot of time on the preceding well-known moves, so Ivanchuk's move-order can be considered a practical success.

15 h3 ♗h5 16 g4

After 16 ♗f4 Black can carry out the aforementioned manoeuvre 16...♘d8 17 g4 ♘e6 18 ♗g3 ♗g6 19 ♘h4 c5!, with a pleasant position for Black, Timofeev-Lastin, Sochi 2005.

16...♗g6 17 ♘d2 *(D)*

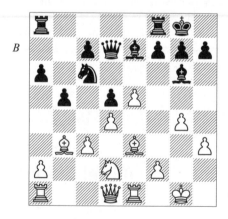

Preparing a pawn-storm with f4, when the position of the g6-bishop might cause Black some problems.

What should Black play now? One possibility is 17...♘a5, when White would play not 18 ♗c2, but 18 f4, allowing Black to capture on b3 and intending to recapture with the pawn.

On the other hand it is clear that 'at some point' Black will have to play ...f5 or ...f6; the only question is the timing of this. Ivanchuk plays a third possibility, 'related' to the ones discussed.

17...a5!

Ivanchuk wants to exchange the light-squared bishops before playing ...f5; this would be a good transaction for Black, getting rid of his uncomfortably placed g6-bishop in exchange for the generally strong 'Spanish bishop'.

17...f5 has been played several times.

18 f4

White does not oppose Black's idea, judging that the advance of his kingside pawns is the priority.

Another idea was to prevent it by playing 18 a4. The reply would be 18...b4, when 19 c4?! is inappropriate since the d4-pawn is left very weak after 19...dxc4. Ivanchuk commented that the position after 19 ♖c1! bxc3 20 ♖xc3 ♗b4 21 ♖c1 f6 22 f4 is difficult to evaluate. Black has good tactical chances against the powerful phalanx of white pawns. For example, there might follow 22...fxe5 23 dxe5 ♔h8 *(D)*.

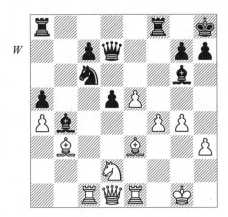

In this position, as in the game, the advance of the white pawns threatens to overwhelm Black's kingside, but this advance is not without its risks, since White's own castled position has also become airy.

Ivanchuk suggests unpinning with 24 ♖f1 and after 24...d4 25 ♘f3 the game is complicated. Both kings are insecure, White's because he has advanced his pawns, and Black's because of the threat of being overwhelmed by these advanced pawns.

The impulsive 24 f5?! shows that Black can hit back hard by sacrificing material with 24...♘xe5!, gaining a strong attack after 25 fxg6 ♕d6 26 ♔g2 ♘xg6.

18...a4 19 ♗c2 ♗xc2 20 ♕xc2 f5! *(D)*

Necessary for restraining the pawn-storm. Ivanchuk also considered 20...f6, in order to take on e5 and then strike back with ...h5.

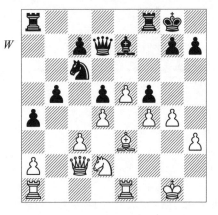

21 exf6

This renounces the space advantage in return for reviving the e3-bishop. In the event of the gambit move 21 ♖f1 it is risky accept the pawn sacrifices since after 21...fxg4?! 22 f5 gxh3 23 ♔h2!, followed by ♖f3, and then bringing the a1-rook to the kingside, White has fair compensation. It is safer and probably better to exploit the fact that the e3-bishop has become passive; Black can play in a similar manner to what we have already seen with 21...♘d8! followed by ...g6 and ...♘e6, and the preparation of an attack against the white centre with ...c5.

21...♗xf6 22 ♘f3 ♖ae8 23 ♗f2

Controlling e4, although the course of the game shows that the direct 23 ♘e5 ♗xe5 24 dxe5 was better. After 24...g5!? the white centre loses its stability but, with both kings exposed, the result remains hard to predict.

23...h5!

Black decides to offer battle on the kingside as well, showing that the white king is no better protected than its black counterpart.

24 ♕g6 *(D)*

Played after long reflection. The alternative was 24 f5 hxg4 25 hxg4, when Black again opens lines against both kings with 25...g6. Although complex, the position is balanced. Ivanchuk gives this illustrative line: 26 ♗h4 gxf5 27 ♖xe8 ♕xe8 28 ♗xf6 ♖xf6 29 g5 ♕e3+ 30 ♔g2 ♖g6 31 ♕xf5 ♘e7, when there is no clear advantage for either side.

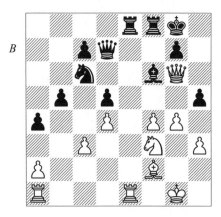

How should Black respond to the attack on the h5-pawn? The opening of the h-file is not in Black's favour, nor was this the idea behind 23...h5.

24...♖e4!

"The white pawns look strong, but this is only at first sight. In fact the black pieces are well placed and are ready to strike at White's most fortified point." – Ivanchuk.

It is noteworthy that Ivanchuk rejects the apparently 'automatic' move 24...hxg4 without comment, not granting it any importance. This decision is fully justified. Concrete calculation proves that Black need not fear a capture on h5, since White does not have time to do so favourably. In contrast, Black can take on g4 when necessary. Generally the so-called 'favourable tension', as in this case, works in favour of the attacking side. In this case it is the reverse, although here the roles of attacker and defender are not 100% clear.

25 ♖xe4?!

It is better to force Black to abandon the e4 outpost with 25 ♘d2!, when Black's advantage is only slight.

25...dxe4 26 ♘h2? *(D)*

A decisive error, allowing a brilliant finish by Ivanchuk, who commented that if 26 ♘e5 then after 26...♗xe5 27 fxe5 hxg4 28 hxg4 Black can defend the e4-pawn with the powerful centralization 28...♕d5!, simultaneously hitting the a2-pawn, and not ruling out a timely ...b4.

26 ♘g5 is necessary, and after 26...♗xg5 27 ♕xg5 there are several options, of which the most natural is 27...hxg4 28 hxg4, although the outcome is unclear. Here 27...b4?! is wrong, since White can safeguard his centre with 28 d5 ♘e7 29 c4 but a deeper examination reveals that this idea can be prepared by 27...♕d6!. After 28 f5 hxg4 29 hxg4 Black can now play 29...b4! in favourable circumstances, destroying White's structure, since now 30 d5 is not possible. If 28 ♗e3 Black can play 28...hxg4 29 hxg4 ♘e7, or 28...♘e7 immediately, offering a promising sacrifice of the b5-pawn, since the exposure of White's poorly defended castled position gives Black grounds for optimism.

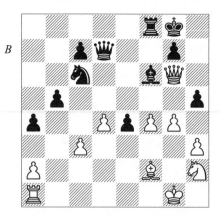

Having defended the g4-pawn, White threatens 27 ♕xe4, which would be the answer to 26...b4, for example. What is the best way to defend the e4-pawn? The fact that, unlike White, Black has all his pieces in play should surely help.

26...♘xd4!!

Rather than a central break to counter an attack on the wing, as the books recommend, this is a central demolition, striking at an apparently well-defended point.

Let us note that the a1-rook is not only out of play but also a tactical weakness, preventing White from capturing twice on d4.

27 cxd4 ♗xd4 28 ♖b1

Other rook moves are no better; for instance, 28 ♖f1 loses to 28...e3, while after 28 ♖e1 ♗xf2+ 29 ♔xf2 ♕d2+ 30 ♖e2 ♖xf4+ 31 ♔g3 h4+ 32 ♔xh4 ♕xe2 there is no perpetual: 33 ♕e8+ ♖f8 34 ♕e6+ ♔h8.

28...e3! 29 ♗g3 h4! *(D)*

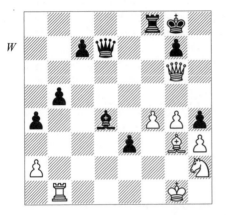

Another elegant move to bring about the fall of the f4-pawn, and with it the whole position. Now we can see how important it was not to play ...hxg4 automatically at some previous point.

30 ♗xh4

The counter-attack 30 ♘f3 hxg3 31 ♘g5 fails to 31...♖xf4! and Black's king is well defended; e.g., 32 ♕h7+ ♔f8 33 ♕h8+ ♔e7 winning.

30...♖xf4 31 ♕d3 *(D)*

If 31 ♗e1 it is easy to see that the white king cannot be defended; for example, *Deep Junior 10* pointed out the line 31...e2+ 32 ♔g2 ♕d5+ 33 ♔g3 ♗e5! (or 33...♖f6) 34 ♔h4 ♖f6 35 ♕e8+ ♔h7 36 g5 ♕e4+ 37 ♘g4 (or 37 ♔h5 ♖h6+! 38 gxh6 g6+ 39 ♔g5 ♕f4#) 37...♖h6+! 38 gxh6 ♗f6+ 39 ♔g3 ♕xe8 and Black wins. This is not the only winning line, but is definitely the most spectacular, as Maxim Notkin commented in *Chess Today*.

31...♕d5!

Another strong centralization, threatening to win with 32...e2+.

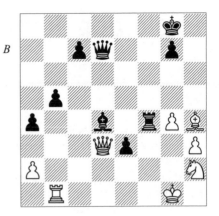

32 ♘f1

If 32 ♕e2 then 32...♖f2! 33 ♗xf2 exf2+ 34 ♔f1 ♕h1#. After 32 ♖b4 there is more than one way to win, such as the simple 32...c5 as well as the more complex 32...♖f2 33 ♗xf2 exf2+ 34 ♔f1 ♕h1+ 35 ♔e2 ♕e1+ 36 ♔f3 ♕xb4.

32...♖f2! 33 ♘xe3

Here 33 ♗xf2 exf2+ 34 ♔h2 ♗e5+ costs White his queen.

33...♖g2+ 34 ♔h1

No better is 34 ♔f1 ♕f3+ 35 ♔e1 ♗c3+! 36 ♕xc3 ♕e2#.

34...♕f3!

The most crushing. Now if 35 ♘xg2 then 35...♕xd3, with the double threat of capturing the b1-rook and mating with 36...♕xh3#.

0-1

We saw in this game that even such a natural advance as that of a kingside pawn-majority has its risks. In every attack, the principle of economy of defensive and aggressive measures is fundamental. Black's spectacular fireworks – 23...h5!, 24...♖e4!, 26...♘xd4!!, 29...h4! – should not blind us to the fact that an important factor was White's failure to involve the a1-rook in the struggle.

The version of 'favourable tension', working in Black's favour, that occurred after 23...h5! is very curious.

Note that rather than there being a separate section of exercises for this chapter, they are combined with those for the next chapter, and start on page 119.

4 Exploiting Temporary Advantages

It often happens that one side builds up strength on one wing at the expense of ceding terrain on the other, and the result is a sort of race to see who can bring the struggle to a head on the wing where he has the advantage.

In several openings the players make semi-automatic moves that extend even into the middlegame. Examples can be found in such lines as the Mar del Plata Variation of the King's Indian Defence, or in the King's Indian Attack. These positions have a specific character, with tactical motifs and thematic manoeuvres which influence the game and which, if only for practical reasons, it is useful to know, because there can be unexpected similarities between positions arising from different openings.

In a way, in these games the side that is attacking on one wing has a temporary advantage, and has to try to profit from this because the opponent also has a similar superiority on the other wing, and the side that gets there first is generally close to victory.

In this chapter we shall be looking at games with less typical positions, where one side achieves a temporary advantage on the kingside, for various reasons, whether in an attacking race, as described above, or because he has eliminated some important defenders of the king.

Game 16
Sergei Kariakin – Loek van Wely
Foros 2007
Sicilian Defence, Najdorf Variation

This game starts quietly, with manoeuvres which give White a slight advantage, but nothing serious, until a rash move by Black allows White to concentrate his forces against Black's castled position and unleash an irresistible storm upon the enemy king.

1 e4 c5 2 ♘f3 d6 3 d4 cxd4 4 ♘xd4 ♘f6 5 ♘c3 a6 6 ♗e3 e5 7 ♘f3

White avoids the fashionable continuation 7 ♘b3.

7...♗e7 8 ♗c4

This bishop can be deployed actively on the open a2-g8 diagonal, because 8...b5? is not playable, owing to 9 ♗d5 ♘xd5 10 ♕xd5, winning.

8...0-0 9 0-0 *(D)*

9...♘c6

The main alternative is 9...♗e6, probing the intentions of the c4-bishop, which cannot retreat

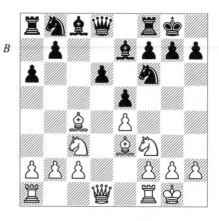

to f1. Let us look at a few examples which will help us understand the events of the main game:

a) 10 ♗b3 ♘c6 (now there is a latent possibility of ...♘a5 to eliminate the b3-bishop, while retaining the e6-bishop to guard d5) 11 ♗g5

♘d7 (offering the exchange of his worse bishop and retaining a knight that can easily be activated) 12 ♗xe7 ♕xe7 13 ♘d5 ♕d8 *(D)* and now:

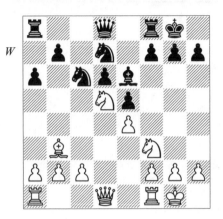

a1) Anand-Leko, Wijk aan Zee 2006 continued 14 c3 (preparing the retreat of the b3-bishop) 14...♘a5!. It turns out that 15 ♗c2 is not advantageous because Black continues with 15...♘c4 16 b3 ♘a3!, catching the bishop. Anand pointed out that 17 ♗d3 is not effective because of 17...♗xd5 18 exd5 f5!, creating counterplay.

a2) de la Riva-Bologan, Spain 2006 saw 14 ♕e2 ♘c5 15 ♖fd1 and here Black used another plan worth considering: 15...♔h8, with the idea of ...f5. After 16 c3 f5 17 exf5 ♗xf5 18 ♘e3 Black could have played simply 18...♗g6, threatening ...♗h5 and intending to answer 19 ♗d5 by 19...♘e7, with equal chances. Bologan chose to complicate with 18...♗d3 19 ♖xd3 e4, which he criticized in his comments in *Informator*.

b) 10 ♗xe6 fxe6 *(D)* is an exchange that generally speaking brings White no advantage, since it strengthens the black centre and Black regains control of the weak d5-square.

The doubled pawns cannot be exploited, but Black is slightly behind in development in this position and Ivanchuk, that inexhaustible inventor of new ideas, found that White has the annoying leap 11 ♘a4, illustrating that there is a weakness on b6 as well as e6. Now 11...♘bd7? is not playable because of 12 ♘g5, and the capture 11...♘xe4?! is not convincing either after,

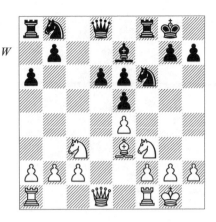

for instance, 12 ♘b6 ♖a7 13 ♕d3 ♘c5 (or 13...d5 14 ♘xd5 exd5 15 ♗xa7 ♘c6 16 ♗b6! and Black's compensation is not sufficient) 14 ♗xc5 dxc5 15 ♕b3, winning.

Ivanchuk-Topalov, Morelia/Linares 2007 continued 11...♘g4 12 ♕d3 (agreeing to the exchange of the bishop, but retaining control of b6 for the time being, and speeding up his own development) 12...♘xe3 13 ♕xe3 b5 14 ♘b6 ♖a7 15 ♘d5! ♖b7 16 ♕d2! (notice that White is in no hurry to take on e7, so as not to allow Black to coordinate his forces easily) 16...♘c6 17 ♖ad1 ♖d7 18 ♕c3! ♘b8 19 ♘xe7+ ♕xe7 (White finally had to exchange the d5-knight, but in return the black knight remains badly placed, and now White is ready to exert pressure on the weakness at d6) 20 ♖d3 h6 21 ♖fd1 ♖fd8 22 h4 and White is better, forcing Black on to the defensive, and with the problem of the b8-knight still without a solution.

10 ♖e1 b5 11 ♗f1 ♖b8

White's possible ♘d5 leap persists in various stages of the game, and Black anticipates it with this move, which defends the b6-square, so that 12 ♘d5? can now be answered by 12...♘xe4! 13 ♗b6 ♖xb6 14 ♘xb6 ♘xf2!, with advantage to Black.

12 ♗g5 *(D)*

Ready to eliminate the defender of the d5-square.

12...♘g4

As in the examples seen earlier, Black does not agree to give up his f6-knight, which is more useful than the passive e7-bishop. This leap is better than 12...♘d7, since in that case

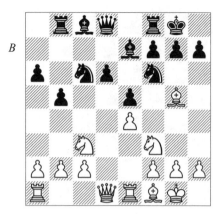

after 13 ♗xe7 it is necessary to recapture with the queen in order not to lose the d6-pawn, handing a free tempo to the opponent after 13...♕xe7 14 ♘d5.

13 ♗c1

The exchange 13 ♗xe7 ♘xe7 gave White nothing in Short-Ehlvest, Horgen 1995, which continued 14 a3 ♗b7 15 ♕d2 ♕c7 16 ♖ad1 ♖fd8 17 h3 ♘f6 18 ♕e3 ♗c6, and Black had all his pieces on good squares, with no problems.

13 ♗d2 seems a more logical retreat. In the game Anand-Topalov, Morelia/Linares 2007, 13...♗e6 14 ♘d5 was played and although White did not achieve much, Kariakin commented that he was more anxious about Black's 13...f5 break, which can be played here in better circumstances than in the de la Riva-Bologan game that we saw earlier.

13...♕b6 (D)

In this position, 13...f5? is inadvisable because of 14 exf5!, when to avoid losing a pawn, Black must play the dubious-looking 14...♖xf5. He cannot recapture by 14...♗xf5? because 15 ♕d5+ wins (but not, of course, immediately 14 ♕d5+? ♔h8 15 ♕xc6?? because of 15...♗b7).

14 ♕d2

White defends the attacked f2-pawn, but this move is also directed against ...f5. The d6-pawn is under pressure on the d-file, and the possible check on d5 creates difficulties for Black (for example, if Black plays 14...f5 then White can reply 15 ♘d5).

14...♘f6

Since h3 is almost certainly coming, Black retreats, to have more options; now he threatens 15...♗g4.

15 h3

This move appears very natural, defending against Black's threat of ...♗g4. However, the unusual configuration of the pieces enables White to manoeuvre in non-routine fashion here with 15 ♘d5! ♘xd5 16 exd5 ♘a5. Then Black would like to expand on the kingside with ...f5, but White could play 17 ♕b4!, with threats of 18 ♘xe5 or 18 a4; Kariakin thinks that White would have retained some pressure this way.

15...♖e8

Now that the e7-bishop is defended there is no longer any fear of 16 ♘d5, since after 16...♘xd5 17 exd5 Black does not have to play his knight to the edge but can reply 17...♘d4 18 ♘xd4 exd4, with good play.

16 ♕d1 (D)

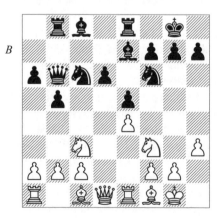

Renewing the threat of ♗g5.

16...h6 17 b3

White has only one clear plan, which is the ♘d5 leap. There is no hurry with this, so first he prefers to control the c4-square, to deprive the (future) black a5-knight of mobility.

17...♗f8 18 a4

Another useful preparation; Black loses all control of the c4-square and the f1-bishop increases its influence on the queenside.

18...b4 19 ♘d5 ♘xd5 20 exd5 ♘a5 21 ♗e3 *(D)*

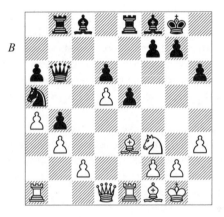

Now that the structure has been changed, Black has a clear plan to play ...f5, but first he has to decide where to retreat the queen. The most natural is to retreat to c7, putting pressure on the backward pawn on c2, but before taking a decision it is useful to ask yourself what the opponent would do in that case.

21...♕c7?!

If we look more carefully at the dynamic possibilities of the white pieces, we see that he has one piece without any good prospects, and that is the f3-knight, which lacks a good square. With 21...♕b7! Black could have avoided the following manoeuvre.

22 ♘d2!

Now White has a clear plan to play ♘c4, getting rid of his inactive piece and reviving the bishops. It is true that the a5-knight is not doing much either, but in contrast to the f3-knight, it does not stand in the way of Black's plan, which is to play ...f5 and make progress on the kingside.

22...f5 23 ♘c4 *(D)*

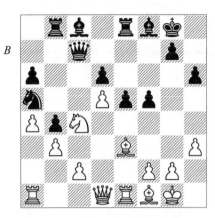

What now? The a6-pawn requires defence, which complicates the task of moving forces to the kingside. 23...♘xc4 24 ♗xc4 ♕f7 is possible, when the advance of the black pawns to f4 and e4 must be handled carefully. White would probably play the prophylactic 25 ♗d2!, to prevent 25...f4 from coming with tempo, and to be able to take advantage of the weakness thus created on the b1-h7 diagonal and prevent 26...e4. White could open the game on the queenside with c3 at an appropriate moment.

Another typical idea in this structure is to play 23...g6, in order to occupy the long diagonal.

23...♗e7?

Black prefers to leave the pawns untouched, and wants to occupy the diagonal with ...♗f6. There is also the possibility of offering to exchange bishops later by ...♗g5. In fact, though, this is the decisive error.

If 23...g6 Kariakin intended to play on 'his' wing, opening lines with 24 ♖c1! followed by c3, with some advantage.

24 ♕h5! *(D)*

The most powerful piece moves to the kingside with gain of time. Admittedly this does not look very dangerous yet, because it is not obvious how White's other pieces can arrive in support.

24...♖f8

If 24...♗d7 White has 25 ♗xh6! gxh6 26 ♕g6+ ♔f8, and now the support arrives in the shape of 27 ♗e2!, with a winning attack after,

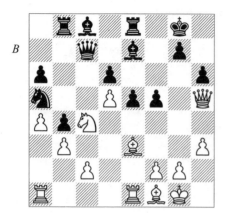

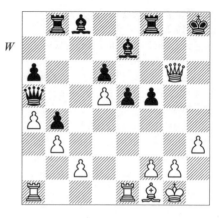

for example, 27...罩ed8 28 皇h5 皇e8 29 營xh6+ 含g8 30 ②xa5 營xa5 31 皇g6! 皇xg6 32 營xg6+ 含h8 33 營h6+ 含g8 34 營e6+ 含f8 35 營xf5+, followed by the entrance into play of the e1-rook, mating quickly.

25 ②xa5 營xa5 (D)

The black queen is a long way from the kingside, which increases the impact of White's small attacking force.

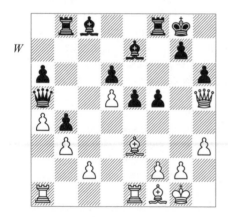

26 皇xh6! gxh6?!

Black thought that there was no more than a perpetual check, because the white queen alone cannot deliver mate, and Black requires only one tempo to come to his king's defence. This is not the case, however, although the reason is not obvious.

It was better not to take the bishop and just play on in a miserable position a pawn down.

27 營g6+ 含h8 28 營xh6+ 含g8 29 營g6+ 含h8 (D)

And now, which piece can help the lone white queen? There is no immediate way, so that it has to be contrived by tactical means, and with great speed; there is no time to manoeuvre, since the black pieces stand ready to assist the defence.

A trained tactical eye discovers that the white bishop can join in the attack decisively after the combination 罩xe5, d6, 皇c4, etc. Once this idea has been spotted, the next task is to work out the correct move-order.

30 罩e3!!

A fantastic preparatory move. In contrast, if White plays the immediate 30 罩xe5? Black is not obliged to capture the rook and can defend by bringing his queen back to defend with 30...營d8!.

30...f4

Preventing 31 罩g3; if 30...罩f6 White mates quickly with 31 營h5+ and 32 罩g3+.

31 罩xe5!

Now this works; with ...f4 played and the fifth rank cleared, the threat is 32 罩h5#.

31...dxe5 32 營h6+ 含g8 33 d6! (D)

Despite the extra rook, and even with the a1-rook taking no part in the attack, the entrance of the bishop at c4 is decisive.

33...罩f7

If 33...含f7, then 34 營h7+ wins.

34 皇c4 皇f5

If 34...營d8 White wins with 35 dxe7 營xe7 36 營g6+, when after 36...含f8 37 皇xf7 營xf7 38 營d6+ the b8-rook drops, while in case of 36...含h8 37 皇xf7 營f8 either entrance of the rook, 38 罩e1 or 38 罩d1, wins.

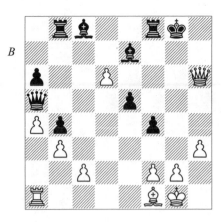

35 dxe7 1-0

Black had a playable position, but just one mistake (23...♗e7?) granted White the tempi required to turn his numerical superiority on the kingside into the decisive factor, aided by the fact that neither the distant black queen, nor any of the other four black pieces, was able to come to the defence of the king.

The beautiful combination, to which the key is the preparatory 30 ♖e3!!, forcing the decisive weakening of the castled position with 30...f4, is aesthetically very striking.

Game 17
Viswanathan Anand – Magnus Carlsen
Morelia/Linares 2007
Ruy Lopez, Chigorin Defence

In this game White gains the advantage thanks to the black pieces being slightly misplaced. White exploited this momentary lack of coordination to make progress on the kingside. In this case it was not possible to breach the defences of the castled position by direct methods, such as advancing pawns or quickly transferring pieces the kingside by means of a sacrifice, as in the previous game.

The manoeuvres carried out by White to force a way through are very instructive. First the struggle develops on the queenside, and only after the advantage (of mobility in this case) has been gained there does the course of the battle change abruptly and focus on the other wing.

This game clearly shows that the concept of which pieces to exchange or retain loses much of its relevance when the safety of the king is involved.

1 e4 e5 2 ♘f3 ♘c6 3 ♗b5 a6 4 ♗a4 ♘f6 5 0-0 ♗e7 6 ♖e1 b5 7 ♗b3 d6 8 c3 0-0 9 h3 ♘a5 10 ♗c2 c5 11 d4 ♘d7 *(D)*

This idea of Paul Keres's was not regarded favourably by Fischer, who commented in his book *My 60 Memorable Games* that Black loses time in transferring his knight to b6 and the kingside is weakened.

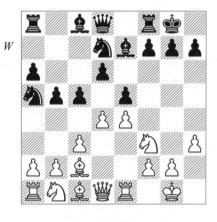

This did not prevent it from being employed later on occasion by Kramnik, Mamedyarov, Adams, Ponomariov, Portisch and other strong players.

12 d5

White decides to close the position. The main alternatives are 12 dxc5, employed successfully by Fischer against Keres in round 7 of the Curaçao Candidates tournament in 1962, and 12 ♘bd2.

After 12 ♘bd2, among other things, Black has the line 12...exd4 13 cxd4 ♘c6 14 d5 ♘ce5, which according to the theory of the time was not easy to breach.

With 12 d5 the central tension is resolved and the game is closed, giving way to a manoeuvring struggle. Now it is possible to 're-cycle' the a5-knight with 12...♘c4, but Black continues with Keres's original idea.

12...♘b6 (D)

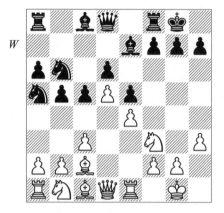

Black prepares the eventual break ...f5, and at the same time controls a4 to discourage White's thematic a4 break.

What now? Should White allow ...f5 or restrain it with 13 g4?

13 ♘bd2

On the basis of another game Fischer-Keres, played in round 22 at Curaçao 1962 (with Fischer curiously replacing his successful 12 dxc5 of the seventh round with 12 d5), it was considered that 13 g4 was not very effective in this position, because White does not have enough pieces on the kingside to support this advance.

There is a thin line between labelling 13 g4 as a useful move restraining enemy counterplay and a move that weakens the position, but the second definition seems to be closer to the truth after 13...h5!, and now to support g4 White has to allow his opponent's dark-squared bishop to be activated: 14 ♘h2 hxg4 15 hxg4 ♗g5! 16 ♘d2 g6 (to occupy the h-file with the rook) 17 ♘df3 ♗xc1 18 ♕xc1 ♔g7 (D).

Black has made progress following 13...h5, having exchanged his usually passive e7-bishop for the c1-bishop, which makes the weaknesses caused by 13 g4 more glaring. Now with 19 ♕g5 Fischer sought the exchange of queens to curb Black's initiative on the kingside or to

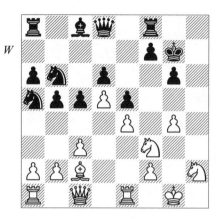

enable the queen to defend the dark squares after 19...f6 20 ♕h4 and ♕g3. Black did not object to the queen exchange, regrouping his pieces with 19...♘b7 and after 20 ♕xd8 ♖xd8 21 a4 bxa4 22 ♗xa4 ♘xa4 23 ♖xa4 ♗d7 24 ♖a2 c4 25 ♘d2 ♗b5 26 ♘hf1 ♖h8 27 ♘e3 ♖h4 28 ♔g2 ♖ah8 29 ♘f3 ♖h3 30 ♘f1 ♘c5 Black obtained a good position and achieved victory after a long struggle. Later in F.Blatny-Filip, Prague 1963, Black did not allow White to play a4 and replied with 19...♕xg5 20 ♘xg5 ♗d7, aiming to make progress subsequently on the queenside: 21 ♔g2 c4 22 ♘h3 ♘b7 23 f4 f6 24 ♔g3 ♘c5 25 ♘f3 ♘ba4 26 ♖ab1 a5, with advantage to Black, who went on to win.

We now return to 13 ♘bd2 (D):

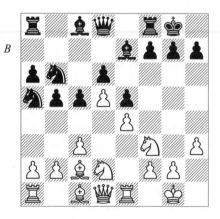

13...g6

Continuing to prepare the ...f5 break.

The immediate 13...f5 is playable, although in general exchanging the light-squared bishops and handing over the e4-square to an enemy knight is not to be recommended, even though Black gains the f-file in return, which would happen after 14 exf5 ♗xf5 15 ♗xf5 ♖xf5 16 ♘e4. In this case the justification for 13...f5 is that the d5-pawn is left rather weak, although the black pieces are not well placed to put pressure on d5. The game Acs-Gschnitzer, Bundesliga 2005/6 continued 16...♕d7 (to bring the queen's rook to f8) 17 ♘fg5 ♗xg5 18 ♗xg5 (the white pieces are not sufficiently developed to maintain the knight on e6 after 18 ♘xg5 ♖af8 19 ♖e2 h6 20 ♘e6?! ♖8f6, when there is no good defence against the threat of 21...♘xd5) 18...♘b7 19 ♗e3 (putting pressure on the g1-a7 diagonal, to lend force to an eventual b4) 19...♘c4 20 ♗c1 a5?! (this allows the structure to be changed radically in White's favour) 21 a4! b4 22 b3 ♘b6 23 c4 (the weakness of the d5-pawn has disappeared, whereas the strength of the e4-knight persists) 23...♖af8 24 ♖a2 ♘c8?! (D).

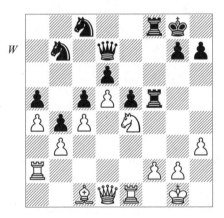

Occupying the e6-square with the e4-knight, once f2 is protected and d5 consolidated, is a dream; is it possible to make it come true?

Yes, it is! 25 g4! is the way to do it (and not with 25 ♘g5, which allows 25...♘d8). The weakness of White's castled position is of no importance, now that the white pieces are strong on the kingside. 25...♖f3 26 ♘g5 ♖3f6 27 ♕d3 ♖g6 28 ♘e6 ♖e8 29 f4 (the moment has arrived to open the game; all the white pieces have maximum activity, which cannot be said of their black counterparts) 29...exf4 30 ♖ae2 ♘d8 31

♘xf4 ♖xe2 32 ♕xe2 ♖f6 33 ♘h5 ♖f7 34 ♗b2 ♔f8 35 ♕d3 ♘e7 36 ♕xh7 ♘g8 37 ♗xg7+ ♖xg7 38 ♖f1+ ♔f7 39 ♕g7+ ♔e7 40 ♖e1+ ♘e6 41 ♕xg8 1-0.

14 b4

A weighty decision. White has a plan in mind and clarifies the position, temporarily giving up the c4-square to the black knight.

The modest 14 b3, restricting the a5-knight by preventing it from reactivating itself via c4 and b6, is typical in this sort of position.

14...cxb4 15 cxb4 ♘ac4 16 ♘xc4 ♘xc4 *(D)*

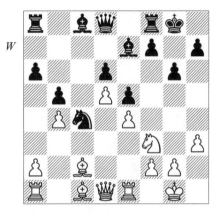

What should White play now? We have already seen that the move ...f5 does not solve all Black's problems, so there is no need to impede it with 17 g4; a lazy solution would be immediately to play 17 ♗h6 and think afterwards. However, Leko-Mamedyarov, Moscow 2006 showed that it does not achieve much after 17...♖e8 18 ♗b3 ♗d7 (18...f5?! is risky here; just how risky is illustrated by the variation 19 exf5 gxf5 20 ♖c1, when Black cannot retreat with 20...♘b6? because of 21 ♘xe5!) 19 ♕e2 ♘b6 (exchanges are gradually coming) 20 ♖ac1 ♖c8 21 ♗e3 ♖xc1 22 ♖xc1 ♕b8 23 ♘d2 ♖c8 24 ♖xc8+ ♘xc8 25 f4 ♕c7 26 ♘f3 ♕c3 27 ♕d2 ♕xd2 28 ♗xd2 f6 and the game later ended in a draw.

17 ♗b3!

An extraordinary move. White does not let himself be tempted by 17 ♗h6 and leaves that square in reserve for the bishop, believing that at the moment the best square for the bishop is e3, from where it operates powerfully against the queenside.

Of course, White reached this conclusion after analysing and evaluating the later course of the struggle; it is not possible merely to glance at the position and deduce something that looks so unnatural at first sight.

17...♘b6

The possibility of White capturing on c4 at an appropriate moment makes it advisable to retreat the knight. This is a success for White's previous move, which cleared the c-file, and we have already seen the influence of the b3-bishop on the a2-g8 diagonal, closed at the moment, if Black opens it by moving his f-pawn.

18 ♗e3

"The bishop belongs on e3." – Anand.

18...♗d7 19 ♖c1 *(D)*

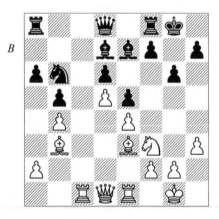

First of all, White occupies the open file; this also discourages Black from breaking with ...f5, since it is difficult to fight simultaneously on two fronts.

19...♖c8

Black follows suit, but his position will suddenly become uncomfortable.

Given the course of the game, 19...♕b8! was better, with the idea of 20...♕b7 and only then ...♖fc8, as Anand indicated.

20 ♖xc8

Creating a slight lack of coordination among the black pieces, which White will use to regain control of the c-file, if only temporarily.

20...♗xc8

20...♘xc8 21 ♕c2 ♘b6 transposes to the game, while the e3-bishop shows its usefulness by preventing the queen from recapturing.

21 ♕c2 ♗d7 22 ♖c1

This is the complement to the previous exchange of rooks – the knight is forced to retreat to the awkward a8-square, since it is essential to prevent an invasion via c7. For example, if 22...♕b8? then 23 ♕c7 ♖c8 24 ♕xb8 ♖xb8 25 ♗xb6 ♖xb6 26 ♖c7 wins. Of course, this is only a temporary advantage, and if White plays indecisively he will not be able to take advantage of the short time that the knight requires to return to the fray and Black will be able to regroup successfully.

22...♘a8 *(D)*

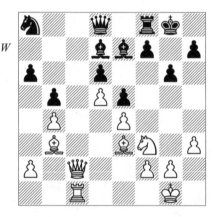

Now Black needs two tempi (23...♕b8 and ...♖c8) to contest White's domination of the c-file. How can White use these two tempi?

23 ♕d2

An obvious move? It might appear so. The queen leaves the c-file in anticipation of Black playing a future ...♖c8, but in fact White's motivation is much deeper than it seems.

Another tempting idea that attracted White was 23 ♘e1, with the intention of sacrificing a piece with ♘d3-c5. When Black takes on c5, the recapture bxc5 would create a very strong pawn-roller. It is true that this allows the exchange of the passive e7-bishop, although Anand indicates that after 23...♗g5 24 ♕d2 ♗xe3 25 ♕xe3, 25...♕b8 26 f4 leaves White slightly better. Even less enticing is 25...f5?! 26 ♘f3! fxe4 27 ♘g5 with a clear advantage to

White after either ♘xe4 or ♘e6 as appropriate. Here we can once again see the influence of the b3-bishop.

23...♛b8 *(D)*

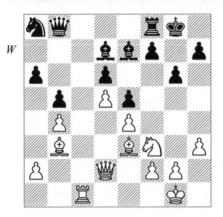

W

So, what was the idea behind Anand's 23 ♛d2 then?

24 ♗g5!!

Earlier White was afraid of the exchange of bishops, but now he seeks it; why? For tactical reasons: White needs to exchange this bishop to speed up his attack on Black's castled position. One point is to bring the queen into the attack via h6. This exchange would hardly be good in 'normal' positions but here it is the best way to create another battlefront and exploit the momentary remoteness of Black's queen and knight.

The exchange of 'good' or 'bad' pieces is something that should be considered in context, and not as an absolute truth.

24...♗xg5?!

If 24...♗d8?! White achieves a strong attack after 25 ♗xd8 ♛xd8 26 ♛h6. This is the main idea of 24 ♗g5; let us see one of the lines given by Anand: 26...f6 27 ♖c6! ♗c8 28 h4! ♖f7 29 h5 ♖g7 (or 29...g5 30 ♘xg5 fxg5 31 ♖xd6, with a winning advantage) 30 hxg6 hxg6 31 ♘h4 g5 32 ♘f5 ♗xf5 33 exf5, "and the rook can never be shifted from c6." – Anand.

24...f6, to avoid the exchange of bishops, is met by 25 ♘xe5!, winning material; the b3-bishop makes its presence felt yet again.

The best move for Black is 24...♛d8!, bringing the queen into the defence, although after

25 ♛e3 (25 ♗xe7?! improves the position of the queen and indeed the whole black position after 25...♛xe7, since 26 ♛e3 is answered by 26...♖c8!, when all the entrances are guarded) 25...♗xg5 26 ♘xg5 ♛e7 27 f4, White has the initiative.

25 ♘xg5

In contrast, 25 ♛xg5? is met by 25...f6! and Black manages to defend his kingside without allowing any pawn-breaks.

25...♖c8 *(D)*

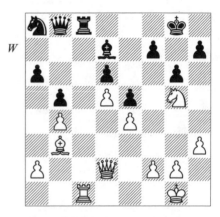

W

26 ♖f1!

The general rule is that it is necessary to retain pieces for the attack, but tactical considerations also apply, and must be checked. White had to calculate quite a lot to make this logical move, which prepares f4.

The alternative, an attractive one, was 26 ♖xc8+ followed by f4.

26...h6 *(D)*

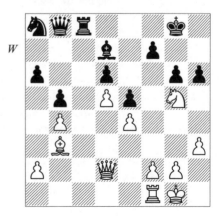

W

27 ᐃe6!

This pretty sacrifice was part of White's calculations, and the reason why he chose 26 ᗅf1. In contrast, the passive 27 ᐃf3? allows Black to solve his difficulties after 27...ᗏg7.

27...ᗏh7

Best. After the capture 27...fxe6 28 dxe6 ᗡe8 the strongest is 29 ᗏxh6!. Here is an illustrative line given by Anand: 29...ᐃb6 30 e7+ ᐃc4 31 ᗏf8+ ᗏh7 32 f4 (we have the computer to thank for the 'inhuman' move 32 ᗡd1) 32...ᗏa8 33 ᗅf3 ᗏxe4 34 f5 gxf5 35 ᗅg3 and wins.

28 f4 ᗏa7+ 29 ᗏh2 *(D)*

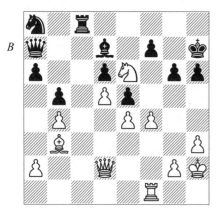

29...ᗡe8

The capture of the knight, although it looks dubious, always has to be considered. Let us see the line indicated by Anand: 29...fxe6 30 dxe6 ᗡe8 31 f5 gxf5 (worse is 31...ᗏd4? 32 ᗏxd4 exd4 33 f6 ᐃb6 34 f7 ᗡxf7 35 ᗅxf7+ ᗏg8 and, as Anand indicates, since Black has not captured on f5, his king has to go to a passive square, such as g8: 36 ᗅd7 ᐃc4 37 e7 ᗅe8 38 ᗅxd6 ᗅxe7 39 ᗅxd4 ᗅc7 40 ᗅd6! and wins) 32 exf5 ᗏd4. Here there are several moves; Anand was intending to enter the endgame with 33 ᗏxd4 exd4 34 f6 ᐃb6 35 f7 ᗡxf7 36 exf7 ᗅf8 37 ᗡe6! (before the bishop is blunted by ...d5 or ...ᐃc4) 37...ᐃc4 38 ᗅd1 ᐃe5 39 ᗅxd4 ᐃxf7 *(D)* and once again it is necessary to take a crucial decision:

a) It is a mistake to go into the rook ending at once, since after 40 ᗡxf7? ᗅxf7 41 ᗅxd6 Black plays 41...ᗅf4! 42 a3 a5! 43 bxa5 ᗅa4, confirming the saying "all rook endings are drawn".

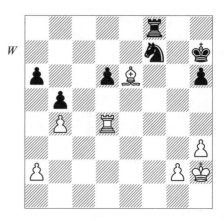

b) The correct way is to enter the pawn ending with 40 ᗅf4! and after 40...ᗏg7 41 ᗡxf7 ᗅxf7 42 ᗅxf7+ ᗏxf7 43 ᗏg3 the ending is winning, since White can create a passed pawn that will deflect the black king and allow the white king to reach the queenside first, viz.: 43...ᗏe6 44 ᗏf3 ᗏe5 45 g4 d5 46 h4 d4 47 g5 hxg5 48 hxg5 ᗏf5 49 g6 ᗏxg6 50 ᗏe4.

30 f5 gxf5 31 exf5 f6 *(D)*

31...fxe6 32 dxe6 transposes to the previous note.

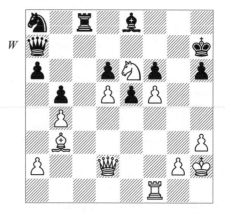

It is obvious that the f1-rook has to be brought into the attack, but how?

32 ᗅe1!

It is easier for Black to defend against an attack along the third rank after 32 ᗅf3 with 32...ᗡf7 33 ᗅg3 ᗅg8, than against invasion via the fourth rank. The threats are ᗅe4-h4 and ᗅe4-g4.

32...ᐃc7

After 32...♘b6 33 ♖e4, 33...h5 fails to 34 ♕e1 ♘c4 35 ♗d1, and there is no defence against ♗xh5 followed by ♖h4, which quickly decides. If 33...♘c4 the most straightforward is 34 ♘f8+!, which wins after 34...♔g7 35 ♖g4+ ♔xf8 36 ♕xh6+ ♔e7 37 ♖g7+ ♗f7 38 ♖xf7+ ♔xf7 39 ♕h7+.

33 ♖c1! (D)

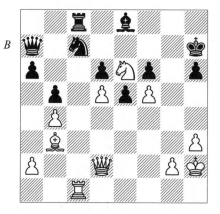

Of course, if the pin allows the rook to take a short cut, it should do so.

33...♗d7 34 ♖c3 e4

Of course, 34...♘xe6 35 dxe6 ♖xc3 gives White a winning protected passed pawn; furthermore, among other things, 36 exd7 would win.

35 ♖g3

Another way to win was to reinforce the pin with 35 ♕c1, but one win is enough.

35...♘xe6

Obviously Black's position is not defensible after 35...♖g8 36 ♖xg8 ♔xg8 37 ♕xh6.

36 dxe6 ♗e8 (D)
37 e7!

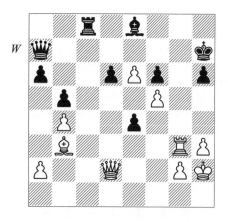

The quickest, threatening 38 ♗g8+.
37...♗h5 38 ♕xd6 1-0

After 38...♖e8, 39 ♕xf6 ♕xe7 40 ♗g8+ wins.

The general rules, such as that just one badly placed piece seriously impairs the position, are almost always valid. This applied to Black's a8-knight in this game.

But there are exceptions; the value of a 'good' or 'bad' bishop ceases to be important when it is exchanged. With 24 ♗g5! White exchanged his 'good' bishop for his opponent's 'bad' one, but once they left the board the only bad thing left was the position of the black king, which had lost an important defender. As always, this decision had to be supported by tactics, and the key was in the correct evaluation of the sacrifice 27 ♘e6!.

White refrained from making two obvious moves, 17 ♗h6 and 32 ♖f3; in both cases these moves, which could have been made almost automatically, were replaced by the superior 17 ♗b3! and 32 ♖e1!.

Game 18

Alexander Grishchuk – Gata Kamsky

FIDE World Cup, Khanty-Mansiisk 2005
Ruy Lopez, Anti-Marshall 8 h3

In this game the absence of black pieces from the kingside is less extreme than in the previous one, so White's advantage is correspondingly smaller. On the other hand, White dominates an open file and, with the little time available to him, manages to increase the tension on the kingside. Finally after an inaccuracy by Black, White wins brilliantly.

1 e4 e5 2 ♘f3 ♘c6 3 ♗b5 a6 4 ♗a4 ♘f6 5 0-0 ♗e7 6 ♖e1 b5 7 ♗b3 0-0 8 h3

In view of the difficulties that White has in confronting the Marshall Attack, some new systems which were previously considered passive have become popular, enriched with new ideas.

8...♗b7 9 d3 *(D)*

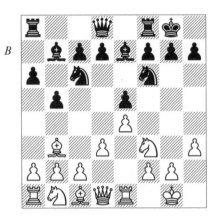

White gives up the idea of playing d4 for the time being; this is an important difference from the 'normal' lines.

9...d6

Here we have an alternative in 9...♖e8, to keep the option of activating the bishop outside the pawn-chain, either on b4 or c5. White can choose between many moves, such as 10 a3 or 10 ♘c3, given the unforcing character of the position. In Supplementary Game 18.1, Svidler-Leko, FIDE World Ch, San Luis 2005, we take a brief look at 10 a4. Black achieved good play in that game.

10 a3

Once Black has defended the e5-pawn, White has to defend against ...♘a5, in order to retain the 'Spanish bishop', which furthermore remains active on the a2-g8 diagonal, whereas in the main lines of the Ruy Lopez it often has to leave this diagonal to support the e4-pawn.

10...h6 *(D)*

Aronian is very fond of moving the c6-knight to make way for the c-pawn to advance, but not to the a5-square, since he seeks a more active role for it in the centre and on the kingside. He

has carried out the ...♕d7 and ....♘d8-e6 manoeuvre on several occasions in similar positions. We examine an example with 10...♕d7 in Supplementary Game 18.2, Bologan-Aronian, Stepanakert 2005.

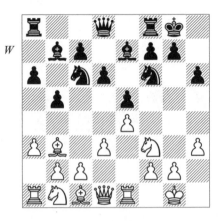

11 ♘c3

Here we have another big difference compared to the more usual lines: since White has not played c3, this square can be occupied by the queen's knight, which does not now have to manoeuvre via d2 and f1.

11...♖e8 12 ♘d5 ♘xd5

In Svidler-Naiditsch, Dortmund 2004, Black chose the natural 12...♗f8 and the game continued 13 c3 (White has not abandoned the idea of occupying the centre) 13...♘b8 14 ♘xf6+ ♕xf6 *(D)*.

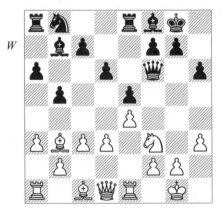

As a result of forcing the exchange of the d5-knight, Black has fallen slightly behind in development. Where should White strike? It is not possible to play d4, but let us note that, in comparison with the normal lines of the Spanish, the b3-bishop is active, but it can do little on its own; how can White give it some support?

With the switch 15 ♘h2!, White plans ♖e3-f3 and if possible also ♕h5, when the strong b3-bishop will provide very effective support, so much so that Svidler considers that Black does best now to play 15...♗c8, in order to oppose the b3-bishop with ...♗e6. A sample continuation is 16 f4 exf4 17 ♘g4 ♕g6 18 ♗xf4 ♗e6 19 ♗c2, and White has the slightly preferable position according to Svidler. Naiditsch did not want to move another piece backwards and after 15...♘d7 16 ♖e3, to meet the threat of 17 ♖f3, he sacrificed a pawn with 16...d5 but did not manage to achieve clear equality. It is worth pointing out that in the event of 16...♕h4 17 ♖f3, Black cannot play the natural defence 17...♘f6? because his queen is cut off and after 18 ♖f5! he loses material due to the threat of 19 ♘f3.

13 ♗xd5 *(D)*

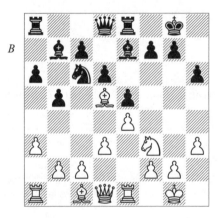

13...♕c8

In order to neutralize the d5-bishop, Black makes a small concession, which is to place his pieces passively; as there is no central tension, this is not serious.

Against 13...♕d7, with the same intention of 14...♘d8, White can play 14 d4 without any preparatory moves, creating tension in the centre, which favours him since he has slightly the more active pieces.

14 c3 ♘d8 15 d4!

Instead of retreating, White believes he can exploit the passive position of the black pieces and advances in the centre.

15...♗f6?! *(D)*

In the event of 15...♗xd5 16 exd5, the d8-knight is left with very limited scope.

Grishchuk thinks that Black should choose 15...c6 16 ♗a2 ♕c7, even though White is then slightly better.

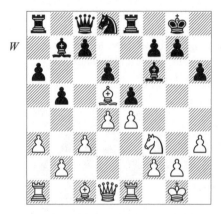

With the text-move, Black bolsters his centre, although all his pieces are for the moment in passive positions. How can White make progress? 16 ♗xb7 is interesting, as 16...♕xb7 17 d5 c6 18 ♗e3 leaves the d8-knight passive; in fact the same can be said of the bishop and the other black pieces. The black knight is similarly restricted after 16...♘xb7 17 d5 c6 18 b4!.

White preferred to keep the central tension, since if Black takes on d5 he will just be swapping one problem for another, as the d8-knight would lose mobility.

16 ♘h2!

The same move that we saw in Svidler-Naiditsch, but with a different idea. Now the ♘g4 leap will create serious trouble for Black's castled position, since it has few defenders.

16...exd4 17 ♘g4!

A *zwischenzug* that should be made almost without thinking, since it is virtually a 'free' move, given that Black normally cannot allow his pawns to be doubled, and must waste a tempo.

17...♗g5

Restraining the c1-bishop; in the event of 17...♗h4?! it is necessary to consider sacrifices on h6, such as 18 ♗xh6.

After the sceptical 17...♗xd5 18 ♘xf6+ gxf6 19 exd5, Black's castled position is weakened, but his queen can come to its defence with 19...♖xe1+ 20 ♕xe1 ♕f5, after which White can gain the advantage with the attractive manoeuvre pointed out by Grishchuk: 21 ♗xh6 ♔h7 22 ♗d2 ♕xd5 23 ♕e7! (forcing the black king to go to the g-file, to defend f7 and make room for the d8-knight) 23...♔g7 24 ♕e2!, with the idea of playing ♕g4 with check and then bringing the a1-rook to the centre, when Black pays the price for his weak king.

18 cxd4 (D)

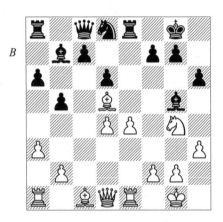

18...♗xd5

This will bring a pawn to d5, which will cause serious problems for Black's development, since the d8-knight will need several tempi to get back into play.

It is not possible to try to improve the knight first with 18...♘e6 because White dominates the whole board after 19 ♗xb7 ♕xb7 20 d5, followed by 21 ♗xg5 and 22 ♕d2.

19 exd5 ♖xe1+ 20 ♕xe1 ♔f8

If Black guards against the incursion of the white queen by 20...♕d7 then a possible line is 21 ♗xg5 hxg5 and White can either dominate the open e-file by 22 ♕e3 f6 23 ♖e1 or else put pressure on the backward c7-pawn with 22 ♖c1; in that case White's dynamic advantage prevents Black from eliminating the d5-pawn with 22...c6?! 23 ♕e3 f6 24 dxc6 ♘xc6 25 ♕f3

♖c8, since here White has the blow 26 ♕xf6!, because 26...♕xg4 fails to 27 ♕xd6.

21 ♗xg5 hxg5 22 ♕e3

Making way for the a1-rook to come to the open e-file. Grishchuk commented that it is even better to put pressure on the queenside first, to worsen the black pieces and improve his own at the same time, with 22 ♖c1! ♕d7 23 ♕c3!, turning his attention back to the kingside later.

22...f6

Weakening, but making room for the d8-knight, so that the a8-rook can come into play.

23 ♖e1 ♕d7 (D)

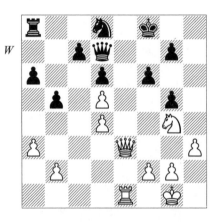

It is essential to sharpen the game before Black can regroup with ...♘f7 and ...♖e8. Infiltrating with 24 ♕d3 ♘f7 25 ♕h7 does not achieve much, since 25...♖e8 brings the last piece into play with no great problems.

24 h4!

Since piece-play is insufficient, White brings the h-pawn to bear, in order to weaken the black structure.

24...♘f7

It is not possible to play 24...gxh4 in view of the devastating attack unleashed with 25 ♘xf6! gxf6 26 ♕h6+ ♔g8 (if 26...♔g7? then 27 ♖e8+ wins) 27 ♕xf6 ♕f7 28 ♕g5+! ♔f8 29 ♕h6+ ♔g8 30 ♖e4.

25 ♕e6! (D)

White prevents ...♖e8 in the most paradoxical manner, offering Black the chance to exchange queens, but only at the cost of giving White a passed pawn on e6.

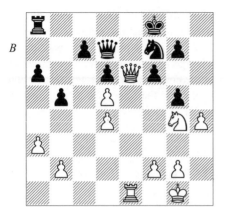

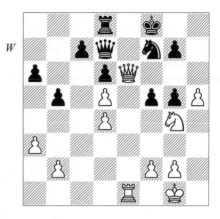

25...Rd8?!

Black does not want to play an inferior endgame after 25...Qxe6 26 dxe6 Nh6. Grishchuk indicates that Black faces a difficult task in the ending after 27 Ne3 gxh4 28 Rc1 c5 29 dxc5 dxc5 (worse is 29...Rc8? 30 c6 Ke7 31 Nd5+ Kxe6 32 Nb6 Rc7 33 Na8 Rc8 34 c7, followed by 35 Nb6) 30 Rxc5 Re8 31 Rc6.

26 h5!

The pawn is now used as a battering-ram, and Black must make another decision.

26...f5? *(D)*

This brings about a crisis on the kingside, where the invasion by the h5-pawn will be decisive.

It was essential to exchange queens with 26...Qxe6 27 dxe6 Re8 28 d5 Ne5 29 Nxe5 fxe5, although White can then take advantage of the distraction caused by the passed pawn on e6 to break in with his king. In order to eliminate the e6-pawn, Black will have to allow the creation of another passed pawn by playing ...c6, so 30 Kh2! Ke7 31 Kg3 c6 32 dxc6, with advantage to White, but in an endgame.

27 Nf6!

The poor coordination of the black pieces allows this combinative solution.

After 27 Ne3, Black is worse, but can defend for the time being with 27...Nh6 28 Qg6 g4.

27...gxf6

Black cannot play 27...Qxe6 28 dxe6 gxf6 29 e7+, so the capture of the knight is forced, making the h-pawn passed.

28 Qxf6

Black cannot cast off White's tremendous pressure. It will be the h-pawn that delivers the *coup de grâce*.

28...Re8 29 Re6! *(D)*

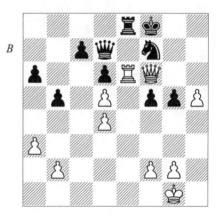

29...Qd8

If 29...Re7 the h-pawn is decisive after 30 h6 Ke8 31 h7.

30 Qxf5 g4

30...Qd7 31 h6, followed by 32 Qf6, wins for White.

31 Rf6 Re7

If 31...Re1+ 32 Kh2 Qe7, once again 33 h6 decides; the same occurs after 31...Qe7 32 h6, followed by Qg6, and Black is paralysed.

32 h6 Qd7 33 Qg6 1-0

Black's manoeuvre to dislodge the d5-bishop with 13...Qc8 and 14...Nd8 left Black's pieces badly placed. Black then made an inaccuracy with 15...♗f6?!. It was essential for White to strike quickly to prevent Black from successfully regrouping and bringing his remote pieces to the kingside. First White employed piece manoeuvres, starting with 16 ♘h2!, and then made the decisive invasion with a fresh attacker by 24 h4!.

It is noteworthy that in order to prevent Black from freeing his position, since he had almost completed his regrouping, White had to offer the exchange of queens with 25 ♕e6!, admittedly at the cost to Black of entering a difficult endgame, since the queen exchange created a white passed pawn on e6.

Supplementary Game 18.1
Peter Svidler – Peter Leko
FIDE World Ch, San Luis 2005
Ruy Lopez, Anti-Marshall 8 h3

1 e4 e5 2 ♘f3 ♘c6 3 ♗b5 a6 4 ♗a4 ♘f6 5 0-0 ♗e7 6 ♖e1 b5 7 ♗b3 0-0 8 h3 ♗b7 9 d3 ♖e8 10 a4 h6 11 ♘c3 b4 12 ♘d5 ♘a5 *(D)*

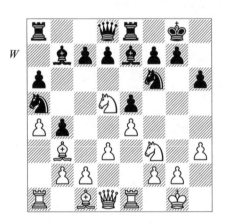

Black does not fear the exchange of his dark-squared bishop; after 13 ♘xe7+ ♕xe7 14 ♗a2 he has 14...d5!, occupying the centre, and after 15 exd5 ♕d6 he regains the pawn with good piece-play.

13 ♗a2 ♗c5 14 ♗d2

Svidler criticized this move and considered that it was better to limit the activity of the c5-bishop with 14 ♗e3.

14...♗xd5 15 ♗xd5 ♘xd5 16 exd5 *(D)*

16...♕f6

Now there is no time to exploit the advanced b4-pawn and the e1-a5 diagonal with 17 ♖e4, since Black has 17...c6!, and then if 18 ♕e1 there is time for 18...d6, and the a5-knight gets back into the fray. After 19 ♖xb4 cxd5 20 ♖g4

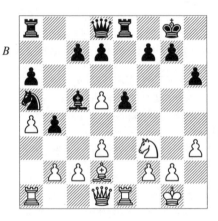

♘c6 the black pawn-centre is worthy of respect, as it is supported by the centralized black pieces.

Svidler therefore chose...

17 c3

This move plans d4. Here Black could have achieved a good position with 17...♖b6!. After, for example, 18 cxb4 Black can play solidly with 18...♗xb4 19 ♗xb4 ♕xb4 20 ♘xe5 (the white queen becomes overloaded in the event of 20 ♖e4? ♕xb2 21 ♕e1 d6!, when the a5-knight is indirectly defended) 20...♕d6, with a balanced game. Black can also enter complications with 18...♗xf2+ 19 ♔h1 ♘b7! 20 ♖xe5 ♗g3! since he has an active game after 21 ♖xe8+ ♖xe8 22 ♗c3 ♕g6.

Leko preferred to play **17...bxc3** first, which activated the d2-bishop, although the game remained complicated. White won after a further mistake by Black.

Supplementary Game 18.2
Viktor Bologan – Levon Aronian
Stepanakert 2005
Ruy Lopez, Anti-Marshall 8 h3

1 e4 e5 2 ♘f3 ♘c6 3 ♗b5 a6 4 ♗a4 ♘f6 5 0-0 ♗e7 6 ♖e1 b5 7 ♗b3 0-0 8 h3 ♗b7 9 d3 d6 10 a3 ♕d7 11 ♘c3 ♘d8 12 ♘e2 ♘e6 13 ♘g3 g6 *(D)*

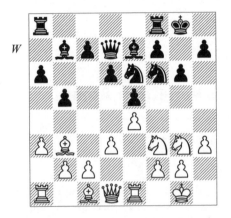

14 c3!

Gelfand-Shirov, European Clubs Cup, Rethymnon 2003 went 14 ♗h6 ♖fe8 15 ♘g5 ♗f8 16 ♗xf8 ♖xf8 17 ♘xe6 fxe6 18 ♕d2 c5 19 f4 exf4 20 ♕xf4 d5 21 ♕e5 c4 22 ♗a2 ♕c6 with a good game for Black, who has expanded on the queenside, shutting in the white bishop for the time being, and at no cost to himself. But we can see that White's impetuous manoeuvre based on ♗h6 and ♘g5 led only to the exchange of bishops, so instead of 14 ♗h6 (do you remember Game 17?) Bologan preferred to occupy the centre.

14...c5 15 d4 c4 16 ♗c2 ♕c7 17 ♗e3

Here 17 a4!?, to avoid the closure of the queenside, was interesting.

17...a5! 18 ♕d2 a4 19 ♘g5 ♘e8

It is typical of this line that the doubled pawn on e6 is not an important weakness, while the f-file gives Black dynamic play.

20 ♘xe6 fxe6 21 ♗h6 ♖f7 22 ♘e2 ♘f6 23 ♕e3 *(D)*

23...♘h5

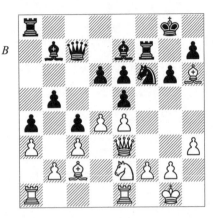

How should White continue? Black has moved his knight to h5 to control f4, and plans to bring the a8-rook to the f-file, after dislodging the h6-bishop with ...♗f8.

24 g4?

Sometimes the cure can be worse than the illness. White seriously weakens his castled position and, since he can make no progress in the attack, this advance constitutes not an improvement but a deterioration of the white position. The simple 24 ♖ad1 was preferable; then Bologan considers that after 24...♗f8 25 ♗xf8 ♖axf8 26 f3 White retains a stable advantage.

24...♘f6 25 f3 d5!

Black exploits White's weakened castled position by breaking in the centre.

26 dxe5

After 26 ♖f1 exd4 27 cxd4 e5, White's position has not improved and his centre and kingside are subject to very unpleasant pressure.

26...dxe4! *(D)*

27 fxe4

White loses after 27 exf6 ♗c5 28 ♘d4 ♕g3+ 29 ♔f1 exf3, while if 27 f4 ♘d5 28 ♕g3 ♗f8 29 ♗xf8 ♖axf8 30 ♗xe4 ♘xf4 31 ♘xf4 ♖xf4 White has weakened his king as well as his e5-pawn, which drops after 32 ♗xb7 ♕xb7 33 ♖f1 ♕b6+ 34 ♔g2 ♕c6+ followed by ...♕c5+.

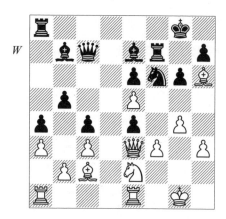

27...♘d7 28 ♘d4 ♘xe5 29 ♖f1 ♖xf1+ 30 ♖xf1 ♘f7!

With this exchange Black takes over the dark squares.

31 ♔g2 ♘xh6 32 ♕xh6 ♕e5 33 ♘f3 ♗xe4

and Black won.

The obvious statement 'pawns cannot move backwards' is especially valid for the pawns that guard the king. Although there was no immediate punishment, 24 g4? decisively weakened White's castled position. Black broke in the centre with 25...d5!, after which White had no satisfactory defence.

Game 19

Rustam Kasimdzhanov – Viswanathan Anand

Linares 2005

Sicilian Defence, 2 ♘f3 d6 3 c3

In this game White has a slight disadvantage in queenside development, which at first does not seem worrying, given that in the scheme chosen this happens frequently. However, there are some differences compared with the 'normal' positions and Black exploits these to prolong White's difficulties in bringing all his queenside pieces into play. This advantage is increased with unexpected but excellent pawn-play, until the decision comes with an elegant kingside attack, taking advantage of the enforced passivity of White's queenside pieces.

1 e4 c5 2 ♘f3 d6 3 c3 ♘f6 4 ♗e2 ♗g4 (D)

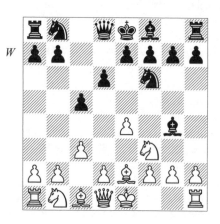

5 d3

Kasimdzhanov has played this little-explored continuation a few times, perhaps without any great hopes of obtaining an opening advantage. Previously he had played 5 0-0 e6 6 d3 ♘c6 7 ♘bd2 d5 8 h3 ♗h5 9 e5 ♘d7 10 d4 ♗e7 11 ♖e1 0-0, as in Kasimdzhanov-Belov, Internet 2004, reaching a sort of Advance Caro-Kann where Black had completed his development and stood well.

In this game Kasimdzhanov wanted to play the manoeuvre ♘bd2-f1-g3 before castling, so as not to have to spend a tempo on ♖e1.

5...e6 6 ♘bd2 ♘c6 7 ♘f1 d5 8 exd5 (D)

White had to decide what to do with the centre. Allowing ...dxe4 and exchanging queens is harmless, and reaching a Caro-Kann-type position with 8 e5 now is more than dubious, since after the simple 8...♘d7 White doesn't have any good way to support his centre. So White captured on d5.

Now, which way should Black recapture?

8...♘xd5!

This brings about Indian-type positions with colours reversed, which are very comfortable for Black. This is better than 8...exd5, which was played in Kasimdzhanov-Sadvakasov, Calvia

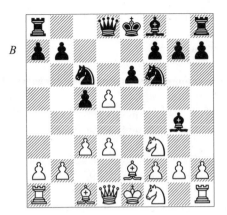

B

Olympiad 2004; after 9 ᐸe3 ᘺe6 10 d4 ᘺd6 11 dxc5 ᘺxc5 12 ᐸc2! 0-0 13 0-0 ᖴe8 14 ᘺe3 ᘺd6 15 ᐸfd4 the structure had changed to that of the Tarrasch French with an isolated d-pawn, and White gained an advantage.

9 ᗺa4 ᘺh5 10 ᐸg3

The absence of the c8-bishop from the queen-side could bring problems on the a4-e8 diagonal, but this is not the case here. Anand indicates that after 10 ᐸe5 ᘺxe2 11 ᗈxe2 (after 11 ᐸxc6 ᗺd7 12 ᗈxe2 ᐸe7! Black regains the piece with an harmonious game, which cannot be said of White's position with his king stuck in the centre) 11...ᖴc8 Black has a slight advantage. Once again the white king in the centre is a problem, and winning a pawn with 12 ᐸxc6 ᖴxc6 13 ᗺxa7, sidelining the queen, is not to be recommended.

10...ᐸb6 (D)

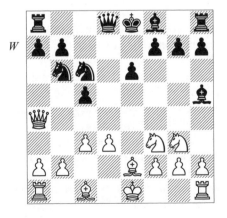

W

11 ᗺd1?

This retreat is the start of his difficulties; the white pieces begin to lack space.

White should have played 11 ᗺb5!, pro-voking 11...a6, so that the b6-knight would no longer enjoy the protection of the a7-pawn, and after 12 ᗺb3 ᘺg6 13 0-0 ᘺe7, not 14 ᘺe3?! ᐸd5!, but 14 ᘺg5!, with good play af-ter 14...ᘺxg5 15 ᐸxg5 0-0 16 ᐸ5e4, when White has no problems as regards space or de-velopment.

11...ᘺg6 12 0-0 ᘺe7 13 a4

White gains space on the queenside. It is not appropriate to try to shed the weak d3-pawn with 13 ᘺe3 0-0 (or 13...ᐸd5 immediately) 14 d4 owing to 14...ᐸd5!.

Now Black must decide what to do about the threat of 14 a5: allow it or prevent it?

13...0-0!

It is better to let the pawn advance, rather than weaken the light squares with 13...a5, which would be answered by 14 ᗺb3, exerting pres-sure down the b-file.

In contrast with other 'Indian' positions, since there is no bishop on g2 and thus no pres-sure on the long diagonal, the pawn's arrival on a5 does not bring White any particular benefit.

14 a5 ᐸd5 15 ᗺa4 (D)

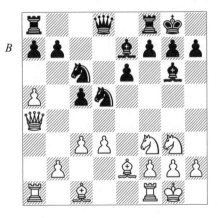

B

15...ᗺc7!

The threat of 16 a6 could be parried with 15...a6 but then 16 d4 would follow, leading to exchanges which would free White's game. Since the advance 16 a6 is not that trouble-some in itself (which it would be, if it forced a weakening of the black structure), it can be neutralized with the move in the game, which defends the c6-knight and is a much more useful move, since it vacates the d8-square for a rook.

16 d4

White gets rid of his backward pawn. No better is 16 a6 b6 17 ♗d2, intending ♖ad1 and ♗c1, since White is still passive. First Black would place a rook on d8 and then, in total freedom, he could try to make progress on either wing.

16...cxd4 17 ♘xd4 ♘xd4 18 ♕xd4 *(D)*

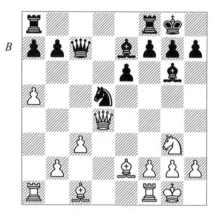

White has moved his queen several times and this is felt especially by the c1-bishop, which has still not moved, while the advance of the a-pawn has not brought any benefit whatsoever; it is under threat and ties the a1-rook to its defence. It is possible to shed this burden by playing a6, but after ...b6 Black's queenside is solid and he can focus on making progress in the centre and on the kingside.

Black has a development advantage and a pawn-majority on the kingside which he utilizes with energy and speed. 18...♖ad8 is a logical move but after 19 ♕c4 Black does not have anything immediate.

With his next move Black shows that there is a second weakness in the white camp, in addition to the almost zero contribution of the c1-bishop and the a1-rook.

18...f5!

Black mobilizes his pawn-majority in an untypical manner. The unusual position of the g3-knight is what makes this favourable for

Black, enabling him to gain time as well as space.

19 ♕a4

Another queen move, but:

a) The dubious manoeuvre 19 ♘h5 ♗d6 20 ♕h4 f4 is of no help.

b) If 19 ♕c4? White is forced to place the g3-knight in a difficult position after 19...f4 20 ♕xc7 ♘xc7 21 ♘h1, etc.

c) If 19 ♗f3, threatening ♗xd5 and controlling e4, Black could play 19...♖ad8, and the white queen has problems on the d-file. Then 20 ♖e1? allows 20...f4! followed by ...♘e3, winning material. 20 ♕a4 is better, but then Black can straighten out his pawns with 20...e5.

d) 19 ♖e1 is perhaps best, making f1 available for the g3-knight and retaining the option of ♕c4 after 19...♖ad8.

19...♖ad8 *(D)*

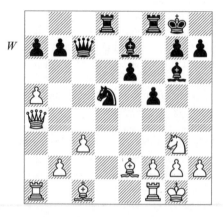

Unhurried; before embarking on more important actions, Black brings another piece into the struggle, controlling the vital d-file.

20 ♖d1?!

White does not want to surrender control of the open file without a fight, but the tension created on the d-file and the subsequent exchange of rooks will help Black's attack.

If 20 ♗f3 there once again follows 20...e5, advantageously occupying the centre, and if 20 ♖e1, strengthening control of e4 and restraining the latent threat of ...f4, Black also plays 20...e5 21 ♗c4 ♔h8. If Black can play ...e5 without any problems, it is clear that he has made progress.

The pressure of the d1-rook now prevents 20...e5? because of 21 &c4, and preparing ...e5 with 20...&h8 allows White to improve his position with 21 &f3.

20...f4!

This gives away the e4-square, but White's pieces are so awkwardly placed he will not find it particularly useful, and meanwhile Black gains space.

21 ♘e4 ♕e5

A strong centralization that creates extra work for the white queen.

22 &f3 (D)

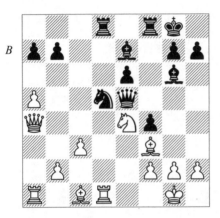

White's pieces are tied to the defence of the e4-knight and the d1-rook, which means that there is a latent possibility of mate on the back rank. How can Black exploit this? There are many possible attempts.

Black gains little from an exchange of pieces: if 22...♘f6? then 23 ♖xd8 must be answered with 23...&xd8 to keep the f-pawn guarded. After 24 ♘xf6+ ♖xf6 White gains an extraordinary sensation of relief with the modest 25 &d2.

Black can win a pawn with 22...&xe4 23 ♕xe4 ♕xe4 24 &xe4 ♘xc3 but after 25 ♖xd8 ♖xd8 26 &f3! White could regain the pawn almost immediately, but even if he does not do so, his strong light-squared bishop will keep him out of danger.

22...♘b4 seems somewhat more promising, although once again the simplifications after, for example, 23 cxb4 &xe4 24 ♖e1 ♖d4 25 &d2 ♖xd2 26 ♖xe4 ♕xb2 27 ♖xe6 &h4 28

♔h1 &xf2 29 ♖f1 leave White with a strong bishop on f3 securely defending g2, and with his pieces active, White's disadvantage is minimal.

22...b5!!

This beautiful deflection exploits the fact that the white queen is overloaded. Black will not win material immediately, but will significantly worsen the position of the white pieces.

In the previous line, White succeeded, at the cost of a pawn, in bringing his two queenside pieces into play; now this will not happen.

23 ♕c2 (D)

The queen has to fall back. If 23 ♕xb5 &xe4 24 ♖e1 (or 24 ♕e2 ♘f6 25 ♖e1 ♕d5, keeping the material advantage), then 24...&d3! wins.

It is also insufficient to give up the queen with 23 axb6 ♘xb6 24 ♖xd8 (24 ♕c2 &xe4 costs White a piece) 24...♘xa4 25 ♖xf8+ ♔xf8 26 ♖xa4 ♕b5 27 ♖d4 (worse is 27 ♖xa7? &xe4 28 &xe4 ♕e2) 27...e5 28 ♖d1 ♕b3 29 ♖e1 a5 and White is defenceless.

After 23 ♕d4 ♕b8! there is no escape for the queen.

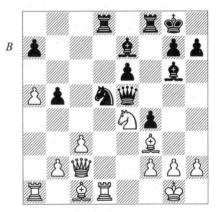

23...♘f6!

"Cleaning up the position". Unlike on the previous move, after this exchange White will not be able to complete his development, and Black's dynamic advantage will become clearer.

Anand had a long think at this point, pondering the alternative 23...♘b4. After 24 ♕e2 ♖xd1+ (if 24...&xe4? the pin against the black queen allows 25 &d2!, for example) 25 ♕xd1 ♖d8 26 ♕e2 ♘d3 (but not 26...&xe4?! 27 h3, and the worst is over for White) Black has the advantage. The endgame after 24 cxb4 ♗xe4 25 ♖e1 ♗xc2 26 ♖xe5 ♗d1! is also difficult for White, whose queenside pieces remain lifeless.

24 ♘xf6+ ♕xf6 25 ♕b3 ♖xd1+

Further simplification to gain a dynamic advantage. The black rook will rule the open file.

26 ♕xd1

If 26 ♗xd1 then 26...♕e5!, when 27 ♗d2 fails to 27...♖d8, winning. Let us note that in this and other lines White misses the c1-bishop and, even more, the a1-rook.

26...♖d8 *(D)*

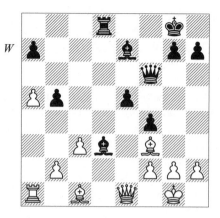

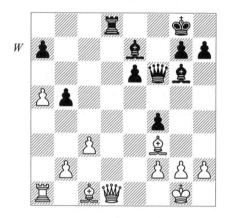

27 ♕e2

If 27 ♕b3, then 27...♕e5! and there is no good way to defend the first rank.

On e2 the queen is exposed to attack, as we shall see, but if White plays 27 ♕e1 right away then after 27...e5 the c1-bishop cannot be developed, since if 28 ♗d2 then 28...♕d6! 29 ♗c1 e4! and White is bottled up.

27...♗d3 28 ♕e1

White's consolation is that the d8-rook is obstructed for now.

28...e5! *(D)*

The pawn-storm arrives before White can bring his queenside pieces to the defence. The queen's bishop has to remain hemmed in, since if 29 ♗d2 then once again comes 29...e4!.

29 ♗e2

It is useful to make *luft* with 29 h3, but the position does not improve after, for example, 29...a6 30 b4 ♕f5 31 ♗g4 ♕g5 32 ♗f3 ♗f6 33 ♗e4 ♗xe4 34 ♕xe4 ♕g6 and the exchange of

queens leaves White's two remaining pieces out of play.

29...♗xe2 30 ♕xe2 e4!

The speed with which Black manages to open lines against White's castled position is admirable. The pawn-storm will produce a passed pawn that will decide the struggle.

31 g3 *(D)*

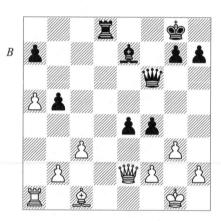

31...e3!

Black does not want to allow any opportunity for the bishop to come into play, which would happen after 31...f3 32 ♕e1 ♕e6 33 ♗e3; although the white position is still not safe, there is no point in allowing this.

32 fxe3

If 32 gxf4 then 32...♕g6+ 33 ♔f1 exf2! wins, since all the black pieces can exploit the opening of the game to take part in a winning attack; for example, 34 ♔xf2 ♗c5+ 35 ♗e3 ♖e8 36 ♗xc5 ♖xe2+ 37 ♔xe2 ♕h5+.

32...f3! *(D)*

This pawn will act as a tremendous wedge. It is also promising to open up the defence with 32...fxg3 33 hxg3 (not 33 &d2? ♕f2+, winning) 33...♕g6, although Anand commented that this would not be as strong as the text-move.

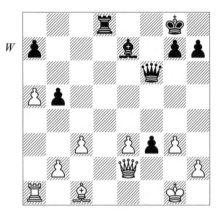

33 ♕xb5

After 33 ♕f1 Black has several ways to win; for example, 33...f2+ 34 ♕xf2 ♖d1+ 35 &g2 ♕c6+ 36 &h3 (36 ♕f3 loses the queen to 36...♖g1+) 36...♕e6+ 37 &g2 ♕e4+ 38 &h3 g5 (or 38...♖d5) 39 ♕e2 (if 39 g4 then 39...♖d6) 39...h5! 40 ♕xh5 ♕f5+ 41 g4 ♕f3#.

33...f2+ 34 &g2 *(D)*

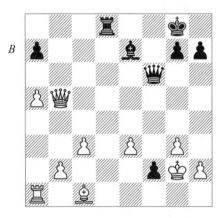

34...♖f8!

Now is the moment to abandon the d-file in order to support the f2-pawn.

35 ♕d5+

If 35 ♕f1 then 35...♕f3+ 36 &h3 ♖f5 wins. If White plays the immediate 35 &f1 then Black plays 35...♕f3, which this check is designed to prevent.

35...&h8 36 &f1 *(D)*

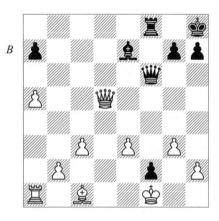

36...♕h6!

Black wants to 'shake up' the white pawns in order to be able to infiltrate later, much as one shakes a tree to dislodge the ripe fruit.

37 &d2

At last the bishop comes out but by now it is too late to help. If 37 h4 instead, one way to win is 37...♕g6 38 &d2 ♕xg3 39 &g2 ♕d6, hitting the d2-bishop and threatening 40...♕d3#.

37...♕h3+ 38 &g2 ♕f5! 0-1

The f1-a6 diagonal cannot be defended; if 39 &e2 then 39...♕b5+.

There are many lessons to be drawn from this game. It is noteworthy that the passive 11 ♕d1? was the start of White's difficulties, after which he had problems developing his queen-side.

Surrendering a central square to an enemy knight is not generally a good idea, but with 20...f4! Black made a great step forward, since the defects of White's position, especially not having vital pieces such as the c1-bishop and the a1-rook in play, prevented him from gaining any benefit from his possession of this square, and he remained with his pieces awkwardly placed. 20...f4! was an illustration of Miguel Najdorf's dictum: "To gain squares, you have to give squares".

Simplifying with 23...♘f6! was the best method for the remaining black pieces to prevail over the uncoordinated white pieces.

The finish, with the pawn-storm 30...e4!, 31...e3! and 32...f3!, is as clear as Black's whole strategy.

Finally, "If one piece is bad, the whole position is bad" applies to the c1-bishop and equally to the a1-rook, but the bad position of the g3-knight was also an important factor, since it had no future, which became clear from 18...f5! onwards.

Game 20

Magnus Carlsen – Alexander Beliavsky
Wijk aan Zee 2006
Ruy Lopez, Arkhangelsk Variation

In the previous games, the attacking side benefited from the absence from the kingside of important pieces such as the queen. In this game the pieces 'missing' from the defence of the castled position are not as powerful, but after some inaccuracies the effect is equally explosive.

1 e4 e5 2 ♘f3 ♘c6 3 ♗b5 a6 4 ♗a4 ♘f6 5 0-0 b5 6 ♗b3 ♗b7 7 d3 ♗c5 *(D)*

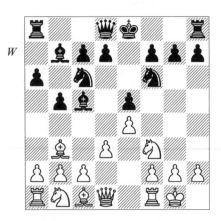

In the Arkhangelsk Variation, in contrast to the majority of the other lines of the Ruy Lopez, Black's king's bishop is developed actively at c5.

8 ♘c3

White cannot immediately exploit the absence of the black bishop from the kingside by the pin 8 ♗g5, since after 8...h6 9 ♗h4 0-0 10 ♘c3, threatening 11 ♘d5, Black 'changes his mind' with 10...♗e7!.

8...d6

The most usual move here is 8...0-0; the text-move was criticized by Beliavsky, who described it as dubious, but this seems an exaggeration. Black does not actually spoil anything with this move; it is true that the c5-bishop cannot go back to e7 now, but this is not the main idea of the line, and Black has enough resources to achieve a good position without having to bemoan the absence of the dark-squared bishop.

9 a4

Creating tension on the queenside, to force the b5-pawn into a decision, and, since Black has now defended his e5-pawn, to make room for the retreat of the b3-bishop, in case it is attacked by ...♘a5.

9...♘a5

Offering the b5-pawn.

The most common move here is the immediate 9...b4, when White usually replies 10 ♘d5, although 10 ♘e2 *(D)* is also playable. Then several continuations are possible:

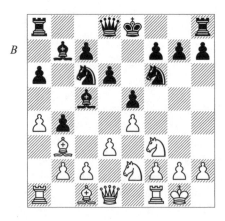

a) In the event of 10...0-0, the pin 11 ♗g5 comes into consideration, since after 11...h6 12 ♗h4, 12...g5? is more than dubious because of 13 ♘xg5! hxg5 14 ♗xg5, when the pin is too strong.

b) 10...h6 is more circumspect, preventing the pin, to which White can reply 11 a5, preventing ...♘a5, or 11 ♘g3, continuing to recycle the knight. Let us look at an example: Nisipeanu-Sturua, Bucharest 2002 continued 11 a5 0-0 12 ♘g3 ♗c8 (getting off the b-file, where in a short while it will feel uncomfortable, controlling the f5-square, and creating the possibility of neutralizing the pressure of the a2-bishop along the a2-g8 diagonal with a timely ...♗e6) 13 c3 (now is the right time to probe the intentions of the b4-pawn) 13...♗a7 (after 13...bxc3 14 bxc3 ♖b8, White reveals another virtue of 11 a5, which is to fix the weakness at a6 and put pressure on it by 15 ♗c4, with a slight advantage to White) 14 ♗a4 ♗d7 15 h3 (capturing the pawn with 15 ♗xc6 ♗xc6 16 cxb4 ♖b8 17 ♗d2 is an interesting alternative, with the plan of slowly preparing the d4 break with ♗c3, h3, ♖e1, etc.) 15...♖b8 16 ♕e2 (Nisipeanu indicates that 16 d4?! is not appropriate here on account of the typical manoeuvre to occupy e4 with 16...bxc3 17 bxc3 exd4 18 cxd4 d5 19 e5 ♘e4, when White must be regretting his central break 16 d4) 16...♖e8 and one of the defects of playing ...h6 came to light, which is that it weakens the castled position and leaves the f5-square indirectly weaker after 17 ♘h4.

We now return to the position after 9...♘a5 (D):

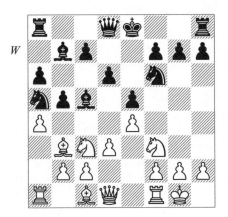

10 ♗a2

Both players agreed that after the acceptance of the pawn with 10 axb5 ♘xb3 11 cxb3 axb5 12 ♖xa8 ♗xa8 13 ♘xb5 h6 Black has enough compensation for White's extra pawn, which is doubled on b3.

10...b4

Abstaining from this advance with 10...c6?! leaves the black pieces very awkwardly placed following 11 ♗d2 0-0 12 ♘e2. After 12...bxa4? White won a piece by 13 ♕e1! ♗b6 14 b4! axb3 15 ♗b1! ♘c4 16 dxc4 b2 17 ♖a2 ♘xe4 18 ♖xb2 in Savon-Bronstein, Odessa 1974.

11 ♘e2 (D)

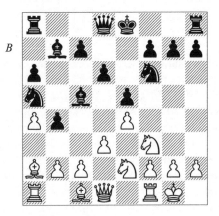

11...♗c8

Here opinion diverges once again. Carlsen considers that this idea is good positionally but mistimed, while Beliavsky thinks that it is worth consideration. The course of the game, or more accurately what could have happened, supports the veteran's view more than that of the young star. We are already aware of the virtues of manoeuvring the bishop back to the c8-h3 diagonal, controlling f5 and with attractive posts not only at e6 but also at g4, eliminating any danger against his castled position by pinning the f3-knight.

11...d5 has been played, but Black does not have enough compensation after 12 ♘xe5 0-0 13 d4 ♗d6 14 exd5 ♘xd5 15 ♘f4, as in Short-Lalić, European Team Ch, Pula 1997.

Carlsen prefers the move-order 11...0-0!? 12 ♗g5 h6 13 ♗h4, and only now 13...♗c8. Instead, 13...g5?! is possible, but very risky of course; only with computer assistance is it possible to stay afloat after 14 ♘xg5 hxg5 15 ♗xg5 *(D)*.

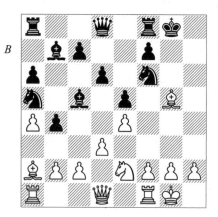

Let us examine the main line, where Black survives after 15...d5 (not 15...b3? 16 ♘g3!) 16 ♘g3 dxe4 17 ♘h5 ♗e7 18 ♗xf6 ♗xf6 19 ♕g4+ ♔h8 20 ♕f5. At first sight Black appears to lose decisive material: if 20...♗g7? then 21 ♘xg7 ♔xg7 22 ♕xe5+ and the a5-knight drops. However, with 20...♗c8! 21 ♕xf6+ ♕xf6 22 ♘xf6 exd3 23 cxd3 b3 24 ♗b1 ♘c6! the position becomes complicated; 25 d4 is then almost forced, to prevent the b1-bishop from being shut out of play for the rest of the game, and the position remains unclear.

The positional sacrifice with ...b3, to blunt or eliminate the a2-bishop, is an idea to be considered in various positions, but here 11...b3?! is dubious due to 12 ♕e1! and after 12...♗b6 13 cxb3 White can quickly play b4, unblocking the a2-bishop.

With the same idea, 11...♖b8!? is interesting, to answer 12 c3 with 12...b3!?.

We now return to 11...♗c8 *(D)*:

12 c3

If 12 ♗e3, looking to open the f-file and thus adding another element to the pressure of the a2-bishop and the knights on the kingside, Black replies with the same recipe, 12...♗xe3 13 fxe3 ♗e6!, followed by ...0-0, with a good position.

With the text-move, White prepares to occupy the centre with d4 at an appropriate moment.

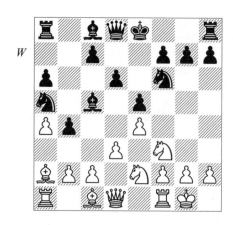

12...bxc3 13 bxc3 ♗b6

Black anticipates the attack with d4. If Black played 13...♗e6 instead, then after 14 d4 ♗xa2 15 ♖xa2 ♗b6 White would have the annoying 16 ♗g5!, with an uncomfortable pin. Breaking the pin with 16...h6 17 ♗h4 g5, on the grounds that his king is not yet castled, is far too risky: 18 ♗g3 ♘xe4 19 dxe5 ♘xg3 20 ♘xg3.

14 ♘g3 *(D)*

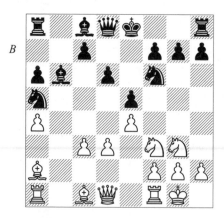

When deciding upon his next move, it is essential for Black to clarify what happens after 14...0-0 15 ♗g5 and decide what should be done following 15...h6 16 ♗h4.

14...♗e6?!

Black wastes another tempo to neutralize the annoying a2-bishop, but it will become more and more evident that the two black pieces on the queenside are not fulfilling any useful function with regard to the centre and even less the kingside.

Best was 14...0-0! and then after 15 ♗g5 h6 16 ♗h4 Black should play 16...♗g4! to eliminate the f3-knight before it can be sacrificed on g5. After 17 h3 ♗xf3 18 ♕xf3 g5 19 ♘h5 (the sacrifice 19 ♘f5 gxh4 20 ♘xh6+ ♔g7 is not clear) 19...♘xh5 20 ♕xh5 (D) Black can, with care, solve his problems:

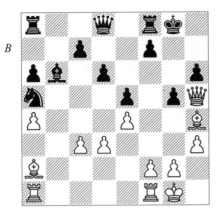

a) Accepting the sacrifice with 20...gxh4? gives White an irresistible attack: 21 ♕g6+ ♔h8 22 ♕xh6+ ♔g8 23 ♖ae1! (with the idea of playing ♖e3-f3 and ♖f5; after the attempt to open the f-file with 23 ♔h1!? Black must avoid 23...♕e7?, which loses to 24 g3!, opening the g-file) 23...c6 (to enable the a8-rook to come to the defence of the second rank) 24 ♖e3 d5 (not 24...♗xe3?, which loses to 25 fxe3 d5 26 ♖f5) and now rather than 25 ♖f3, as given by Magnus Carlsen, the simple 25 exd5 wins in straightforward fashion; for example, 25...cxd5 26 ♖xe5.

Carlsen points out the great power of the 'Spanish bishop' in many of these lines, whose continued presence was ensured with 9 a4.

b) The cautious continuation 20...♕f6! 21 ♗g3 ♔g7, followed by 22...♕g6, is the correct solution.

15 d4 (D)

The central tension favours White.

15...♗xa2

If 15...0-0 then 16 ♗g5 follows, while in the event of 15...♘d7 White is able to breach the kingside with 16 ♗xe6! fxe6 17 ♘g5 ♕e7 18 d5! ♘c5 19 ♘xe6 ♘xe6 20 ♘f5, and Black's position collapses.

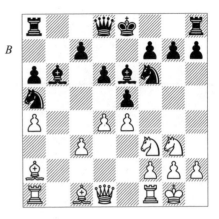

16 ♖xa2

The rook is better here than on a1 because it can be activated along the second rank with a timely ♖d2 or ♖e2.

16...0-0

Improving the position of the a5-knight with 16...♘c6 would be a good idea, but the tactical possibilities offered by the king in the centre can be exploited with 17 a5! ♘xa5 (or 17...♗xa5? 18 ♕a4 ♕d7 19 d5 and White wins) 18 dxe5 dxe5 19 ♖d2, followed by ♗a3 and/or ♘f5, when, trapped in the centre, the black king will not survive.

If 16...♘d7, supporting the centre for the time being, Carlsen indicates the line 17 dxe5 dxe5 (or 17...♘xe5 18 ♘xe5 dxe5 19 ♕g4 with strong pressure) 18 ♘f5 g6 19 ♘g7+ ♔e7 (or 19...♔f8 20 ♗h6 ♔g8 21 ♖d2 winning) 20 ♕d5, when the twin threats of 21 ♘xe5 and 21 ♗g5+ cannot be parried.

In these lines, the opening of the d-file is almost decisive, but preventing this with 16...exd4 17 cxd4 and then 17...0-0 is not a solution; Beliavsky indicated 18 ♖e2, with advantage to White, which is certain, since White has a good centre and better pieces, but it seems even stronger to carry out White's main idea with 18 ♗g5, when 18...h6 19 ♗h4 g5 is met by our well-known recipe 20 ♘xg5! hxg5 21 ♗xg5 ♘c6 22 ♘h5 ♗xd4 23 ♕f3, and there is no defence.

17 ♗g5! (D)

17...exd4?

This speeds up his defeat, but it is difficult to suggest anything better. 17...h6 18 ♗h4 exd4 gives White a pleasant choice:

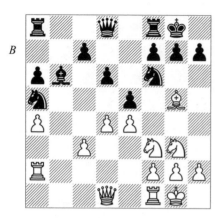

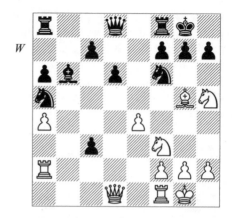

a) 19 cxd4 ♖e8 (of course, 19...g5 is met by 20 ♘xg5 hxg5 21 ♗xg5 and there is no defence) 20 ♖e2 and White consolidates a comfortable advantage through his more active pieces and good centre.

b) White can also seek complications in the zone where his forces outnumber Black's with 19 ♘h5. After 19...g5 20 ♘xg5 ♘xh5 21 ♕xh5 hxg5 22 ♗xg5, 22...♕d7? is not possible since 23 ♗f6 leads to mate, while 22...f6 23 ♗h6 ♕e8 24 ♕g4+ ♔f7 25 ♗xf8 ♔xf8 26 cxd4 leaves the black king very exposed – White's attack is very promising.

18 ♘h5!

The b6-bishop and the a5-knight can do nothing to halt the approaching deluge of white pieces.

18...dxc3 (D)

White's superiority on the kingside is overwhelming. One promising continuation here is to weaken Black's castled position with 19 ♗xf6 gxf6 20 ♕c1, threatening ♕h6. After 20...♔h8 21 ♕xc3! ♖g8 22 ♘xf6 ♖g6 23 e5! d5 24 ♘h4 ♖g7 25 ♘f5 ♖g6 26 ♕h3 ♖xf6 27 exf6 ♕xf6 28 ♖e1 White has a strong attack.

However, Carlsen finds something even more crushing.

19 ♘h4!

With the threat of 20 ♗xf6 and ♕g4+.

19...♔h8 20 ♘f5 1-0

Although Black resignation appears somewhat premature, in fact there is no defence. Let us examine some defensive tries:

a) 20...♘c4 21 ♘fxg7 ♘xh5 22 ♗xd8 ♘xg7 23 ♗f6.

b) 20...♘c6 21 ♘fxg7 ♗d4 22 ♘f5 ♗e5 23 f4.

c) 20...♘xh5 21 ♗xd8 ♖axd8 22 ♕xh5 g6 23 ♕h4 gxf5 24 ♕f6+ ♔g8 25 ♖a3 and White wins.

Black decided to postpone castling and with 11...♗c8 he initiated a manoeuvre that was sound, but hard to carry out accurately from the practical point of view.

Precise defence was essential to prevent White from exploiting the absence of the dark-squared bishop from the defence of the kingside. With 14...0-0! Black would have solved his problems, but after 14...♗e6?! the pin on the h4-d8 diagonal had a devastating effect at maximum speed with 17 ♗g5!, 18 ♘h5! and 19 ♘h4!.

Rarely has a great player of Alexander Beliavsky's class and experience been routed so devastatingly.

In all the examples we have examined in this chapter there were powerful reasons for one side to launch an attack. As we remarked in the introduction, it is not a question of wanting to attack; it depends on whether the position allows or even 'requires' it. It is also important to pay some attention to the defence of the queenside, so as not to give up too much ground there before making sufficient progress on the kingside.

To conclude, we shall briefly look at a case where this premise of combining attack and defence is not fulfilled, and White launches the attack before it is advisable.

Game 21
Alexei Fedorov – Garry Kasparov
Wijk aan Zee 2001
Sicilian Defence, Closed

1 e4 c5 2 d3 ♘c6 3 g3 g6 4 ♗g2 ♗g7 5 f4 d6 6 ♘f3 ♘f6 7 0-0 0-0 8 h3 *(D)*

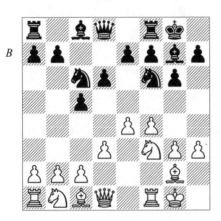

The Closed set-up against the Sicilian Defence is a dangerous one. There are many classic examples; it is sufficient to recall the spectacular victories of Spassky over Geller in their 1968 Candidates match (see Supplementary Game 28.1 for one example).

This position is not standard; the b1-knight has not been developed, and White plans a pawn-storm against Black's castled position. Black can also make easier progress on 'his' wing, i.e. the queenside.

8...b5!

Kasparov discovered that it was not necessary to evade the pressure on the long diagonal with 8...♖b8 before making this advance. But we might wonder: if there is no knight on c3, how is such a slow attack to be followed up?

9 g4

If White advances in the centre with 9 e5, Kasparov pointed out that Black secures good compensation for the exchange with 9...dxe5!? 10 ♘xe5 ♘xe5 and now 11 fxe5 ♘d5 12 c4 ♘c7 13 ♗xa8 ♘xa8 or 11 ♗xa8 ♗xh3 12 ♗g2 ♗xg2 13 ♔xg2 ♘c6.

9...a5 10 f5 b4 11 ♕e1?!

Kasparov indicated that it was preferable to pay some attention to development and queenside defence with 11 ♘bd2 a4 12 ♖b1.

11...♗a6 *(D)*

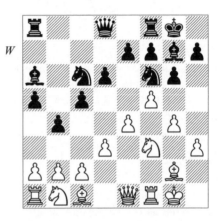

12 ♕h4?

White's idea is well-known: ♗h6, ♘g5 and then choose the right move-order for invading at h7 with ♗xg7, fxg6 and ♖xf6. This is why White has not played 12 ♘bd2, so as not to obstruct the c1-h6 diagonal. But Black has three tempi to spare, which if used well are an eternity. So where should Black strike back?

12...c4!

Black exploits the fact that this advance, opening lines in the centre and on the queenside, has not been prevented. Black also opens the g1-a7 diagonal for his queen.

13 ♗h6?

Consistent, but bad. Of course, abandoning his original plan and resigning himself to 13 ♖d1 was very difficult to do, even more so since after 13...cxd3 14 cxd3 ♕b6+ 15 ♕f2 (worse is 15 ♔h1 ♘e5 16 ♘xe5 dxe5, when the white position is a mess and d3 is very weak) 15...♕xf2+ 16 ♔xf2 ♖fc8, followed by ...♘d7, the white position is full of weaknesses.

13...cxd3 *(D)*

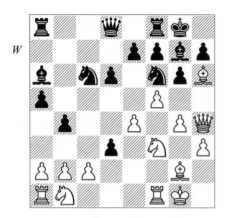

14 cxd3

The main idea of White's attack simply does not work; for example, 14 fxg6 hxg6 15 ♘g5 dxc2 16 ♘d2 ♗xf1 17 ♖xf1 ♘e5 18 ♗xg7 ♔xg7 19 ♖xf6 ♖h8 and Black wins.

14...♗xd3 15 ♖e1

One of White's main attacking pieces abandons the offensive.

15...♗xh6

With this exchange Black diverts the white queen even further from the centre. In other circumstances this would be a mistake, bringing the attacking queen closer to the king, but here it is appropriate because Black's castled position is easily defended.

16 ♕xh6 ♕b6+ 17 ♔h1 ♘e5! *(D)*

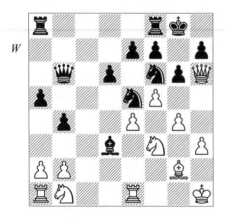

The centralized knight defends everything and if it is exchanged, another file is opened for Black. Now the c-file is clear of obstructions.

18 ♘bd2 ♖ac8 19 ♘g5 *(D)*

Of course 19 ♘xe5 dxe5 20 ♕e3 ♕xe3 21 ♖xe3 ♖fd8 is hopeless for White.

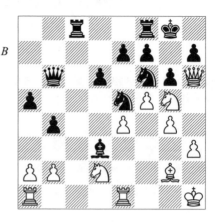

19...♖c2 20 ♖f1 ♗xf1 21 ♖xf1 ♖fc8 22 fxg6 hxg6 23 ♘b3 *(D)*

Kasparov indicates that 23 ♘xf7 ♔xf7 24 g5 fails to 24...♕e3 25 ♕h7+ ♔e6 26 gxf6 exf6 27 ♕g7 ♕g5, with an easy victory. The e5-knight is master of the board.

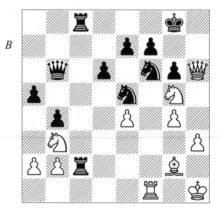

23...♖xg2!

Black returns some material to enable the other pieces to attack, and they meet no opposition as White's pieces are totally offside.

24 ♔xg2 ♖c2+ 25 ♔g3 ♕e3+ 0-1

This is a clear example where a premature attack against a sound position, even though it appears dangerous, is condemned to failure if it is inadequately prepared and if insufficient care is taken to defend the other wing.

Exercises

25
W

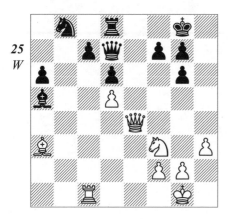

28
W

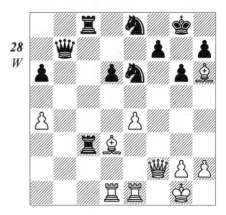

26
W

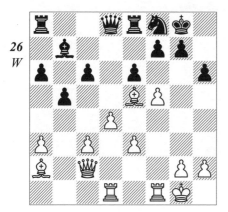

29
B

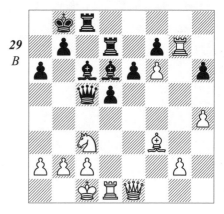

27
W

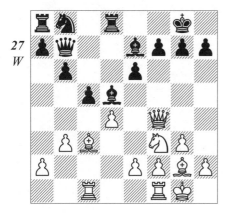

30
W

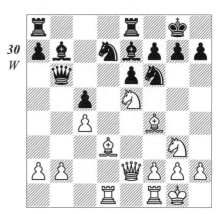

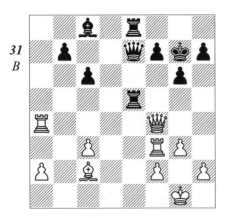

31
B

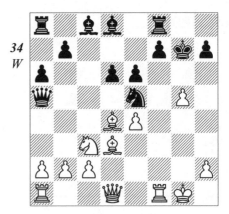

34
W

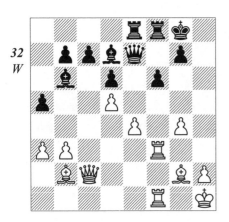

32
W

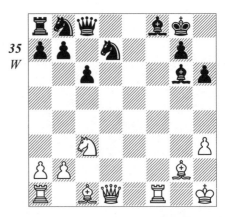

35
W

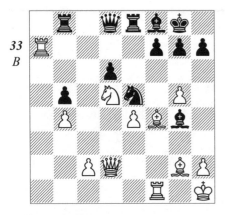

33
B

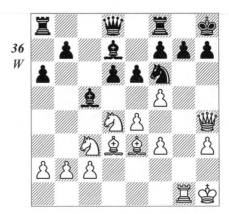

36
W

Choose between:
a) 23...♞c6
b) 23...♞c4
c) 23....♝e6

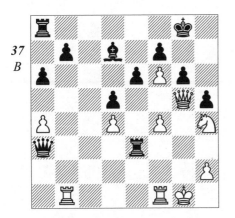

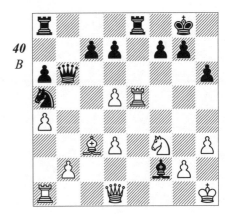

1) How should one evaluate this position?
Choose between:
   a) White has a winning attack.
   b) Black repels the attack and equalizes.
   c) Black is better.
2) Indicate Black's best move.

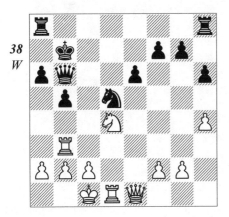

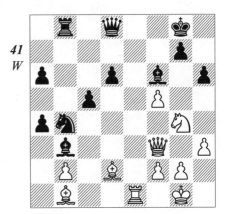

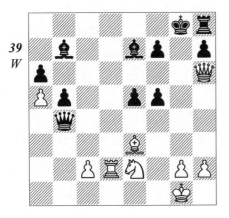

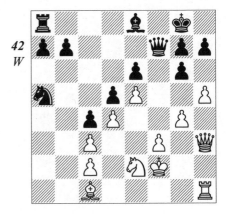

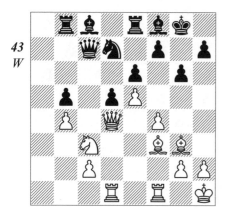

43
W

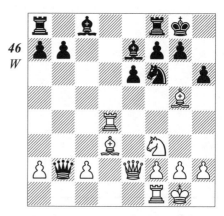

46
W

Evaluate the position, choosing between:
a) White has a winning position.
b) White has the advantage.
c) The position offers chances for both sides.
d) Black has the advantage.

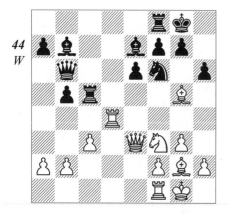

44
W

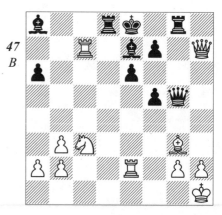

47
B

White threatens 28 ♖xe7+. What is the best defence?

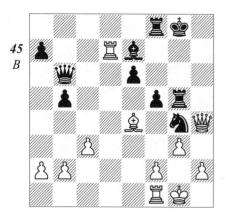

45
B

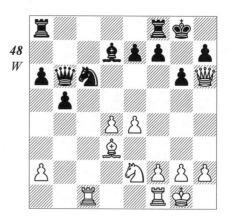

48
W

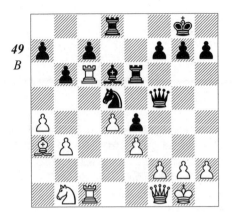

49
B

5 Horwitz Bishops

Aron Nimzowitsch defined 'Horwitz Bishops' as "two bishops raking two adjacent diagonals and thus together bombarding the enemy's castled position" and he gave as an example white bishops placed at b2 and d3.

If the bishops' diagonals are open, the danger is clear. This type of position is generally reached from the Queen's Gambit or the Queen's Indian Defence but it also can arise from the Sicilian Defence, with a white pawn on e4 that might disappear, and other openings.

The best-known example of the power of these bishops is perhaps the game Lasker-Bauer, Amsterdam 1889, in which White carried out a brilliant combination involving the sacrifice of both bishops. For reference, it is worth citing this game in full (without notes):

Emanuel Lasker – Johann Bauer
Amsterdam 1889

1 f4 d5 2 e3 ♘f6 3 b3 e6 4 ♗b2 ♗e7 5 ♗d3 b6 6 ♘f3 ♗b7 7 ♘c3 ♘bd7 8 0-0 0-0 9 ♘e2 c5 10 ♘g3 ♕c7 11 ♘e5 ♘xe5 12 ♗xe5 ♕c6 13 ♕e2 a6 14 ♘h5 ♘xh5 (D)

15 ♗xh7+ ♔xh7 16 ♕xh5+ ♔g8 17 ♗xg7 ♔xg7 18 ♕g4+ ♔h7 19 ♖f3 e5 20 ♖h3+ ♕h6

21 ♖xh6+ ♔xh6 22 ♕d7 ♗f6 23 ♕xb7 ♔g7 24 ♖f1 ♖ab8 25 ♕d7 ♖fd8 26 ♕g4+ ♔f8 27 fxe5 ♗g7 28 e6 ♖b7 29 ♕g6 f6 30 ♖xf6+ ♗xf6 31 ♕xf6+ ♔e8 32 ♕h8+ ♔e7 33 ♕g7+ ♔xe6 34 ♕xb7 ♖d6 35 ♕xa6 d4 36 exd4 cxd4 37 h4 d3 38 ♕xd3 1-0

Then in Nimzowitsch-Tarrasch, St Petersburg 1914, the same theme was repeated:

Aron Nimzowitsch – Siegbert Tarrasch
St Petersburg (preliminary) 1914

1 d4 d5 2 ♘f3 c5 3 c4 e6 4 e3 ♘f6 5 ♗d3 ♘c6 6 0-0 ♗d6 7 b3 0-0 8 ♗b2 b6 9 ♘bd2 ♗b7 10 ♖c1 ♕e7 11 cxd5 exd5 12 ♘h4 g6 13 ♘hf3 ♖ad8 14 dxc5 bxc5 15 ♗b5 ♘e4 16 ♗xc6 ♗xc6 17 ♕c2 ♘xd2 18 ♘xd2 d4 19 exd4 (D)

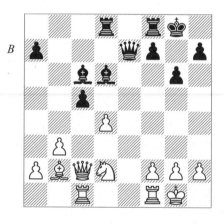

19...♗xh2+ 20 ♔xh2 ♕h4+ 21 ♔g1 ♗xg2 22 f3 ♖fe8 23 ♘e4 ♕h1+ 24 ♔f2 ♗xf1 25 d5 f5 26 ♕c3 ♕g2+ 27 ♔e3 ♖xe4+ 28 fxe4 f4+ 29 ♔xf4 ♖f8+ 30 ♔e5 ♕h2+ 31 ♔e6 ♖e8+ 32 ♔d7 ♗b5# (0-1)

Several masters have shown a great predilection for this scheme: Paul Keres, Lajos Portisch and Miguel Najdorf were its greatest 'fans', but since it can arise from the Queen's Gambit 'Hanging Pawns' structure, there are examples from the practice of many other great players.

Even Anatoly Karpov, when he was world champion in the early 1980s, experienced difficulties as Black in blitz games with Najdorf when he played the Queen's Indian and Najdorf played the line with e3 and b3 against him. As a result, Karpov made a thorough study of this line and began to play it himself with White, gaining some beautiful victories with this set-up.

Of course, the mere possession of these bishops does not in itself guarantee a successful attack. The power of the Horwitz Bishops depends on many factors, although they frequently do offer attacking chances.

Game 22
Boris Spassky – Mikhail Tal
Montreal 1979
Queen's Indian Defence, Classical Variation

In our first game we shall see both sides developing their bishops according to the theme of this chapter. The structure of the centre pawns dictates the plans for both sides, and in this game it is Black who benefits more from his bishops.

1 d4 ♘f6 2 c4 e6 3 ♘f3 b6 4 e3 ♗b7 5 ♗d3 d5 6 b3 *(D)*

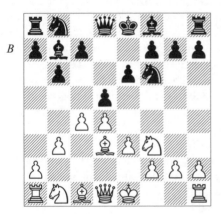

6...♗d6

The first important decision that Black has to make is where to place this bishop. From d6 it not only controls the e5-square but also aims at the kingside; this will be very important in the course of the game, although to a great extent it is due to the changes to the structure in the centre brought about by White.

Black's main alternative is 6...♗e7, which we will examine in two supplementary games:

Spassky-Sigurjonsson, German Open Ch, Munich 1979 is 22.1 and Keres-Spassky, Gothenburg Interzonal 1955 features as Game 22.2.

7 0-0 0-0 8 ♗b2 ♘bd7 9 ♘bd2 *(D)*

This goes against Keres's rule of thumb (see Supplementary Game 22.1), although the position is different, since the black bishop is on d6. White wants leave the long dark diagonal open, in order to have ♘e5 available. More active is 9 ♘c3, which has often been used by Petrosian, Portisch, and Spassky himself.

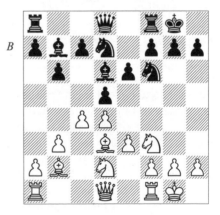

9...♕e7

This useful move connects the rooks, intending to centralize them. White's idea can be seen in the event of 9...♘e4 10 ♕c2 f5 11 ♘e5!, when White is slightly better, since he can dislodge the e4-knight with f3.

10 ♖c1

Now if 10 ♕e2, 10...♘e4 is playable, while if 10 ♕c2 Black could play 10...c5, followed by ...♖ac8.

10...♖ad8

Black has more useful moves available than White. Once again he delays 10...♘e4, which could be answered by 11 ♕c2 f5 12 ♘e5.

11 ♕c2

Finally preventing ...♘e4, which would have been the answer to 11 ♕e2; another possibility is 11 ♘e5!?.

11...c5 *(D)*

Black had also held back this move, since the c5-square can be useful for a knight. However, the position of the white queen on c2, where it can be subject to pressure from a rook on c8, persuades Black to increase the central tension.

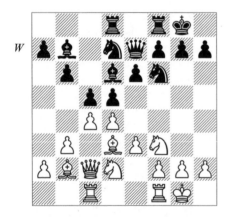

12 cxd5

White decides to create hanging pawns, but this decision is a debatable one, since his pieces are not well placed either to put pressure on hanging pawns or to restrict their advance adequately.

The alternatives were 12 ♖fd1 and 12 ♘e5, to which Black intended to respond with 12...cxd4 13 exd4 ♖c8. Tal felt that the tempo-loss was less important than the discomfort caused to the white queen.

12...exd5 13 dxc5?!

Tal considered that 13 ♗f5 or 13 ♗b5 was preferable. In *My Great Predecessors* Kasparov agreed with this, and added that for "psychological reasons" the decision to create hanging

pawns was not the best, because Tal loved dynamic positions.

'External' factors such as character, or predilection for a certain type of position, are perhaps not important for the objective evaluation of the position, but can definitely have an effect on the game.

13...bxc5 *(D)*

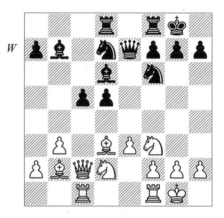

14 ♕c3

A very provocative move, since the thematic break ...d4 can be made at an appropriate moment with gain of time. Furthermore, the less typical break ...c4 is also possible, given that Black can answer bxc4 with ...♗b4.

Spassky believed that his position was already dubious and that he had nothing to lose, but 14 ♖fd1, followed by ♘f1, would have been more solid.

14...♖fe8

Bringing another piece into play and lending more force to the eventual ...d4 break.

15 ♖fd1 *(D)*

15...d4

The black pieces are ideally placed for this break, although objectively, and with computer assistance, it is not clear that this is the best move. But from the practical point of view it is very strong; White has to enter complications and put his king in danger to try to refute it.

16 exd4 cxd4 17 ♕a5?

17 ♕xd4?! fails to 17...♘c5, winning material.

White must try for a refutation with 17 ♘xd4!, when the sacrifice 17...♗xh2+ needs to

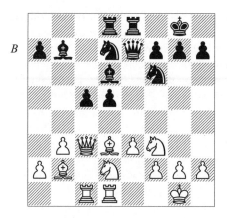

be examined. After 18 ♔xh2 ♘g4+, the retreat 19 ♔g1 ♕h4 20 ♘2f3 (20 ♗xh7+ is better) 20...♕xf2+ 21 ♔h1 appears to allow Black good play after 21...♘de5 22 ♖d2 ♕g3, so White should go forward with 19 ♔g3; e.g., 19...♕e5+ 20 f4 ♕e3+ 21 ♘2f3. One of the defensive points is the counter-sacrifice ♗xh7+; for example, 21...♗xf3?! 22 ♗xh7+! ♔xh7 23 ♕xe3 ♘xe3 24 ♖h1+ followed by 25 ♔xf3 with a healthy extra pawn.

Tal had a reserve possibility (in case in the end he was not convinced by the bishop sacrifice) in 17...♕e5 18 ♘4f3 ♕h5, when he felt that Black had compensation for the pawn. Kasparov does not agree with this view.

17...♘e5 *(D)*

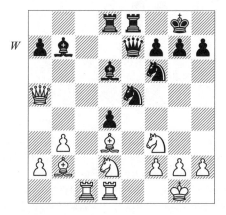

18 ♘xe5

After 18 ♖e1 ♗xf3 19 ♘xf3, instead of weakening White's position with 19...♘xf3+, *Fritz 10* considers that it is stronger first to play

19...♗c7! and only after 20 ♕d2 to continue 20...♘xf3+ 21 gxf3 ♕d6, with a strong attack. After 22 f4 Kasparov indicates the line 22...♘d5 23 ♖xe8+ ♖xe8 24 ♖e1 ♖e6, when White has a difficult position. Another idea is 22...♖xe1+ 23 ♖xe1 ♕d7 (threatening 24...♕g4+) and after 24 f3 ♘d5 the position of the white king is very bad.

18...♗xe5 19 ♘c4 *(D)*

Tal commented that Black's initiative is very strong after 19 ♘f1 ♘d5 20 ♘g3 ♘f4 21 ♗f1 h5!. Kasparov indicates that the most tenacious defence was to seek resources such as 19 ♗a3, but after 19...♕e6 20 ♘f1 ♗f4 21 ♖b1 ♕c6 22 f3 ♖d5 White's position, with the kingside weakened, is difficult to hold.

If 19 ♖e1 Black gains a decisive attack with 19...♘g4!; for example, 20 g3 ♕f6! 21 f3 (or 21 f4 ♗xf4! 22 gxf4 ♕h4) 21...♘xh2!.

In all these lines, Black's forces outnumber White's on the kingside, which allows them to force weaknesses in White's castled position. The white queen in particular is a long way from the kingside.

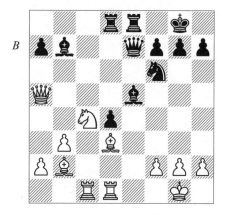

19...♖d5!

The rook comes into play with gain of time, and all the black pieces are now aiming at the kingside.

20 ♕d2

After 20 ♗a3 ♕e6! 21 ♕xa7 Black sets up a mating attack with 21...♗xh2+! 22 ♔xh2 ♖h5+ 23 ♔g1 ♖h1+! 24 ♔xh1 ♕h3+ 25 ♔g1 ♕xg2#.

20 ♕e1 is no better, as Black uses a similar recipe: 20...♗xh2+! 21 ♔xh2 ♕c7+ 22 ♘e5

♕d6, and the white king remains very exposed after 23 f4 ♖exe5 24 fxe5 ♖xe5 25 ♔g1 ♖xe1+ 26 ♖xe1 g6, followed by 27...♘g4.

20...♗xh2+! 21 ♔xh2 ♖h5+

Also good is 21...♘g4+ 22 ♔g3 ♖g5 with a winning attack.

22 ♔g1

If 22 ♔g3 the quickest way is 22...♘e4+! 23 ♗xe4 ♕h4+ 24 ♔f3 ♕xe4+ 25 ♔g3 ♕h4#.

22...♘g4! 0-1

Spassky resigned, since if 23 ♖e1 Black mates with 23...♖h1+! 24 ♔xh1 ♕h4+ 25 ♔g1 ♕h2+ 26 ♔f1 ♕xg2#, while 23 ♕f4 ♕h4 does not prevent mate either.

On this occasion, both sides lined up Horwitz Bishops, but the hanging pawns gave Black more space, and his pressure on the kingside was much more important than anything the white bishops could produce. It is easy to see that the d3-bishop would have been much better placed defending the kingside, ideally on g2.

White's method of fighting against the hanging pawns was not the most effective, to put it mildly; the manoeuvre involving 14 ♕c3 and answering 15...d4 by sending his queen to a5, is not worthy of imitation.

From the practical point of view, the thematic break 15...d4 was effective; even though in this case objective analysis can show it to be questionable, it also demonstrates the tremendous latent power of the Horwitz Bishops.

Let us see another example from Spassky:

Supplementary Game 22.1
Boris Spassky – Gudmundur Sigurjonsson
German Open Ch, Munich 1979
Queen's Indian Defence, Classical Variation

1 d4 ♘f6 2 c4 e6 3 ♘f3 b6 4 e3 ♗b7 5 ♗d3 ♗e7 6 0-0 0-0 7 b3 d5 8 ♗b2 ♘bd7 9 ♘c3

There is a general rule, formulated by Paul Keres, about where this knight should go. Keres recommended waiting to develop it until Black commits his b8-knight; if it goes to c6, then White should play ♘bd2, prophylactically defending the c4-pawn, which can become a target after ...♘a5. On the other hand, if, as in this game, the b8-knight develops to d7, it is possible to play more actively with ♘c3, which is what Spassky does.

9...c5 *(D)*

Keres did not approve of this move when Black has played his knight to d7, since it does not exert enough pressure on the centre

10 ♕e2 cxd4 11 exd4 ♖e8 12 ♖ad1 ♗f8 13 ♘e5

One of the virtues of this structure is the active piece-play that White obtains in the middlegame.

13...g6

In this way the d3-bishop is nullified to a great extent and the weakness of the dark squares is

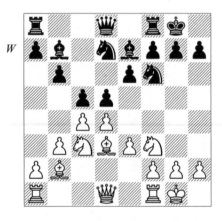

not serious, given that Black can control these by employing the manoeuvre ...♖e8, ...♗f8 and then ...♗g7. Furthermore, Black has not yet opened the long diagonal by playing ...dxc4, so that the scope of the b2-bishop remains limited.

14 f4 ♖c8 15 ♖f2

A strange move, defending g2 even though this is not strictly necessary. It seems more logical to play 15 ♕e3 immediately, so that the queen overprotects d4 and can transfer to the kingside at an appropriate moment.

15...♞b8 *(D)*

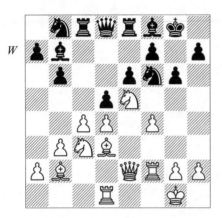

Intending ...♞c6, to improve the passive knight.

16 ♕e3 ♞c6 17 ♗e2 *(D)*

Forcing this retreat is a small triumph for Black, but White manages to support his centre.

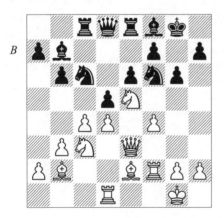

17...♗b4

The threat is 18...♗xc3 and 19...♞e4; with each exchange of pieces of the same value, the white centre pawns become weaker.

18 ♗f3

Therefore White controls e4.

18...♞a5 19 cxd5 ♞xd5

Not 19...♗xc3? 20 dxe6!, winning.

20 ♞xd5 ♗xd5 21 ♗xd5 ♕xd5 *(D)*

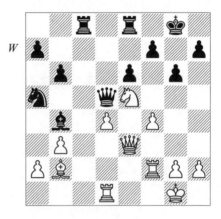

At first sight White's strategy has been a complete disaster. He has exchanged his better bishop, he has a useless isolated pawn on d4 that blocks his b2-bishop, etc. This assessment would be correct if the b4-bishop were not so far away from his castled position (for example, if it were on g7). White immediately takes advantage of this.

22 ♞g4! ♗e7 23 ♗a3!

and White won in the complications.

Let us look briefly at a classic example which is also instructive:

Supplementary Game 22.2

Paul Keres – Boris Spassky

Gothenburg Interzonal 1955

Queen's Indian Defence, Classical Variation

1 d4 ♞f6 2 c4 e6 3 ♞f3 b6 4 e3 ♗b7 5 ♗d3 ♗e7 6 0-0 0-0 7 b3 d5 8 ♗b2 ♞bd7 9 ♞c3 c5 10 ♕e2 dxc4?!

This exchange revives the b2-bishop, which is much more dangerous than the b7-bishop, the diagonal of which has also been opened;

the c4-pawn has lost its protection, but in this position the creation of 'hanging pawns' is quite typical and, if well supported by the pieces, they are strong; furthermore, with this formation the pieces have more room to manoeuvre. However, it is another story in the endgame, where the hanging pawns are a weakness.

11 bxc4 ♕c7 12 ♖ad1 ♖ad8?! *(D)*

It was better to preface this move with the preliminary 12...cxd4.

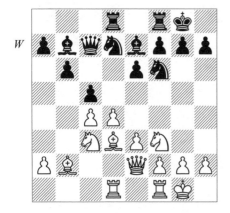

13 d5!

"Experience teaches us that White always gets an advantage in such positions when he can carry out the thrust d5 without incurring a disadvantage elsewhere. This is in fact the case in the present game. Black cannot now continue with 13...exd5 14 cxd5 ♘xd5 15 ♘xd5 ♗xd5, since 16 ♗xh7+ ♔xh7 17 ♖xd5 ♘f6 18 ♖g5! gives White a most dangerous attack" – Keres.

Playing d5 with the inclusion of the moves ...cxd4 and exd4 is less clear, since it gives Black the c5-square, which is not the case here.

13...a6

Preventing ♘b5, thus parrying the threat of 14 d6, and also envisaging closing the centre with ...e5.

14 dxe6! fxe6 15 ♘g5 ♕c6 16 f4 h6 17 ♘f3 ♕c7 *(D)*

White has succeeded in creating an important weakness on g6. Meanwhile, Black lacks good squares for his pieces, and his only possibility lies in the advance ...e5, around which the following phase revolves, according to Keres.

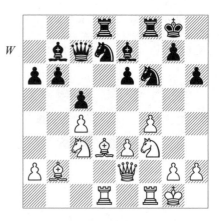

18 ♘h4 ♗d6 19 ♗b1

19 ♗g6! is better, preventing the following manoeuvre.

19...♖fe8 20 ♕f2 ♘f8 21 ♕g3 ♘h5 22 ♕h3 ♘f6 23 ♘g6 e5 24 ♘d5!

Opening the diagonals for the Horwitz Bishops.

24...♗xd5 25 fxe5 ♗xe5 26 ♘xe5?!

Keres commented that he should have played the devastating 26 ♗xe5! ♖xe5 27 ♘xe5, since if 27...♗e6 then 28 ♗f5! (the move he overlooked) leaves White the exchange ahead and with a winning position. Instead, the game now becomes complicated.

26...♗e6 27 ♕g3 ♖xd1 28 ♖xd1 b5 29 ♖f1 ♘6d7? *(D)*

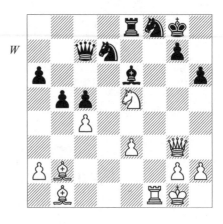

A mistake in a worse, but not lost, position.

30 ♕xg7+! 1-0

White wins a piece after 30...♔xg7 31 ♘xd7+ ♔g8 32 ♘f6+ ♔f7 33 ♘d5+.

Game 23
Viktor Bologan – Sergei Movsesian
Sarajevo 2005
Slav Defence, 4 e3 a6

In this game, it was only White who placed his bishops according to the pattern that we are studying.

In the pawn-structure of the Classical Queen's Indian, it is common for the central tension to be maintained for a considerable time. Both sides can change the structure by creating hanging pawns, as White did in the previous game, or else continue to improve the position of the pieces. If the structure remains unchanged, the side with the Horwitz Bishops has two main plans: one is to open the centre with e4, the other is to place a strong knight on e5, if possible supported by a quick f4.

The game that we shall see now (and some of the game fragments included within it) revolves round these themes.

1 d4 d5 2 c4 c6 3 ♘f3 ♘f6 4 e3 a6

This apparently modest move has been used at all levels since 1990. Black plans a timely ...b5 and, continuing with the main idea of the Slav Defence, he leaves open the possibility of developing his c8-bishop outside the pawn-chain.

5 ♕c2 (D)

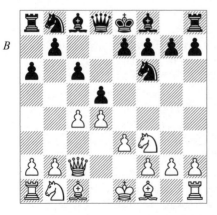

5...e6
A change of plan.

With 5...g6 and 6...♗g7 the game would reach a form of Schlechter Variation, which is a reasonable alternative here, given that, with the move-order used, the c1-bishop cannot develop powerfully to f4 or g5.

As we have said, developing the c8-bishop outside the pawn-chain is one of the main ideas of the Slav. Here White has taken measures against this by 'unpinning' in advance, so that now if 5...♗g4 White plays 6 ♘e5. After 6...♗h5 he can try to take advantage of the fact that the bishop is no longer on c8 by playing 7 ♕b3 (7 ♗d3 does not cause Black any problems after 7...e6 8 ♘d2 ♘bd7 9 ♘df3 ♘xe5 10 ♘xe5 ♘d7 11 ♘xd7 ♕xd7 12 0-0 ♗g6 13 b3 ♗e7 14 ♗b2 0-0 15 e4 dxe4 16 ♗xe4 ♗f6 17 ♖ad1 ♖fd8 and Black has a healthy position, Khalifman-Kasparov, Moscow 2002) 7...♕c7 *(D)* and now:

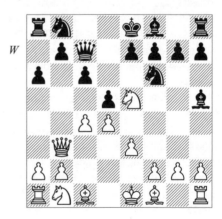

a) 8 cxd5 cxd5 9 ♘c3 e6 10 ♗d2 ♗d6?! 11 ♖c1?! (11 ♕a4+, with ♘b5 ideas, is critical; Black could have avoided this by 10...♘c6) 11...♘c6 12 ♘a4 (White opts for queenside play; instead, supporting the e5-knight with 12 f4 is standard) 12...0-0! (Black seeks to unbalance the game and takes risks, allowing his pawn-structure to be weakened; he could reach an acceptable, although quiet, position by playing 12...♗xe5 13 dxe5 ♘d7) 13 ♘xc6 bxc6 14 ♕b6 ♕e7 15 ♗d3 *(D)* (if 15 ♗xa6 Black plays 15...♘e4, with a strong initiative).

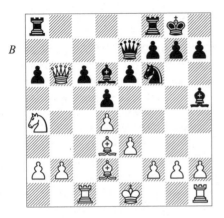

15...♗g6 16 ♗xg6 fxg6! (this move indicates that Black does not believe that the game will reach an ending; any endgame would now be difficult for Black, but he is relying on his better piece-coordination and advantage in development; the previously safe white king on e1 is less so now) 17 f3 ♘e4! 18 fxe4 ♕h4+ 19 g3? (19 ♔d1 was necessary; now follows a tremendous display of strength by Kasparov) 19...♕xe4 20 ♔e2 ♕g2+ 21 ♔d3 ♖f2 22 ♕a5 ♖b8 23 a3 ♗c7! 24 ♕xc7 ♖xd2+ 25 ♔c3 ♖dxb2! 0-1 Azmaiparashvili-Kasparov, Crete (rapid) 2003.

b) Later Azmaiparashvili tried to improve his play with 8 ♘c3 e6 9 ♗d2 ♗d6 10 c5 ♗e7 11 e4, but Black has good resources after 11...♘bd7 12 ♗f4 ♕c8 13 ♗d3 0-0 14 0-0 ♘xe5 15 ♗xe5 ♗g6, and Black is better in a complex game, Azmaiparashvili-Illescas, Dos Hermanas 2005.

6 ♘bd2

This piece set-up discourages one of the basic ideas of 4...a6, which is to play ...b5, because from d2, instead of c3, the knight has quick access to the weakened c5-square via b3.

6...♘bd7 7 b3 *(D)*

7...♗e7

Alternatively, this bishop can be developed at d6 with 7...♗d6, and after 8 ♗b2 Black can play 8...♕e7, preparing ...e5.

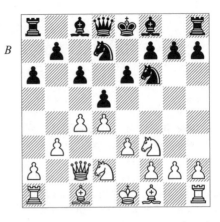

7...c5 is also playable, although somewhat riskier: 8 cxd5 (not allowing the capture on c4; after 8 ♗b2 dxc4 9 bxc4 ♗d6 10 ♗d3 0-0 11 0-0 h6, in Inarkiev-Amonatov, Russian Team Ch, Sochi 2005, White charged into the attack with 12 ♘e5 ♕c7 13 f4 b6 14 ♖f3) 8...exd5 9 ♗b2 b6 10 ♗d3 ♗b7 11 ♗f5 (anticipating that Black will restrict the d3-bishop with ...g6, the importance of which we shall examine more deeply in Game 24) 11...♗e7 12 0-0 0-0 13 ♖fd1 g6 14 ♗h3 ♖e8 15 ♖ac1 ♗f8 16 ♘e5 ♖c8 17 ♕b1 and White has some pressure and a slight advantage, Sakaev-S.Ivanov, Russian Team Ch, Sochi 2004.

8 ♗b2

The deployment of the white bishops is clear: one will go to b2 and the other to d3. The order does not seem to make much difference. Thus it is possible to play 8 ♗d3, which creates the additional possibility of playing e4; then after 8...c5 9 ♗b2 we reach the 'normal' structure with 9...cxd4 10 exd4 (it is essential to control the centre; if 10 ♘xd4 then 10...♘e5 11 ♗e2 dxc4) 10...b6 11 0-0 ♗b7. In Karpov-Mecking, Buenos Aires 2001, Black played 9...0-0?! 10 cxd5 exd5 11 0-0 h6 *(D)* (Karpov indicated that 11...b6 was better, although White gains a slight advantage after 12 e4 dxe4 13 ♘xe4 ♗b7 14 dxc5 ♗xe4 15 ♗xe4 ♘xe4 16 ♕xe4 ♘xc5 17 ♕g4 ♗f6 18 ♖ad1 ♕e7 19 ♖fe1, since his pieces are slightly more active; another typical idea is 12 ♘e5, followed by f4).

12 ♖ad1 (Karpov considered that it was better to play 12 dxc5! ♗xc5 13 ♖ad1 b6 and now exploit Black's delay in playing ...♗b7 with 14

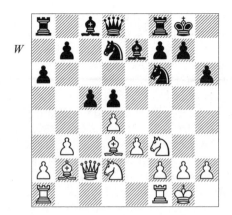

e4!; after 14...♗b7 15 exd5 ♘xd5 16 ♘e4 ♗e7 17 ♗c4 ♖c8 18 ♕e2 the white pieces are very active, while Black's are placed very awkwardly, in particular his queen) 12...b6 13 e4 ♗b7 14 dxc5 ♘xc5 15 e5 ♘fe4 16 ♕b1 ♘xd3 17 ♕xd3 ♖c8?! (17...♘c5! 18 ♕e3 a5 is better, seeking counterplay on the queenside) 18 ♘d4 ♕d7?! (it was still possible to hold the game with 18...♗b4! 19 ♘xe4 dxe4 20 ♕g3 ♕g5, according to Hübner) 19 ♘xe4 dxe4 20 ♕g3 ♗c5 21 b4! ♗xd4 (if 21...♗xb4 White wins material by 22 ♘c2 ♕e7 23 ♘xb4 ♕xb4 24 ♗a3) 22 ♖xd4 ♕e7 23 ♖d6!, with advantage to White, who is better on both wings.

We now return to 8 ♗b2 *(D)*:

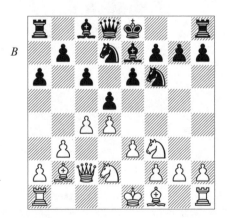

8...0-0 9 ♗d3 h6?!

This move, which we have already seen played by Mecking, is directed against one of White's typical plans, which is to play ♘e5 and f4. The e5-knight cannot be exchanged because

after fxe5 the f6-knight has to retreat and the h7-pawn will drop; for example, if 9...b6!? then 10 ♘e5 ♗b7 11 0-0 and 12 f4. Although this is playable for Black after 11...♖c8, followed by ...c5, a different type of position is reached, one in which White has a space advantage and attacking chances but has significantly advanced his forces, so that if his offensive is not successful he will be left with many weaknesses in his camp.

The immediate 9...c5 transposes to Karpov-Mecking above.

10 0-0 c5 *(D)*

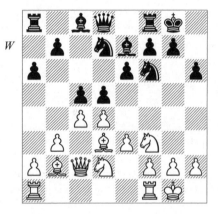

What now? Is the position ready for 11 ♘e5? Is it necessary to exchange on d5, seeking to weaken Black's structure? Or should White just maintain the position with a strengthening move?

11 ♖ad1!

White brings another piece into play, while not yet determining the structure of the centre pawns. However, this is not such an easy decision in itself, as it is not easy to know which is the best position for the rooks, which can go to c1 and d1, or d1 and e1.

On d1 the rook lends more force to a possible ♘e5, since if he then plays f4 the king's rook is useful on the f-file; the f1-rook can also go to e1 if White plays e4 instead of ♘e5.

The capture 11 cxd5 is always an option to be considered. If Black had to recapture with the pawn, his pieces would be badly placed, especially the passive d7-knight (which should be on c6 in that structure). However, he can play

11...♘xd5!, based on the fact that White's knight is on d2 instead of c3. Thus the resolution of the central tension does not give White anything special; after 12 ♗h7+ ♔h8 13 ♗e4, Black can play quietly with 13...b6, not fearing 14 ♗xd5 exd5 15 dxc5 bxc5, since in return for creating hanging pawns in the black camp, White has given up his valuable light-squared bishop. On the other hand, if White tries to reverse the order of moves with 14 dxc5, Black replies 14...♘xc5!, to be able to recapture on d5 with the queen.

If 11 ♘e5 then after 11...cxd4 12 exd4 dxc4 13 bxc4 ♘xe5 14 dxe5 ♘d7, the b2-bishop is an inactive piece, and the attempt to attack by placing the queen in front of the d3-bishop can be defended satisfactorily after 15 ♘b3 with the simple 15...b6, followed by ...♗b7; Bologan also indicates the line 15...♕c7 16 ♕e2 ♖d8, followed by 17...♘f8 and ...b6.

11...b6 (D)

It is not appropriate for Black to change the central structure with 11...cxd4, since with 12 ♗xd4! ♕c7 13 ♕b2, White gains strong pressure with his strong centralized pieces, both against Black's castled position and in the centre.

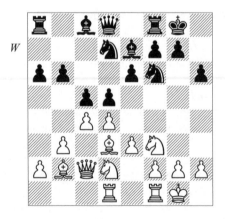

12 e4

It was worth considering the insertion of 12 cxd5 and then if 12...exd5 White can play 13 e4 dxe4 14 ♘xe4 ♕c7 15 dxc5 with a clear advantage. But 12...♘xd5 13 dxc5 ♘xc5 (13...♘b4? is bad, in view of the obvious 14 ♕c3) 14 ♗h7+ ♔h8 15 ♘c4, threatening 16 e4, is not at all

clear after 15...f5!, when the invading bishop on h7 is in a dubious position. After 16 ♗g6 ♗b7 17 ♘ce5 ♔g8, followed by a quick ...♖c8, Black's position seems satisfactory.

12...dxe4?!

Opening the game favours White. If 12...♗b7 Bologan intended 13 exd5 exd5 14 ♗f5 ♖e8 15 ♘e5 ♕c7 16 ♘xd7 ♘xd7 17 cxd5 ♗xd5 18 ♘c4, though the pawn sacrifice 18...♗xc4 19 ♕xc4 b5 and 20...c4 gives Black counterplay.

13 ♘xe4 ♕c7 (D)

Black can still not finish his development, since if 13...♗b7?! White has 14 dxc5 bxc5 15 ♘xf6+ ♗xf6 16 ♘e5, exploiting the strength of the d1-rook. Hence the queen moves off the d-file. Opening the d-file with 13...cxd4 is equally untrustworthy, since although Black eliminates the annoying light-squared bishop after 14 ♘xf6+ ♘xf6 15 ♗e4 ♘xe4 16 ♕xe4, the centralized white pieces are very active. Bologan indicates that if then 16...♕c7 17 ♗xd4 ♗b7 White gains the advantage with the manoeuvre 18 ♕g4 g6 19 ♘e5 ♔h7 20 ♕g3 ♗d6 21 ♕e3, when 21...♗xe5 is almost forced and after 22 ♗xe5 ♕c6 23 f3 the opposite-coloured bishops make White's attack more dangerous.

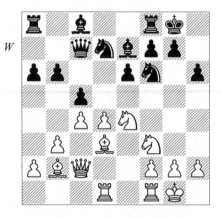

And now? Is there anything better than acquiring the better structure and a small endgame edge with 14 dxc5? Then Black cannot recapture with a piece, since this allows his kingside to be weakened, so he has to play 14...bxc5.

14 d5!

This is more ambitious. There is nothing more tempting than to open the game for the two bishops and exploit Black's delay in development.

14...exd5 15 cxd5 *(D)*

White goes ahead with his sacrifice.

15 ♘xf6+ is interesting. After 15...♘xf6 (this recapture allows Black to blockade on d6 at an appropriate moment with the bishop; instead, 15...♗xf6 16 cxd5 ♗b7 17 d6 allows White to try to make use of his passed pawn, granting him the initiative) 16 cxd5 (if 16 ♗e5 ♕d8 17 cxd5 then 17...♗d6, with reasonable play) 16...♗g4 17 ♗e5 (there is also a quieter option for White, namely 17 ♗e2, threatening 18 ♗e5) 17...♗d6 18 ♗xf6 ♗xf3 19 gxf3 gxf6 20 ♔h1! White's threats against Black's castled position are more serious, since he is helped by being one move ahead in starting action, as well as by the weakness of h6. Now 20...♗xh2? is a mistake on account of 21 d6! ♗xd6 22 ♗c4!, with the twin threats of ♕g6+ and ♕f5 followed by ♗d3, so that 22...♔h8 loses to 23 ♕f5.

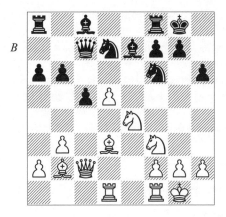

B

15...♘xd5

Accepting the challenge. Instead, 15...♗b7? loses to 16 d6, while 15...♘xe4 16 ♗xe4 ♗d6 17 ♖fe1 ♗b7 leaves the b7-bishop very badly placed, doing nothing more than attack the d-pawn, but this does not prevent White from making further progress on the kingside. For example, 18 ♗h7+ ♔h8 19 ♕f5!? leaves Black uncomfortably placed, as with the white queen hitting f7 it is not possible for Black to contest the e-file, and White has a lot of pieces on the kingside. If then 19...♖ad8?, for example, White can play 20 ♕g4, giving his opponent insoluble

problems. So Black must play 19...♕d8, when White has the initiative after 20 ♘d2.

16 ♗c4!

The combination 16 ♘xc5?! ♕xc5 17 ♗h7+ does not work: 17...♔h8 18 ♖xd5 ♕xd5 19 ♗e4 ♕c5 20 ♕d2 ♗f6, and Black can defend, as pointed out by Bologan.

16...♘b4? *(D)*

The decisive error, which will be punished on the spot.

16...♘5f6? is also unsatisfactory, since after 17 ♘g3! the threat of ♘f5 is very strong.

Black can challenge White to prove the correctness of the sacrifice by 16...♘f4. Then White must carefully find the right path; not, for example, 17 ♖xd7? on account of 17...♕xd7 18 ♕c3 ♗g4!. Bologan noted the following pretty line, which is not easy to find over the board: 17 ♘g3 ♗b7 18 ♘f5 ♗f6 19 ♘xh6+ gxh6 20 ♕f5 ♗xb2 21 ♖xd7 ♕b8 22 ♗xf7+ ♔h8 23 ♖fd1!, intending 24 ♖1d6, with an irresistible attack; if 23...♗d5, then 24 ♖1xd5 ♘xd5 25 ♘g5! ♘f6 26 ♕g6, and mate in a few moves.

There are more stubborn defences, but in general White's initiative justifies the sacrifice 14 d5!.

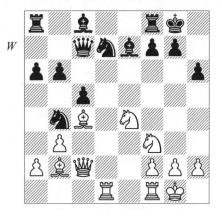

W

17 ♖xd7!!

With the disappearance of one of the defenders of the f6-square, Black's castled position, which now lacks protection, will fall without a struggle.

17...♕xd7

17...♗xd7 is also answered by 18 ♕c3, to which there is no defence.

18 ♕c3 *(D)*

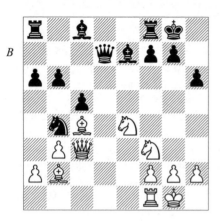

18...♕g4

Since Black's knight is on b4 instead of f4, Black is not threatening mate on g2, so White has time to prevent the black queen from defending g7.

19 ♘fg5!

Now Black has no choice except to give up his queen.

19...♕xg5 20 ♘xg5 ♗f6 21 ♕f3 ♗xb2 22 ♘xf7

Black has obtained very little material for the queen; the rest is a rout.

22...b5 23 ♘xh6++ ♚h7 24 ♕xf8 bxc4 25 ♕xc5 1-0

It is not clear whether 9...h6 is justified. Admittedly it restrains White's ♘e5 manoeuvre, but the weakness of the castled position was important later on, and this loss of tempo, added to 4...a6 and later the semi-forced 13...♕c7, gave White a dynamic advantage.

The point where White opted to increase the tension in the centre with 11 ♖ad1!, before deciding what to do about the centre, is instructive.

The thematic d5 break was carried out by means of a pawn sacrifice, but the prospects for White were clearly good, given Black's lag in development, which meant that the c8-bishop still remained on its original square. On the other hand, nearly all the white pieces were aimed at Black's castled position, with the vital support of the centralized rook, which finally delivered the *coup de grâce*.

The refutation of 16...♘f4 given by Bologan is complicated but very beautiful. The blunder 16...♘b4? shortened the black king's suffering.

In the type of position that we have seen in the two previous games, the Horwitz Bishops are menacing and dangerous, but are of course no guarantee of success, or even of an attack.

In the next example the side fighting against the Horwitz Bishops (Black) finds an effective recipe for neutralizing them, and at the end of the game it is Black who goes on the attack.

Game 24

Boris Gulko – Jaan Ehlvest

Horgen 1995

Queen's Indian Defence, Classical Variation

1 c4 e6 2 ♘c3 b6 3 b3 ♗b7 4 ♗b2 ♘f6 5 e3 ♗e7 6 ♘f3 0-0 7 d4 d5 8 ♗d3 ♘bd7 9 0-0 *(D)*

By a transposition of moves we have reached a position very similar to the ones we have already seen. We already know that Keres did not approve of 9...c5, because when the b8-knight is developed on d7, instead of c6, it does not attack the centre; nevertheless, this has often been played, even by some famous names.

Occupying the centre with 9...♘e4, with the idea of ...f5, is playable, but naturally this might not be the best course of action when White has ♘e2 available, so that ...f5 can be answered with ♘f4.

What other useful move can Black come up with here?

9...♖e8!

In his comments in *New in Chess Magazine*, Ehlvest awarded this move an exclamation mark, and I am not going to remove it, even though when annotating the game for the *Informator* he marked it merely as 'interesting'. It is

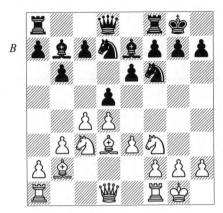

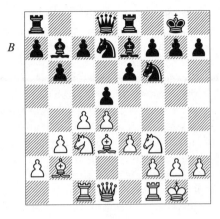

more than likely that it will transpose to known positions, because ...♖e8 is a useful move, and very probably would be played at some point soon.

Let us read his explanation: "A useful move in Black's set-up. Paul Keres played this system very often during his long chess career. Of course I was quite familiar with this system, and it was obvious that Gulko did not sense the danger."

In fact it can be verified that Gulko was also familiar with this type of position; let us recall, for example, the instructive game Garcia Martinez-Gulko, Cienfuegos 1976. But the implication that he lowered his guard seems very plausible.

The move ...♖e8 is doubly useful; in the first place it permits the regrouping ...♗f8, and then, if appropriate, ...g6 and ...♗g7, putting pressure on the hanging pawns if White should decide to play with these. This is a typical manoeuvre, although it is not carried out in full in the game. Everything depends on what happens to the pawn-structure in the centre. The best options for the bishop depend on how the centre ends up. Furthermore, the e-file might become open in the future, and Black is anticipating such a turn of events.

10 ♖c1 *(D)*

White occupies the c-file, and has in mind the possibility of opening the file later with pressure on c7. How should Black respond?

10...a6

"The question is: what direction is White going to take?" commented Ehlvest. This move

anticipates two of White's ideas: in the first place it rules out ♘b5, allowing Black to play ...♗d6, and it also prevents the manoeuvre ♕e2 followed by ♗a6 to weaken Black's structure, after exchanging on d5.

11 ♕e2

Another common idea is to manoeuvre the c3-knight to the kingside with 11 cxd5 exd5 12 ♘e2 ♗d6 (preventing 13 ♘e5) 13 ♘g3. In this position Black has to respond with the prophylactic 13...g6! restricting the g3-knight; in that case the natural break ...c5 is on the agenda, but only after taking the necessary precautions and keeping an eye on the dangerous b2-bishop.

11...c5

Now there is no better option than to create tension in the centre. 11...♗f8 prematurely determines the position of this bishop; we have already seen that d6 is a more active position and there is no reason to rule it out.

12 cxd5 exd5 13 ♖fd1?! *(D)*

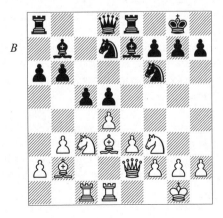

This natural move is an error, which might seem surprising, since how can it be bad to centralize a rook, and at the same time create pressure against the black queen?

The weakness of this move does not lie so much in the move itself, which viewed in isolation is a good one, but in the fact that it takes no account of what Black can play. This highlights the usefulness of 'prophylactic thinking', as discussed by Dvoretsky in his books. It is important to keep asking yourself "what can my opponent do, or what does he want to do?".

If the opponent's planned move cannot be prevented, or is not harmful to us, we should continue with our own plans relatively independently. But if the opponent intends to play something unpleasant, it is essential to react accordingly, if possible with a move that advances our own plans and at the same time removes the venom from the opponent's idea.

White is planning ♘e5, when exchanging knights on e5 would be inadvisable for Black on account of the pressure from the d1-rook. How can Black reduce White's prospects?

13...g6!

Black could prevent ♘e5 with 13...♗d6, but the seemingly modest text-move is more ambitious: Black prepares a reply to 14 ♘e5, while the future of the d3-bishop will be very poor after this excellent move; its activity is now restricted on both diagonals, by the g6- and a6-pawns.

Neutralizing the d3-bishop is much more important than the weakness created on the long dark diagonal, because White does not have enough pieces to exploit this, and because opening the diagonal with dxc5 would leave Black with strong hanging pawns. The strength of these pawns in similar positions where White (in this case) is not in a position to attack them can be seen by comparing the position with that in Game 22.

As well as simply restricting the d3-bishop, ...g6 has other virtues, as we shall see.

Looking back, it is now clear that the right move was 13 ♗f5! instead of 13 ♖fd1?!, so that the bishop could remain active on the h3-c8 diagonal.

14 ♘e5 *(D)*

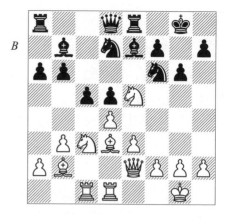

This was the idea of White's previous move. Now White wants to play 15 f4, fortifying the strong e5-knight.

14...cxd4!

It is always difficult to know the right moment to resolve the central tension. Here Black has a concrete idea to combat White's plan to entrench the e5-knight.

15 exd4 ♘h5! *(D)*

This is the other part of Black's defensive concept. White has weakened the f4-square and now, unexpectedly, we see another virtue of 13...g6!: control of the h5-square.

The late Spanish GM David Garcia Ilundain used to emphasize that good moves have additional and unexpected virtues.

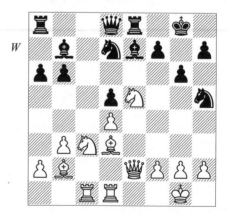

16 ♘xd7

Black will not occupy f4, but has forced the exchange of the strong e5-knight, which improves his position.

16...♕xd7 *(D)*

Not taking any drastic measures. On the other hand, it should not be forgotten that the kingside has been weakened; although Black can gain material with 16...♗g5, Ehlvest commented that after 17 ♘e5 ♗xc1 18 ♗xc1 f6 19 f4 White has good compensation for the exchange: he has a pawn, the black king is somewhat exposed, largely owing to 13...g6, and the open files for the black rooks are not very important for the moment.

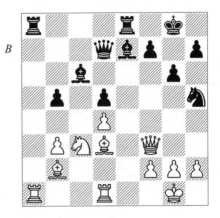

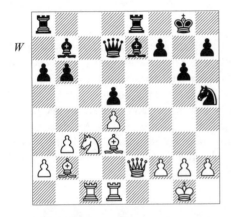

17 ♕f3 b5

17 ♘a4? was not playable on account of 17...♗g5, winning material 'for free', but now it is appropriate to prevent the c3-knight from becoming a nuisance at a4.

Other moves, such as 17...♗g5, forcing 18 ♖b1, do not offer anything special.

18 a4

What now? Gain space or keep the tension?

18...♗c6!

For the time being it is still best not to advance the b-pawn, so as not to simplify White's task. The tension favours Black, since he can continue to make progress with his pieces in a much clearer way than White can.

19 axb5 axb5 20 ♖a1 *(D)*

20...♘f6

The task of the knight on h5 has now been fulfilled. It is not yet necessary to take any concrete measures. It is better to make this 'essential' move that reactivates the h5-knight, before taking any other decisions. The knight is naturally very keen to land on e4.

There are other moves to consider, such as dislodging the c3-knight with 20...b4, but it seems better to leave them for the future. On the other hand, 20...f5?!, with the idea of ...♘f6-e4, is probably over-ambitious, since opening the position so much with so many pieces still on the board looks rash.

21 ♕e2

If 21 ♘e2 then 21...♘e4 is now the logical response; White wants to maintain the pressure on b5.

21...♖xa1 22 ♖xa1 ♗d6 *(D)*

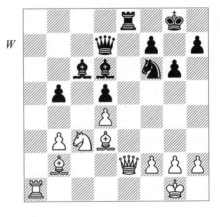

Activating the bishop 'for free'.

23 ♕f1 b4

The moment has arrived to ascertain the intentions of the c3-knight. In contrast, 23...♖b8 is unnecessary, as well as very passive. 23...♘g4 is premature, since after 24 g3 it is not obvious how to continue.

24 ♘a4?! *(D)*

Previously this move would have been annoying for Black, but now it leaves the knight badly placed. 24 ♘e2 was better, keeping it close to the main battlefield, which will be the kingside.

The white knight wants to become active on the queenside, but after Black's correct reply it will remain separated from the future focus of operations. 24 ♘b5?! is just as dubious as the text-move, if not more so, since after 24...♗b8 the knight is a tactical weakness.

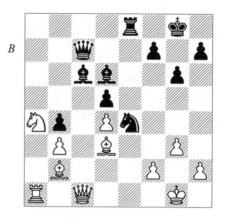

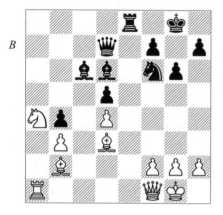

24...♕c7!

Seeking to create weaknesses in White's castled position as a first measure, since how best to proceed will become clearer once White has decided what to do with his kingside structure.

White now has a difficult decision to make. Which is better, to blunt the d6-bishop with 25 g3, or to leave the bishop active with 25 h3 (this avoids weakening f3 but does not create any real *luft*)? There is no clear answer.

25 g3 ♘e4

There are no further useful *zwischenzugs*, so Black occupies the centre. 25 h3 would have been answered in the same way.

26 ♕c1 *(D)*

If White plays 26 ♖c1 to pin the bishop, apparently restricting Black's freedom to manoeuvre, the weakness of the f3-square created by 25 g3 is revealed; Black can exploit this tactically with 26...♘d2 27 ♕d1 ♖e1+! 28 ♕xe1 ♘f3+, winning.

How should Black make progress? The black pieces are very active, while the a4-knight and

the a1-rook are mere spectators, and you could say the same about the b2-bishop. But of course this is just a temporary advantage and in a short while White could regroup.

How can the tension on the kingside be increased? It is easy to see that the black pieces occupy their almost optimal positions. A new element is required.

26...h5! *(D)*

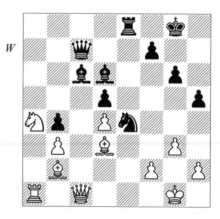

In this game it will not be the Horwitz Bishops that play the starring roles in the attack.

The new element added to the struggle is a powerful one. It will succeed in creating weaknesses in the structure of White's castled position. This move is a logical consequence of having provoked 25 g3.

27 ♕c2

A queenside counter-attack by 27 ♘c5 h4 28 ♖a6 fails to distract Black from the weakness of

White's castled position: 28...♘c3! 29 ♗xc3 bxc3 30 ♕xc3 hxg3 31 hxg3 ♗xg3! 32 ♖xc6 ♗xf2+! 33 ♔xf2 ♕f4+ 34 ♔g1 ♖e3 35 ♕d2 ♖g3+ 36 ♕g2 ♕xd4+ 37 ♔f1 ♖xg2 38 ♔xg2 g5, when Black's queen and pawns prevail.

27...h4 28 ♖c1 hxg3! *(D)*

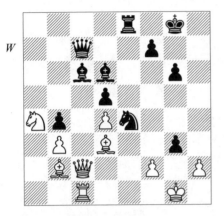

"In for a penny, in for a pound!"

29 ♕xc6

This loses, but there was no defence. If White plays the submissive 29 hxg3 then there would follow logically 29...♗xg3 30 ♗xe4 (if 30 ♕xc6 then both 30...♕f4! 31 ♕xe8+ ♔h7 and 30...♗xf2+ 31 ♔h1 ♕d8 32 ♕c7 ♕g5! win for Black) 30...♖xe4 31 ♔g2, when Black wins by, among other things, 31...♖g4 32 ♕xc6 ♕f4, with a mating attack.

29...gxh2+ 30 ♔g2 ♕xc6

The simplest, although 30...♕e7, with the idea of transferring the queen to the kingside, also wins, as does 30...h1♕+ 31 ♔xh1 ♕e7, forcing 32 ♕xe8+.

31 ♖xc6 ♘xf2! 0-1

The double threat of queening and capturing the d3-bishop is decisive.

Many lessons can be drawn from this struggle:
- It is essential to pay attention to the opponent's plans.
- It is not enough for a move to look good; it is always necessary to consider what the opponent can play in reply, as with 13 ♖fd1?! instead of 13 ♗f5!.
- Restricting the moves of the enemy pieces, and at the same time making progress with your own plans, is an indication that you are on the right track (13...g6! and 17...b5).
- Before undertaking any major commitments, it is important to create the appropriate conditions, such as by regrouping scattered forces (20...♘f6) or making a preparatory move, such as 24...♕c7!, creating weaknesses in the enemy camp.
- It is no less vital to take advantage of opportunities and to take concrete decisions when the position demands it (26...h5! and 28...hxg3!).
- "If one piece is bad, the whole position is bad" is not a warning to be taken lightly; White's a4-knight can testify to that.

Game 25

Vasily Smyslov – Curt Hansen

Biel Interzonal 1993

Sicilian Defence, Taimanov Variation

Horwitz Bishops are not exclusive to queen's pawn openings; they can also appear in other structures, as we shall now see.

1 e4 c5 2 ♘f3 e6 3 d4 cxd4 4 ♘xd4 ♘c6 5 ♘c3 a6 6 ♘xc6

This line, which was for years considered innocuous since it strengthens Black's centre, is now very fashionable. White speeds up his development on the assumption that the black centre is not so strong after all, and can be assailed.

6...bxc6 7 ♗d3 d5 8 0-0 ♘f6 *(D)*

The knight develops to its most natural square, not fearing the advance e5, which would determine White's pawn-structure rather prematurely. This does not mean that in the future, when White's pieces are well developed, this will not be an option to be regarded with

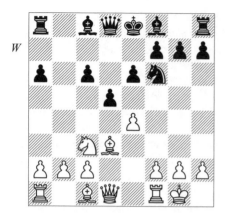

interest, given that it opens the diagonal of the d3-bishop.

9 ♕e2

This was a novelty at the time. The most usual move now is 9 ♖e1. Both moves maintain the central tension. We shall take a look at an instructive example with 9 ♖e1 in Supplementary Game 25.1, Reinderman-Ivanchuk, Wijk aan Zee 1999.

9...♗e7 10 b3

The bishop goes to the long diagonal, where it might have more of a future than on the c1-h6 diagonal.

10...0-0 11 ♗b2 a5 *(D)*

This is an ambitious move, preparing an eventual ...a4, getting rid of the weak pawn, although admittedly it weakens b5.

11...♗b7, followed by 12...♕c7 with the plan of ...c5, is also playable. We examine this in Supplementary Game 25.2, Svidler-Volokitin, Turin Olympiad 2006.

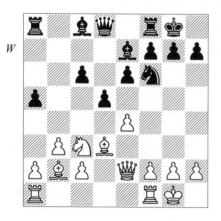

12 ♖ad1

As Smyslov commented, White rejected the complications that follow 12 f4, since after 12...a4 13 ♘xa4 dxe4 14 ♗xe4 ♖xa4 15 bxa4 ♕b6+ 16 ♔h1 ♕xb2 17 ♗xc6 ♕c3 Black gains good piece-play.

12...♕c7 13 ♘a4 *(D)*

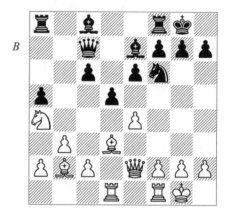

We have already seen this idea; White wants to play c4.

13...♗b7?!

Black does not want to spoil his structure, but Smyslov pointed out that it was possible to play 13...dxe4 14 ♗xe4 ♘xe4 15 ♕xe4, freeing his game at the cost of this small concession.

14 c4 ♖fd8?! *(D)*

Once again 14...dxe4 15 ♗xe4 ♘xe4 16 ♕xe4 c5 was playable, with just a slight advantage to White after 17 ♕e3 ♖fd8 18 ♗e5 ♕c6 19 f3.

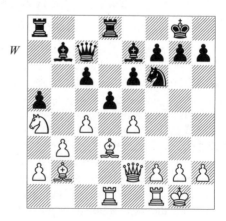

The central tension is almost at its peak. Black has been unwilling to exchange on e4 so far, waiting for a more opportune moment.

15 e5!

White is unable to increase the pressure on the black centre, so he is the first to change the central structure. He gains space, at the cost of dashing the b2-bishop's dreams of aggression against Black's castled position – at least for the time being, but this does not mean that it is going to remain passive.

15...♘d7 16 cxd5!

This is the complement to the previous advance: White opens the c-file and is the first to occupy it.

16...cxd5 17 ♖c1 (D)

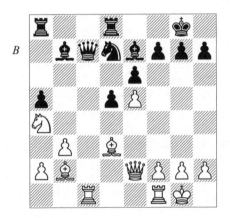

17...♕b8

The black queen is badly placed; Black is relying on this being only temporary.

18 ♗d4!

"The white bishops occupy good central squares, while Black's position is cramped" – Smyslov.

18...♗a3?! (D)

Black wants to dislodge the rook and control the c1-square, to prevent White from doubling rooks on the c-file, but this just helps White, and it is yet another piece that has moved away from the kingside.

It is better for Black to contest the open file with 18...♖c8, which leaves Black's position uncomfortable but does not help the opponent. White could then exchange on c8 and play 20 f4 to try to break with f5, since there are few

black pieces ready to rush to the defence of his castled position.

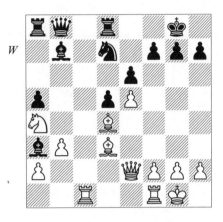

19 ♖c3!

White has not forgotten about the kingside, which has few defenders following the eviction of the f6-knight. After moves such as 19...♖c8? White gains a winning attack with 20 ♗xh7+!; for instance, 20...♔xh7 21 ♕h5+ ♔g8 22 ♖h3 ♔f8 23 ♖f3!.

19...h6 20 ♗b5!

With the threat of 21 ♗xd7 followed by 22 ♘b6, winning material. Furthermore, the pressure on the d7-knight paralyses the d8-rook, and by moving the bishop White clears the way for the transfer of the c3-rook to the kingside, relying on the absence of defenders to make itself felt in one way or another.

20...♘f8 21 ♖g3

The idea is clear, to build up piece pressure with ♕h5 and ♗d3.

21...♘g6

Having sown the seeds earlier, is it time now to reap the harvest by winning some material?

22 ♘b6! ♖a7 23 ♘d7! ♕a8 (D)

24 ♖xg6!!

No, it is not yet harvest time.

The manoeuvre 22 ♘b6! and 23 ♘d7! was not to capture material but to misplace Black's pieces.

The hasty 24 ♗xa7 ♕xa7 leaves the d7-knight badly placed, and although the black king is still weak, and 25 h4 appears to give good prospects, White prefers to keep the black queen on a8 and leave the a7-rook *en prise* in

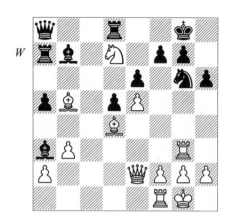

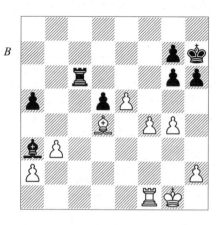

32 f4! ⅏c6 33 g4! *(D)*

order to attack the castled position, which does not have even a single defender.

24...fxg6 25 ♕g4 ♗a6

If 25...⅏f7 then 26 ♘b6 ♕b8 27 ♗d3 g5 28 f4! and, as Smyslov commented, White's attack is irresistible.

26 ♕xe6+ ⅏h7 27 ♗xa6 ♖xa6

Of course if 27...♖axd7 then 28 ♗d3, with a quick decision. In this position the Horwitz Bishops are worth much more than the exchange.

28 ♕f7

With the strong threat of 29 e6, forcing the return of the exchange, but even stronger was 28 ♘f6+! gxf6 (or 28...⅏h8 29 ♕f7) 29 ♕f7+ ⅏h8 30 e6, and there is no defence.

28...♖xd7 29 ♕xd7 ♕c6 30 ♕f7 ♕e6 31 ♕xe6 ♖xe6 *(D)*

To avoid a worse fate for his king, Black decided to enter an endgame a pawn down, but the extra pawn is very strong and White is quick to exploit it.

33...♗c5

Black did not think he could defend with 33...♖c2 34 ♖f2 ♖c1+ 35 ⅏g2 ♖d1 36 ♗c3, but his chances in the rook ending are no better.

34 ♖d1 h5 35 gxh5 gxh5 36 f5 ♗xd4+ 37 ♖xd4 ♖c1+ 38 ⅏f2 ♖c2+ 39 ⅏f3!

With the active king and the passed pawn on e5, it does not require the technique of a Smyslov to win the game.

39...♖xa2 40 ♖xd5 ♖a3 41 ⅏f4 ♖xb3 42 ♖xa5 1-0

Sometimes a small but acceptable evil, such as a slight structural disadvantage, is better than continuing to maintain the tension; Smyslov's suggestions at moves 13 and 14 are good illustrations of this.

This game is a good demonstration of how dangerous the Horwitz Bishops can be when the enemy's castled position is short of defenders.

Supplementary Game 25.1
Dmitri Reinderman – Vasily Ivanchuk
Wijk aan Zee 1999
Sicilian Defence, Taimanov Variation

1 e4 c5 2 ♘e2 ♘c6 3 d4 cxd4 4 ♘xd4 e6 5 ♘c3 a6 6 ♘xc6 bxc6 7 ♗d3 d5 8 0-0 ♘f6 9 ♖e1 ♗b7

9...♗e7 is more usual nowadays.

10 e5 ♘d7 *(D)*

11 ♘a4

Beginning a typical plan to create favourable tension with c4. The reason it is favourable is that White is not afraid of Black taking on c4, since that would worsen Black's structure. In

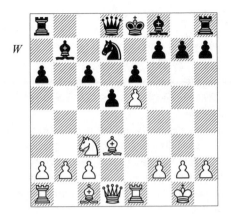

contrast, White can make progress at an appropriate moment by opening the c-file. As a result, White has more freedom of action. This feature of the position was exploited to perfection by White in Game 25, although it should not be forgotten that this is only a rule of thumb, and it is necessary to check its validity in each case.

11...c5

Bringing the b7-bishop to life.

12 c4 d4 13 b3 ♕c7 (D)

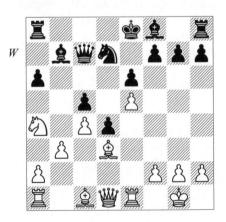

How should White defend e5? We have three options: 14 f4, 14 ♕e2 and 14 ♗f4.

14 f4 has lost some of its venom, because it is not clear whether White will be able to follow up with f5 in view of the weakness of e5; it also restricts the c1-bishop. Ribli suggested 14...h6 in reply, with the idea of an eventual ...g5, trying to combine the b7-bishop with a future ...♖g8, although in this position it looks rather

risky for Black. It is clear though that, by not having castled on the kingside, Black has gained some extra possibilities.

In Ivanchuk's opinion the best move is 14 ♕e2, although Black has reasonable play after 14...♗e7 15 ♗d2 0-0.

However, White chose...

14 ♗f4?!

This is an instructive error. Admittedly it develops a piece, but it does not take into consideration the fact that the f4-bishop becomes a tactical weakness which can be exploited by Black to improve his position.

14...f5!

Thanks to the pin on the e5-pawn, Black succeeds in closing the diagonal of the d3-bishop and controlling the e4-square.

15 ♕d2 ♕c6 16 f3 (D)

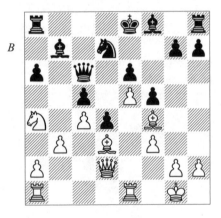

16...♖g8!

Here we have a version of Ribli's idea; Black threatens to open the g-file.

17 h4 h6 18 h5

If White's king tries to flee with 18 ♔f2 Black can continue 18...g5! and after 19 hxg5 hxg5 20 ♗xg5 there is the beautiful combination 20...♗h6! 21 ♗xh6 ♖xg2+! 22 ♔xg2 ♕xf3+ 23 ♔h2 ♕h5+, mating quickly.

18...♗e7 19 ♕e2 g6!

The g-file is opened.

20 hxg6 ♘f8

It is more useful to take on g6 with the knight, attacking the f4-bishop.

21 g7 ♖xg7 22 ♗xh6 ♖g8 23 ♗xf8 ♔xf8 24 ♔f1 ♖h8 (D)

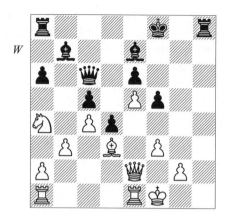

Black gains tremendous pressure on the king-side, with all his pieces coordinating perfectly.

25 ♕f2 ♕c7 26 ♕g3 ♖h6! 27 ♕f4 ♔g7 28 ♔e2 ♖ah8 29 ♖g1 ♖g6 30 g4 ♗g5 31 ♕g3 ♗h4 32 ♕f4 ♗g5 33 ♕g3 f4 34 ♕f2 ♗h4 35 ♕g2 ♕xe5+ 36 ♗e4 ♗xe4 37 fxe4 f3+! 38 ♕xf3 ♖f6 0-1

This game gives us another demonstration of something we covered in the first chapter of the book, i.e. that having his king in the centre was an advantage to Black, who was able to attack on the kingside very easily and with tremendous force.

Supplementary Game 25.2
Peter Svidler – Andrei Volokitin
Turin Olympiad 2006
Sicilian Defence, Taimanov Variation

1 e4 c5 2 ♘f3 e6 3 d4 cxd4 4 ♘xd4 ♘c6 5 ♘c3 a6 6 ♘xc6 bxc6 7 ♗d3 d5 8 0-0 ♘f6 9 ♕e2 ♗e7 10 b3 0-0 11 ♗b2 (D)

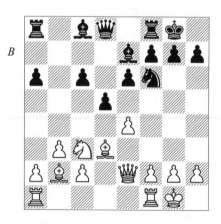

11...♗b7

Black intends 12...♕c7 with the plan of ...c5.

12 ♖ad1

L.Dominguez-Andersson, Havana 2001 continued 12 ♘a4 ♕c7 13 e5 ♘d7 14 c4 and here Black made a concession by playing 14...dxc4! but after 15 ♗xc4 ♘b6! 16 ♘xb6 ♕xb6 17 ♕g4 ♖ad8 18 ♖ad1 a5 19 ♗c1 ♖xd1 20 ♖xd1 ♖d8 the concession of having spoiled his pawn-chain

was not important, and Black achieved a balanced game.

Black must be willing to make this type of 'mini-concession' to free his game, since it is more difficult for him to maintain the tension in the centre and on the queenside because he has less space and is more passively placed.

With the text-move, White plans a potent response to the immediate ...c5, but Black is undeterred...

12...c5?! 13 ♘a4

Threatening to double Black's f-pawns or win the c5-pawn with 14 ♗xf6. We reach a standard type of position, but with Black slightly behind in development.

13...♕c7 (D)

Black defends the c5-pawn. 13...d4 is also possible. After 14 f4 ♕c7 White highlights one of the drawbacks of Black's early ...d4 with 15 c3!?.

How should White make good use of the Horwitz Bishops?

14 exd5!

Opening lines for the bishops.

14...♘xd5

It is not possible to retain a healthy structure with 14...exd5? for tactical reasons, viz. 15

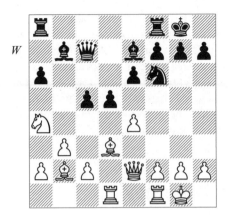

W

罝fe1 盒d8 (if 15...罝ae8 then 16 盒xf6, exploiting the e-file pin) 16 盒a3. And if 14...盒xd5 15 c4 盒c6 then both 16 盒xf6 盒xf6 17 ②xc5 and the complications arising from 16 ②xc5!? are unsatisfactory for Black.

15 盒e5 豐c6

If 15...盒d6 White cashes in on the d-file pin with 16 盒xd6 豐xd6 17 c4 ②f4 18 盒xh7+.

16 盒e4! *(D)*

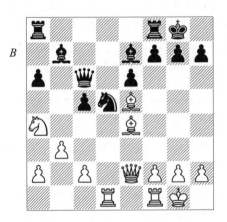

B

Keeping the bishops active and pointed dangerously towards Black's castled position, as well as threatening 17 c4.

16...f6

This does not look very good, since the black king is exposed, but 16...②f4? fails to 17 豐g4 with a double attack.

17 c4!

Ignoring the attack on his bishop, White enters favourable complications.

17...罝fd8

To provide a retreat-square for the king. In the event of 17...fxe5 18 cxd5 豐b5 White finishes off the game in simple fashion based on the inadequate defence of Black's castled position: 19 豐h5 g6 20 盒xg6 hxg6 21 豐xg6+ 含h8 22 罝d3.

18 豐h5! fxe5 19 豐xh7+ 含f8 20 cxd5 exd5 *(D)*

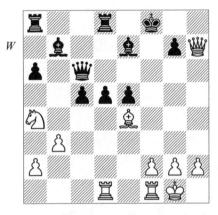

W

The queen cannot give mate on her own, but the black king has been left exposed and at no cost to White in material. It is true that the e4-bishop is attacked, and in an endgame the black centre pawns would be fearsome. However, no endgame will be reached, as White succeeds in introducing another attacking piece:

21 f4! exf4

If 21...dxe4 Svidler indicates that Black is defenceless after 22 fxe5+ 盒f6 23 exf6 gxf6 24 豐h8+ 含e7 25 豐g7+ 含e8 26 罝c1!, but the move played prolonged the game for only a few more moves.

22 盒g6 豐e6

If 22...盒f6 to give the king the e7-square then White plays the *zwischenzug* 23 罝fe1!.

23 豐h8+ 豐g8 24 罝xf4+ 盒f6 25 罝xf6+ 1-0

It is noteworthy that White did not need the a4-knight in the attack, although it had an influence in various phases of the game by putting pressure on the c5-pawn, and in the line 21...dxe4 by lending support to 26 罝c1!.

This provides another excellent example of the Horwitz Bishops' power when the opponent's castled position is short of defenders. Also, L.Dominguez-Andersson (note to White's

12th move) again illustrates the point, emphasized after the main game, that sometimes it is better to accept a small evil, in terms of a slight structural disadvantage, than maintaining 'unfavourable' tension.

As we have stated, the Horwitz Bishops are not the exclusive birthright of closed openings based on 1 d4, nor is it essential that one side quickly develops his bishops on the b1-h7 and a1-h8 diagonals (or their black counterparts). They can also arise from openings that you would not expect, as in the following game, where a world champion lowered his guard and overlooked the power of the bishops that are the subject of our chapter.

Game 26

Judit Polgar – Anatoly Karpov

Hoogeveen 2003
Petroff Defence, Main Line

1 e4 e5 2 ♘f3 ♘f6 3 ♘xe5 d6 4 ♘f3 ♘xe4 5 d4 d5 6 ♗d3 ♗e7 7 0-0 ♘c6 8 c4 ♘b4 9 ♗e2 0-0 10 a3 ♘c6 11 cxd5 ♕xd5 12 ♘c3 ♘xc3 13 bxc3 *(D)*

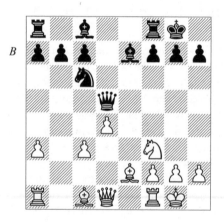

The position is asymmetrical; let us examine some of its features.

If the c7-pawn were on e6, we would 'almost' have hanging pawns, but with a pawn on c7 there are differences; in the first place the c8-bishop does not have to try to develop with ...b6 and ...♗b7, but can already come into play along its original diagonal. White's structure consists of three pawn-islands, while Black has only two, but the white pawns are mobile and, since the c-file is closed, they are not as weak as in the hanging-pawns structure.

As regards the c6-knight, this prevents both the counter-blow ...c5 and the restraining move ...c6, so that one of White's aims is to mobilize his c- and d-pawns, dislodging Black's pieces such as the queen on d5 and the c6-knight in the process.

Naturally Black would like, ideally, to blockade the white pawns on c3 and d4 or, if this proves impossible, to be able to withdraw his pieces to acceptable positions and still blockade the c- and d-pawns, even when they have advanced a step.

The open and half-open files constitute another important factor. The e-file is normally not a decisive factor, because neither side can afford to abandon it to the opponent without gaining something in return. White's half-open b-file and Black's half-open d-file fulfil two very different functions. White can play ♖b1 to put pressure on b7 and even in some cases to be able to swing the rook to the centre or to the opposite wing with ♖b5. Black will play ...♖d8, basically to put pressure on d4 and hinder the d-pawn's advance.

What is Black's best move here? 13...♗f5 has been the most common move for many years. It continues Black's development and prevents ♖b1, while against an eventual ♗f4 by White, attacking c7, Black can play ...♗d6. Another idea is to delay development and try to blockade the white pawns with 13...♘a5.

13...♕d6?!

This was a novelty which did not meet with much success. Polgar will demonstrate that it limits Black's possibilities without achieving anything in return. Black wants to post his bishop on the a2-g8 diagonal to blockade the pawns, but this gives White great freedom of action, compared with the more usual options.

After 13...♗f5 14 ♖e1 ♖fe8 we examine two game extracts in the form of Supplementary Games 26.1 (Akopian-Dominguez, Turin Olympiad 2006) and 26.2 (Svidler-Kramnik, Dortmund 2006).

14 ♖b1

Taking advantage of the fact that Black has not prevented it, White activates the rook with gain of time. There is no reason not to do so; in fact it is an 'essential' move, in the sense that it is useful in itself, but does not commit any of the other pieces or restrict White's plans. Hence it is a move that should be made first, and White can decide later what to do with the other pieces.

14...b6 *(D)*

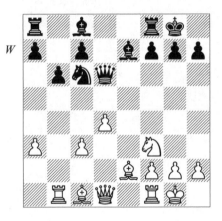

Now White must decide what to play. One idea is to prevent ...♗f5 with 15 ♗d3, occupying the splendid b1-h7 diagonal, pointing at Black's sparsely defended castled position. Another logical move is to occupy the open e-file with 15 ♖e1. Which is the better move in this position?

15 ♖e1!

If 15 ♗d3 there is no clear way for White to continue after the pin 15...♗g4; in the event of 16 h3 ♗h5 the bishop helps defend the castled position, with the possibility of offering the exchange of the dangerous d3-bishop by playing ...♗g6 at an appropriate moment.

15...♗e6

Possibly this modest deployment was the idea behind 13...♕d6. In any case Black does not seem to have a better alternative, since now in the event of 15...♗g4 White can arrange his pieces in a more promising way, first with 16 h3!, not fearing 16...♗xh3? 17 gxh3 ♕g6+ 18 ♔h1 ♕xb1, since the awkward position of the black pieces can be exploited by 19 ♗d3 ♕a2 20 ♕a4! ♕d5 21 ♗e4 ♕h5 22 ♘g1 b5 23 ♕c2, and White wins material. If Black retreats with 16...♗h5 then White plays 17 ♖b5! with tempo, and after 17...♗g6 18 ♗c4! Black will perhaps be sorry to have abandoned the c8-h3 diagonal.

Something similar can happen after 15...♗f5 16 ♖b5, when 16...♗g6 is met by 17 ♗c4!. It is worth noting how much harm has been done with the apparently 'healthy' move 14...b6. The weakening of the h1-a8 diagonal means that Black has to be especially careful. In this line, 16...♕g6? fails to the surprising sacrifice 17 ♖xf5! and after 17...♕xf5 18 ♗d3 ♕f6 19 ♗e4, threatening 20 ♗xc6, Black cannot avoid material loss, since the weakness of the c6-knight, as well as of the a8-rook, means the e7-bishop is doomed.

16 ♗d3 *(D)*

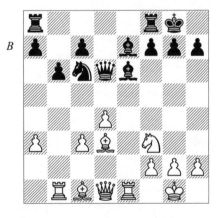

Now White is able to achieve an ideal set-up. The b1-rook is keen to help the d3-bishop by transferring to the kingside via the fifth rank. It is not certain that this will happen, but it is essential to consider it.

16...♖ae8

A strange decision; if this rook is not exchanged, the f8-rook will remain out of play. It would seem that the best square for the f8-rook is e8, and the a8-rook ought to be earmarked for d8 or c8.

Polgar considered that the best move was 16...♖fe8, with a slight advantage to White after, for instance, 17 ♗e4 ♗d5 18 ♗f4 ♕d7 19 ♗xd5 ♕xd5 20 ♕d3.

On the other hand, after the provocative 16...♗d5 White can get her centre moving with the pawn sacrifice 17 c4!. If 17...♗xf3 18 ♕xf3 ♖ae8 19 c5! (preventing the queen from occupying the c5-square) 19...bxc5 20 ♗f4 ♕f6 21 ♕e4!, White wins material: 21...♕g6 22 ♕xg6 fxg6 23 ♗b5 or 21...g6 22 ♗h6 ♘xd4 23 ♗xf8 ♔xf8 24 ♖b7 and Black does not have enough for the exchange.

17 ♖b5 *(D)*

In hindsight, it was better to prevent White's following manoeuvre with 17...a6!, since Polgar's first idea 18 ♘g5 is not very dangerous in view of 18...♗xg5 (not 18...axb5? 19 ♖xe6! fxe6 20 ♗xh7+ ♔h8 21 ♕h5 and wins) 19 ♖xg5 ♗b3! 20 ♕d2 ♘a5! and the attack has vanished; in the post-mortem both players reached the conclusion that Black has a reasonable position.

After 17...a6, sending the rook to the kingside with 18 ♖h5?! does not achieve anything after the simple 18...g6, so Polgar was intending to play 18 ♖b2!? and after 18...♗d5 19 ♖be2 ♗xf3 20 gxf3 a complex position is reached where White's greater dynamism compensates for the damaged structure.

18 ♖be5 *(D)*

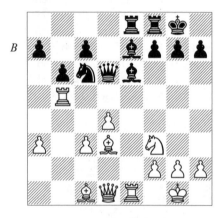

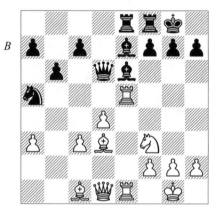

The rook comes into play, with the idea of switching to the kingside and lending more force to the ♘g5 leap. It is necessary to resort to calculation now to assess how dangerous White's threats are.

17...♘a5?

Black considers (wrongly) that his king is in no danger and so he continues with his blockading manoeuvre, but the loss of control of the e5-square allows White to carry out an ideal regrouping.

This is a noteworthy error by Karpov, whose prophylactic treatment of the game has always been one of his strong points, that is to say his ability to nullify the opponent's ideas before they can become harmful, and continue improving his own position.

Controlling the e-file.

18...♘c6

A sad retreat. In the event of 18...♗f6, White can take advantage of the unequal balance of forces on the kingside. Polgar was intending to continue with 19 ♘g5! ♗xg5 (19...♗xe5? loses to 20 dxe5, followed by 21 ♗xh7+ and ♕h5) 20 ♗xg5 ♘c6 (not 20...f6? 21 ♕h5) 21 ♕h5 h6 (if 21...g6 then White has the pretty 22 ♗f6!, with a quick mate; in this case Black would regret having played 16...♖ae8 instead of 16...♖fe8) 22 ♗xh6 ♘xe5 23 ♗xg7 ♘g6 24 ♗e5 ♗g4 25 ♕xg4 ♖xe5 26 ♖xe5, winning.

19 ♖5e2

A difficult decision. White prefers to leave the c1-h6 diagonal open, rather than play 19 ♖5e3, with the idea of tripling on the e-file.

19...♗d7 *(D)*

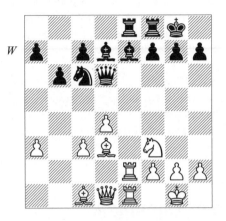

20 d5

Unlike in the Kramnik game that follows (Supplementary Game 26.2), here the black pieces are badly placed to deal with this advance, and White gains squares for improving her pieces. The first result is the control of the e5-square.

20...♘a5 21 ♘e5 ♗f6 22 ♗f4 *(D)*

White has noticeably improved the activity of her pieces, but the time is still not ripe to derive maximum benefit. If 22 ♘xf7? then 22...♔xf7 23 ♖e6 ♕xd5!, with great advantage to Black after 24 ♖xe8 ♖xe8 25 ♖xe8 ♗xe8 26 ♗g6+ ♔e6. Instead, 22 ♘xd7 ♕xd7 23 ♗f5 ♕d8 24 ♕d3 g6 25 ♗e4 ♘b7 is slightly better for White, but does not justify the simplification.

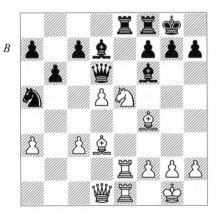

The text-move forces the exchange of the e5-knight and White's pieces 'expand' a little more.

22...♗xe5 23 ♗xe5

White prefers to keep the rooks on, given that the f8-rook is a hindrance to Black. In the event of 23 ♖xe5 ♖xe5 24 ♗xe5 ♕xa3 25 ♕h5 h6, it is not clear how to continue. There are alternatives such as 25 d6 or 25 ♕b1 attacking h7, followed by 26 ♕b4, but they do not lead to a clear advantage, so White once again keeps the tension, which favours her because she has more space and the more active pieces.

23...♕xa3 *(D)*

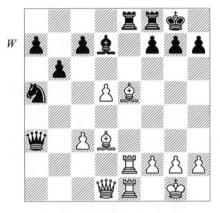

The exchange of the a3-pawn for the one on c7 favours White, who gains a passed pawn, but if 24 ♗xc7 then Black has 24...♗g4! and after 25 ♗xh7+ ♔h8, although the position of the black king is suspect, it is hard to see any way of taking advantage of this.

24 ♖e3

White escapes the possible skewer (...♗g4), while renewing the threat of ♗xc7 with gain of time.

24...♕c5??

In horrendous time-pressure, Black overlooks the most serious threat. He had to play 24...♖xe5 25 ♖xe5 and now, not 25...♕xc3?! 26 ♖e7, and the vital c7-pawn drops after 26...♗c8 27 ♕c2, but 25...♘b7!, trying to blockade on d6. Then White has to find the attractive shot 26 d6!, suggested by Ivan Sokolov, to prevent the blockade. The pawn is less important than opening the game; then 26...♘xd6 is met by 27 ♖e7, while 26...♕xd6? loses to 27 ♖d5!. 26...cxd6 seems best, to which White replies advantageously with 27 ♖5e3.

25 ♗xh7+!

"Surprise, surprise" – Polgar.

25...♔xh7 26 ♕h5+ 1-0

Black resigned without waiting for the Lasker recipe of 26...♔g8 27 ♗xg7! and a quick mate.

Karpov's novelty 13...♕d6?! was not a very good one, but only after a further inaccuracy (17...♘a5?) was Polgar able to regroup her pieces to ideal positions. When Black was faced with a difficult defensive task, the dreadful time-pressure that he was in meant that he over-looked the double-bishop sacrifice, a combination first created by Emanuel Lasker against Bauer in Amsterdam 1889.

We shall now examine two supplementary games that are also highly relevant to several of the themes we have seen in this game. In the first, White's central majority played a principal role:

Supplementary Game 26.1
Vladimir Akopian – Lenier Dominguez
Turin Olympiad 2006
Petroff Defence, Main Line

1 e4 e5 2 ♘f3 ♘f6 3 ♘xe5 d6 4 ♘f3 ♘xe4 5 d4 d5 6 ♗d3 ♘c6 7 0-0 ♗e7 8 c4 ♘b4 9 ♗e2 0-0 10 ♘c3 ♗f5 11 a3 ♘xc3 12 bxc3 ♘c6 13 ♖e1 ♖e8 14 cxd5 ♕xd5 15 ♗f4 ♖ac8 *(D)*

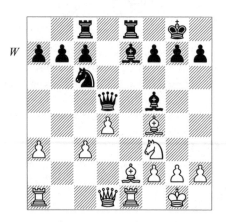

Reaching a modern 'tabiya' where there are many moves for White, who innovated here with...

16 ♗f1

Depriving the black queen off the e4-square, in preparation for playing c4. For the main move, 16 ♗d3, see Supplementary Game 26.2 below.

16...♗d6 17 ♖xe8+ ♖xe8 18 c4 ♕e4

The queen cannot go to a5 since 18...♕a5?? loses a piece after 19 ♗d2 ♕b6 20 c5.

19 ♗xd6 cxd6 *(D)*

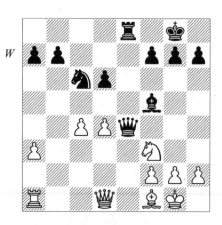

20 ♕d2

Now White threatens to win with 21 ♖e1. Black did not want to enter complications by moving the queen away with 20...♕c2, when White has 21 ♕f4 or 21 ♖e1, although the outcome is not absolutely clear. Instead he opted to retreat with...

20...♕e7?!

Dominguez considers this to be an error, since it allows White to make progress and gain an unpleasant initiative without any difficulties.

21 ♖e1 ♕d7 22 ♖xe8+ ♕xe8 23 ♕f4 ♕d7 24 d5! ♘e7 25 ♘d4! ♗g6 26 ♘b5 ♘c8

Here the centre pawns proved their worth with the help of tactics:

27 c5! dxc5 28 ♕b8 ♗f5 29 ♘xa7

White's pressure has allowed him to win a pawn and after a hard-fought endgame he eventually achieved victory.

Supplementary Game 26.2
Peter Svidler – Vladimir Kramnik
Dortmund 2006
Petroff Defence, Main Line

1 e4 e5 2 ♘f3 ♘f6 3 ♘xe5 d6 4 ♘f3 ♘xe4 5 d4 d5 6 ♗d3 ♘c6 7 0-0 ♗e7 8 c4 ♘b4 9 ♗e2 0-0 10 ♘c3 ♗f5 11 a3 ♘xc3 12 bxc3 ♘c6 13 ♖e1 ♖e8 14 cxd5 ♕xd5 15 ♗f4 ♖ac8 16 ♗d3 *(D)*

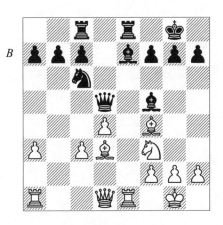

This is the main move. The idea is to activate the queen's rook at b1.

16...♕d7

Kramnik had good results with 16...b5!?, another method of blockading the white pawns. In J.Polgar-Kramnik, Sofia 2005, White subsequently tried to lift that blockade with a4, but Black resisted this.

17 ♖b1 ♗xd3

Black exchanges bishops before playing ...b6 in order to nullify the tactical possibilities of a possible ♗b5. The consequences of allowing ♗b5 are not at all clear, but the text-move is safer, even though it activates the white queen.

18 ♕xd3 b6 19 d5 ♗f6 20 c4 ♘e7 21 ♘e5 ♗xe5 22 ♗xe5 *(D)*

White has achieved something. His bishop is slightly better than the knight. After, for

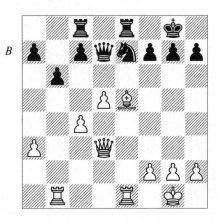

example, 22...♘g6 23 ♗g3 the bishop is active, aiming at the c7-pawn, and if Black tries to escape the pressure by playing ...c6, the bishop can support the advance of the d5-pawn, which would become passed; in contrast, nothing positive can be said about the g6-knight.

How should Black defend? It is essential to find somewhere better for the knight, where it will have more activity than on the useless g6-square.

The search for a better square throws up d6, but if 22...♘f5 Black has to consider 23 ♗xc7, when Black's back-rank weakness allows White to regain the piece and remain with a passed pawn on d5.

Kramnik found a better idea:

22...f6!

Black creates *luft* for his king and succeeds in carrying out the desired manoeuvre.

23 ♗f4 ♘f5 24 c5

The blockade does not appeal to White, who succeeds in highlighting the weakness of the c7-pawn with this advance.

24...bxc5 25 ♕c4 g5!?

Forcing the bishop to move to an exposed position, although the fact that the king's position is now draughtier will restrict Black's options in the future.

26 ♗d2 ♘d6 27 ♕xc5 ♘e4 (D)

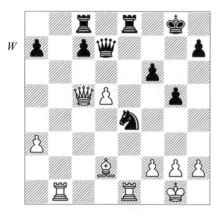

28 ♕a5

If 28 ♕d4 then with 28...c5 29 ♕d3 c4 Black is able to create a passed pawn to match White's d5-pawn.

28...c6

The simplification 28...♘xd2 29 ♕xd2 does not suit Black now, since his weakened king would be a negative factor. With the text-move he maintains the tension, exploiting the pin on the d5-pawn and awaiting a better moment to make the game safe.

29 ♗e3

Now Black easily solves his problems by forcing a general liquidation, but it is hard to see anything that offers White chances of advantage.

29...cxd5 30 ♕xa7 ♕xa7 31 ♗xa7 ♘c3 32 ♖xe8+ ♖xe8 33 ♖b8 ♖xb8 34 ♗xb8 d4 35 ♔f1 ♔f7 36 ♗a7 d3 37 ♔e1 d2+ 38 ♔xd2 ♘b1+ 39 ♔d3 ½-½

The mobility of the c3- and d4-pawns was covered to some extent in the main game and also in the two supplementary games. In both J.Polgar-Karpov and Akopian-L.Dominguez, Black was unable to solve the problem of the advance of these pawns, whereas Kramnik succeeded in neutralizing them.

Exercises

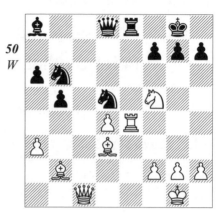

50
W

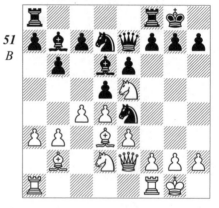

51
B

1) Evaluate the position.
2) What do you think of 12...♗xe5?

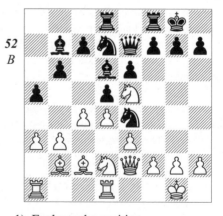

52
B

1) Evaluate the position.
2) What do you think of 14...♗xe5?

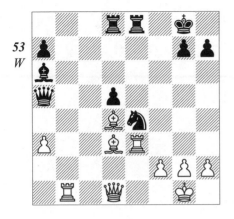

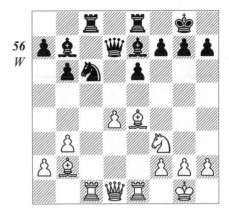

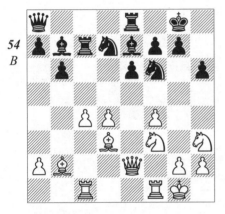

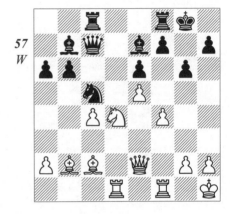

1) How do you assess the position?
2) Indicate Black's best move.

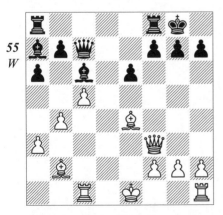

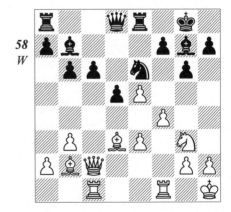

1) Evaluate the position, choosing between:
a) White is better.
b) White has a winning position.
c) The game is approximately equal.
2) Indicate White's best move.

59
W

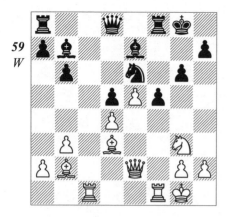

61
W

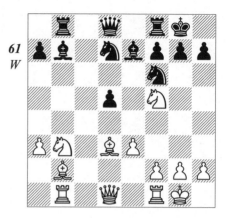

60
W

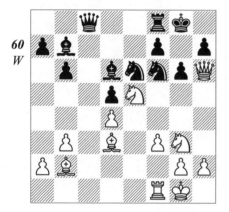

62
W

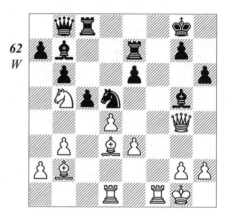

6 Miscellaneous Themes

There are countless actual and (especially) potential strategic and tactical themes in a game of chess.

In this final chapter we shall examine a number of attacking games using various elements that can have decisive influence in an attack, such as:

- the power of a white knight on f5 (or a black knight on f4);
- major-piece manoeuvres; and
- attacks based on a strong pawn-centre.

The Power of the f5-Knight

Game 27
Boris Spassky – Wolfgang Unzicker
Piatigorsky Cup, Santa Monica 1966
Ruy Lopez, Breyer Defence

There are certain games in which the possibilities seem infinite. Games, for example, where few pieces have been exchanged, where there are no exploitable weaknesses on either side, the game is closed, and it is not yet clear on which wing it would be appropriate to take the initiative.

This is the case, according to Spassky, at the start of this encounter. After a manoeuvring phase and an alteration to the pawn-structure, the position changes completely and there are many factors in play.

We shall see an example of the importance of a knight on f5 in the attack on the enemy castled position. Admittedly this is not the only factor, but it is one of the most important.

1 e4 e5 2 ♘f3 ♘c6 3 ♗b5 a6 4 ♗a4 ♘f6 5 0-0 ♗e7 6 ♖e1 b5 7 ♗b3 0-0 8 c3 d6 9 h3 ♘b8

The Breyer Variation continues to be one of Black's most solid defences.

10 d4 ♘bd7 11 ♘bd2 ♗b7 12 ♗c2 ♖e8 13 ♘f1 ♗f8 14 ♘g3 g6 15 ♗g5

The most popular continuations at that time were 15 a4 c5 16 d5 c4 17 ♗g5 and 15 b3.

15...h6

Necessary, before White gains a paralysing grip with 16 ♕d2.

16 ♗d2 ♗g7 *(D)*

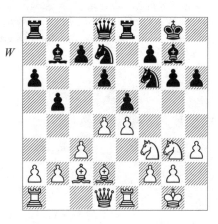

White has carried out the typical manoeuvre ♘bd2-f1-g3 and developed his c1-bishop. Now it is necessary to decide the next step; what should be his plan?

17 ♖c1

What is the explanation for this passive, odd-looking rook move? Let us hand over to Spassky:

"Where can White gain the victory, on the queenside or the kingside? In the present instance, with the configuration of pawns not clarified, I decided to make a move to bide time. Such a move should prove useful in the proper circumstances. ... Often in the Ruy Lopez one must be patient, wait and carry on a lengthy and wearisome struggle."

17 ♕c1 ♔h7 18 h4 has also been played here.

However, with the experience of years of practice (and proving that positions can have different interpretations, sometimes of similar value), in a game of great historical importance White decided here and now on which wing to make progress: in Fischer-Spassky, Match (game 1), Sveti Stefan/Belgrade 1992, 17 a4! was played – we examine this in detail as Supplementary Game 27.1.

17...c5 *(D)*

The relative harmlessness of 17 ♖c1 was shown in the line given by Unzicker in his annotations for the book *Second Piatigorsky Cup*, where he suggested 17...d5 18 ♘xe5 ♘xe5 19 dxe5 ♘xe4 20 ♘xe4 dxe4 21 ♗xe4 ♗xe4 22 ♖xe4 ♗xe5 23 ♕e2 ♗g7 24 ♗f4, and White has only an insignificant space advantage; this assessment was confirmed in Morović-Wong, Thessaloniki Olympiad 1984, in which Black had no problems.

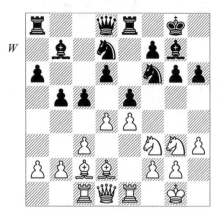

18 d5

White gains a slight space advantage and blunts the b7-bishop, although the disappearance of the central tension allows Black greater freedom to regroup.

18...♘b6

Unzicker criticized this move, which threatens 19...♘c4; it is more natural to play 18...c4 followed by ...♘c5. Subsequently Black returned to that scheme, and although he took two more moves to do it, these 'wasted' tempi were used by White to play 'neutral' moves, so that although 18...♘b6 was unnatural, it was not actually bad.

19 ♗d3 ♕c7 *(D)*

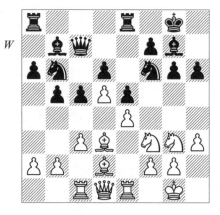

20 ♘h2

Another typical move in the Spanish, with two basic ideas: making way for the f2-pawn to advance to f4 at an opportune moment, and playing ♘g4. Here, since White has played d5, ♘g4 would not, as in other cases, help in the fight for the d5-square; it merely applies pressure to Black's kingside. White does not fear the exchange with ...♘xg4, because generally bringing the h-pawn closer to the centre and opening the h-file are more important than the creation of a doubled pawn.

20...♘a4 21 ♖b1

This defence is more flexible than 21 ♕c2, since White has envisaged another role for the queen, on the kingside. Black would reply in the same way as in the game, 21...c4 22 ♗f1 ♘c5, putting pressure on the e4-pawn, and the white bishop seems to be placed worse on f1 than c2.

21...c4 22 &c2 &c5 23 &g4 &h7 *(D)*

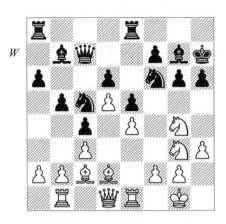

24 &f3

White continues with his manoeuvring game. 24 &xh6 &xg4 25 &xg7 &xf2! 26 &xf2 &xg7 would give White the half-open f-file, but grant Black the better structure.

24...&xg4

An important decision. Unzicker believed it to be almost forced, while Spassky was not so sure that the exchange of knights was better than 24...&g8. Both players considered the main move then to be 25 h4!, followed by 26 h5, since it is not possible to block with 25...h5? owing to 26 &xh5! gxh5 27 &f5+, winning. Black has to defend with 25...&e7 26 h5 &f8, when White may have to turn his attention back to the queenside with the break 27 b4, or 27 b3.

25 hxg4 &e7?! *(D)*

Black starts a plan that will be instructively punished by White. It was better to keep playing on the queenside with 25...a5.

How should White attack? Or rather, how should he prepare the offensive against Black's castled position? The h-file is half-open, but there is no obvious way to utilize this.

26 b3!

There is a time for everything; first White exchanges the c4-pawn and rules out a possible ...&d3 leap.

26...cxb3 27 axb3 &f6?!

This was the idea behind 25...&e7; the exchange of dark-squared bishops would suit Black, since it would leave many weak squares in White's camp. However, he does not manage

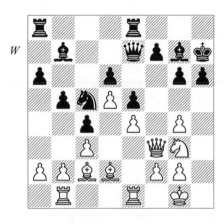

to carry it out, and it was better to regroup with 27...&c8 followed by 28...&d7.

28 &f1!

A multi-purpose move; the most immediate intention is to go to e3, preventing the exchange of bishops.

28...&g5 29 &e3 *(D)*

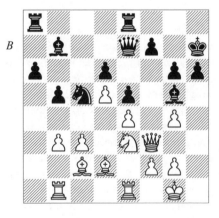

The other idea behind 28 &f1! is to prepare the f4 break with g3, taking advantage of the insecure position of the g5-bishop.

29...&c8 30 g3 &d7?!

Black decides to give battle on the kingside and prevent f4, by making the g4-pawn a target.

In view of the failure of this idea, it will become clear that 30...a5 was better, followed by ...&d7, retaining harmony among his forces.

31 &e2 &f6 32 f3

Black has managed to prevent the immediate threat, which was the f4 advance, but White has a plan, and Black does not. After, for instance, 32...♗d7 33 ♔g2 ♔g7, White could play on both wings; in the first place he could force through his idea of playing f4 by preparing it with 34 ♖f1, in unhurried fashion; or else he could paralyse the queenside with 34 ♗d3, followed by doubling rooks on the a-file.

32...h5? *(D)*

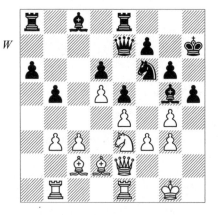

Black does not want his initiative to fizzle out, so he increases the tension on the kingside, where he has a lot of pieces, but where his king is not as well protected as White's and the unguarded g5-bishop is a tactical weakness.

The tactical complications do not appear to be in Black's favour, since the general rule says "you should not move the pawns on the wing where you are worse", but this phase of the game requires concrete calculation, not general principles. How should White reply?

It is clear that 33 gxh5 ♘xh5 only favours Black, who succeeds in improving the coordination of his forces, while 33 ♘f5? is met with the saving move 33...♕a7+!.

33 ♔g2!

Now the defensive resource of the check on the diagonal has gone, so 34 ♘f5 becomes a real threat. White also clears a path for his rook to occupy the h-file. This move was overlooked by Unzicker when he began his plan of becoming active on the kingside with 30...♘d7.

33...♕d8

33...hxg4 is met by 34 ♖h1+. After 34...♔g7 35 ♘f5+!, the dark squares fall into White's hands with devastating effect, while if 34...♔g8

then 35 ♘f5! still comes, and the pin on the f6-knight is more or less decisive.

34 ♖h1 ♔g8 35 ♖bf1! *(D)*

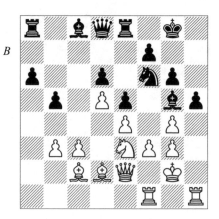

The f4 advance is still on the agenda.

35...♗h6 *(D)*

Now if 35...hxg4 White wins with 36 f4 exf4 37 gxf4, when the sacrifice 37...♘xe4 38 ♗xe4 ♖xe4 39 fxg5 ♕xg5 is unsound, since White unpins and simultaneously attacks f7 with 40 ♕f2!, proving that Black is really missing the a8-rook and the c8-bishop. If then 40...♕e7, Unzicker gave 41 c4, planning 42 ♗c3, with a winning advantage, or 41 ♖h6, while 40...f5 is refuted by 41 ♘xf5! ♕xf5 42 ♕h4 ♕f3+ 43 ♔g1 and White wins.

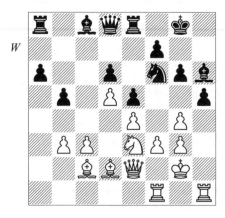

White has all his pieces on the kingside, and furthermore Black has somewhat weakened his position on that wing. How should White break through?

36 ♘f5!

This pretty sacrifice decides the struggle. The weakened squares in Black's castled position will be at the mercy of the white pieces.

36...♗xd2

Black must accept the sacrifice; in the event of 36...♗f8? White can gain a winning attack in several ways. Spassky gives 37 ♘h6+ ♔g7 38 gxh5 ♘xh5 39 ♖xh5 (or the simple 39 ♘f5+ ♔g8 40 ♖h2) 39...gxh5 40 f4; for example, 40...♔xh6 41 f5+ ♔g7 42 ♕xh5, followed by 43 ♖h1, or 43 f6+, mating quickly.

37 ♕xd2 (D)

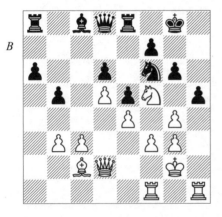

37...gxf5

Spassky offers a convincing line against 37...♘h7: 38 ♕h6 ♕f6 39 g5 ♕h8 40 ♘xd6 ♖d8 41 ♘f5! gxf5 42 ♖xh5 ♕g7 43 ♕b6 ♗d7 44 ♖fh1 ♘f8 45 ♕f6!, and the black king cannot escape mate after 45...♘g6 46 exf5.

38 ♕h6!

Threatening 39 g5 followed by ♖xh5.

38...fxe4 39 fxe4 ♗xg4

The opening of the h-file with 39...♘xg4 40 ♕xh5 ♘e3+ 41 ♔g1 leads to immediate mate.

40 ♖xf6

With the regaining of the piece, any hope of salvation for Black is dashed.

40...♕e7

If 40...♕c7 then 41 ♕g5+ ♔f8 42 ♖h6, mating.

41 ♕g5+ ♔f8 (D)

Now it only requires a tiny breath of air to bring Black's house of cards tumbling down. Where is this to come from?

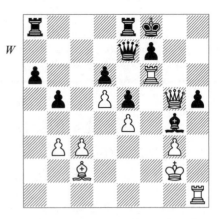

42 ♗d1!

The exchange of the only defender of the kingside quickly decides the struggle.

42 ♖hf1 was also good, with the idea of the quiet but deadly manoeuvre 43 ♕g6 and 44 ♕h7.

42...♗xd1 43 ♖xd1 ♖ec8 44 ♖df1 ♖xc3 45 ♕xh5 ♖c2+ 46 ♔h1 1-0

White gained the advantage after the move 26 b3!, the importance of which could easily pass unnoticed, but which was vital to wrest control of the d3-square from Black, after which the c5-knight became a harmless piece.

Black did not want to wait passively while White made progress on the kingside, and with the 25...♕e7 manoeuvre, planning ...♗f6 and ...♗g5, followed later by ...♘d7-f6 and ...h5, Black increased the pressure on the kingside to the maximum, but the tension on that wing could not possibly conclude in his favour, since his king was in a worse position, and his activity was limited to just three pieces, whereas White had all his forces in place.

Of course, a game is not won with general considerations alone; one should always remember the importance of confirming a positional advantage by tactical means, whether it be with a quiet move such as 33 ♔g2!, or a brilliant move like 36 ♘f5!.

The importance of the f5-knight was clear; with Black's kingside weakened, the presence of the knight was intolerable, but its capture led to an irreparable weakening of Black's king position, and White had no problems in winning, thanks to the opening and then occupation of the three kingside files by his major pieces.

Spassky said that one of his contributions to chess knowledge is the help that his games provide towards our understanding of the typical structures of the Ruy Lopez. The game we have just examined provides an excellent demonstration of this.

Supplementary Game 27.1
Bobby Fischer – Boris Spassky
Match (game 1), Sveti-Stefan/Belgrade 1992
Ruy Lopez, Breyer Defence

1 e4 e5 2 ᗾf3 ᗾc6 3 ♗b5 a6 4 ♗a4 ᗾf6 5 0-0 ♗e7 6 ♖e1 b5 7 ♗b3 d6 8 c3 0-0 9 h3 ᗾb8 10 d4 ᗾbd7 11 ᗾbd2 ♗b7 12 ♗c2 ♖e8 13 ᗾf1 ♗f8 14 ᗾg3 g6 15 ♗g5 h6 16 ♗d2 ♗g7 17 a4!

This move creates pressure on the b5-pawn, which is one of the most common plans in the Ruy Lopez.

17...c5 18 d5 c4 *(D)*

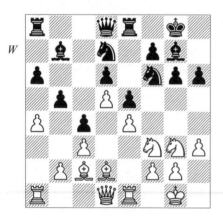

This advance is also typical. Black gains the c5-square for his d7-knight and is able to improve the coordination of his pieces, which are rather sluggish at the moment.

19 b4!

Now Black has to decide whether to take on b3.

19...ᗾh7?!

He opts not to do so, but Black's lack of mobility now proves more important than the discomfort that the black pieces would experience after 19...cxb3 20 ♗xb3 ᗾc5 21 c4. Kasparov wrote that Black can emerge from his slight inferiority with 21...bxa4 22 ♗xa4 ♖f8 and then regroup with ...♕c7, ...♖fb8, ...ᗾfd7, etc., with adequate control of the queenside.

20 ♗e3 h5 21 ♕d2 ♖f8 *(D)*

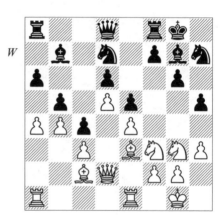

22 ♖a3!

This doubling of rooks on the closed a-file bears a certain resemblance to the manoeuvre employed in Karpov-Unzicker, Nice Olympiad 1974, although the motivation in that game was to be able to continue manoeuvring without allowing an exchange of rooks until it suited White. In this game White has a different, more concrete idea.

22...ᗾdf6 23 ♖ea1 ♕d7 24 ♖1a2 ♖fc8 25 ♕c1!

White will not just double but triple on the a-file.

25...♗f8 26 ♕a1 ♕e8 *(D)*

Black has made all his preparations to deal with White's invasion along the a-file, which would now only lead to simplification. However, White shows that there is an important weakness in Black's position, namely the b5-pawn;

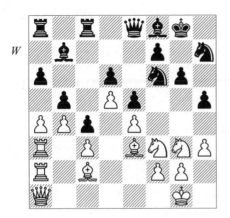

he now begins a knight manoeuvre to attack and capture it with a timely ♘a3 after the exchange of all the major pieces on the a-file.

27 ♘f1! ♗e7 28 ♘1d2 ♔g7 29 ♘b1!

Black's position is at critical point.

29...♘xe4!?

Spassky decides to prevent the aforementioned manoeuvre (which would occur after, for instance, 29...♘d7 30 axb5 axb5 31 ♖xa8 ♖xa8 32 ♖xa8 ♕xa8 33 ♕xa8 ♗xa8 34 ♘a3) by giving up a piece.

30 ♗xe4 f5?!

Black defends badly in the follow-up to his sacrifice. Kasparov pointed out that instead of this weakening advance, 30...♘f6 was better.

31 ♗c2 ♗xd5 32 axb5 axb5 33 ♖a7 ♔f6

Another move queried by Kasparov, who suggested 33...♖xa7 34 ♖xa7 ♖a8. Fischer will take brilliant advantage of the black king's position.

34 ♘bd2 ♖xa7 35 ♖xa7 ♖a8 *(D)*

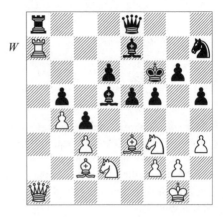

36 g4!

Opening up the king's position and increasing the power of the c2-bishop.

36...hxg4 37 hxg4 ♖xa7 38 ♕xa7 f4 39 ♗xf4 exf4 40 ♘h4! ♗f7 41 ♕d4+ ♔e6 42 ♘f5! ♗f8 43 ♕xf4 ♔d7 44 ♘d4 ♕e1+ 45 ♔g2 ♗d5+ 46 ♗e4 ♗xe4+ 47 ♘xe4 ♗e7 48 ♘xb5 ♘f8 49 ♘bxd6 ♘e6 50 ♕e5 1-0

Game 28
Vasily Smyslov – Alexander Kotov
Moscow Ch 1943
Sicilian Defence, Closed

In this game we shall see another example of the importance of ♘f5 (or ...♘f4) in the attack on the enemy king. The ♘f5 leap will have a different effect here from that in the previous game.

We shall also see, in less depth and as a supplementary game, one of the most brilliant attacking games ever carried out using the Closed Sicilian.

1 e4 c5 2 ♘c3 ♘c6 3 g3 g6 4 ♗g2 ♗g7 5 d3 d6 *(D)*

White can choose between various piece deployments. Regarding the development of the g1-knight, we have three possibilities, the squares f3, e2 and h3. Another possibility is to postpone this decision by playing 6 ♗e3, and finally it is also possible to play f4.

Each of these has points for and against. On h3 the knight keeps the d1-h5 diagonal open, although it is a long way from the centre; Spassky played his knight to h3 several times, while Chigorin preferred to bring it out to e2. Playing f4 seems the most logical, since this advance is carried out anyway in a very high percentage of games; its negative side is that it prematurely

closes the c1-h6 diagonal, making it impossible to threaten to exchange the dark-squared bishops, at least in the immediate future.

It is worth noting that this type of position is often reached with colours reversed from the English Opening.

The choice is to some extent a matter of taste.

6 ♘f3

White opts for the most natural development. We examine 6 f4 in Supplementary Game 28.1, Spassky-Geller, Candidates match (game 6), Sukhumi 1968.

6...e6 7 ♗g5

White delays castling in order to retain the option of attacking along the h-file with an eventual h4-h5.

7...♘ge7 8 ♕d2 *(D)*

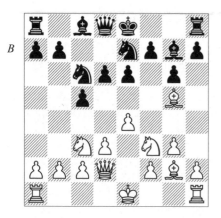

8...h6

This eviction is necessary to prevent ♗h6, which could be followed by the aforementioned

opening of the h-file with h4-h5. The price Black pays is that he is going to be tied to the defence of the h6-pawn. Now there begins a duel in which both sides make as many useful moves as possible, while delaying a decision about the h6-pawn as long as possible.

9 ♗e3 e5

Black decides to develop his c8-bishop along the h3-c8 diagonal, after which he could castle queenside and also play ...d5, depending on circumstances. The negative aspect of this is that it presents White with a clear plan, which is the possibility of breaking with f4.

10 0-0

Now there are no moves more useful than castling and White prepares to break with f4.

10...♗e6 11 ♘e1 ♕d7 *(D)*

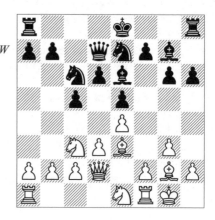

And now what is best? 12 f4 is the most consistent move with what has gone on before, but Black can respond with 12...exf4 13 ♗xf4 0-0-0, when all the black pieces are harmoniously placed, the pressure on h6 is futile, and Black can play ...g5 and ...f5.

As Dvoretsky's books show, it is useful and even necessary to ask yourself about the opponent's intentions, and to combine progress with your own plans with placing obstacles in the way of the opponent's plans, if these would harm your cause.

12 a3!

This modest move completely discourages queenside castling by Black, since ♖b1 and b4 would follow, immediately opening lines against the black king.

12...♗h3 13 f4 *(D)*

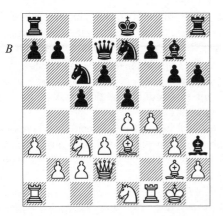

Now all flexible measures are exhausted and there is no better move than this break, prepared with 11 ♘e1.

13...♘d4

Black continues to delay the decision about where to put his king. Keeping the king in the centre here is correct, but it merely delays the decision about the best place for the king in the long run, because, as we have already seen in the earlier chapters, it is not advisable to leave the king in the centre for very long, even when the position is not open.

14 ♖b1

Played in the same spirit as Black's last move, but with a more aggressive idea, which is to break with b4, if appropriate.

14...exf4 15 ♗xf4 ♗xg2 *(D)*

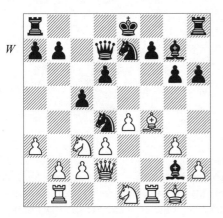

16 ♕xg2

White opts to maintain the harmony of his pieces, even though it allows Black to castle on the kingside, assuming that he will be able to attack the black king there.

Smyslov does not mention in his annotations the possibility of maintaining the pressure on h6 by playing 16 ♘xg2. Admittedly, the knight is inactive on g2, but Black is left with the dilemma of where to put his king. Then 16...0-0?, exchanging the h6-pawn for the one on c2, is no good because White achieves a devastating attack, thanks to the weakness of Black's castled position and the exchange of its main defender; after 17 ♗xh6 ♗xh6 18 ♕xh6 ♘xc2 White can play 19 ♘f4, followed by ♘cd5, or 19 ♖f6, and Black's castled position cannot be defended.

Against 16 ♘xg2 Black would possibly have played 16...g5, followed by 17...0-0, with a reasonable position.

16...0-0 17 g4

White slowly starts his attack, but the centre is not closed, so Black does not lack defensive resources.

17...♖ad8

Preparing the central break ...d5.

18 ♔h1 ♘e6 19 ♗d2 d5 20 ♘f3 *(D)*

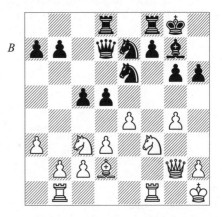

Black has succeeded in occupying the centre. What should he do about the central tension? Should he gain space with 20...d4, or occupy the centre with 20...dxe4 and 21...♘d5? In the latter case White too strongly centralizes a knight with 21 ♘xe4.

20...d4?!

Black chooses the option of gaining space and makes the c3-knight passive for the moment. This looks understandable but is in fact a debatable decision.

The drawback of this decision is that White has a concrete plan of attack, taking advantage of the fact that Black's castled position is slightly weakened.

White's plan looks rather slow, but it is also true that he can make progress without any obstacles. Black cannot take advantage of this slowness to create counterplay, or even solidify his position.

These are general explanations, of course, and concrete calculation is essential to make the correct decision at this critical moment.

The course of the game shows that it was better to keep the centre open with 20...dxe4 21 ♘xe4 ♘d5.

After the text-move, the structure is now like a King's Indian Defence with reversed colours, where White has carried out a favourable exchange of bishops and can make rapid progress on the kingside, whereas Black has made no progress on the queenside.

21 ♘e2 ♘c6 22 ♕h3!

White puts pressure on one of the weaknesses in Black's castled position, forcing him to place the king in a vulnerable position. This move also vacates the g-file, the importance of which will be seen in the near-future.

22...♔h7 23 ♘g3 f6 (D)

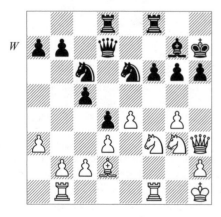

Black controls all the entry points and, as Smyslov commented, it would seem that once

he has played ...♘e5 he will have solidified his position.

It is true that it is not possible for White to make progress on the kingside by 'normal' means. There are no pawn-breaks, and although the black kingside pawns have all taken a step forward, and thus become weaker, there is no open file that could be used to exploit this, nor any point of entry.

However, in this type of position, where one side has so many pieces lined up against the opponent's castled position, tactics make their appearance.

24 ♘f5!

Smyslov described the sacrifice in these words: "A typical piece sacrifice in such positions. The special feature of it in the given instance is that White will not try to regain the sacrificed material immediately, but will build up his attack by systematic pressure. Here one has to rely on an evaluation of the position based on general principles, rather than calculate specific variations."

It could be added that after the first phase, when the moves based on general considerations have finished, exact calculation will be required to finish the task.

24...gxf5 25 gxf5 (D)

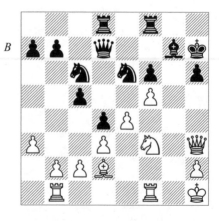

25...♘c7

The importance of the pressure from the white queen against the black king is evident in the line 25...♘g5 26 ♗xg5 fxg5 27 ♘xg5+, followed by ♘e6, regaining the material with interest.

26 ⌖g1 *(D)*

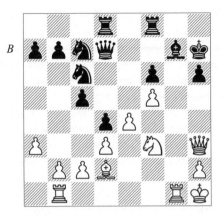

Planning to occupy the open file and put pressure on the weak points g7 and h6.

26...♘e8?

Preparing the flight of the king to the queenside while covering g7. If 26...♖h8?, looking to escape with ...♔g8, Smyslov gives 27 ♗xh6! ♗xh6 28 ♖g6 ♕g7 29 ♖xg7+ ♔xg7 30 ♕g3+, winning. 26...♘e5? loses to 27 ♘xe5 fxe5 28 ♗xh6 ♗xh6 29 ♖g6, amongst other things. 26...♖f7! is more resilient, as the rook can defend along its second rank. After 27 ♗xh6 ♗xh6 28 ♖g6 ♔h8! 29 ♖xh6+ ♖h7 30 ♖g1 White has strong pressure, but the position remains complex.

27 ♖g6?

Smyslov relies on general ideas (doubling rooks on the open file and putting pressure on h6), but this move is ineffective, whereas the immediate 27 ♗xh6! should win. After 27...♗xh6 28 ♖g6, 28...♘g7 loses to 29 ♖xh6+ ♔g8 30 ♖g1, so Black has to give up his queen.

27...♖f7?

27...♖h8! is a much better defence. White still has enough pressure for the sacrificed material, but there is no obvious way through after natural moves like 28 ♗xh6 ♔g8 29 ♖bg1 ♖h7.

28 ♖bg1 ♔g8 29 ♖xh6 ♔f8 30 ♖h7 ♔e7 *(D)*
31 ♕h5!

There are several other strong moves here, such as 31 ♖g6, but this move seems most natural. The pressure on the f7-rook helps the further opening of lines against the black king.

31...♔d6

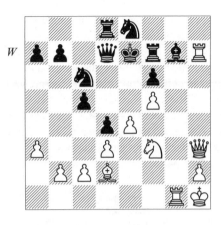

The black king continues its flight towards the queenside, although of course in the centre it will be more exposed.

If 31...♖c8, seeking to escape via d8, White gains a devastating attack with 32 ♘g5! fxg5 33 ♗xg5+. For example, if now 33...♘f6, then among other things there is a win with 34 ♗xf6+ ♔xf6 35 ♕h4+ ♔e5 36 ♖g6, and mate in a few moves. 33...♔d6 also loses, to 34 ♗f4+ ♔e7 and now 35 f6+ ♘xf6 36 ♖gxg7 ♘xh5 37 ♖xf7+ ♔e6 38 ♖xd7 ♘xf4 39 ♖xb7 with a winning endgame according to Smyslov. Also very strong is 35 ♖gxg7 ♘xg7 36 f6+, given by the computers, but Smyslov's line is conclusive enough.

32 ♗f4+ ♘e5 *(D)*

32...♔e7 33 ♘g5! fxg5 34 ♗xg5+ leads to similar lines.

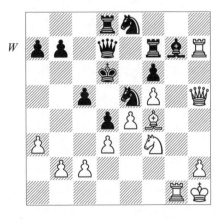

Now Smyslov says that the worst seems to be over for Black since the deadly h2-b8 diagonal has been closed. How can White demonstrate that this impression is mistaken?

33 ♗xe5+!

Several moves ago the common-sense moves came to an end, making way for concrete variations. White now breaks through with two well-calculated blows. As a first step White exchanges a pinned piece, something that should never be done without a definite reason.

33...fxe5 34 f6! *(D)*

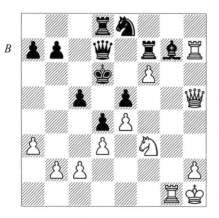

A beautiful problem-like move, based on the tactical themes of pinning and interference; any capture on f6 by Black loses him material.

34...♘xf6 35 ♕xe5+ ♔c6 36 ♖hxg7! *(D)*

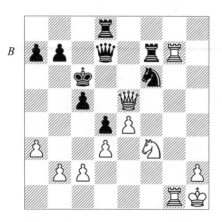

Regaining the piece, and now White has a material advantage and a winning attack.

36...♔b5 37 ♘xd4+ ♔b6

37...♖xd4 38 ♕xd4 cxd4 39 ♖xf7 is also lost.

38 b4 ♖c8

If 38...cxd4 then White mates in two with 39 ♕c5+ ♔a6 40 ♕a5#.

39 ♖xf7 ♕xf7 40 ♕d6+ ♖c6 41 ♘xc6 ♘xe4 42 bxc5+ 1-0

There are various lessons in this game that began as a manoeuvring struggle and ended as a violent combinative game.

Capablanca, annotating his endgame against Ragozin from Moscow 1936, demonstrated a way to analyse that consisted of working out the opponent's plan and then deciding how to place your pieces to prevent it, while continuing to make progress yourself. In that endgame, each side had only a rook and minor piece. On White's 24th move, Smyslov did something similar, but in the middlegame, and by sacrificing a piece. This shows that, even in the middlegame, on certain occasions it is possible and even to be recommended to ask yourself about the ideal position for the pieces; of course this has to go hand in hand with a careful tactical check.

There are useful moves that can pass unnoticed if you do not ask yourself what the opponent wants to do. That type of questioning helps you find the right direction for your own plans, as with 12 a3!.

Determining the pawn-structure is a critical decision that has to be pondered deeply. Black made a bad decision with 20...d4?!, which allowed White an attack 'for free'.

Of course, for the attack to bear fruit, it required a sacrifice with 24 ♘f5!, the consequences of which were difficult to evaluate, as well as quiet moves such as 31 ♕h5!, increasing the pressure on Black's most important defences.

General measures, such as occupying an open file, doubling rooks on it, etc., gave way to concrete calculation, such as with the combinations on g7 at Black's 26th move, or the ♘g5 leap in various lines given in the notes to moves 31 and 32 which prevented various black defences, and finally the sequence with 33 ♗xe5+!, 34 f6! and 36 ♖hxg7! that was actually played.

The following spectacular game should be in any book about attacking chess:

Supplementary Game 28.1

Boris Spassky – Efim Geller

Candidates match (game 6), Sukhumi 1968

Sicilian Defence, Closed

1 e4 c5 2 ♘c3 d6 3 g3 ♘c6 4 ♗g2 g6 5 d3 ♗g7 6 f4

This is the most popular move. The main game featured 6 ♘f3.

6...♘f6

Black too can choose between various set-ups; for example, with 6...e6 or 6...e5 and then ...♘ge7.

7 ♘f3 0-0 8 0-0 ♖b8 *(D)*

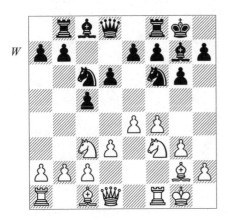

Black has a clear plan of advancing his b-pawn, but what about White?

9 h3!

White prepares a kingside pawn-storm with g4.

9...b5 10 a3!

It is essential to combine attack and defence; if 10 g4 then 10...b4 11 ♘e2 c4! followed by ...♗a6, and Black has managed to create favourable tension in the centre and on the queenside.

10...a5 11 ♗e3 b4 12 axb4 axb4 13 ♘e2 ♗b7 *(D)*

What now? White's plan is to play g4 and f5, combined with ♕d2, followed possibly by ♗h6. A logical question is to ask yourself which is the best move-order. But this is not the only question to ask yourself; the other is to consider

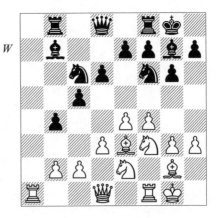

what Black is going to do, and then find the best way to combining opposition to the opponent's plans with making progress with your own.

In the fourth game of this match White played 14 ♕d2 ♖a8 15 ♖ab1 (it is typical to move the rook to this square, where it defends in advance against any discovered attack on b2 by the bishop) 15...♕a5 16 b3 and here instead of 16...♖fc8 it was possible to change the structure and disrupt White's plans by 16...d5 17 e5 d4 18 ♗f2 ♘d5; with 16...♖fc8 Black also gained reasonable play, but Spassky overcame Geller in the resulting complex middlegame, demolishing his castled position.

Here Spassky chose a different plan, pre-empting the inevitable attack on b2:

14 b3! ♖a8 15 ♖c1!

White has defended the new weakness on c2 in advance.

15...♖a2 16 g4 *(D)*

16...♕a8?!

An optimistic move. Black has 'physically' come first in the race between the attacks on opposite wings, but he has made little real progress and the damage inflicted on White's queenside is minimal. It would have been better to play either the sharper 16...♕a5, followed by ...♕b5 and ...♖fa8, with the plan of ...♖a1 to exchange

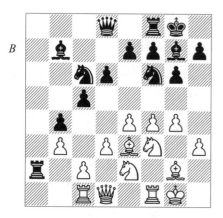

the rooks, which are vital pieces for White's attack, or 16...♕c7.

With the text-move, the queen strays too far from the kingside, so that when the attacking race reaches its crisis-point, Black will miss his queen and the duel will be settled in White's favour.

17 ♕e1 ♕a6?!

Geller thought that he could have resisted better with 17...d5 18 e5 ♘d7 19 ♕h4 e6.

18 ♕f2 ♘a7?! *(D)*

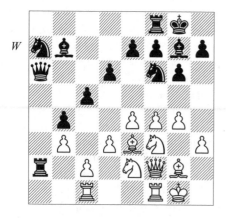

Black continues to play consistently, with the aim of attacking the weakness at c2, but White's first step beyond his fourth rank foreshadows a devastating attack.

19 f5!

"The beginning of the end; White's attack develops so quickly that Black does not even have time to capture the superfluous c2-pawn" – Geller. White opens the f-file as the first step

towards the goal of invading the black position at h7.

19...♘b5 20 fxg6 hxg6?

Geller thought that capturing the other way would not have changed anything, but many years later Kasparov's analysis showed that in fact the unnatural 20...fxg6 was more tenacious.

21 ♘g5

White continues with his aim of reaching h7; this is the second step.

21...♘a3 22 ♕h4

And now the queen arrives.

22...♖c8 *(D)*

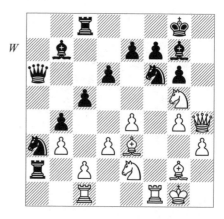

Which enemy piece is preventing White from concluding the invasion at h7?

23 ♖xf6!

That's right; we need to get rid of the f6-knight, although on its own this is not enough.

23...exf6 24 ♕h7+ ♔f8 *(D)*

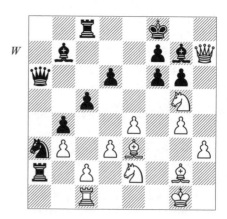

We've said check, but now what? What had Spassky planned here?

25 ♘xf7! ♖xc2?!

Now taking the knight is of no use: 25...♔xf7 26 ♗h6 ♖g8 27 ♘f4 and White obtains a winning attack; for example, 27...d5 28 e5!, as Polugaevsky indicated, or 27...♖xc2 28 ♖f1! g5 29 ♕g6+ ♔e7 30 ♗xg7 gxf4 31 ♗xf6+ ♔d7 32 ♕xg8 ♕xd3 33 ♕f7+ ♔c6 34 ♕d5+ ♕xd5 35 exd5+ ♔d7 36 ♗e4, as pointed out by Kasparov.

26 ♗h6! ♖xc1+

Or 26...♕xd3 27 ♕xg7+ ♔e8 28 ♖xc2 ♘xc2 29 ♘f4.

27 ♘xc1 ♔xf7

27...♗xh6 28 ♘xh6 ♔e8 also loses: 29 ♘g8! ♔f8 30 ♘e7 ♔e8 31 ♘xg6.

28 ♕xg7+ ♔e8 29 g5! f5 30 ♕xg6+ ♔d7 31 ♕f7+ ♔c6 32 exf5+ 1-0

After a series of exchanges on b7, White will play f6.

Manoeuvring with the Major Pieces

In the following games we shall see examples of the important role that the major pieces can play in the attack on the king, specifically the manoeuvres to transfer the rooks to the wing where the enemy king is located.

It is does not happen very often but on certain occasions this method of attack can even be played automatically, as in the following example, which follows a well-known theoretical path well into the middlegame. It can be said that the middlegame starts in a standard, even almost routine, fashion but then it becomes exceptional, original, very creative, and brilliant in its execution.

Game 29

Viswanathan Anand – Michael Adams

FIDE World Ch, San Luis 2005

Ruy Lopez, Zaitsev Variation

1 e4 e5 2 ♘f3 ♘c6 3 ♗b5 a6 4 ♗a4 ♘f6 5 0-0 ♗e7 6 ♖e1 b5 7 ♗b3 d6 8 c3 0-0 9 h3 ♗b7 10 d4 ♖e8 11 ♘bd2 ♗f8 *(D)*

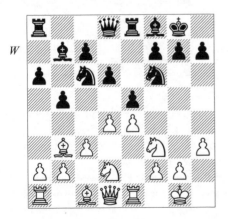

The Zaitsev Variation was often debated in the matches between Kasparov and Karpov.

That prolific creator of ideas, Igor Zaitsev, discovered that Black is not obliged to play ...h6 as a preparation for ...♖e8, since the 11 ♘g5 leap is not to be feared – provided that a draw is not a bad result in the sporting sense after 11...♖f8 12 ♘f3 ♖e8 13 ♘g5 ♖f8.

At the top level, the computer has become more and more important in opening preparation, since it can provide definite answers to what previously might have been evaluated as 'with compensation for the material' or 'with an attack'. If the position is very tactical, that sort of abstract assessment has almost disappeared altogether, since the combined analysis of the best chess-players in the world, their seconds and the computers can arrive at more definitive conclusions.

At present this line is not high fashion, nor was it when this game was played, so that it would have seemed a good choice by Black from the point of view of concrete opening preparation; it would not have seemed logical that the most intensive preparation of the white side would be in a line with a great deal of history but which is now in a certain sense a secondary line.

Furthermore, the analysis carried out in the 1980s or early 1990s did not have the depth and certainty of today, because the engines were not as strong, and thus a fundamental aid was lacking.

12 a4

This was the main continuation in the duels between Kasparov and Karpov. White creates typical tension on the queenside, with an extra idea, as well as maintaining the pressure on f7.

There are several alternatives, such as 12 a3 (preparing both the retreat of the b3-bishop and the b4 advance), 12 d5 and 12 ♗c2.

12...h6 13 ♗c2 exd4

This is another important decision. Black opens the game and occupies the queenside, in return for giving up the centre.

The alternative is to play in the spirit of the Breyer and recycle the c6-knight to another square with 13...♘b8.

14 cxd4 ♘b4 15 ♗b1 c5 16 d5 ♘d7 17 ♖a3 (D)

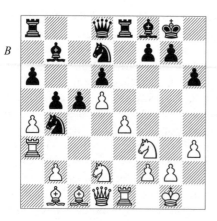

This is another of the consequences of 13...exd4; White gains good prospects for the rook along the third rank. As I once heard David Bronstein say about a similar position, the board is too small to be able to develop the queenside in a natural way. The a1-rook suffers

most from the position of the three minor pieces on the queenside, which prevent it from coming into play via the first rank, so that it has to find an alternative route, already prepared with 12 a4.

17...c4

With this advance, Black makes room for the d7-knight, and gains access to the d3-square, in return for giving up control of d4. 17...f5 is a sharp alternative.

18 axb5

This capture might appear illogical, since the opening of the a-file does not suit White. However, there is a tactical justification: in the event of the natural 18 ♘d4 Black can play 18...♕f6 19 ♘2f3 ♘d3 20 ♗xd3 b4!, when he obtains very good compensation for the pawn after 21 ♖a1 cxd3 22 ♕xd3 ♘c5 23 ♕c4 a5! 24 ♘b5 ♖ac8. There are alternatives, naturally, such as 21 ♗xc4, which was the choice of Anand himself against Kamsky in their match in Las Palmas 1995, or 21 ♖b3, which was successful in Enders-Lukacs, Budapest 1995.

18...axb5 19 ♘d4 (D)

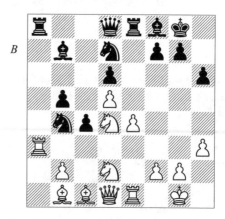

This clears the third rank and, again for tactical reasons, Black does not have time to exchange rooks. Now the b5-pawn is threatened.

19...♕b6 20 ♘f5 ♘e5

The threat of ♘xh6+, followed by ♕g4+ and the capture of the d7-knight, prevents Black from playing 20...♖xa3, and forces him to allow the transfer of White's a3-rook to the kingside.

21 ♖g3 g6

The concentration of white forces on the kingside is very great. Let us see a crushing refutation of 21...♔h7?: Marcinkiewicz-Zundell, corr. 2002 continued 22 ♘f3 ♘bd3 23 ♗e3 ♕a5 24 ♗xd3 ♘xd3 25 ♗xh6! gxh6 26 ♘g5+! ♔g6 27 ♕h5+!!, and Black resigned in view of the sequence 27...♔xh5 28 ♘h7! ♕xe1+ 29 ♔h2, when there is no defence to the mate.

22 ♘f3 ♘ed3 *(D)*

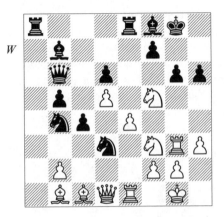

We are still in familiar territory, with Adams playing very quickly and Anand struggling to recall analysis from a decade before, and which did not seem very important at the time.

What should White play here? It seems obvious that he should avoid the exchange of the c1-bishop and defend f2 by playing 23 ♗e3 'and think later'. But that isn't what happened.

23 ♕d2!!

A marvellous idea, found by one of Anand's analytical team, Artur Yusupov, ten years earlier. It is even more admirable that it was found without any help from a computer.

The exchange is not a great price for all the white pieces being able to participate in the attack.

Objectively, after much calm analysis with computers, it is not clear that this move gives White a definite advantage, but finding the correct path for Black over the board, in a fiendishly difficult position, was in practice an almost impossible task for Adams.

23...♗xd5?

Understandably Black does not find the only move to stay in the game.

Anand commented that the only defence was 23...♘xe1!, when the main line goes 24 ♘xe1 ♘xd5! 25 ♘xh6+ ♗xh6 26 ♕xh6 ♖a1! 27 ♖xg6+ fxg6 28 ♕xg6+ ♔f8 29 ♕f5+ and the game ends in a draw. For the details, the reader is recommended to consult Anand's deep analysis in *Informator 94*.

24 ♘xh6+!

Anand is still on what to him is known ground.

24...♗xh6 25 ♕xh6 ♕xf2+ 26 ♔h2 ♘xe1 *(D)*

If 26...♘xc1 White wins with the pretty sequence 27 exd5! ♘cd3 (or else 27...♖xe1 28 ♗xg6!) 28 ♖e6!.

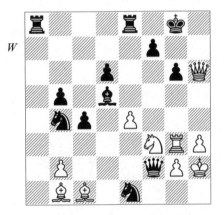

By now Anand was finally out of his extraordinary preparation. The obvious 27 ♖xg6+? fxg6 28 ♕xg6+ ♔f8 29 ♕f6+ is only a draw.

27 ♘h4!

A fresh reinforcement of the attack, with decisive effect.

27...♘ed3 28 ♘xg6 ♕xg3+ 29 ♔xg3 fxg6 30 ♕xg6+ ♔f8 31 ♕f6+ ♔g8 32 ♗h6 1-0

If 32...♖a7 then 33 ♕g6+ decides.

In addition to its sporting significance, this brilliant attacking game shows a duel between White's attack on the kingside and Black's offensive in the centre and on the queenside.

The inclusion of the a1-rook in the attack via a3 and g3 was of supreme importance.

Even in our era of very deep theoretical preparation, rarely has a game really 'begun' so late. Anand started to play 'on his own' well past move 20, with the rook already situated on g3, while Adams's preparation ended earlier. However, this does not detract from the game's beauty or instructive value.

In the following game, the struggle leaves theoretical lines far earlier than in the previous game, so both sides have to think for themselves from an early stage.

Game 30

Nigel Short – Gata Kamsky

PCA Candidates match (game 6), Linares 1994
Ruy Lopez, Arkhangelsk Variation

1 e4 e5 2 ♘f3 ♘c6 3 ♗b5 a6 4 ♗a4 ♘f6 5 0-0 b5 6 ♗b3 ♗b7 7 ♖e1 *(D)*

White plays in a more direct manner in the centre than in Game 20, where White chose 7 d3, although, as we saw, this line is not exempt from danger. Here White protects the e4-pawn in order to be able to occupy the centre with c3 and d4.

The main alternative, leading to very complex (and much-studied) positions, is 7 c3.

based on the assumption that White cannot take advantage of the weakness thus created. The Arkhangelsk Variation is not used much at present, but these two last possibilities seem to be the most robust.

10...0-0 11 ♘bd2 *(D)*

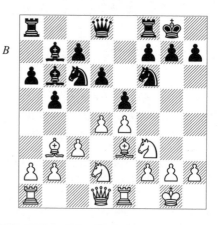

What should Black do now? There are various ideas, such as ...♖e8 to put pressure on the e4-pawn; preparing the ...c5 break also seems reasonable, for which Black must first defend the e5-pawn and then move the c6-knight. There are several options for the c6-knight; instead of the almost automatic ...♘a5, as in other lines of the Ruy Lopez, Black now has access to e7, which is a very tempting location since it can serve as a springboard to g6 and thence to f4 or h4.

However, it should be noted that the distant posting of the b6-bishop has left some kingside dark squares unprotected, and these now require some care; if 11...♘d7?! then 12 ♗g5! ♘e7 13 ♘f1 ♔h8 (planning to chase away the

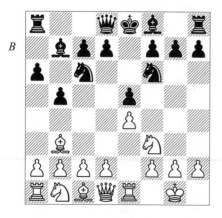

7...♗c5 8 c3 d6 9 d4 ♗b6 10 ♗e3

White once again avoids an early theoretical debate. The main alternative is 10 ♗g5, seeking to take advantage, with the pin, of the absence of the dark-squared bishop from the kingside.

Black can reply 10...h6 11 ♗h4, and then play in many ways, such as castling queenside after 11...♕d7, for which the great specialist in the Arkhangelsk Variation, Alexander Beliavsky, never showed great enthusiasm. Another way is to play 11...0-0, not fearing the pin, and yet another is 11...g5 followed by kingside castling, g5-bishop; after 13...c5?! 14 dxe5!, 14...♘xe5 15 ♘xe5 dxe5 is answered by 16 ♕h5, followed by ♖ad1, with an obvious advantage, while 14...dxe5 15 ♕d6 ♘c8 16 ♕d2 ♕e8 17 ♖ad1 also gives White a clear advantage; in both cases White gains a much more dynamic game) 14 ♘g3 f6 15 ♗e3 c5 and here the unpleasant 16 ♗e6! gave White the advantage in Khalifman-Mikhalchishin, Kuibyshev 1986. Thus Black needs to make a preparatory move.

11...h6

Control of g5 has been shown to be essential to allow Black to manoeuvre.

12 h3 ♘d7 *(D)*

This idea is a deviation from the most common one, which is 12...exd4 13 cxd4 ♘b4, followed by ...c5. There is also 12...♖e8, after which the main line is 13 d5 followed by 14 ♗xb6, when the doubled pawns are not a serious weakness.

Beliavsky devised 12...♖b8 here, with the idea of answering 13 d5 with 13...♗xe3, since now there is no 15 dxc6 and 16 cxb7, hitting the a8-rook.

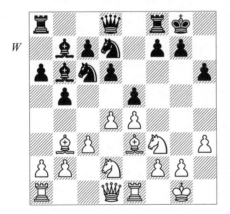

13 a3

White prevents ...♘b4, and seeks to restrain ...c5 by playing b4, while maintaining the Spanish bishop on the a2-g8 diagonal.

It is also possible to continue with the typical knight tour with 13 ♘f1. In Ljubojević-Beliavsky, Reggio Emilia 1991, Black gained reasonable play by carrying out the plan mentioned above with 13...♘e7 14 ♘g3 c5 and after 15 ♖e2 ♕c7 16 ♖d2 ♘f6 17 ♗c2 ♖ad8 18 ♖c1

♘g6 19 a4 ♖fe8 Black had an harmonious game, although 15 ♘h4 seems rather more promising, to attempt to exploit the weakness of f5.

13...♘e7 14 ♗a2 *(D)*

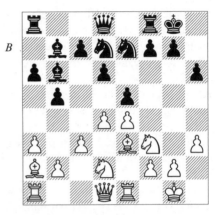

14...♔h8

After half an hour's reflection, Black changes plan and instead of 14...c5, he seeks to take advantage of the possibility of playing ...f5.

It is not clear what Kamsky feared that caused him to reject 14...c5. Fedorowicz, Kamsky's second, disliked 15 dxc5 dxc5 16 c4, when after 16...b4 17 ♗b3 ♘c6 18 ♗a4 the black bishops are restricted and White has the advantage, but there does not seem to be anything seriously wrong with 16...♘g6, followed, for example, by ...♕e7 and ...♖fd8.

15 b4 *(D)*

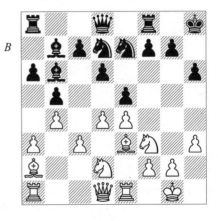

And now? Is it time to play ...f5?

No, not yet; if 15...f5?! then 16 dxe5 ♗xe3 (or 16...dxe5 17 ♘g5!) 17 ♖xe3 and after both 17...dxe5 18 ♗e6 and 17...♘xe5 18 ♘d4 the opening of the centre has handed over some important squares to White.

15...a5!

Setting up tension on the a-file, to create a distraction and prevent White's central domination from being the only important element and to stop White from manoeuvring unhindered.

16 ♕c2?!

White decides to maintain the tension, but this is not the most flexible square for the queen. 16 ♕e2 is better, with one eye on b5 and another on the d1-h5 diagonal, which we have already seen was important for tactical reasons in the 15...f5?! line.

Hübner, who was Short's second, indicated that White could obtain a slight advantage by releasing the central tension with 16 dxe5; his main line continued 16...♗xe3 17 ♖xe3 ♘xe5 (if 17...dxe5, controlling d4, White occupies the queenside with the knight after 18 ♘b3) 18 ♘d4. Weaker are both 16...♘xe5 17 ♗xb6, followed by 18 ♘d4, and 16...dxe5 17 ♗xb6 cxb6 18 ♘f1, when the doubled pawns on the queenside are a definite weakness.

16...axb4 17 axb4 (D)

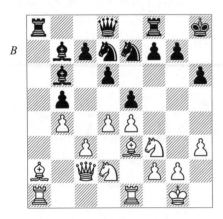

17...f5!

All the preparatory moves have been made and Black can break on f5 without fearing the weakness it creates in his pawn-structure. The next three moves for both sides are almost forced.

18 dxe5 ♗xe3 19 ♖xe3 ♘xe5 20 ♘xe5 dxe5 21 ♖ae1?! (D)

White increases the pressure on e5; however, this pressure is fictitious, since to exploit it White will have to play exf5, which, as we shall see, has serious defects. 21 ♖d1 is interesting, as is 21 ♖ee1, followed by neutralizing the pressure on the a-file with ♗b3.

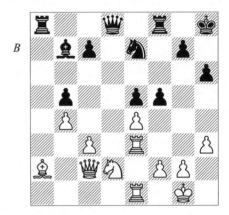

Structurally, White has everything in his favour, but the dynamic assessment is quite different. The a2-bishop is out of play. The white king is rather lacking in protection, but this does not seem important because there are no threatening black pieces, except possibly for the b7-bishop. Which other black piece can come to the kingside?

21...♖a6!

Of course! The rook heads for f6 or g6, and also makes room for ...♕a8 in some lines.

22 exf5?

Consistent, but also the decisive error; White wins a pawn, but his king will come under a hail of fire.

22 ♖d3?! only helps Black, as then 22...♕c8 puts pressure on the h3-pawn.

Bolstering e4 with 22 f3 seems reasonable, but Black is in a position to gain a strong attack by opening the f-file and then seeking to transfer the a6-rook, the e7-knight and his queen to the kingside. There are various ways to attempt this; for example, 22...fxe4 23 ♘xe4 (23 fxe4 is no better in view of 23...♘g6 24 ♘f3 ♕e7, followed by ...♘f4) 23...♘f5 followed by ...♕h4 and ...♖g6. Another interesting idea is

22...♖g6!?; then if 23 ♘b3?! Black plays the strong 23...fxe4 24 fxe4 ♘f5! with advantage, since 25 exf5 fails to 25...♖xg2+ 26 ♕xg2 ♗xg2 27 ♔xg2 ♕a8+ and the a2-bishop drops.

Perhaps 22 ♗b1 is the most solid; this would also be answered by 22...♖g6.

22...♘xf5 (D)

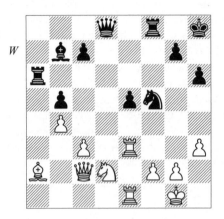

23 ♖xe5

White cannot exploit the b1-h7 diagonal with 23 ♗b1 since Black would close it by 23...e4!, after which the attack continues along familiar lines; for instance, 24 ♖3e2 ♖g6 25 ♘xe4 ♘h4 26 ♘g3 ♗xg2 and, as Hübner indicates, 27 ♕c1 ♖g5 28 ♕c2 fails to the simple 28...g6.

23...♘h4! (D)

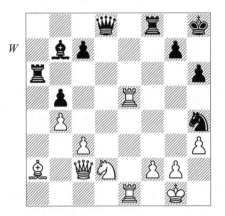

There is no way of coping with the pressure on g2; if 24 ♗b1 then 24...♖g6 25 g3 ♕xd2!, followed by 26...♘f3+, while if 24 f3 then 24...♖g6 and there is no defence.

24 ♘e4 ♖g6 25 ♘g3 ♗xg2

The weaknesses created in White's castled position are irreparable, Black threatens both 26...♗xh3 and 26...♗a8.

26 ♖1e3 (D)

If White plays 26 ♗f7 intending to win the queen with ♖e8, the refutation is 26...♖f6! 27 ♖e8 ♖xe8 28 ♖xe8+ ♕xe8 29 ♗xe8 ♘f3+ 30 ♔xg2 ♘e1+, regaining the queen with a decisive material advantage.

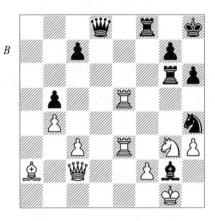

26...♖d6!

Threatening both 27...♖d2 and 27...♖d1+.

This is not the only winning idea; 26...♕a8 was also effective, with the idea of 27...♗h1, but the choice is influenced by practical considerations: Black does not want unnecessary complications.

27 ♗b1 g6 28 ♖h5

If 28 ♔h2 then 28...♖d2 wins easily for Black.

28...♗f3 29 ♖xh6+ ♔g7 30 ♖xh4 ♕xh4

Black already has a material advantage, his king can easily be defended and his pressure continues unabated.

31 ♔h2 ♗g4 32 ♘e4 (D)

32...♗f5!

The knight is the main support of f2 and of the whole position in fact, so Black puts maximum pressure on it, taking advantage of the nuisance caused by the pin against the white queen.

33 ♔g2 ♖e6 34 ♕e2 ♖fe8 35 f3 ♕xh3+

With this capture the task is simplified; Black is easily winning now.

B

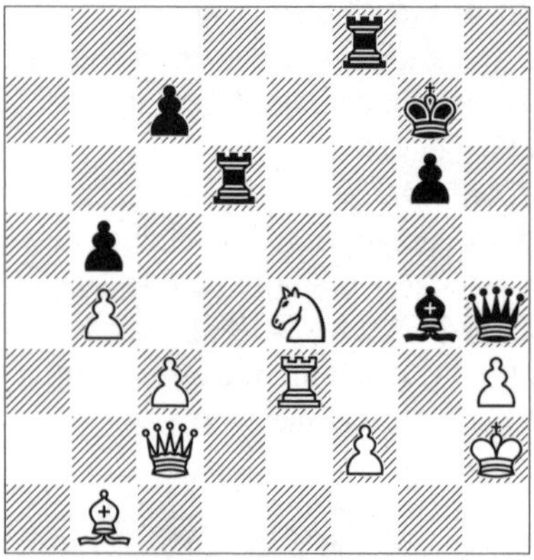

36 ♔g1 ♖h8 37 ♕g2 ♕xg2+ 38 ♔xg2 ♖d8 39 ♔f2 ♖d1 40 ♗d3 c6 41 ♔e2 ♖a1 42 ♔d2 ♖a2+ 43 ♔c1 ♖h2 44 ♖e1 ♖e8 45 ♗c2 ♖eh8 0-1

Helped by the closed character of the game, Black showed great flexibility in finding the best moment to become active with 14...♔h8, 15...a5! and 17...f5!.

In contrast, White failed in this respect with 16 ♕c2?! and especially 22 exf5?, which gave Black the opportunity to launch a whirlwind attack on White's castled position; this move opened the f-file and the long diagonal, improving the b7-bishop and helping the attack on g2, all at the absurdly low price of one pawn.

The manoeuvre to transfer the a8-rook to the kingside, begun with 15...a5! and 21...♖a6!, was not on the agenda from the start, nor was it certain that it could be achieved; it just arose during the struggle. Once again we can state that king safety is the most important element in the evaluation of the struggle.

Game 31
Magnus Carlsen – Teimour Radjabov
Biel 2007

Pirc/Philidor Defence

In the previous game, a rook-lift was employed to very good effect. However, when there are still many pieces on the board that can harass the rook, it is not always appropriate to transfer the major pieces to the centre and kingside via the third or fourth rank. It is essential to calculate the results of such a manoeuvre accurately. If it does not achieve anything concrete, the rook can end up badly placed, but if it is appropriate, then the attacking side will have extra firepower in the combat zone. A well-known example of it succeeding is the 4th game of the 1908 World Championship match between Tarrasch and Lasker. Here is a more modern example, between two rising superstars.

1 e4 d6 2 d4 ♘f6 3 ♘c3 e5 4 ♘ge2

4 ♘f3 transposes to the main line of the Philidor Defence. It is curious that Carlsen commented that he did not feel prepared "for the line 4...♘bd7 5 g4!? without adequate preparation", without considering the usual alternatives to the violent 5 g4.

4...♘bd7 5 g3 c6 *(D)*

W

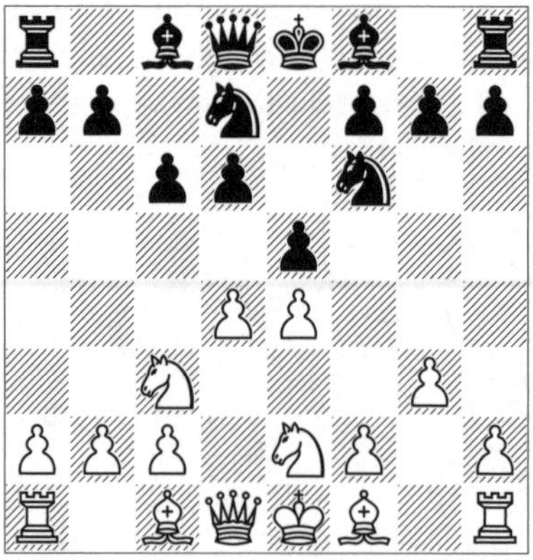

6 ♗g2

The standard move is 6 a4, in order to restrain Black's following expansion. Then Black can prepare to carry out the same advance, only more slowly, with ...b6, ...a6, ...♗b7 and ...b5, depending on circumstances.

6...b5!

Carlsen commented that this advance does not weaken Black's position, and he was not sure whether allowing it was a mistake, although he soon began to feel uncomfortable.

7 a3 ♗e7 8 0-0 0-0 9 h3

Carlsen was taken by surprise in the opening, which does not often happen, and he was already practically on his own, although the position had often been played before. This move is generally played with the idea of ♗e3 and ♕d2, without having to worry about the reply ...♘g4, but here Black will not allow this.

9...a5 (D)

Black plays the most ambitious move, seeking to make progress on the queenside. This seems correct, because Black does not need to worry about the centre or the kingside, and can start activity on 'his' wing. The quieter 9...♗b7 has also been played, but the text-move is sharper.

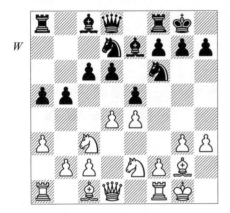

10 g4

The preparation of ...b4 by Black forces Carlsen to play this move, which was not his original idea, but is a common method of giving the e2-knight some mobility. In this case it solves the problem of what to do with the c3-knight in a reasonable manner.

10...♗a6

The move-order employed allows this unusual activity, exerting pressure along the f1-a6 diagonal. 10...♗b7, followed by 11...b4, is also playable.

Now, how should White deal with the unpleasant threat of 11...b4?

11 ♘g3

This is the solution that White had already prepared. There is a more radical way to restrict Black's activity, namely 11 b4 (D).

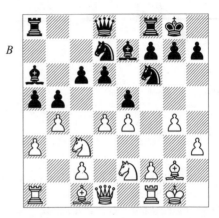

The a6-bishop remains shut in and the black pieces have lost a lot of the dynamism that would have been gained after playing ...b4.

The main drawbacks of playing b4 are that it weakens the c4-square, which is in reach of the d7-knight, and that it provides Black with favourable tension on the queenside since he has already carried out the break ...a5.

Beliavsky-Mokry, European Team Ch, Haifa 1989 continued 11...♗b7 12 ♖b1 axb4 13 axb4 ♘e8 (it is possible for Black to play the immediate 13...♘b6 14 ♘g3 g6 but Black wants to prevent White from playing 15 ♗h6 before he has the reply ...♘g7 available) 14 ♘g3 g6 15 ♗h6 ♘g7 16 ♘ce2 ♘b6 17 f4 exf4 18 ♘xf4 and here Black has the simple 18...♘c4! with a reasonable position after, for instance, 19 ♕c1 ♖e8, keeping ...♗g5 in reserve. Instead, the game continued 18...♗g5?, which is positionally 'correct' but fails tactically: 19 ♗xg5 ♕xg5 20 e5! dxe5 (20...d5 leaves the b7-bishop 'dead') 21 ♘e4 ♕e7 22 dxe5 ♕xe5 (worse are both 22...♖ad8? 23 ♘f6+ ♔h8 24 ♕e1, followed by ♕h4, and 22...♘c4? 23 ♘f6+ ♔h8 24 ♕e1 ♕xe5 25 ♕h4 h5 26 ♖be1, with a mating attack in both cases) and White gained a strong initiative with 23 ♕d6!, when the g7-knight is out of play and the g2-bishop is very strong.

We now return to the position after 11 ♘g3 (D):

11...b4

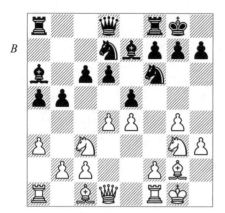

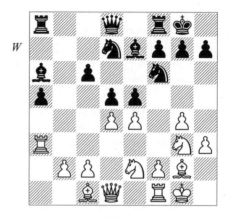

Consistent, but Black's development advantage can be exploited with 11...exd4!, when 12 ♕xd4 leaves the white pieces awkwardly placed and allows 12...b4 13 ♘ce2 bxa3 14 bxa3 (or 14 ♖xa3 d5) 14...♘xg4! 15 hxg4 ♗f6. Perhaps White's best practical chance lies in giving up a pawn by 12 ♘ce2 c5 13 ♘f5, planning ♘eg3 and an eventual g5, as suggested by Notkin in *Chess Today*. In any case, this speculative sacrifice was not Carlsen's original idea, as his annotations made clear.

12 ♘ce2 bxa3?!

Black possibly considered that White was practically forced to recapture with 13 bxa3, after which the white structure loses its solidity.

With 12...d5 Black would have achieved a comfortable game; for example, after 13 exd5 ♘xd5 14 ♖e1 bxa3 the black pieces are active, which is what he was seeking when he played 12...bxa3.

13 ♖xa3!

A surprising reply. White places his rook where it is exposed to a discovered attack by the e7-bishop following ...d5, after which the central tension seems to favour Black, on account of the pin on the e2-knight.

13...d5 *(D)*

What was the idea of 13 ♖xa3?

14 ♖e3!

Carlsen was aware that the rook was exposed, but he calculated correctly that he could solve the problem of harassment by Black's minor pieces, in which case the influence of his rook in the centre will be considerable.

14...dxe4

It is important that 14...exd4?! can be answered with 15 ♘xd4!, when 15...♗xf1? 16 ♘xc6 ♕e8 17 exd5 is winning for White. Increasing the pressure in the centre with 15...♗c5 is not much better, since somewhat surprisingly White has a winning attack after 16 ♘xc6! (as indicated by Notkin) 16...♕b6 17 exd5 ♗xf1 18 ♗xf1 ♗xe3 19 ♗xe3 ♕xb2 20 g5 ♘e8 21 ♗d3 *(D)*.

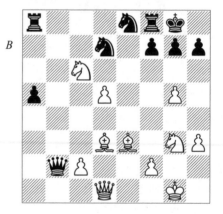

We see here that the development disadvantage that White had a few moves ago has been converted, at the cost of sacrificing two exchanges, into an overwhelming dynamic advantage. How can this be explained?

In addition to being able to force the retreat of the f6-knight to the awkward e8-square, where it obstructs Black's movements (a rather unforeseen consequence of 10 g4), White has managed to exchange one rook that was out of play on a1 for one of Black's agile minor pieces, and his other rook similarly. The result is that now his five pieces are attacking the black king, which cannot be defended with the queen so far away from the struggle, and with his pieces so passive.

It is important that all the aforementioned conditions are fulfilled for White to be successful, since two exchanges constitutes a large investment.

15 ♖e1! *(D)*

The drawback of having the rook in the centre becomes apparent after 15 ♘xe4?! ♘d5, followed by ...exd4. In contrast, now this rook evades the pressure of the a6-bishop and gives strong support to the e3-rook – excellent coordination between his forces.

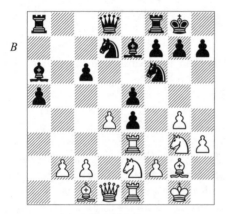

15...♕c7?!

Harassing the e3-rook with 15...♘d5 16 ♖xe4 ♘5f6 17 ♖e3 achieves nothing, as now 17...♘d5 is answered with 18 ♗xd5 and 19 dxe5.

15...♗xe2 16 ♖3xe2! exd4 17 ♕xd4 is not satisfactory either, since White's pieces escape the pressure and he has two very strong bishops and active pieces.

After 15...h6 White shows another of the virtues of the centralized rook with 16 ♘f5 ♖e8 17 ♖g3, when the combinations on h6 or the break g5 are clearly very dangerous.

The best move is the prophylactic 15...♖e8!, with only a slight advantage to White, although it is clear that White has emerged successfully from the duel following 13 ♖xa3, when the rook could best be described as somewhere between suicidal and active.

16 ♘f5 ♗d8?

A very surprising move; Black discoordinates his pieces. The natural 16...♖fe8 is better, vacating f8 for the e7-bishop, although is true that White is already substantially better.

17 g5 ♘d5 18 ♖xe4 *(D)*

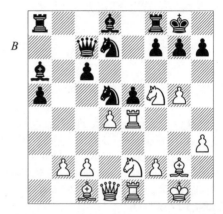

18...f6

The increased tension in the centre and kingside naturally favours White. "It did not make much sense to me to open the position when White is so much better prepared for it" as Carlsen commented, although he admitted that not he could not see a satisfactory continuation for Black.

The pressure on e5 will be intolerable, and taking on d4 just brings more difficulties for the black king. After 18...exd4? 19 ♕xd4 f6 20 ♘f4 ♘xf4 21 ♗xf4, followed by ♗d6, White wins precisely because of his control of the e-file.

19 ♘eg3

Giving support to the f5-knight and clearing the e-file; the shot ♘xg7 is now in the air.

19...g6

19...fxg5 is more tenacious, although after 20 dxe5 the passed pawn is a new source of worry for Black.

20 ♘h6+ ♔g7 *(D)*

The lack of coordination among the black pieces and the concentration of absolutely all the white forces against Black's castled position indicate that the end is near.

21 dxe5

Opening the position. There was more than one effective way to attack here; an alternative

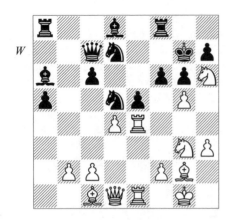

path, pointed out by Kavalek, is 21 gxf6+ ♘5xf6 22 ♖4e3 with tremendous pressure on e5, after which 22...exd4 23 ♕xd4 is hopeless for Black, and 22...♔xh6? leads to mate after 23 ♘f5+!! gxf5 24 ♖g3+ f4 25 ♖xe5 ♘xe5 26 ♗xf4#.

21...fxg5 22 e6! *(D)*

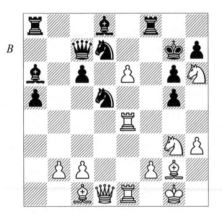

The pawn clears the way for the other forces. There is no need to retreat the knight from h6.

22...♔xh6 *(D)*

If the d7-knight moves, the accumulation of White's forces crystallizes with the combination of several tactical ideas, especially the double attack and the pin, after 22...♘7f6 23 e7! ♗xe7 24 ♖xe7+! ♘xe7 25 ♖xe7+ ♕xe7 26 ♘hf5+.

Something similar occurs after 22...♘7b6, when White wins with, among other things (such as the simple 23 ♘f7) 23 e7! ♗xe7 24 ♖xe7+! ♘xe7 25 ♕d4+ ♖f6 (or 25...♔xh6 26 h4 and there is no defence) 26 ♖xe7+! ♕xe7 27

♘hf5+! gxf5 28 ♘xf5+ ♔f7 29 ♘xe7 ♔xe7 30 ♗xg5.

Carlsen indicated that the computer thinks 22...♕a7 is the most tenacious, but Black's position is equally desperate after 23 ♘f7 or 23 ♕d2.

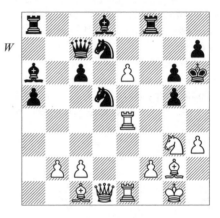

Is there anything stronger than regaining the piece with 23 exd7?

23 e7!

The pawn acts as a battering-ram, sacrificing itself to make way for its followers.

23...♕b6

If 23...♖e8 White wins easily with 24 exd8♕ ♖exd8 25 ♕d4!, cutting off the king's retreat to g7, with the unstoppable threat of 26 ♖h4#, while after 23...♗xe7 24 ♖xe7 ♘xe7 25 ♖xe7 ♖ad8 26 ♕d4, there is no defence against the threats of mate on g7 and h4.

24 exf8♕+ ♘xf8 *(D)*

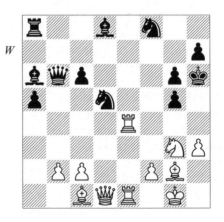

25 c4

Evicting the centralized knight, after which White gains access to more squares.

With the advantage of the exchange and an attack it is logical that there should be several ways to win, such as the incursion 25 ♖e8. Kavalek indicated another one: 25 ♖e6! (threatening 26 ♘f5#) 25...♘xe6 26 ♖xe6 ♘f6 (if 26...♔g7 then 27 ♗xd5 wins) and now the king is drawn out with 27 ♗xg5+! ♔xg5 (or 27...♔g7 28 ♖xf6 ♗xf6 29 ♕d7+ ♔g8 30 ♕e6+) 28 ♕d2+ and mate.

25...♘f4 (D)

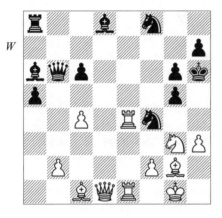

What is the quickest way for White to finish the game?

26 ♕d6!

Of course – this why the knight was expelled from d5. Now there is a double threat of 27 ♕xf8# and 27 ♘f5+ ♔h5 28 ♕d1+, mating.

26...♔g7 27 ♗xf4 gxf4 (D)

28 ♖e7+ 1-0

Black resigned in view of the mate that ensues after 28...♗xe7 29 ♖xe7+ ♔g8 30 ♕f6.

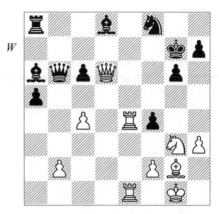

Black achieved a promising position after the opening, with a quick deployment on the queenside, and unpleasant pressure on the f1-a6 diagonal. White had to play in very committal fashion with 10 g4 and 11 ♘g3, which is a rather inflexible but not necessarily bad deployment, and in the event of White emerging from Black's initiative unharmed, it could even help a future attack against the enemy king.

Playing with White allows you to take certain liberties without necessarily being punished. Perhaps as a result of excessive optimism, Black overlooked the manoeuvre 13 ♖xa3! and 14 ♖e3!. This required precise calculation on White's part, as the rook was left in an awkward position. After another strong move, 15 ♖e1!, nullifying the pressure of the a6-bishop and gaining greater control of the e-file, Black's position deteriorated with surprising speed.

After some errors or inaccuracies in succession (including 15...♕c7?! and 16...♗d8?) White showed that his pieces were much better coordinated and he won brilliantly.

The Pawn-Centre

In Chapter 5 we saw a piece set-up, the 'Horwitz Bishops', which facilitated the attack on the kingside. In the following games we shall see that a strong pawn-centre can play a similar role. However, as was the case with Horwitz Bishops, on its own, a strong pawn-centre is not enough to guarantee a successful attack; instead we have a struggle in which each side tries to make his trumps count.

The best-known example of the triumph of the attack based on a central pawn-majority is surely Botvinnik-Capablanca, Rotterdam (AVRO) 1938. Because of its extreme thematic importance, I shall quote this famous game, but without notes.

Mikhail Botvinnik – Jose Capablanca
Rotterdam (AVRO) 1938

1 d4 ♘f6 2 c4 e6 3 ♘c3 ♗b4 4 e3 d5 5 a3
♗xc3+ 6 bxc3 c5 7 cxd5 exd5 8 ♗d3 0-0 9
♘e2 b6 10 0-0 ♗a6 11 ♗xa6 ♘xa6 12 ♗b2
♕d7 13 a4 ♖fe8 14 ♕d3 c4 15 ♕c2 ♘b8 16
♖ae1 ♘c6 17 ♘g3 ♘a5 *(D)*

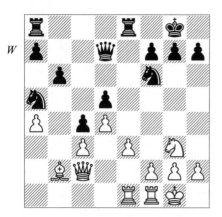

18 f3 ♘b3 19 e4 ♕xa4 20 e5 ♘d7 21 ♕f2
g6 22 f4 f5 23 exf6 ♘xf6 24 f5 ♖xe1 25 ♖xe1
♖e8 26 ♖e6 ♖xe6 27 fxe6 ♔g7 28 ♕f4 ♕e8 29
♕e5 ♕e7 *(D)*

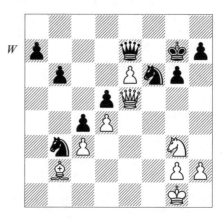

30 ♗a3 ♕xa3 31 ♘h5+ gxh5 32 ♕g5+ ♔f8
33 ♕xf6+ ♔g8 34 e7 ♕c1+ 35 ♔f2 ♕c2+ 36
♔g3 ♕d3+ 37 ♔h4 ♕e4+ 38 ♔xh5 ♕e2+ 39
♔h4 ♕e4+ 40 g4 ♕e1+ 41 ♔h5 1-0

The triumphs of the side fighting against the central majority are generally less spectacular; perhaps one of the most elegant was Ståhlberg-Keres, Bad Nauheim 1936, although in that game White soon decided to change the structure.

Game 32
Miguel Najdorf – Mikhail Botvinnik
Staunton Memorial, Groningen 1946
Nimzo-Indian Defence, 4 ♕c2

In this well-known but very instructive game, the structure we are studying was reached in a rather unexpected way. Both sides had various alternative plans available, but by mutual consent they arrived at a position displaying many typical features, where a large part of the struggle revolved round the e4-square. White made better use of his resources, despite not having played the opening in the best manner.

1 d4 ♘f6 2 c4 e6 3 ♘c3 ♗b4 4 ♕c2 d5 5 cxd5 exd5 *(D)*

6 a3

The strongest move here is considered to be 6 ♗g5, which Najdorf himself had played earlier.

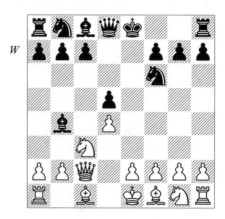

However, the player of the white pieces was aware that he should leave the beaten track as soon as a reasonable alternative presented itself, in order to be able to fight on an equal footing, since there was a significant difference in knowledge and preparation of the openings between the two players.

For a celebrated example of 6 ♗g5, see Supplementary Game 32.1, Keres-Botvinnik, Leningrad/Moscow 1941.

6...♗xc3+

Retreating the bishop just presents White with the extra move a3, which is not a weakness and can prove useful, e.g. for starting the minority attack with b4, with no further preparation required.

7 bxc3 c5

Hitting the centre and making way for the queen to harass the white pawns.

8 ♘f3 ♕a5 9 ♘d2 *(D)*

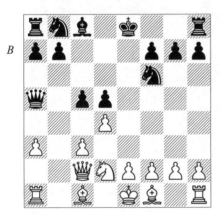

To be able to answer ...cxd4 with cxd4, keeping his structure healthy, although of course at the cost of moving an already-developed piece again. Najdorf was so pleased with his position and of his success in having "taken Botvinnik out of the books" that he got up from the board and in his typically bubbly fashion told anyone who would listen that he had a winning position. He knew that this was not true, but truth mattered little to him in this situation; in reality it was just his way of psyching himself up.

9...♗d7

As Kasparov indicated, there is a certain similarity here with the Winawer French, which was one of Botvinnik's defensive weapons for several decades. Black plans ...♗a4 blockading the queenside.

9...0-0 is also playable, not fearing 10 ♘b3 ♕a4 11 dxc5 since Black will regain the pawn with a good game after, for example, 11...♘a6.

Another idea was to retreat from the possible attack by ♘b3 with 9...♕c7, threatening ...cxd4, and after 10 ♕b1 0-0 11 e3, to prepare the exchange of the annoying white bishop with 11...b6 followed by ...♗a6.

10 ♘b3 *(D)*

Another move by a developed piece, but this time without loss of time. White did not like 10 e3 on account of 10...♗a4 followed by ...♘bd7, ...0-0 and ...♖fc8, when harmony reigns among the black forces.

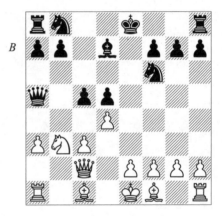

10...♕a4 11 ♕b2 ♘a6

This is not the most active position for the knight, but it is another developing move, and Black's advantage in this department is already considerable.

12 e3 *(D)*

White threatens 13 ♗xa6 followed by 14 ♘xc5. How should Black defend?

12...c4

This advance came in for a lot of criticism, since after closing the position all his development advantage disappears.

Perhaps it did not suit Black, who needed a win in this game to make sure of first place in the tournament, to reach a good but simplified position with the most natural move 12...cxd4. After 13 cxd4 (if 13 ♘xd4 then 13...♘c5, followed

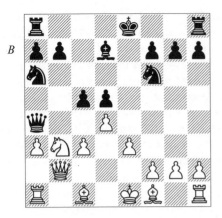

by ...0-0 and ...♖fc8, with good play) 13...0-0 14 ♗d3 ♖fc8, the idea of offering the exchange of bishops by ...♗b5 gives Black good play.

13 ♘d2 0-0 14 ♗e2 (D)

White cannot develop his bishop on d3, but Black's bishop has also lost a large part of its mobility.

Not, of course, 14 ♕xb7?? due to 14...♖fb8.

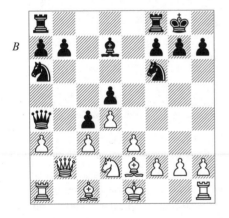

14...b5?

This ambitious idea of eventually advancing on the queenside with ...a5 and ...b4 is a more serious error. White will have more freedom to play in the centre and on the kingside, while Black will not be able to complete his plans on the queenside.

It was better to leave the b5-square vacant and play, as Kasparov indicates, 14...♘c7, with the idea of 15...♘b5. Then if 15 ♗d1 ♕a5 16 a4, Black plays 16...♗f5!, activating his bishop. After 17 0-0 ♗d3 18 ♖e1 ♖fe8 the game remains

complicated. White can try to make progress in the centre and on the kingside, but Black's pieces are well placed for a fight in that area. If we compare this position with the course of the game, having his bishop on d3 is a clear improvement for Black.

14...♗f5! is also attractive, preventing the following regrouping.

15 ♗d1!

There is no risk in delaying castling; it is much more important to prevent the d7-bishop from becoming entrenched in White's camp. If 15 0-0?! then 15...♗f5!.

15...♕a5 16 ♗c2!

Now ...♗f5 is ruled out, and the bishop starts to gaze, timidly for now, towards the kingside.

16...♖fe8 17 0-0 ♖ab8 (D)

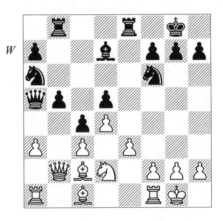

As Botvinnik himself showed on many occasions, the white structure 'yearns' to advance with f3 and e4. Thus one naturally considers 18 f3, or possibly 18 ♖e1 followed by f3.

For years it was thought that 18 f3 was not playable immediately owing to 18...♖xe3 19 ♘e4 (not 19 ♘xc4? because of 19...bxc4, hitting the queen) 19...♘xe4 20 ♗xe3 ♘xc3 and now the line continued 21 ♗d2(?) ♘e2+ 22 ♔h1 c3!. But instead, White can gain the advantage with 21 ♖fe1!, since although Black is well off materially, the majority of his pieces are badly situated.

Kasparov indicated that after 18 f3, 18...♗c6 is better, preventing e4, and we then have the typical struggle around the e4 advance following 19 ♖e1 ♖e6 20 ♘f1, and later ♘g3 and ♗d2.

Thus both 18 ♖e1 and 18 f3 are satisfactory. Najdorf found a third, equally good, possibility.

18 ♘f3!?

Instead of playing the knight to f1 and g3, White wants to take advantage of the fact that Black does not control the e5-square, so he postpones for a few moves the plan of breaking with e4.

18...♕c7 19 ♘e5 ♗e6

Black could try 19...♘c5, reasoning that White will not want to exchange his strong e5-knight for the passive d7-bishop. However, Tarrasch's rule "it's not what leaves the board that's important, it's what stays on" remains valid. The important factor is then White's bishop-pair, which grows in strength after 20 ♘xd7! ♘cxd7 21 f3, and later e4, even if this requires the sacrifice of a pawn.

20 f3! *(D)*

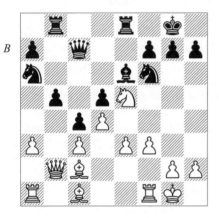

Now this, since there are no longer any alternatives.

20...♘c5 21 ♗d2 ♘a4

As in the French Defence, the a4-knight puts pressure on c3 and blockades White's game; however, the knight is also straying out of play.

There are strong arguments in favour of 21...♘cd7, to eliminate the strong e5-knight, but it is not clear whether this is an improvement. After 22 ♘xd7 ♗xd7, White's dark-squared bishop becomes very active with 23 ♗e1 followed by ♗g3 and ♗e5, after which White carries on with the preparation of e4. Kasparov proposes another idea for White, worth considering in this and similar positions: after 23

♖ae1 ♕b7 24 ♖e2 ♖e6, since it is not easy to play e4 without giving up material, the other idea is 25 g4!?, making progress on the kingside. For the time being the white centre serves to restrain any central counter-blow, without ruling out its advance in the future, if he can manage to distract Black's forces. Opening the game with 23 e4!? should also be considered; White has strong pressure after 23...dxe4 24 fxe4 ♘xe4 25 ♗f4 ♘d6 26 ♕b4, followed by ♖ae1, as Kasparov indicated.

22 ♕b1!

The queen retreats to the most annoying square, where it prevents 22...♘d7 through its pressure on h7.

22...♖b6 *(D)*

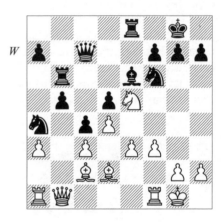

And now? How should White make progress?

The most straightforward is 23 e4, which is a good move, but White prefers to improve his pieces first, keeping the b1-h7 diagonal open for now.

23 ♕e1!

Heading for h4, after which the pressure on the kingside will increase considerably.

23...♘d7 24 ♕h4 ♘f8

Black has beaten off the first offensive and gets ready to expel the e5-knight.

25 e4 *(D)*

All according to the blueprint of Botvinnik-Capablanca. There is no longer any reason to postpone the central break. White plans in the future to play e5 and then f4-f5.

25...f6

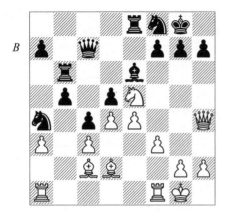

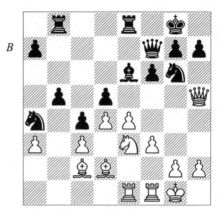

The e5-knight has to retreat, but it will not be inactive; it will head for e3, where it will increase the pressure on d5.

26 ♘g4 ♘g6 27 ♕h5 ♕f7 *(D)*

Against the threat of 28 exd5, Kasparov found some interesting tactical resources. After 27...♗f7!?, according to his analysis White has a strong attack after 28 e5! ♘f8 29 ♕h4 h5 30 exf6!, but of course the position is very sharp, and precise calculation is essential.

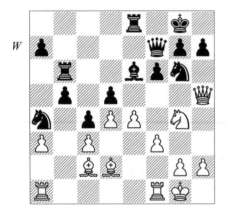

28 ♖ae1

The last piece comes into play, threatening to win a pawn with 29 exd5, since after 29...♗xd5? 30 ♖xe8+, the black queen is overloaded and cannot defend both the bishop and the e8-rook.

28...♖bb8 29 ♘e3 *(D)*

What is the best defence against the threat of 30 exd5?

29...♖bd8? fails to 30 exd5 ♗xd5 31 ♘xd5 ♖xe1, and here the *zwischenzug* 32 ♘xf6+ wins.

29...♘f4 does not work either, since Black has no answer to the white centre supported by the bishop-pair: after 30 ♕xf7+ ♔xf7 31 ♘xc4! ♘xg2 32 ♔xg2 dxc4, Fine indicated 33 ♖b1, while Kasparov preferred 33 ♗f4 ♖b7 34 ♖e3 with an equally favourable evaluation.

29...♘e7?

This was considered to be the final error. Black guards the d5-square and seeks simplification, which would eliminate his king's problems.

With a similar idea, it is better to recycle the inactive a4-knight with 29...♘b6!. Kasparov indicates that White still has a clear advantage after 30 ♘f5! ♖bd8 31 ♕g4 ♕d7 32 ♕g3. However, 29...♘b6 gives Black good practical chances of successful defence, since White can easily stray from the correct path, such as with the natural but premature 30 f4?!, when Black has 30...♘e7!. Now if White retreats with 31 ♕h4, Black can play 31...dxe4 32 ♗xe4 f5! and White's bishop-pair, in particular the dark-squared one, has been neutralized, while the endgame after 31 ♕xf7+ ♗xf7 32 e5 fxe5 33 dxe5 ♘c6 is unclear. Black has several ideas, such as playing ...d4, attacking the c3-pawn with ...♘a4, and mobilizing his majority with ...a5, etc.

30 ♕h4 f5 *(D)*

If 30...♘g6 then 31 ♕g3, with the additional idea of attacking with h4-h5.

31 g4!

A decisive blow, after which White succeeds in opening up the defences of the black king.

31...f4?!

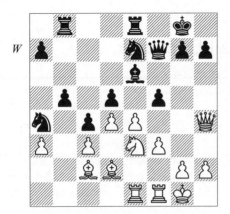

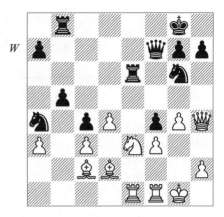

Against the more prudent 31...g6 32 gxf5 gxf5 White can win a pawn with 33 exf5 ♘xf5 (or 33...♗xf5 34 ♗xf5 ♘xf5 35 ♕g5+ ♘g7 36 ♘xd5) 34 ♗xf5 ♗xf5 35 ♕g5+ ♘g6 36 ♘xd5. Nevertheless, most probably White, in the spirit of the game, would have chosen 33 ♔h1!, using the g-file as a new avenue of attack.

32 exd5! *(D)*

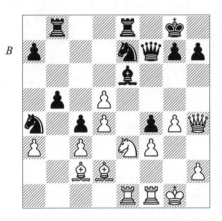

Winning material, since now h7 and the e6-bishop are both attacked.

32...♘g6

32...fxe3 is hopeless after, for example, 33 ♕xh7+ ♔f8 34 dxe6 ♕xe6 35 ♖xe3.

33 dxe6 ♖xe6 *(D)*

A piece down, Black could resign here, but given the tremendous competitive importance of this last-round game, Botvinnik played on, in case Najdorf committed some serious error in time-pressure, but once the time-control was reached he resigned.

34 ♗xg6 hxg6 35 ♘g2 ♖be8 36 ♖xe6 ♖xe6 37 ♘xf4 ♖f6 38 ♕g5 ♘xc3 39 ♗xc3 ♖xf4 40 ♔g2 1-0

In the end this defeat did not prevent Botvinnik from winning the tournament, half a point ahead of his pursuer Euwe, who was also beaten in the last round, by Kotov.

The clash of ideas resulted in a complete triumph for White. After an uncertain start by White, some questionable decisions by Black (12...c4 and especially 14...b5?) allowed White to gain the advantage with some strong preparatory moves, such as 15 ♗d1! followed by ♗c2, improving the bishop.

White then continued to prepare the thematic break e4 with 20 f3!, after rejecting 18 f3 in favour of 18 ♘f3!?, aiming for e5; this was an unusual decision, but in line with the slightly untypical character of the position, since neither black knight was controlling e5, and furthermore the white knight rarely has this possibility, since it is almost always placed on e2, rather than d2.

Another important point was the transfer of the white queen to the kingside with 22 ♕b1!, 23 ♕e1! and then ♕h4, with which the attack now took on a definite shape and crystallized with the blow 31 g4!.

We should note the possibility suggested by Kasparov in the comments to Black's 21st move, which is to play the advance 25 g4!? since e4 was not easy to accomplish.

Now we will take a brief look at the famous game mentioned in the note to White's 6th move.

Supplementary Game 32.1
Paul Keres – Mikhail Botvinnik
Leningrad/Moscow 1941
Nimzo-Indian Defence, 4 ♕c2

1 d4 ♘f6 2 c4 e6 3 ♘c3 ♗b4 4 ♕c2 d5 5 cxd5 exd5 6 ♗g5 h6 7 ♗h4 c5 8 0-0-0? *(D)*

The correct move here is 8 dxc5!, suggested at the time by Najdorf, and successfully employed many years later by Kasparov among others.

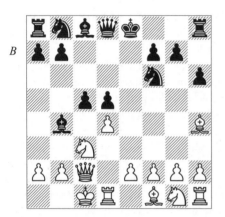

Mikenas had beaten Botvinnik with the ambitious idea of castling queenside in the previous year's USSR Championship. Botvinnik had responded in 'normal' fashion with 8...0-0?! but after 9 dxc5 ♗xc3 10 ♕xc3 g5 11 ♗g3 ♘e4 12 ♕a3 ♗e6 13 f3 ♘xg3 14 hxg3 ♕f6 15 e3 ♖c8 16 ♔b1 ♘d7 17 ♘e2 ♖xc5 18 ♘d4 a6 19 ♗b5! ♖ac8 20 ♗xd7 ♗xd7 21 g4 ♕g6+ 22 ♔a1 White had a clear advantage thanks to his strong d4-knight (much superior to Black's 'bad' bishop), the open h-file, etc., although the game was decided in a queen ending.

Of course Botvinnik analysed the cause of his defeat afterwards, although amazingly Ragozin informed him that the two of them had already analysed and refuted the dubious idea of queenside castling in 1936.

Despite Mikenas's success, the idea is suspect. The kingside is undeveloped and the white king is several tempi away from safety; the c-file is clearly a bad location for the king, but b1

is not at all satisfactory either, since it is vulnerable along the b1-h7 diagonal.

The problem is putting theory into practice, i.e. it is not enough to have a correct idea; relevant calculation is essential to find the best move-order and the appropriate moves.

8...♗xc3!

"The white knight on c3 is the enemy No. 1. It has to be destroyed in order to secure the centre, and also to open up the c-file" – Botvinnik.

9 ♕xc3 g5! *(D)*

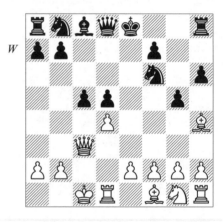

The f6-knight is supporting the centre, and Black discovered that this weakening was not serious, since White cannot exploit it.

10 ♗g3 cxd4!

The third move of the plan; the c-file must be opened. In Belavenets-Simagin, Moscow 1940, 10...♘e4 was played, which does not fit in with the plan of speeding up the attack on the white king before White's kingside is developed.

11 ♕xd4 ♘c6 12 ♕a4 ♗f5

Controlling the b1-h7 diagonal and cutting off the king's retreat.

13 e3 ♖c8 14 ♗d3?! *(D)*

Keres did not find the best defence, which is to plug the c-file with 14 ♘e2! followed by ♘c3 if appropriate.

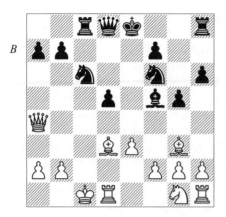

Is there anything better than 14...0-0, unpinning and completing development?

14...豐d7!

Yes, this method of unpinning is much better. Now the threat is a deadly discovered check, and the black queen comes suddenly into play. There is no defence now.

15 當b1 ♗xd3+ 16 罝xd3 豐f5

This forces White to give up material.

17 e4 ♘xe4 18 當a1 0-0!

Not 18...♘c5?! on account of 19 罝e3+.

19 罝d1 b5!

Giving White no respite; all Black's queenside pieces pounce on the weak white king, while White's kingside pieces are no more than distant onlookers.

20 豐xb5 ♘d4 21 豐d3 ♘c2+ 22 當b1 ♘b4 0-1

Game 33

Garry Kasparov – Judit Polgar

Tilburg 1997

Nimzo-Indian Defence, 4 e3

In this game, the structure that we are examining was reached straight from the opening, although, given Black's early 8...c4, it very soon lost its 'normality' and White had to play in a slightly different way from the standard.

1 c4 e6 2 ♘c3 d5 3 d4 ♗b4 4 e3 c5 5 a3 ♗xc3+ 6 bxc3 ♘f6 7 cxd5 exd5 8 f3 c4

Black prevents White's 'normal' piece development of ♗d3 and ♘e2, which is very dangerous and has given White some spectacular triumphs, such as the classical model game Botvinnik-Capablanca, Rotterdam (AVRO) 1938 that I previously quoted.

This early release of the tension inconveniences White, who is now unable to develop harmoniously. However, as we saw in the previous game, it is not all good news for Black, since she gives up the pressure on d4 and relinquishes the eventual opening of the c-file. Thus Black's counterplay is also restricted.

9 ♘e2 ♘c6 (D)

How should White develop his kingside? It is essential to castle, but first White has to decide where to put the f1-bishop and perhaps also the e2-knight.

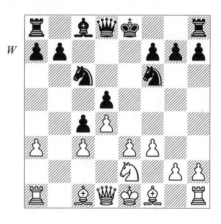

10 g4!

White's aim, as well as breaking with e4, is to play on the kingside. The move-order in the game allows White to gain space on that wing with this advance, instead of playing more modestly with ♘g3 or ♘f4, followed by ♗e2.

We shall recall that this advance was suggested by Kasparov in the note to Black's 21st move in the previous game, when White had problems in playing e4. Here the motivation is different: to proceed with his development, but the idea of preparing an offensive on the king-side is equally valid.

How should Black play now? Restrain g5, or not?

10...h6?

A very significant decision. Black secures the position of the f6-knight, but at the cost of granting White a contact-point on g5. The disadvantage outweighs the advantage; it is much more serious to grant a contact-point on the kingside than to prevent the eventual eviction of the f6-knight. Furthermore, it is not clear that this is even an imminent threat, since a premature g5 on White's part would lose control of some squares and could weaken his structure.

It is better to continue making useful moves; the natural 10...0-0 is playable, but the most flexible idea is to make use of one of the benefits of having played ...c4, which is that it controls the b3-square. Hence Black should first play the 'essential' move 10...♘a5, followed by 11...♘b3, when the knight hinders White's manoeuvres and, if necessary, can be exchanged at an appropriate moment for the c1-bishop, which solidly defends the e3-pawn, and which will increase in strength if White opens the c1-h6 diagonal with e4.

11 ♗g2 (D)

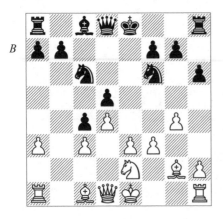

This was the main idea of the g4 advance; on g2 the bishop does not get in the way of White's other pieces.

11...♘a5 12 0-0 ♘b3 13 ♖a2

Naturally the rook heads for the centre and kingside, taking advantage of the fact that the

second rank will be cleared; this manoeuvre is typical of this type of position.

13...0-0

Was queenside castling a safer alternative?

After 13...♕c7 (D), with the idea of developing the c8-bishop and then castling queenside, White must act quickly. If Black manages to carry out this idea unhindered, his king will be relatively safe and his position will noticeably improve; how can White impede this?

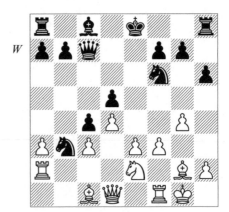

The reply is in part simple: try to break on e4. Black must then either exchange on e4, opening the f-file for White, after which f7 is under pressure, or else allow the advance e5, which is not pleasant for Black.

There are difficulties, however. The g4-pawn is attacked, but this did not seem important to Kasparov, who suggested 14 ♕e1 ♗d7, and here 15 e4 carries the threat of ♗f4 and the b3-knight is badly placed, with all the dark squares under White's control. Thus 15...♘xc1 16 ♕xc1 is forced, and then if Black accepts the sacrifice with 16...dxe4 17 fxe4 ♘xg4, White can play 18 e5, defending h2 and threatening 19 h3, when Black's position becomes critical.

Simply defending the g4-pawn with 14 h3 also seems strong, with a similar idea but without giving up any pawns.

We now return to 13...0-0 (D):

14 ♘g3

'Normal' moves are running out. Before taking any decisions it is essential to place all the pieces on their ideal squares. In this case there is no doubt that the knight has to support the e4

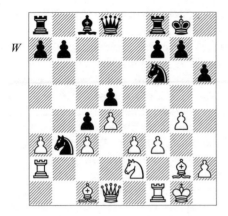

break, as well as 'eyeing up' the squares f5 and h5.

14...♗d7 15 ♕e1

Preparing e4 is the priority, but this move, already mentioned earlier by Kasparov, might appear strange. It is not the first move that comes to mind for preparing e4, but it is not easy to find the ideal way to play e4 without making any concession.

The king's rook clearly has to remain on the f-file in case it opens. The manoeuvre ♖a2-e2 seems the most logical, but then another preparatory move would be required, namely h3, to defend the g4-pawn.

It is not clear now whether 15 h3, defending g4, is a good idea, since Black can reply with the unpleasant 15...♕c7!, when 16 ♕e1? loses a piece to 16...♘xc1, while the self-pin 16 ♔h2? is inherently dubious and all the more so after the reply 16...h5!.

15...♖e8 (D)

So, what was the idea of 15 ♕e1? White could still prepare e4 with the modest 16 h3 but then Black could still play the unpleasant 16...♕c7.

16 e4!

We already know that a pawn is an acceptable price to pay to get a pawn-centre moving, since capturing it would create a very strong mobile pawn-roller on e4 and d4.

Incidentally, here we can clearly see one of the drawbacks of 8...c4; White's d4-pawn is solidly defended, which gives him more possibilities.

16...dxe4 17 fxe4 ♘xg4

Eliminating the c1-bishop with 17...♘xc1 18 ♕xc1 (D) and then taking on g4 is the main alternative, but it is not clear whether this is an improvement.

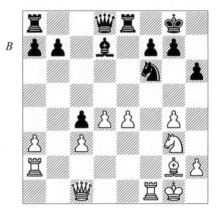

Let us look at 18...♗xg4 for instance, to which White would reply 19 ♖af2, threatening e5 and concentrating many more forces than Black on the kingside. This means that after 19...♖e7 White could destroy Black's castled position with 20 ♖xf6! gxf6 21 ♕xh6 ♕f8 22 ♕h4 ♕g7, and here both 23 h3 and 23 ♖f4, followed by 24 ♘h5, are winning.

18...♘xg4 prevents the a2-rook from coming into play, at least for the moment, but the queen is no less dangerous than the a2-rook, and after 19 ♕f4! White is threatening to capture on f7, to which there is no good defence. The passive 19...♖f8 is answered by 20 e5, threatening 21 h3, and if then 20...♕g5 the g4-knight is almost lost after 21 ♖e2, not forgetting that the b7-pawn is always hanging once White has played e5. No better are 19...♗e6 20 h3 ♘f6 21 d5 and 19...♕f6 20 ♕xf6 ♘xf6 21 e5 ♘g4 22 ♗xb7 ♖ab8 23 ♗e4!, and once again the g4-knight is in danger; as well as having recovered the pawn White has a powerful centre and a central passed pawn.

18 ♗f4

This bishop does not have an opponent, and the b3-knight might be unable to get back to the main combat zone.

18...♕h4

Black remembers that White's castled position has also been weakened, and in theory the pin on the g3-knight hinders White's progress, since exchanging queens when a pawn down is not ideal for White.

19 h3 ♘f6 (D)

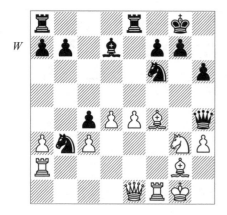

Now the h3-pawn is attacked. It is essential to combine attack and defence; advancing with e5 would unmask the g2-bishop, but the e5-pawn would not actually be threatening to take the f6-knight. So how should White continue?

20 e5!

Kasparov makes the most consistent move, increasing the tension on the kingside, which is to White's benefit, since he has more forces in that sector. Of course, as always in complex positions, the tactical element is of overriding importance, and this advance is backed up by precise calculation.

Defending the pawn with 20 ♔h2 is excessively cautious, as it allows Black to strengthen her position with, for example, 20...♗c6, when

21 e5? is inadvisable in view of 21...♘d5, while 21 d5? fails to 21...♗xd5.

20 ♗e5 also comes into consideration, when 20...♗xh3? is not good in view of 21 ♗xh3 ♕xh3 22 ♗xf6 gxf6, and now the strongest move is 23 ♖f4!, preventing ...♕g4, and with the idea of 24 ♖h2, when the black king's position will be indefensible. It is possible to try to hold the attack with 20...♗e6, but Kasparov suggests immediately frustrating White's attack with the sacrifice 20...♖xe5! 21 dxe5 ♘h5, when for a minimal material investment White's dangerous pawn-centre and strong g2-bishop are neutralized. With a similar idea, 20...♘h5 could be considered, and after 21 ♘xh5 ♕xh5 22 ♕g3 Black can make the same exchange sacrifice 22...♖xe5!?, with similar results.

We now return to 20 e5! (D):

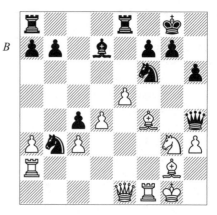

20...♖ad8

Black replies with a developing move which does not create any immediate threat and allows White to continue making progress.

In the first place 20...♗xh3 had to be considered, but Black has serious problems after the simple 21 ♗xh3 ♕xh3 22 ♖h2. Here Kasparov indicates various possibilities; let us see a sample: 22...♕g4 23 ♗xh6! ♘xd4 (if 23...♘d5 Black's castled position is demolished with 24 ♗xg7! ♔xg7 {24...♕xg7 is met by the same reply} 25 ♔h1 ♖h8 {or 25...♖g8 26 ♘f5+ ♔f8 27 ♘h6 ♕g3 28 ♘xg8} 26 ♘f5+ ♔g6 27 ♘h4+ followed by 28 ♖g1) 24 cxd4 ♕xd4+ 25 ♗e3 ♕xe5 26 ♘f5 (Black has four pawns for the piece, but his king has very few defenders and is hounded by too many attacking pieces) 26...♘g4 27 ♖h3 (threatening 28 ♕h4) 27...g6 28 ♗d4! ♕xd4+ 29 ♘xd4 ♖xe1 30 ♖xe1 and White wins.

If 20...♗c6, controlling the d5-square, White can highlight its downside, which is that it abandons the f5-square, with 21 ♕d1!, escaping from the two pins and thus threatening both 22 exf6 as well as invasion with 22 ♘f5. After 21...♘d5 22 ♘f5 ♘xc3 23 ♕c2 ♘xd4 24 ♘xh4 ♘xc2 25 ♖xc2 ♗xg2 26 ♘xg2 ♘d5 27 ♖xc4 White has a clear advantage, since Black has only two pawns for the piece.

21 ♕f2 (D)

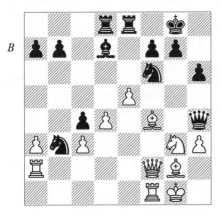

With this unpinning move, White not only threatens 22 exf6 but also sets up a potential attack on the f7-square.

21...♘h5 (D)

Since this active continuation proves unsuccessful, it is natural to suggest the more defensive 21...♘h7, threatening 22...♗xh3, since after the exchange of bishops White will no longer have the strong manoeuvre ♖a2-h2. How should White reply in that case?

Despite being a pawn down, White can enter the endgame with confidence; after 22 ♘e4 ♕xf2+ 23 ♖axf2 b5 24 ♗g3! ♖e7 (to be able to play the other rook to f8; if 24...♖f8 White plays 25 ♘d6 ♘g5 26 ♔h2 and, faced with the threat of h4, Black's position falls apart) 25 ♗h4 g5 26 ♗g3. Kasparov considers that the white position is winning. Black has no play whereas White has several plans, such as d5 and ♘f6+, or ♘d6 and ♔h2 followed by ♗d5,

while the b3-knight remains out of play, and is sorely missed.

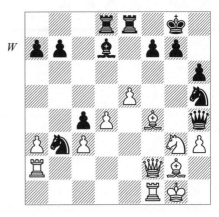

Does the f4-bishop have any good discovery, or is it necessary to keep manoeuvring?

22 ♗xh6!

Yes, this is what 21...♘h7 would have prevented. It is crushing; the white pieces are ready for the final attack. There were other continuations, such as quietly bringing all the pieces to bear with 22 ♘xh5 ♕xh5 23 ♕g3, intending ♖af2, but this is not as strong as the text-move.

22...♖e7 (D)

The h5-knight cannot capture on g3 because this would allow mate in two, while after 22...♕xg3 23 ♕xf7+ ♔h8 24 ♕xh5 gxh6 25 ♕xh6+ ♔g8, it does not take a Kasparov or a computer to see that 26 ♖f6 is decisive.

If 22...♗e6 then White could play 23 ♘xh5 ♕xh5 24 ♗e3, and having recovered the pawn and weakened Black's castled position, White's advantage is overwhelming. The waywardness of the b3-knight continues to be very important; Kasparov pointed out the line 24...♗d5 (or 24...♕g6 25 ♕h4 ♗d5 26 ♗g5, and the a2-rook comes into play decisively on g2) 25 ♗xd5 ♖xd5 26 ♕g2 ♖d7 27 ♖af2 and all the white pieces will attack the black king.

After the text-move (22...♖e7), is there anything better than 23 ♘xh5 ♕xh5 24 ♗e3, with the idea of ♕g3 and ♖af2?

23 ♘f5!

Yes; it is no longer necessary to avoid a queen exchange in order to attack the black king.

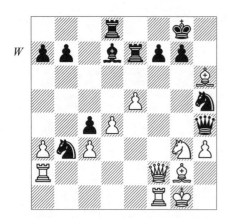

23...♛xf2+ 24 ♖fxf2

The pressure must not be relaxed; if 24 ♖axf2 Black gains some relief by 24...♝xf5 25 ♖xf5 ♞g3. The position after 26 ♝g5 ♖dd7 27 ♝xe7 ♖xe7 28 ♖5f2 ♞xf1 29 ♔xf1 is still advantageous for White, but less so than in the game.

24...♖e6

With the material equalized, Black's king-side weakened and the b3-knight still out of play, simplification is no longer enough to hold the position; in the event of 24...♝xf5 25 ♖xf5 gxh6 26 ♖xh5, followed by ♝e4 and ♖g2, White wins with ease.

25 ♝e3 ♝c6 *(D)*

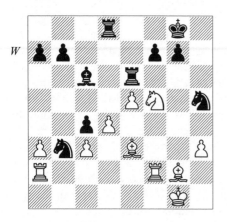

26 ♝f1!

The decisive blow; the threats of 27 ♝xc4 and 27 ♝e2 terminate Black's resistance.

26...f6 27 ♝xc4 ♝d5 28 ♝e2 fxe5 29 ♝xh5 exd4 30 ♝g5 ♖d7 31 ♖ae2 ♝e4 32 ♞xd4 1-0

In this game, a move made without a deep examination of its necessity, 10...h6?, seriously weakened Black's position, showing that the saying "the cure can be worse than the disease" sometimes also applies to chess. It is essential to distinguish between a real threat and an imaginary one. The waste of a tempo with 10...h6? was less important than the creation of a 'contact-point', and curiously one of the decisive blows fell precisely on this square: 22 ♝xh6!.

Flexibility is a very important concept; by first making 'essential' moves, such as 10...♞a5, other possibilities are left open.

Just as important as flexibility is determination. When the position 'requires' a drastic decision, it is necessary to take it, whatever the cost: 16 e4!, 20 e5!, 22 ♝xh6!, and then, even when on the attack, not spurning an endgame if it is an advantageous one: 23 ♞f5!.

Finally, it is never superfluous to recall that "if one piece is bad, the whole position is bad", as Black's b3-knight testified.

Exercises

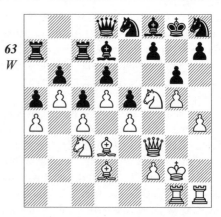

63
W

Indicate the correct plan for increasing White's advantage.

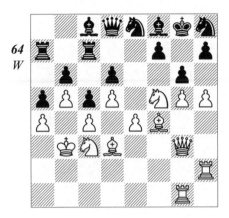

64
W

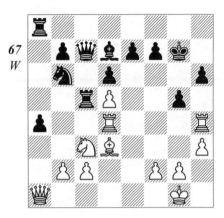

67
W

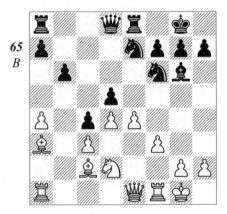

65
B

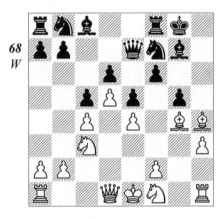

68
W

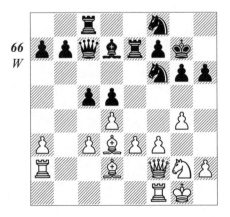

66
W

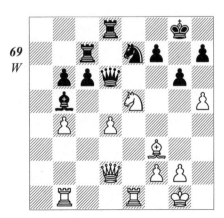

69
W

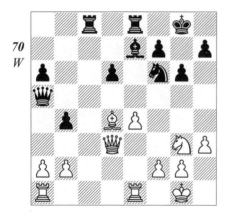

70
W

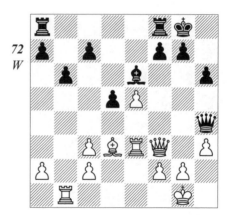

72
W

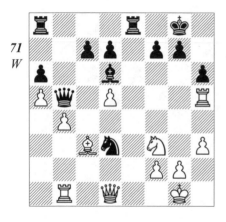

71
W

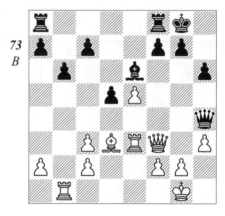

73
B

Solutions to Exercises

Chapter 1

Exercise 1

Averbakh – Panno

Argentina-USSR, Buenos Aires 1954

17 ♔e2!

The solid central barrier means that the king will be secure on e2.

The next stage in the attack is to transfer the major pieces to the h-file and then open it.

17...♖g7 18 ♖h4 ♘d7 19 hxg6 hxg6 20 ♕h1

Now that he has regrouped, White is ready to invade.

20...♗e7 21 ♖h8+ ♔f7 22 ♕h6 ♘f8

Black's king is safe only in appearance; the pieces that surround it are not guarding it very well, and it only requires a spark and the black fortress will explode.

23 ♖h1! ♖b8 24 ♗xf4! *(D)*

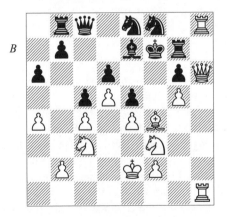

With the threat of 25 ♗xe5!.

24...♕c7

24...exf4 loses to 25 ♖h4; if 24...♘d7 then 25 ♕h3 ♘b6 26 ♗xe5! wins material.

25 ♕h2!

Renewing the threat of capturing on e5.

25...♘d7 26 ♕h3

The triumph of White's plan; the queen succeeds in invading Black's weak squares.

26...♘f8 *(D)*

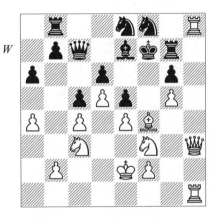

27 ♖xf8+!

The only defender of e6 is eliminated.

27...♔xf8 28 ♕e6 ♖g8 29 ♘h4!

The attack proceeds unabated.

29...♗d8 30 ♘xg6+ ♔g7

30...♖xg6 allows mate by 31 ♖h8+ ♔g7 32 ♕g8#.

31 ♘xe5 1-0

Exercise 2

Averbakh – Panno

Argentina – USSR, Buenos Aires 1954

9...e5?

This natural advance is a serious error. By closing the centre, Black frees the opponent's hands to attack on the kingside. White need not fear any counterattack from Black, as there are no dangerous open lines to attack the white king.

The correct continuation is considered to be 9...e6 10 ♘f3 exd5 11 exd5 ♗g4 12 0-0, with a slight advantage to White.

10 g4!

Thanks to the closed centre, White immediately starts a pawn-storm.

10...♘e8 11 h4 f5

As is typical in the King's Indian, Black seeks counterplay with this break, rather than waiting passively while White makes progress. However, there is a serious drawback in that it weakens Black's king position.

12 h5

With the threat of opening two lines against the king by 13 hxg6 hxg6 14 gxf5 gxf5 15 ♗h5 ♘f6 16 ♗g6, with a strong attack.

12...f4 13 g5! *(D)*

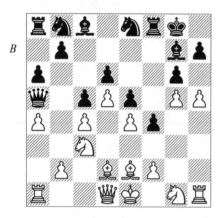

Threatening 14 h6 shutting in the g7-bishop; at the same time it prepares to exchange bishops, after which many light squares in the black camp will be left weak.

13...♖f7 14 ♗g4! ♕d8

An attempt to counter-attack on the queenside would not achieve anything; for example: 14...♗xg4 15 ♕xg4 ♕b4 16 hxg6 hxg6 17 ♕c8! ♖e7 18 b3! and if 18...♕xb3, then 19 ♖b1 followed by ♖xb7.

15 ♗xc8 ♕xc8 16 ♘f3 ♗f8

And thus we arrive at Exercise 1.

Exercise 3

Svidler – Dreev

Russian Ch, Elista 1997

Black is behind in development and has been saddled with a very poor bishop on h7.

White has also expanded on the wing, and Black might create counterplay against the c5-pawn, which could help him complete his development. However, since White controls more space and has a big lead in development,

enabling him to occupy the centre rapidly, he would have reasonable compensation for sacrificing the c5-pawn.

White has to decide whether to focus on preventing the development of Black's queenside or to look for something stronger on the kingside, taking advantage of the strong advanced pawns and Black's two main weaknesses, the king in the centre and the h7-bishop which is out of play.

15 g5!! *(D)*

White abandons the c5-pawn to its fate, and offers another pawn, to open lines against the black king which is still in the centre.

The alternative plan is also good, but not as energetic; for instance, 15 b4 a5 16 b5 0-0.

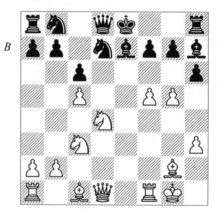

15...0-0

Black solves his main problem. He had many other moves available:

a) 15...♗xg5? 16 ♗xg5 ♕xg5 17 ♘e4 followed by ♘d6+, ♖e1, etc., gives White an overwhelming initiative. Here 17...♕e3+ is like putting one's head in the lion's mouth, since after 18 ♔h1 0-0 19 ♘c2 the queen is lost.

b) The capture 15...hxg5 reveals the usefulness of opening the d1-h5 diagonal: after 16 ♘e6! ♕a5 17 ♘xg7+ the black king has serious problems. Following 17...♔d8 18 ♘e4 the king will not survive in the centre, while sending it to the kingside is scarcely any safer; for instance, 17...♔f8 18 ♘e6+ fxe6 19 fxe6+ ♔g7 (19...♘f6 loses to 20 ♕h5) 20 ♕d4+ ♘f6 21 ♗xg5! ♖xc5 22 ♗xf6+ ♔g8 23 ♗xh8 and the black king will hardly be able to resist the very strong attack; let us analyse a bit further: 23...♘a6 24 ♖f4 ♗d3 25 ♔h1 ♖xd4 26 ♗xd4.

c) If 15...♘xc5 then 16 gxh6 is playable. Svidler thought that it would be even better to play 16 b4! ♘ca6 (after 16...♘cd7 17 g6 fxg6 18 ♘e6 ♕b6+ 19 ♔h1 once again the black king is in a bad way) 17 g6! ♗g8 (17...fxg6 hands over the e6-square to the d4-knight after 18 fxg6 ♗xg6 19 ♕g4 ♕d6 20 ♘e6) 18 b5 and the black pieces are all placed very passively, with the king stuck in the centre too long, so the extra pawn is clearly insufficient consolation.

16 g6 fxg6 17 ♘e6 *(D)*

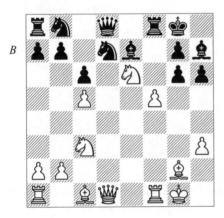

17...♕c8

If 17...♗xc5+ 18 ♔h1 ♕e7 19 ♘xf8 ♘xf8 then 20 ♘e4 is very strong, with the idea of 21 f6 or 21 ♕b3+, and 20...gxf5? fails to 21 ♘xc5 ♕xc5 22 ♕b3+ ♔h8 23 ♕xb7, winning.

18 ♘xf8 ♗xc5+

If 18...♘xf8 then 19 f6! (shutting in the h7-bishop even more and opening lines against the black king) 19...gxf6 (or 19...♗xf6 20 ♘e4 with a very strong initiative) 20 ♗xh6.

19 ♔h1 ♗xf8

19...♘xf8 is met by 20 f6 gxf6 21 ♘e4, with the well-known scenario.

20 fxg6 ♗xg6

And thus we arrive at Exercise 35.

Exercise 4
Anand – Svidler
Linares 1999

Both sides have weaknesses; Black's is his king, which is not under direct attack at the moment, but we know how dangerous open files can be, and there is also an unpleasant intruder at g5; on the other hand, Black's pieces are very well placed.

White has a weak d4-pawn and has a problem with where to put his king, since the queenside not does look safe but it cannot stay in the centre, which can be opened at any moment.

20...♖d6?

Black increases the pressure on the d4-pawn but grants greater freedom to the white pieces; now White has a clearer way forward.

It is better to maintain the tension with 20...♕d7!, as suggested by Svidler, to bring the a8-rook into play. Note that 21 f3? fails to 21...♖xf3!, when the white position collapses.

21 f3! *(D)*

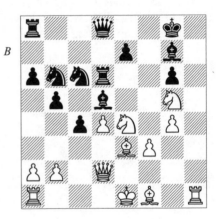

The white queen can now join the attack from h2.

21...♗xe4

21...♘xd4? highlights the black king's difficulties after, for example, 22 ♗xd4 ♗xe4 23 ♗xg7 ♖xd2 24 ♗e5.

22 fxe4

Now the f-file has also been opened and the duel between the exposed kings, White's in the centre and Black's castled, has clearly been decided in White's favour.

22...♘d7 23 ♕h2 ♘f8 24 e5 ♖d7 25 ♘e6 ♕a5+ 26 ♗d2 ♘xe5 27 ♗e2 c3 28 ♗xc3 b4 29 ♘xg7 bxc3 30 ♕h8+ ♔f7 31 0-0+ 1-0

Anand's complete annotations to this game in his book *Vishy Anand: My Best Games of Chess* (Gambit, 2001) can be recommended.

Exercise 5
J. Polgar – Fressinet
Istanbul Olympiad 2000

Black has an extra pawn, but this is not really an advantage, since his king has not yet managed to castle, so that the h8-rook is inactive, and the black queen and the f4-rook are also missing from the defence at the moment.

White has the upper hand, and the first task is an easy one.

20 ♕c6+

Guaranteeing that the king will stay in the centre for some time to come.

20...♚f8

Now White can regain the pawn, but this marks the end of the easy moves for White.

21 ♖xd6 g6

The rook was obviously taboo, but now it gets a bit more difficult; Black a refuge ready for his king, and the g5- and a2-pawns are attacked.

22 ♕c5! *(D)*

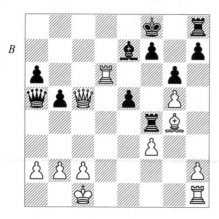

The threat of 23 ♕xe5 prevents the black king from going to g7.

22...♚g8

22...♕b4 is no defence because of 23 ♕xe5 f6 24 ♖xf6+ ♗xf6 25 gxf6. The rook is still immune, since 22...♖xd6? loses to 23 ♕xd6+ ♚g8 24 ♕b8+ ♚g7 25 ♕xe5+.

23 ♕xe5

Winning the exchange is now forced.

23...♗xd6 24 ♕xd6 ♖c4

If 24...♕xa2 White can now bring the h1-rook into play with 25 ♖e1. Polgar indicates

that 24...♖a4 loses to the beautiful line 25 ♕b8+ ♚g7 26 ♕e5+ ♚g8 27 ♗e6!, in a similar manner to what happens in the game.

25 ♕b8+ ♚g7 26 ♕e5+ ♚g8

Now it would be ideal to bring the h1-rook into play as well, but there is no advantage in 27 ♖d1 ♕c7 28 ♕f6 since Black can exchange the queens with 28...♕f4+, while 27 ♖e1 fails to the resource 27...♖c5!.

27 ♕f6! *(D)*

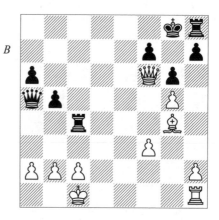

The correct move-order, threatening 28 ♖d1, which would be the answer to 27...♕xa2; for instance, 28...♕a1+ 29 ♚d2 ♕a5+ 30 ♚e3 and White wins.

27...♕c7

Now the e1-square is accessible, after which White's initiative continues. She is technically an exchange down but effectively a piece up, because the h8-rook merely obstructs the black king.

28 ♖e1 ♕c6

Taking on c2 leads to a lost endgame after 28...♖xc2+ 29 ♚b1 ♕c6 30 ♖d1 ♕xf6 31 gxf6 h5 32 ♖d8+ ♚h7 33 ♖xh8+ ♚xh8 34 ♚xc2, followed by the capture of Black's queenside pawns.

If 28...♕b8 White infiltrates by 29 ♖e7 ♖f4 30 ♕c6 ♚g7 31 ♕c3+ ♚g8 32 ♗c8! ♚f8 33 ♖d7, winning.

29 ♗e6! fxe6

The endgame after 29...♖xc2+ 30 ♚b1 ♖c1+ 31 ♖xc1 ♕xe6 32 ♕xe6 fxe6 33 ♖c8+ ♚g7 34 ♖xh8 ♚xh8 35 ♚c2 is also winning for White.

30 ♖d1 1-0

After the forced 30...♕e8 31 ♖d8, White captures the e6- and a6-pawns without the h8-rook being able to enter the struggle.

Exercise 6
Bologan – Svidler
Russian Team Ch, Tomsk 2001

Eliminating the g4-bishop with 19...♘xg4 is satisfactory, with a slight advantage to Black after 20 ♕xg4 ♗g5 21 ♗xf4 ♘e5 22 ♖xc8 ♗xc8. However, Black hopes for more, because the advantage is not very clear, the white king is under no pressure, and the white queen controls the kingside.

19...♘xd5! 20 exd5 ♘e5 21 ♗xc8 ♗xc8 *(D)*

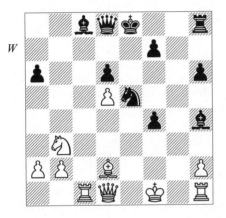

Thanks to the exchange sacrifice, the white king has no safe shelter and will come under strong attack; it is threatened with incarceration in much worse conditions than in Game 1.

22 ♖c3

If 22 h3 Svidler gives 22...♗f5 23 ♖c3 ♗e4 24 ♖g1 f3.

22...♗g4 23 ♕c2

The white queen is now very passive, deprived of mobility by the black minor pieces.

23...♕d7 24 ♗xf4 ♕b5+

Time-pressure raises its head; there was a quicker finish with 24...♗h3+ 25 ♔g1, and now the typical 'long move' which could easily be overlooked, 25...♕a7+.

25 ♔g1 ♕xd5 26 ♗g3

Eliminating the monster on e5 with 26 ♗xe5 is not a solution, since after 26...♕xe5 the h1-rook remains inactive, while the white king

does not have any protection and the h8-rook threatens to come into play via g8.

26...♖g8 *(D)*

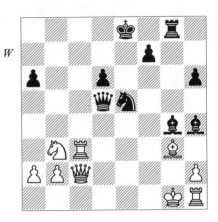

27 ♕g2

If 27 ♘d2, the h4-bishop changes diagonal with decisive effect: 27...♗d8!.

27...♗f3 28 ♖xf3 ♘xf3+ 29 ♔f2 ♖g5!

With the entrance of the rook into the attack, all resistance is broken.

30 ♕h3 ♖f5 31 ♖d1 ♘g5+ 0-1

Exercise 7
Karpov – J. Polgar
Wijk aan Zee 2003

White has just played 16 ♗f1-b5?; the exchange of light-squared bishops would be in his favour, but there is a tactical detail which knocks this idea on the head.

16...♗b4+!

The problems of the uncastled king have only begun.

17 axb4 ♗xb5

With his king stranded in the centre, White has a very difficult defensive task ahead.

18 bxa5 ♗c4 *(D)*

19 ♕a3?

Polgar gave 19 ♕a4 as better. The position is very complex, but she devoted a lot of time to analysing it in detail; let us see a part of the main line of her analysis which demonstrates White's great difficulties in holding the position owing to the bad position of his king: 19...bxa5 20 ♗c3 ♕f6! (looking to infiltrate via the light squares) 21 ♕xd7 ♕g6 22 d5 (if 22

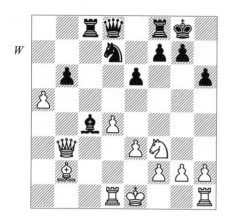

🜚g1 then 22...♕c2 wins quickly) 22...♕c2 23 ♗d2 ♖fd8 24 ♕e7 ♖xd5 25 ♕a3 ♗a6 and the king in the centre will never find peace.

19...bxa5 20 ♕d6?

20 e4 is more tenacious, although after 20...♗b5! (to invade with the rook on the seventh rank) 21 ♕e3 ♖c2 22 ♖d2 ♕c7, Black's initiative continues.

20...♗b5!

Subsequently White managed to transfer his king to the queenside, but it came to no good there either.

21 d5 ♖c2 22 ♖d2 ♕c8 23 ♕a3 ♖xd2 24 ♔xd2 ♘b6 25 ♕c3 ♘c4+ 26 ♔c2 e5 27 ♔b1 ♕g4 28 ♖c1 ♖b8 29 ♖c2 f6 30 d6 ♕xg2 31 ♘d2 ♕h1+ 32 ♔a2 ♘xd6 33 ♕c5 ♖c8 0-1

Exercise 8

Khuzman – Shirov

European Clubs Cup, Izmir 2004

Black has sacrificed his a-pawn but its loss is not serious, since in compensation White has lost his light-squared bishop and his queen is rather awkwardly placed. However, the main drawback of White's position is...

12...♗d3!

Of course! The white king will no longer have a quiet middlegame sheltered on the kingside and in addition the white queen is further discomforted.

13 ♔d2

Shirov marked this move as dubious. White attacks the d3-bishop and wants to play ♖hc1, when giving up castling would not seem to be a great worry.

13...b6!! *(D)*

Of the five options that Shirov gives here, 13...♖a6, 13...♗c4, 13...♗a6, 13...♗g6, and the text-move, this is the strongest.

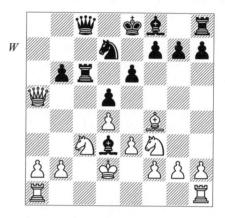

14 ♕a7?

14 ♕a4 is better, although after 14...♖c4 15 ♕a7 ♗b4 White's problems do not disappear. Shirov also gave 14...b5 15 ♕a5 ♗c4 as promising for Black, but after 16 b3! it is not so clear if Black has enough for the pawn.

14...♗b4 15 ♖hc1 ♗b5!! 16 ♔d1 ♗xc3 17 bxc3 ♗a6!!

After this move, incarcerating the queen on a7, Shirov considers that Black has a winning position.

18 a4 0-0 19 a5 b5 20 ♘e1 g5!

Black deprives the white bishop of control of the c7-square and now the white queen will drop.

21 ♗g3 f5 22 ♘d3 f4 23 exf4 ♖c7 24 ♕xc7 ♕xc7 25 fxg5 ♕c4 26 ♘b4 e5 27 ♘xa6 exd4 28 ♘c7 dxc3 29 a6 ♘c5 30 a7 ♕f1+ 0-1

Exercise 9

Dreev – Minasian

European Ch, Warsaw 2005

It can be guessed that Black has captured the b2-pawn with his queen; in return he has fallen behind in development and his king is still in the centre, but now he threatens to castle...

13 ♗xe7!!

After this spectacular blow the black king will be unable to find shelter.

13...♘xe7

No better is 13...fxe4 14 ♗xd6 e3 15 ♕e1 ♕d8 16 ♘g5! and the black king is in a bad way; now 16...♘xf4? fails to, among other things, 17 ♘f7! ♔xf7 18 ♖xf4+ ♔e8 19 ♗c4 with a winning attack.

14 ♘xd6+ ♔f8 15 ♘g5 (D)

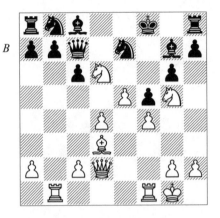

White has only one pawn for the piece, but Black's difficulties in finding a safe place for his king and organizing his forces are insuperable.

15...b6 16 ♕b4 h6 17 ♕b3 ♘d5 18 ♘gf7 ♗e6

If 18...♖h7 then a possible line is 19 ♘xc8 ♕xf7 20 ♘d6 ♕d7 21 ♗c4 (also attractive is 21 g4!? ♘e3 22 gxf5 ♘xf5 23 ♗xf5 gxf5 24 ♔h1! ♗h8 25 ♖g1 ♖g7 26 ♖xg7 ♗xg7 27 ♖g1 and White can do as he wants; Black's queenside pieces are dormant and the f5-pawn is dropping) 21...♕e6 22 ♗e2, followed by c4.

19 ♘xh8 ♗xh8 20 c4 ♘e7 21 g4! ♘d7 (D)

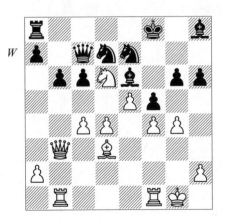

22 ♕a3!

Making the black king uncomfortable. White has available the earlier plan of opening the g-file by exchanging on f5 followed by ♔h1 with even more force than before, since the g1-rook will have no opponent.

22...c5?! 23 d5 ♘xd5 24 cxd5 ♗xd5 25 ♖bd1 1-0

Exercise 10
Pelletier – G. Georgadze
Spanish Team Ch, Olite 2006

White has embarked on a thematic manoeuvre to place his knight on e3, without deciding yet where to place his king. It seems reasonable to leave the king in the centre for the time being, because the position is closed, and if it does open up, the bishop-pair will become a powerful weapon... isn't that so?

15...exd4 16 cxd4 ♘xe4!

"No so fast, buddy!" The e-file which was closed and secure has been suddenly opened up, as in Game 4, and the white king faces a difficult journey to find a comfortable place; as well as the initiative, Black has two pawns for the piece.

17 fxe4 ♗xe4 18 ♖h2 d5! (D)

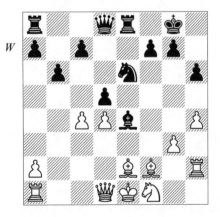

This guarantees that the position will open even more, to the benefit of Black's major pieces, and adding to the worries of the white king.

19 ♘d2 ♗g6 20 ♔f1 ♕f6 21 ♘b3

Moving the knight away. 21 ♘f3 is more natural; then Black continues to put his pieces on good squares with 21...dxc4 (or perhaps 21...♖ad8, after which 22 ♘e5?! dxc4 23 ♘xg6 ♘xd4! is winning for Black) 22 ♗xc4 ♖ad8.

21...♖ad8 22 ♔g1 dxc4 23 ♗xc4 c5 24 ♕f1 cxd4 25 ♗xe6 ♕xe6 26 h5?!

This move 'forces' the g6-bishop to change to a diagonal where its strength increases, but in any case Black's position is easy and pleasant to play, whereas it is not easy to find moves for White with his pieces placed so awkwardly.

26...♗e4 27 ♗xd4 ♗b7 28 ♖h4 ♕d5 29 ♔h2 ♖e6 30 ♖d1 ♖e4 31 ♖xe4 ♕xe4 32 ♖e1 ♕g4 33 ♕f4? ♕xh5+ 34 ♔h4 ♕d5 35 ♖g1 ♖c8 36 ♘d2 ♖c2 37 ♗e3 ♕f3! 38 ♕d4 ♕h5+ 0-1

Exercise 11
Ivanchuk – Vallejo
Morelia/Linares 2006

Black is a pawn up, but his king's defensive shield has advanced very far forward. If he manages to complete his development, his centre pawns will be very strong.

18 ♘f4!! *(D)*

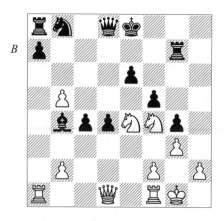

It is necessary to give up material to open lines and prevent Black from bringing his pieces into play to support his centre and his king.

18...♔f7

Let us see some of the beautiful lines given by Ivanchuk:

a) 18...♖e7 19 ♘g5 e5 20 ♕c2!! exf4 (if 20...♕c8 then 21 ♘d5 ♖g7 22 h4 gxh3 23 ♕e2!! wins) 21 ♕xc4 ♗d6 22 ♕g8+ ♔d7 23 ♕d5 and White wins.

b) 18...fxe4 19 ♘xe6 ♕f6 20 ♘xg7+ ♕xg7 21 ♕a4 (21 ♕e2 ♕e7 22 ♕xc4 is also strong) 21...♕e7 22 b6+! ♘d7 (if 22...♔f8 then the spectacular 23 ♕xa7!! ♖xa7 24 bxa7 wins) 23 ♕c6, winning thanks to the pawn that will appear on a7.

19 ♖c1! *(D)*

Better than 19 ♕c2 ♕c7 20 ♖a4 a5!.

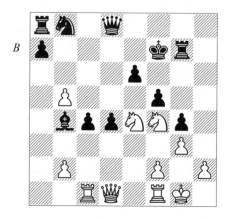

19...fxe4

If 19...a5 there follows a sequence that can also appear in other lines: 20 ♖xc4 fxe4 21 ♖xd4 and, now that the game has opened up, the most important factor is king safety. The position of the black king is beyond saving; after 21...♕c8 22 ♖xe4 ♘d7 23 ♖xe6 ♘f8 24 ♖c6 White has a winning attack.

20 ♖xc4 ♗c5 *(D)*

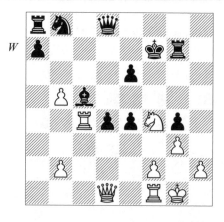

Black returns the piece to retain his pawn and keep the game closed, but it will not be enough.

21 ♖xc5 ♘d7

If 21...♕d6, Ivanchuk pointed out the winning line 22 ♖c8 a5 23 ♖e1 ♕e5 24 ♖d8.

22 ♖h5!

It is important to keep the rook on the fifth rank.

22...♘f6 23 ♖e5 ♕d6 24 ♖xe6

Not only taking a pawn, but in addition opening the a2-g8 diagonal; now after 24...♕d7 or 24...♕c5, 25 ♕b3 is decisive, while if 24...♕b4 then 25 ♖xf6+.

1-0

Exercise 12

Navara – Macieja

Greek Team Ch, Ermioni Argolidas 2006

Black's king is rather uncomfortably placed, but the solid central pawn-mass seems to prevent any immediate attempts to achieve anything. However, Black is lost.

13 exd5!

This simple exchange forces open the e-file.

13...exd5

You will have discovered the mating pattern that follows 13...cxd5, which loses immediately to 14 ♖xe6! fxe6 15 ♗xg6+ hxg6 16 ♕xg6#.

14 ♖e2!

The most logical; White will double rooks, bringing the a1-rook into play. There are other strong continuations, but this is the most natural.

14...♘c5

The only way to close the e-file.

15 ♖ae1 ♘e6 *(D)*

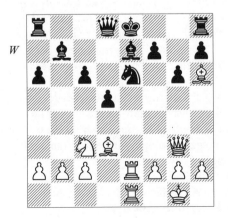

Neither the c3-knight nor the d3-bishop can join in the attack by simple means, but White forces a way through with a fresh sacrifice. The poor position of the black king is what makes this possible, coupled with the b7-bishop being out of play.

16 ♖xe6! fxe6 17 ♕e5! *(D)*

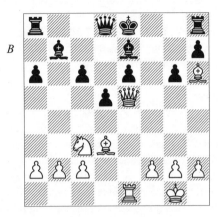

17...♖g8

Or 17...♖f8 18 ♗xf8 ♗xf8 (18...♔xf8 19 ♕h8+ ♔f7 20 ♕xh7+ ♔e8 21 ♕xg6+) 19 ♗xg6+! hxg6 20 ♕xe6+ ♗e7 (20...♕e7 21 ♕xg6+ costs Black his queen) 21 ♖e3! (threatening ♖h3) 21...♗c8 22 ♖xc6+ and White wins.

18 ♕xe6 ♖f8 19 ♗g5 ♖f7 20 ♗xg6! hxg6 21 ♕xg6

The extra rook is not sufficient to defend the black king. White will regain the sacrificed material with interest.

21...♕d7 22 ♖xe7+ ♕xe7 23 ♗xe7 ♔xe7 24 ♘a4! *(D)*

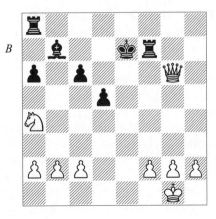

Finally the c3-knight joins in the attack, emphasizing the great difference between the two minor pieces.

24...♖f6 25 ♕g7+ ♖f7 26 ♕e5+ ♔f8 27 ♘c5 ♔g8

27...♖e8 is no better; the queen + knight tandem is very effective in attack. The continuation would be 28 ♘e6+ ♔g8 29 ♕g5+ ♔h8 30 ♕h5+ ♔g8 31 ♕g6+.

28 ♘e6 ♖e7 29 ♕g5+ ♔f7 30 ♕f5+ ♔e8

If 30...♔g8 then 31 ♕g6+ ♔h8 32 ♕f6+.

31 ♕f8+ ♔d7 32 ♘c5+ 1-0

Exercise 13
Wang Hao – Vescovi
Taiyuan 2006

White has given up a piece for only one pawn, but the black pieces are uncoordinated, and the black king is uncomfortably placed. However, a piece is a piece, and unless White can find a way to increase or at least maintain the pressure, his temporary advantage will gradually disappear.

White urgently needs to open lines so that his centralized rooks can show their power and penetrate the black position.

24 c4!

An elegant way to achieve the objective.

24...♗d7

It is not possible to capture the pawn with the bishop in view of the mate on e8, and if 24...♕xc4? then White wins with 25 ♗b6+ ♖c7 26 ♖c1. If 24...bxc3 the d1-rook comes into play on the c-file with 25 ♖c1! f5 26 ♖xc3 and the trapped black king will be unable to resist the attack.

25 ♗xd7 ♕xd7 26 ♗b6+ ♔c8 27 c5! (D)

Before playing ♕e8+, White creates a passed pawn for himself.

27...dxc5 28 ♕e8+ ♕xe8 29 ♖xe8+ ♔d7 30 ♖d8+ ♔e7 31 d6+ ♔e6?

This natural move, to be close to the passed pawn, loses. He had to play 31...♔f6! and the struggle goes on, although White is better. He does not have to hurry with 32 d7 ♖xb6 33 ♖e8 ♗e7 34 ♖xh8. Since Black is almost paralysed, White can improve his position and it looks better to play 32 ♗xc5 ♖g8 33 ♖d5 (threatening 34 f5 and ♗d4#) 33...♔e6 34 ♖e5+ ♔f6 35 h5.

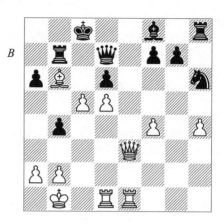

32 d7!

Now the possibility of ♖e8+ changes the situation.

32...♗e7

Also insufficient is 32...♗d6 33 ♖xh8 ♖xd7 34 ♖e8+! ♗e7 35 ♖e1+ ♔f6 36 ♖8xe7! ♖xe7 37 ♗d8.

33 ♖xh8 ♖xd7

Or 33...♖xb6 34 ♖e8 ♖d6 35 ♖xe7+ ♔xe7 36 ♖xd6, with an easy victory.

34 ♖xh6+!

A finale in harmony with the preceding play.

34...gxh6 35 f5+ ♔xf5 36 ♖xd7 1-0

Chapter 2

Exercise 14
Moiseev – Simagin
USSR Ch, Moscow 1951

White has opened the g-file, but exploiting it is a distant dream.

If you recalled Game 4, you will surely have looked for a way to avoid retreating the knight from b4; the motivation is even greater here, where Black has his two bishops boring into White's king position. That is what Black did.

18...c5!

"A piece sacrifice that creates a devastating attack against the white king. Refusing this sacrifice is impossible, since after 19 dxc6 ♘xc6 the attack develops with equal material." – Simagin.

19 ♗xf6

Even so, perhaps 19 dxc6 was better.

19...♕xf6 20 axb4 axb4 (D)

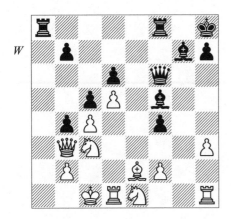

21 ♘b5

Let us look at the other defences indicated by Simagin: 21 ♘a4? fails to 21...♖xa4. In reply to 21 ♘a2 there are several good moves, one being to double rooks with 21...♖a7, when White cannot escape with 22 ♔d2 because of 22...♕d4+. If 21 ♘b1, it is very strong to open more diagonals with 21...f3! 22 ♗d3 (if 22 ♘xf3 then White no longer has ♘c2 to block the f5-bishop after 22...♖a1; 22 ♗xf3 ♗h6+ 23 ♖d2 ♗xd2+ 24 ♔xd2 ♗xb1) 22...♗d7 23 ♕c2 ♖a2.

21...♖a1+ 22 ♔d2 f3!! (D)

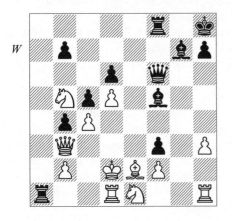

23 ♘c2

23 ♖xa1 is not possible since Black crushes White with 23...♗h6+ 24 ♔d1 fxe2+ 25 ♔xe2 ♗g6! 26 f3 ♖e8+ 27 ♔f1 ♕e5 28 ♕d1 ♕g3 29 ♘g2 ♖f8 30 ♘e1 ♗e3 31 ♕e2 ♗d3!!.

If 23 ♘xf3 ♗h6+ 24 ♔e1 then 24...♗c1, avoiding the exchange of rooks and planning ...♖b1, leaves White virtually paralysed; for

instance, 25 ♖g1 ♖b1 26 ♕a4 ♕xb2 27 ♘xd6 ♕c3+ 28 ♔f1 ♗xh3+ 29 ♖g2 ♕g7 30 ♘e1 ♗xg2+ 31 ♘xg2 ♕g3.

After 23 ♗xf3 there is a move similar to 24...♗c1 in the previous line: 23...♗b1! 24 ♘c7 ♗a2 25 ♕d3 ♕xb2+ 26 ♘c2 ♗b3 27 ♖xa1 ♗c3+.

23...♖xc2 24 ♔xc2

24 ♕xc2 is met by 24...fxe2 25 ♖xa1 ♕f4+ 26 ♔xe2 ♕f3+, mating quickly.

24...fxe2! 25 ♖xa1 ♕g6+ 26 ♔d2

In response to 26 ♕d3 the quickest win is 26...e1♘+! 27 ♖axe1 ♖xf2+.

26...♗h6+ 27 ♕e3

Or 27 ♔xe2 ♕e4+.

27...♖xf2 28 ♖he1 ♗xe3+ 29 ♔xe3 ♕g3+ 30 ♔d2 ♕f4+ 0-1

Exercise 15

Honfi – Tal
Sukhumi 1972

Black has made great progress with his attack and now opens lines in the typical manner.

25...b3!? 26 cxb3

If 26 ♖c3 bxa2+ 27 ♔a1 ♕a5 Black's attack is extremely dangerous in Tal's opinion; Black has in his favour the b-file, the latent threat of ...a3, and the possible tour ...♗c5-d4.

26...axb3 (D)

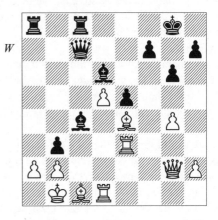

27 axb3?

White should keep the a-file closed with 27 a3!. Then 27...♗xd5!? must be met by 28 ♖c3 (28 ♗xd5?? ♕c2+), when Black is only a little better due to the more exposed white king.

27...♗e2!

A beautiful sacrifice clearing the c-file, which also pulls the white queen onto an unprotected square.

28 ♕xe2

If 28 ♖c3 ♗xd1 29 ♖xc7 ♖xc7 the two rooks are much stronger than the queen, because of the exposed position of the king; the threats are ...♗xb3 and also the attack with ...♖ca7.

28...♕a5 29 ♖c3 ♕a2+! 30 ♔c2 ♖xc3+ 31 ♔xc3 ♗b4+!

This sacrifice is the key to the whole combination.

32 ♔xb4

Of course if 32 ♔d3 then 32...♕xb3#.

32...♕a5+ 33 ♔c4 ♕a6+ 0-1

Exercise 16

Svidler – Glek

Haifa 1996

At first sight the position is just chaotic. The d1-rook is attacked and Black is planning ...g5 and ...g4 to open up the white king's defences. However, at the moment White's forces are better placed. His pieces occupy active positions, the clearest difference being between the major pieces; White's rooks are centralized on open files, unlike Black's on the closed g- and h-files. A single tempo would be enough to change everything, so White must hurry and find some weak point in Black's position.

24 ♖e5!

The vulnerable point is nothing less than the black king on c8. The white queen can combine with the f4-bishop to devastating effect on the h2-b8 diagonal, supported by the centralized rooks.

Black would reply to the 24 ♘e5 leap with 24...♘g4+!, when the position can become complicated. There is a draw by retreating the king to h1, but White can play more effectively, applying a recipe similar to the one used in the game: 25 ♘xg4 hxg4 26 ♖e5!.

24...♗b6

24...♘g4+? loses material: 25 hxg4 hxg4+ 26 ♔g3.

25 ♕d6! *(D)*

25...♘xd1

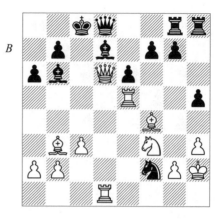

If 25...♗c6 then White wins with 26 ♗xe6+! fxe6 27 ♕xe6+ ♗d7 28 ♖xd7 ♕xd7 29 ♕xb6 (threatening both 30 ♖c5+ and the capture of the f2-knight) 29...♘d3 30 ♖d5.

26 ♖c5+ ♗c6 27 ♖xc6+ bxc6 28 ♕xc6+ ♕c7

28...♗c7 allows another piece to join the attack: 29 ♗a4! (threatening 30 ♕a8+) 29...♔b8 30 ♕b6+ ♔c8 31 ♕xa6+ ♔b8 32 ♘e5!, mating quickly.

29 ♗xc7 ♗xc7+ 30 ♔g1 ♖d8 31 ♕xa6+ ♔b8 32 ♘d4 ♖d6 33 ♘c6+ ♖xc6 34 ♕xc6

The material advantage is enormous and White wins easily.

34...♖d8 35 ♗c2 ♖d6 36 ♕e8+ ♖d8 37 ♕b5+ ♔c8 38 ♕a6+ 1-0

If 38...♔b8 then 39 ♗e4 is decisive.

Exercise 17

Granda – L. Dominguez

Wijk aan Zee 2004

White's attack is not quick; the pawn-storm has only just begun. Of course, if Black did nothing then h4-h5 and g6 would follow, but Black can make progress on the queenside.

18...♗d5!

The ...c4 advance is unstoppable.

19 e4

If White plays the passive 19 ♘d2 then Black can reply 19...cxd4 20 exd4 (20 ♕xd4 leads to a lost endgame after 20...♕xd4 21 exd4 ♗xh2) 20...♖c3 21 ♕b5 ♕c7 with a crushing position.

19...c4 20 ♕e3 c3 *(D)*

Black not managed to open a file, but the pawn on its sixth rank is very strong, tying up

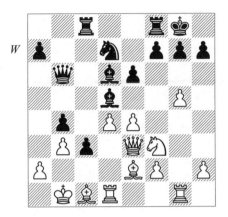

White's pieces and making the white king uncomfortable.

21 &d3

Dominguez commented that the game would follow a similar course if White tried the alternative blockading method: 21 ♘e1 &b7 22 e5 &e7 23 &d3 a5! (files will be opened against the white king well before White makes any progress against the black king) 24 ♕h3 g6 25 ♖g4 ♖fd8 (the difference is that Black can easily defend his weaknesses, unlike White) 26 ♖h4 ♘f8 27 &c2 &d5 followed by ...a4, with a winning attack.

21...&b7 22 &c2 a5 *(D)*

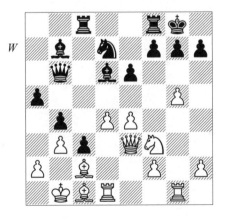

23 g6

After 23 e5 &e7 24 ♕d3 g6 25 h4 &d5 26 h5 a4 27 hxg6 fxg6 28 ♘h4 axb3 29 axb3 ♖f7, Black repels the attack with a winning position, according to Dominguez; a quick mate on the a-file will follow. Let us continue this line a

little further: 30 ♘xg6 hxg6 31 ♕xg6+ ♖g7 32 ♕h5 ♖a8 33 ♖h1 ♔f8 34 &g6 c2+ 35 ♔xc2 (if 35 &xc2 then 35...♕a6) 35...♕c6+ 36 ♔d3 ♖xg6, with a decisive advantage.

23...fxg6 24 ♘g5 &f4 25 ♕e2 &a6 26 ♕g4 &xg5 27 ♕xg5 a4! 28 &e3 axb3 29 &xb3

If 29 axb3 Black wins by occupying the a-file with 29...♖a8, threatening ...&e2 followed by ...♕a6.

29...♕c6 0-1

There is no defence; if 30 &c2 then 30...&c4 wins.

Exercise 18

Akopian – Kramnik
Wijk aan Zee 2004

White has the h-file and a strong knight on f5, but there is nothing to be achieved immediately by 'normal' means. If 29 ♖h2 to double rooks, Black can always simplify by ...♕xb2+, but it is not obvious either what White can do on the h-file after 29...&g6.

29 ♖h7!! *(D)*

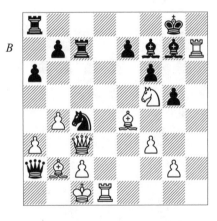

Akopian commented: "This move, which provoked so much admiration on the Internet and in the press, is in fact not at all complicated and it concludes the game in a few moves."

29...♕xb2+

Black also loses after 29...&f8 30 ♖dh1 &e6 31 ♘xe7+ ♖xe7 32 ♖h8+ ♔f7 33 &g6+ ♔xg6 34 ♕xf6#, or 29...♔xh7 30 ♘xe7+ ♔h6 31 ♖h1+ &h5 32 g4, while 29...♘xb2 30 ♖xg7+ ♔f8 31 ♕xb2 ♕xb2+ 32 ♔xb2 e6 33 ♖xf7+

♖xf7 34 ♘d6 ♖d8 35 ♖d3 results in a winning endgame for White.

30 ♕xb2 ♘xb2 31 ♖xg7+ ♔f8 32 ♖h1 1-0

Exercise 19
Grishchuk – Ponomariov
Wijk aan Zee 2005

White's attack is more advanced, but it is essential to choose the correct plan here. If 21 f5, threatening f6, then 21...f6, and Black holds. Pushing the h2-pawn to h5 is not attractive either, since it is very time-consuming. However, White identified the weakest point in Black's position: h7.

21 ♗f6!

Preventing ...f6 or ...f5, and threatening to bring the major pieces to the h-file with ♖d3-h3 and ♕h4. There is no good defence to this, nor can Black's counter-attack arrive in time.

21...♗b7

After 21...b4 22 axb4 ♖xb4 23 ♕h4 (23 ♖d3 h5!?) 23...♖e8 24 ♖d3 there is no defence; if 24...♕b6 then 25 ♗d4.

22 ♖d3 ♖fc8 23 ♖h3 *(D)*

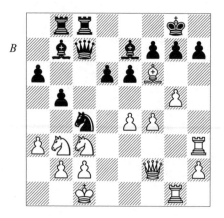

23...♔f8

Giving up the h7-pawn is equivalent to resignation, but there is no defence; for instance, 23...gxf6 24 gxf6+ ♔f8 25 ♖xh7 ♗xf6 (or 25...♔e8 26 ♖g8+ ♔d7 27 ♖xf7 ♖xg8 28 ♖xe7+ ♔d8 29 ♖xc7 ♔xc7 30 ♘d4 with an advantage in material and an overwhelming positional advantage) 26 ♕g3 d5 (if 26...♔e7 there is a mate with 27 ♖xf7+! ♔xf7 28 ♕g6+ ♔f8 {or 28...♔e7 29 ♕h7+} 29 ♕g8+ ♔e7 30 ♕h7+

♔d8 31 ♖g8#) 27 ♕g8+ ♔e7 28 ♕xf7+ ♔d6 29 ♕xf6 ♕xh7 30 ♖g7, winning the queen, and although Black gains two rooks in return, his king is very weak and will not be able to survive.

24 ♖xh7 ♔e8 25 ♗xg7 ♔d7 26 g6

Now White wins easily.

26...a5 27 gxf7 ♔f8 28 ♗xf8 ♖xf8 29 ♖d1 ♗c8 30 f5 e5 31 ♘d5 1-0

Exercise 20
L. Dominguez – Gulko
World Team Ch, Beersheba 2005

White has two options: he can win material, or else try to break on g5.

It is essential for White to evaluate whether the material advantage obtained is sufficient, or whether he should focus on the kingside, not forgetting that Black's attack on the white king is also well advanced.

21 ♖hg1! *(D)*

White chooses the strongest plan, which is to play g5 and open the g-file.

It is not very attractive to win the exchange with 21 ♘b5?! since after 21...♖xb5 22 ♕xb5 ♕xc2+ 23 ♔a1 ♗f6 Black has good counterplay against the white king. Dominguez indicates the variation 24 ♖b1 ♘c5 25 ♖hc1 (25 ♗xc5?! dxc5 26 ♖he1 c4 just adds a new attacker) 25...♕g2 26 e5 ♗xe5 27 f4 ♗f6 28 g5 hxg5 29 fxg5 ♗e5 and the game is unclear.

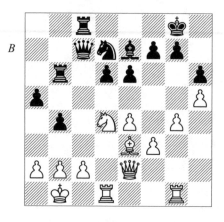

21...♗f6

If 21...♕c4 White was intending to play 22 ♕f2 (he was less convinced by 22 ♕d2, since 22...♗f6 23 g5 hxg5 24 ♗xg5 ♗xd4 25 ♕xd4

♕xd4 26 ♖xd4 ♚f8 leads to the exchange of queens without achieving anything special) 22...a4 23 g5 ♗xg5 24 ♗xg5 hxg5 25 ♖xg5 and White has made progress. Dominguez continues this line 25...♚h8 26 ♕d2 ♖g8 27 ♖a5, now targeting the black queenside pawns, with advantage to White.

22 g5 hxg5 23 ♗xg5 ♚h8 24 ♗xf6 ♘xf6 25 ♖g5! *(D)*

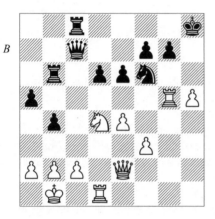

To triple with ♖dg1 and ♕g2.

25...a4 26 ♕d2?!

It was better to continue with the original plan by playing 26 ♖dg1.

26...♕e7 27 ♖dg1 ♖g8 28 ♕g2 ♘e8?

28...♕f8 is better.

29 ♖g6! *(D)*

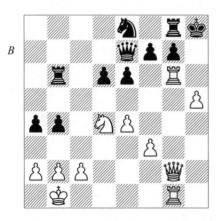

With the idea of playing h6 without allowing ...g6 in reply.

29...♕f8 30 ♘xe6!

Also good is 30 h6! fxg6 31 ♘xe6 ♕f7 32 ♕h3.

30...fxe6 31 h6 ♕f7

If 31...♖b7 then 32 ♖h1 gxh6 33 ♖gxh6+ ♕xh6 34 ♖xh6+ ♖h7 35 ♖xh7+ ♚xh7 36 ♕h3+ ♚g7 37 ♕xe6 with an easy win.

32 ♖h1 1-0

Exercise 21
Ivanchuk – Van Wely
Monaco (Amber blindfold) 2006

White's attack is very far advanced, but the natural break 20 g6 fxg6 21 hxg6 h6 yields nothing special. White carries out an untypical manoeuvre, exploiting some key details of the position, such as the fact that the e8-rook is loose; although this might seem odd, it is very important.

20 b3!

"You should not move pawns on your weaker wing" is a sensible rule in the vast majority of cases, but there are exceptions, such as this one, based on concrete calculation.

20...♖c6 21 ♘d5!! *(D)*

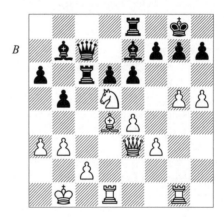

The beautiful complement to White's previous move; the idea of the sacrifice is to lend much more force to the g6 break, which previously was almost harmless. It is worth remembering that this was a blindfold game!

21...exd5

21...♕d8 loses to 22 ♘f6+.

22 exd5 ♖xc2

If 22...♖c5 then 23 g6, and now if 23...fxg6 24 hxg6 h6, the e6-square is available to White, leading to a quick win after 25 ♕e6+ ♚h8 26 ♖h1.

23 g6 hxg6

Or 23...fxg6 24 ♕e6+ ♚f8 25 hxg6 ♗f6 26 gxh7 and White wins.

24 hxg6 ♖f8 25 gxf7+ ♖xf7 (D)

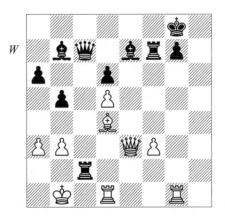

26 ♗xg7!

The final decisive blow. The black king cannot survive.

26...♖xg7 27 ♕e6+ ♚h8 28 ♖xg7 ♚xg7 29 ♖g1+ 1-0

Exercise 22

Kariakin – Anand
Wijk aan Zee 2006

Who is ahead in the race? The bottled-up black pieces on the kingside appear to make it doubtful that it is Black who is in the lead.

24...♘c7!!

A lovely way to come into play; if 25 ♗b6 the knight delivers a fatal blow after 25...♖xa3 26 bxa3 ♘b5.

25 ♕xc7

And now?

25...♖c8! (D)

The knight gave up its life to enable the f8-rook to enter the action. And now this comes to pass, with another piece sacrifice, which has to be accepted, since if 26 ♕b6 then 26...♘c4! is decisive.

26 ♕xe7

Black has achieved his objective of bringing the inactive rook into the attack and deflecting the white queen. With so many pieces aimed at

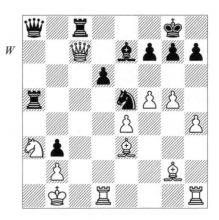

White's castled position, all that is needed is to open some lines.

26...♘c4!

Not the tempting 26...♖xa3?? 27 bxa3 ♕xa3 because of the unexpected 28 ♕a7! and White can defend, with a decisive material advantage to boot.

27 g6

Let us look at the other defences given by Anand:

a) 27 ♗c5 ♖xa3 28 bxa3 ♖xc5 29 a4 ♘a3+ 30 ♚b2 ♖c2+ 31 ♚xa3 ♕b8! 32 ♖a1 b2, and mate follows.

b) 27 ♗d4 ♖xa3 28 bxa3 ♘xa3+ 29 ♚b2 ♘c4+ 30 ♚c3 (30 ♚xb3 leads to mate after 30...♕a3+ 31 ♚c2 ♘e3++ 32 ♚d2 ♖c2+ 33 ♚e1 ♕b4+) 30...♕a2! 31 ♗c5 ♕c2+ 32 ♚d4 dxc5+ 33 ♚d5 ♘e3+ 34 ♚d6 ♘xd1 and Black wins.

27...hxg6 28 fxg6 ♘xa3+ 29 bxa3 ♖xa3 30 gxf7+ ♚h7 31 f8♘+ ♖xf8 (D)

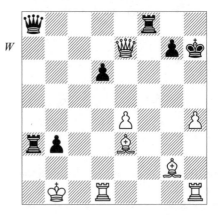

32 ♕xf8

Black delivers mate after 32 ♕xd6 ♖a1+ 33 ♔b2 ♖a2+ 34 ♔b1 ♖c2!.

White now has enough material to compensate for the queen, but with his king so badly defended this is not sufficient.

32...♖a1+ 33 ♔b2 ♖a2+ 34 ♔c3

Now the king will be mated, but if 34 ♔b1 then 34...♕xf8 35 ♗h3 ♕a8 36 ♗f5+ ♔h8 37 ♖c1 ♖a1+ 38 ♔b2 ♕a3+ 39 ♔c3 b2+.

34...♕a5+ 35 ♔d3

Or 35 ♔xb3 ♕a4+ 36 ♔c3 ♖c2+ 37 ♔d3 ♕c4#.

35...♕b5+ 36 ♔d4 ♖a4+ 37 ♔c3 ♕c4+ 0-1

Exercise 23
Svidler – Kariakin
Wijk aan Zee 2007

Black has two open files on the queenside, and already has unpleasant pressure on c2, while White has not achieved much on the kingside.

19...♖ab8!! *(D)*

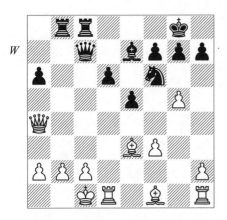

With the occupation of the b-file Black's attack takes a big step forward. White does not have time to capture the knight, since if 20 gxf6? Black's main threat, 20...♖b4, wins.

20 ♗d3?

20 ♕c4? loses to 20...♖b7, since b2, the queen and f3 are all attacked.

The best move is 20 ♗c4, when Black has various possibilities for keeping a slight advantage, but nothing decisive; for instance, 20...♕xc4 21 ♕xc4 ♖xc4 22 gxf6 ♗xf6 23

♖xd6 e4 24 c3 ♖a4 25 a3 exf3 26 ♖f1 ♗e5 27 ♖d7 ♗xh2 28 ♖xf3 f6, when the fight goes on. Black's other possibilities are 20...♘d7 and 20...♘g4.

20...♘d7

The d3-bishop defends c2, but does nothing to protect b2.

21 ♕e4 g6 22 ♗xa6

If 22 h4 then 22...♖xb2! 23 ♔xb2 ♕c3+ 24 ♔c1 d5 wins, while 22 ♖de1 ♘c5 does not solve White's problems.

22...♖b4! *(D)*

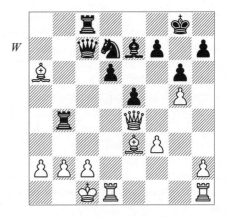

Activating the rook with tempo.

23 ♕d3

There is no salvation in 23 c4 ♕c6 24 ♗xc8 ♖xc4+ 25 ♔b1 ♖xe4 26 ♗xd7 ♕xd7 27 fxe4 ♕a4. As in several positions that we have already seen, the defending side wins enough material for the queen, but at the cost of being saddled with very passive pieces and being left powerless to prevent heavy material losses.

23...♖cb8 24 b3

This weakening is a great gain for Black.

24...♘c5!

This forces the following exchange, after which all the weakened dark squares fall into Black's hands.

25 ♗xc5 ♕xc5 26 ♕d5 ♕a7 27 ♗c4 ♗xg5+ 28 ♔b2 ♖a4 29 a3 ♖a5 30 ♕e4 ♗e3

The entrance of the bishop is decisive.

31 c3 ♖xa3 32 ♖a1 ♖a8 0-1

If 33 ♕xa8+ then 33...♖xa8 34 ♖xa3 ♕xf3 35 ♖f1 ♕g2+ 36 ♔b1 d5 gains more material, while if 33 ♕b1 Black wins with 33...♖xa1 34

♕xa1 ♗c1+! 35 ♖xc1 ♕f2+ 36 ♖c2 ♕xc2+ 37 ♔xc2 ♖xa1.

Exercise 24
Tomashevsky – Alekseev
Russian Ch, Moscow 2006

Castling on opposite wings generally leads to a race to see who can get there first, although sometimes it includes prophylactic measures to help the defence. Here it is necessary to decide whether it is the right moment to launch the attack, or make some improvement to the pieces.

Improving the d2-knight with 13 ♘f3 neglects the e4-square and Black achieves a good position with 13...d5! 14 e5 ♘e4, centralizing the knight with nasty threats, such as 15...♘f2.

As Alekseev indicates, it was best to force Black to retreat to a passive position with the immediate 13 g4! and after 13...a5 14 g5 ♘d7 15 ♘f3 a4 16 ♘bd4 e5 we reach a complex position with chances for both sides.

13 ♔b1?

This allows Black the opportunity to stabilize the centre first, and gain a strong central square.

13...e5!

With the threat of 14...♗g4.

14 f5 a5! *(D)*

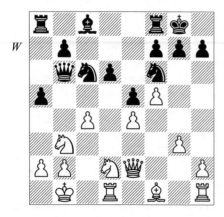

Beginning the attack; White wanted to do the same, but with less justification.

15 g4?

It is no longer appropriate for White to treat the position as an attacking race; in that respect

Black has a big lead. It is better to regroup with 15 ♘f3, defending the d4-square, and after 15...a4 16 ♘c1 ♖d8, the position remains complicated.

15...a4 16 ♘c1

Here Black could have gained a winning advantage with 16...a3! 17 b3 ♕d4 18 ♘d3 b5! (the move that Alekseev overlooked) 19 cxb5 (or 19 ♗g2 ♗a6) 19...♘a7, and White will not be able to resist the black offensive. Alekseev preferred the natural but less strong **16...♘d4?!** and still won.

Chapters 3 and 4

Exercise 25
Alekhine – Consulting team
Amberes 1923

Black is two pawns up, although for the moment the b8-knight and the a5-bishop are out of play, so White needs to hurry. How should White make progress on the kingside? One idea that comes to mind is 26 ♘g5, intending ♕h4, but this is refuted by 26...♗d2.

26 ♗b2!

The a3-bishop was also not doing much; now 27 ♘g5 is a definite threat, since 27...♗d2? loses to 28 ♕d4.

26...♖e8 27 ♕h4 *(D)*

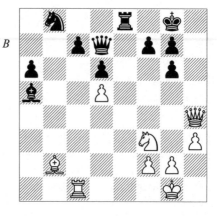

27...f6?

This weakens the e6-square prematurely. Instead, the counter-attack 27...♕b5! was a good defensive resource, attacking the b2-bishop and vacating the d7-square for the b8-knight, which would then enable Black to defend h7 without creating any weakness, with ...♘f8.

28 ♘d4

Heading for the weakness at e6, although White will not be in a hurry to play ♘e6 if Black can play the sacrifice ...♖xe6 in acceptable circumstances.

28...♔f7

Preparing to respond to 29 ♘e6 with the exchange sacrifice. Exchanging rooks is not satisfactory because after 28...♖e1+ 29 ♖xe1 ♗xe1 30 ♕e4! White regains one of the pawns, having weakened the position of the black king.

29 ♖c4!! (D)

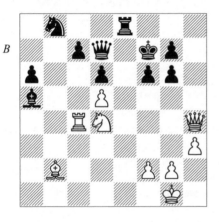

Another piece comes into play. As Alekhine points out, now there is a definite threat to invade e6 since after 30 ♘e6 ♖xe6 31 dxe6+ ♕xe6 32 ♖e4 ♕f5 White has 33 ♗xf6!, winning.

29...♖e5 30 ♘e6 ♖h5

30...♖xd5 loses to 31 ♘xg7!.

31 ♕e4 ♕e7

If 31...♖xd5 then 32 ♘d8+!, winning a whole rook. Now the queen makes room for the b8-knight.

32 ♕d3 ♗b6

White's idea was to reply to 32...♘d7 with 33 ♖e4! ♘e5 34 ♕xa6 ♗b6 35 ♕c8, when all White's pieces are very active while Black's pieces are uncoordinated and his king in danger.

33 ♖e4 ♕d7 34 g4 ♖h8 35 ♖f4!

The pressure from the white pieces keeps growing. Now there are threats of 36 ♗xf6, 36 ♘xg7 and 36 g5.

35...♖e8 36 ♗xf6! gxf6

This leads to mate, but as Alekhine indicates, there was no defence. After 36...♖xe6 37 dxe6+ ♕xe6 38 ♗d4+ ♔g8 White wins with, among other things, 39 ♗xb6 cxb6 40 ♖d4.

37 ♖xf6+! ♔xf6

Or 37...♔e7 38 ♕xg6, and mate in two moves; now there is mate in three.

38 ♕c3+ 1-0

Exercise 26
Réti – Spielmann
Trenčianske Teplice 1928

White has made great progress with his attack. The two bishops exert strong pressure on Black's kingside. In contrast, the b7-bishop is a useless piece, either for attack or defence, and White should try to take advantage of this by speeding up events on the kingside. The first step is to involve more pieces by opening the f-file.

21 fxe6 fxe6

21...♘xe6 loses to 22 ♖xf7! ♔xf7 23 ♕f5+ ♔g8 24 ♗xe6+ ♔h8 25 ♕g6.

22 ♖xf8+! (D)

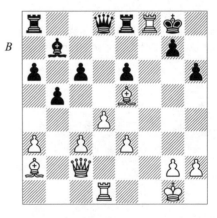

The most effective defender is eliminated, and the other rook will soon take its place.

22...♖xf8

If 22...♔xf8 then White can win with 23 ♕h7 ♕d7 24 ♗xg7+, or 23 ♖f1+, when 23...♔e7 loses quickly to 24 ♕g6, whilst if 23...♔g8 White soon mates after 24 ♗b1.

23 ♗xe6+ ♔h8 24 ♗a2!

Even better than 24 ♕g6 ♖f6 25 ♗xf6 ♕xf6 26 ♕xf6 gxf6, which also wins, but is more long-winded.

24...♕g5 25 ♗b1 ♔g8 26 ♕h7+ ♔f7 27 ♗xg7!

Destroying the last defences of the black king, which will be unable to defend itself against the attack by all White's pieces.

27...♕xe3+

27...♕xg7 loses to 28 ♖f1+.

28 ♔h1 ♕e2 29 ♗e5+ ♔e6 30 ♕g6+ ♔d7 31 ♕d6+ 1-0

Exercise 27
Alekhine/Monosson – Stoltz/Reilly
Nice 1931

Black has rather fallen behind in development. If his b8-knight were on d7 it would be quite different, so White must speed up his activity on the kingside.

15 dxc5!

Opening the diagonal of the b2-bishop, and weakening Black's structure. The lack of coordination caused by the b8-knight shows up in the fact that 15...♗xc5? is impossible because of 16 ♗xg7! ♔xg7 17 ♕g5+, capturing the undefended rook on d8.

15...bxc5 16 e4! *(D)*

The inclusion of this pawn is very important; in contrast, 16 ♘e5 is not so strong in view of 16...f6!.

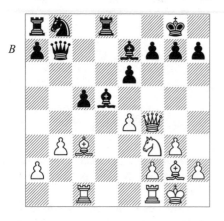

16...♗c6

Not, of course, 16...♗xe4? because of 17 ♘g5!, winning material and gaining an attack;

for instance, 17...♗xg5 18 ♕xg5 f6 19 ♗xe4 ♕xe4 20 ♗xf6 ♖d7 21 ♖xc5.

17 ♘e5 ♗e8

If 17...♗d6 then 18 ♕g4 is strong, while in the event of 17...f6 18 ♘xc6 ♘xc6 19 e5 f5 20 ♕c4 ♕c8 White can play, among other things, 21 g4!, and if 21...fxg4, then 22 ♕e4, winning material.

18 ♘g4!

At this point White has four pieces in the attack, the queen and all the minor pieces, since an eventual e5 will liberate the g2-bishop, against which there is no good defence.

18...♘a6

If 18...♘c6 White wins with 19 ♗xg7! ♔xg7 20 ♕h6+ ♔g8 21 e5 f6 22 ♗e4 f5 23 ♕xe6+. Now the finish is similar.

19 ♗xg7! 1-0

Exercise 28
Alekhine – Fine
Hastings 1936

Black is a pawn up, but the h6-bishop is very strong and both black knights are occupying very passive positions.

30 ♖f1!

The pressure on f7 creates the threat of 31 ♗xa6.

30...♖3c7

If 30...♘c5 31 ♗b1 ♘xa4, Fine indicates the pretty finish 32 ♗a2 ♖3c7 33 ♖b1 ♕a7 34 ♗xf7+!! ♖xf7 35 ♕xa7 ♖xa7 36 ♖f8#.

31 ♖b1 ♕c6 *(D)*

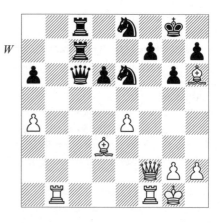

32 a5!

Creating strong pressure on Black's position. He fails to find the most tenacious defence.

32...♘c5?

Giving up the exchange with 32...♕c5 does not seem to be an improvement, since after 33 ♗e3 ♕xa5 34 ♗b6 ♕e5 35 ♗xa6 Black has a difficult defensive task.

The same can be said of 32...♕c3 33 ♗xa6 ♖a8 34 ♗b7 ♖xa5 35 ♗d2, given by Euwe, who also pointed out the following beautiful variation which illustrates the power of all the white pieces and the defensive fragility of the black king: 32...♕a4 33 ♗xa6 ♖a8 34 ♗b7 ♖xa5 35 ♗d5! ♕d7 36 ♖b8! ♕e7 37 ♗xe6 ♕xe6 38 ♕f6! mating.

The best move is 32...♖a8, although after 33 ♖bc1 with the plan of 34 ♗c4 Alekhine prophesied a difficult defensive task for Black.

33 ♗c4

Now White's bishop can be activated without having to carry out any manoeuvres.

33...♕d7 *(D)*

33...♘xe4? fails to 34 ♗xf7+ ♔h8 35 ♕d4+.

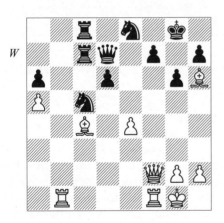

Can you find the best move for White in this position?

34 ♕a2!

With this unexpected switch, making way for the f1-rook, Black's position is left defenceless.

34...♘xe4

Now the capture on f7 is winning. Instead, 34...♘b7 35 ♖xf7 ♕xf7 36 ♗xf7+ ♖xf7 37 ♕e6 does not improve Black's position, and

34...d5 35 ♗xd5 ♘d6 fails to change anything either; the simplest then seems to be 36 ♕a1 ♘e6 37 ♖b6! (threatening 38 ♕f6) and now if 37...♕e7, 38 ♖xa6 wins easily.

35 ♖xf7 ♕xf7 36 ♗xf7+ ♖xf7 37 ♕e6 1-0

Exercise 29

Parma – Bielicki

World Junior Ch, Münchenstein/Basel 1959

White was relying on an indirect defence of f2 after 25...d4 26 ♘e4 ♗xe4 27 ♗xe4, but a surprise awaited him.

25...d4! 26 ♘e4 ♕xc2+!! *(D)*

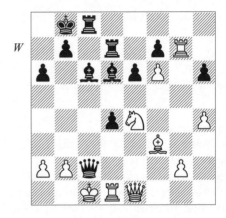

27 ♔xc2 ♗xe4++ 0-1

It is mate after 28 ♔b3 ♗c2# or 28 ♔d2 ♖c2#. This game was of great importance in helping the Argentinean Carlos Bielicki to win the World Junior Championship of that year.

Exercise 30

Tal – Miles

Porz 1982

In positions with a knight on e5, the f7-square generally requires special care. This is especially the case here, since White has several pieces aiming at the kingside and has also occupied the d-file.

15 ♗xh7+!

It was possible to win a pawn with the simple 15 ♘xd7 ♘xd7 16 ♗xh7+ ♔xh7 17 ♖xd7, but White can hope for more than he gets after 17...♕c6 18 ♕d3+ ♔g8 19 f3 ♖ad8 20 ♖xd8 (not 20 ♖d1? ♖xd7 21 ♕xd7 ♖d8, winning material) 20...♖xd8.

15...♘xh7

The importance of retaining the e5-knight, due to its influence on f7, can be seen in the line 15...♘xh7 16 ♖xd7 ♘xd7 17 ♕h5+ ♔g8 18 ♕xf7+ ♔h8 19 ♘g6+ ♔h7 20 ♘xe7.

16 ♖xd7! (D)

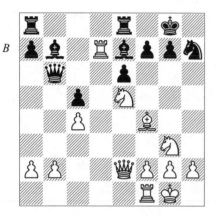

16...g6

No better is 16...f6 17 ♕g4 fxe5 18 ♘h5, when the black king is helpless.

The weakness of g7 and of Black's castled position in general following the disappearance of the vital h7-pawn can also be seen after 16...♘f6 17 ♘h5!! ♘xd7, and once again the blow 18 ♕g4!, to which there is no satisfactory reply.

Now White has an extra pawn and a long-term technical victory, but once again White finds a neat combinative solution to shorten the task.

17 b4!

Opening the long diagonal for the queen; for example, 17...cxb4 18 ♗h6 ♖ad8 19 ♕b2! f6 20 ♕c2 f5, and Black's castled position has become very weak. Although this is advantageous for White, it is Black's best course, since at least he has recovered the pawn.

17...♗c8?

Now the attack continues with an extra pawn and no difficulties.

18 bxc5 ♕xc5 19 ♘e4 ♕b6 20 ♕f3!

Once again the most aggressive, hitting f7, and seeking out the black king.

20...♕b2

20...♗xd7 loses to 21 ♗e3.

21 ♘xf7 ♕g7

If 21...♗xd7 then 22 ♗e5 ♕xa2 23 ♘h6#.

22 ♘h6+ ♔h8 23 ♖c7 ♖f8 24 ♖xe7! 1-0

Exercise 31

Netto – Abente
Asuncion 1983

The white pieces are uncoordinated, but the decisive factor is the weakness of the light squares in White's castled position, combined with the undefended back rank. The theme is well known, but the finish is also beautiful.

1...♖e1+ 2 ♔g2 ♖g1+!! (D)

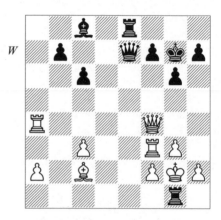

3 ♔xg1 ♕e1+ 4 ♔g2 ♕f1+! 5 ♔xf1 ♗h3+ 0-1

Exercise 32

Lautier – Karpov
Dortmund 1993

There is a pawn missing from each side's castled position. This definitely benefits White, who now has two files for attack. Let us note that the b6-bishop is not helping the defence and that White is not threatening anything; the g2-bishop is hemmed in by its own pawns at e4 and d5, yet is carrying out a vital task defending the e4-pawn.

How should White attack Black's king?

26 ♖h3!

The threat of 27 e5 'forces' the capture of the g4-pawn, after which White obtains a new file to attack down, at the moderate price of a pawn of no immediate importance.

26...♗xg4 27 ♖g3 ♗h5 (D)

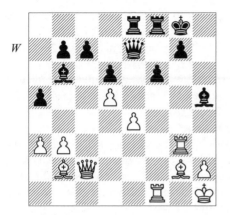

How should White continue? Black has a satisfactory reply against the immediate 28 ♖f5 in 28...♕f7!, threatening 29...♗g6, and after 29 ♖xf6?! ♕xf6 30 ♗xf6 ♖xf6, Black has reasonable compensation for the queen, thanks to his control of the dark squares, the weakness of e4, and having nullified White's attack.

28 ♕d2!

This was the move that Black missed; the white queen joins in the attack with tremendous force.

28...g6 *(D)*

Against 28...♔h7 White plays the manoeuvre started with ♕d2, which is to send the queen on the offensive with 29 ♕f4 ♕f7 30 ♕h4!, threatening 31 ♖f5, with an irresistible attack.

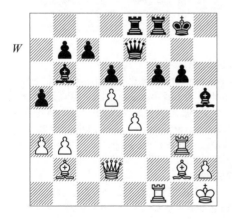

29 ♖f5

The accumulation of White's forces on the kingside is tremendous.

29...♕h7

After 29...♔h7 there are two very strong continuations; one is 30 ♕f4!, when after 30...gxf5 there is a mating attack with 31 ♕xf5+ ♔h8 32 ♕xh5+ ♔h7 33 ♗xf6+. The result is similar using the move-order 30 ♖xh5+! gxh5 31 ♕f4 f5 32 ♖g5! ♕f7 33 ♕h4.

30 ♗xf6 *(D)*

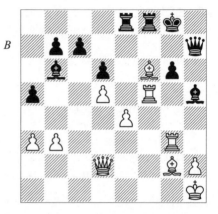

White has an extra piece in the attack and, with the diagonals and files open, the result already seems clear.

30...♖f7 31 ♕g5 c6

Lautier pointed out that after 31...♔f8 one possible continuation is 32 ♖f4 c6 33 ♗h3 cxd5 34 ♕xd5, and Black's position collapses.

32 e5

The g2-bishop links up with the other pieces, and victory is near. There are other strong continuations which are less complex, but White calculated this continuation well.

32...dxe5 33 dxc6 *(D)*

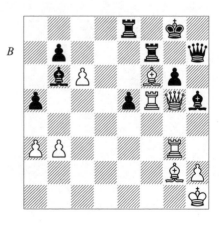

33...♔f8

A more tenacious continuation, especially when you take into account the practical chances offered by White's time-pressure, was 33...e4!?, although White is still winning; for example, 34 cxb7 ♗c7 35 ♗e5! ♖xf5 36 ♕xf5 ♗xe5 (or 36...♖xe5 37 ♕c8+) 37 ♕xe5, and the b7-pawn decides.

34 ♖xe5 ♖xe5 35 ♕xe5 ♗c7 36 ♕e6!

36...♗xg3 is not playable now owing to the mate on c8.

36...♗g4 37 ♕xg4 ♖xf6 38 ♕c8+ 1-0

Exercise 33

Ivanchuk – Topalov
Novgorod 1996

White is slightly better; the d5-knight is strong and there is pressure on f7. Black chose to expel the a7-rook from its annoying position.

23...♘c6?

This will be brilliantly refuted. The imagination displayed by White in the attack is worthy of admiration.

It is not logical to abandon the strong central knight outpost with 23...♘c4? just to attack the queen; after, for instance, 24 ♕f2, the pressure would continue.

The best move is 23...♗e6!, defending the vulnerable f7-square, and only after 24 ♕f2 expelling the a7-rook with 24...♘c6 25 ♖aa1 ♕d7 26 ♗e3 ♘e5, with a normal position, slightly advantageous for White after 27 ♗d4, according to Ivanchuk.

24 g6!! (D)

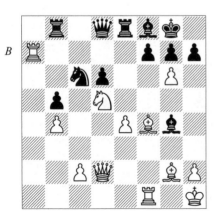

Opening the h4-d8 diagonal. The main idea is to reply to 24...hxg6 with 25 ♖xf7!, when if the rook is captured White plays 26 ♗g5+, while after 25...♗e6 26 ♗g5 ♗e7 27 ♘xe7+ ♘xe7 28 ♕f4 ♕d7 White's build-up of forces is converted into a mating attack with 29 ♖xg7+! ♔xg7 30 ♗f6+.

24...♘xa7

This is the first defence that should be considered. Ivanchuk commented that the most tenacious is 24...f6!?; let us examine the main continuation, in which White gains the advantage after 25 ♖c7! ♗d7 26 ♘xf6+ gxf6 27 ♕d5+ ♔h8 28 gxh7 ♗e7 29 ♖xc6 ♗xc6 30 ♕xc6, since the black king is very exposed.

If 24...fxg6 25 ♗g5 ♗e7 White wins thanks to the pin on the e7-knight after 26 ♘xe7+ ♘xe7 27 ♕f4 ♗e6 28 ♕h4 ♗d7 29 ♗h3.

25 gxf7+ ♔h8 (D)

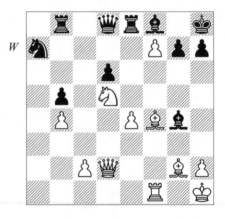

26 ♗g5!!

Looking for more than the positional advantage that could be achieved with 26 fxe8♕ ♕xe8 27 ♘e3, with perhaps ♘f5 to follow; there are several weaknesses in the black camp: the king is rather exposed, the a7-knight is out of play, and the d6-pawn is weak.

26...♕d7

If 26...♖e7 27 ♘xe7 ♗xe7 White can win in various ways, such as 28 ♕f4 or 28 e5.

27 fxe8♘ ♖xe8

Ivanchuk pointed out that after 27...♕xe8 White wins with 28 ♘f6! gxf6 29 ♗xf6+ ♔g8 (or 29...♗g7 30 ♗xg7+ and the a7-knight falls to 31 ♕d4+) and here the only piece that is not yet attacking comes into play and seizes the light squares with 30 e5! ♗e6 31 ♗d5, winning.

28 ♕f2 ♔g8 *(D)*

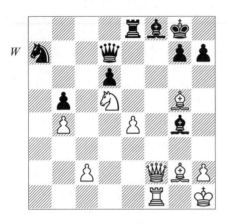

What now? The material is equal, the black king is somewhat exposed, and the a7-knight out of play, although the same can be said of the g2-bishop. How can White continue the attack before the a7-knight returns to the defence?

29 e5!! *(D)*

Now the g2-bishop cannot be said to be out of play.

29 ♗e7 was tempting, since after 29...♗xe7 30 ♕f7+ ♔h8 31 ♘xe7 the defensive try 31...♗e6? fails to 32 ♕f8+ ♗g8 33 ♘xg8! ♖xf8 34 ♖xf8, winning, but Black can defend with 31...♕d8!, and if 32 h3 then 32...♗h5.

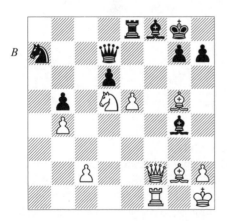

29...h6

29...♗e6 loses to 30 ♘f4! ♗c4 31 e6 ♕c8 32 ♕xa7. The entrance of the g2-bishop is decisive

after 29...♘c8 30 ♘c7 ♕xc7 31 ♗d5+. The same thing happens after 29...dxe5 30 ♘b6 ♕c7 31 ♗d5+.

30 ♘b6 ♕c7 31 ♗d5+ *(D)*

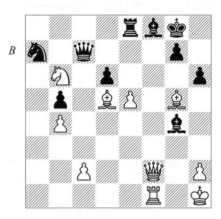

31...♔h7

Or 31...♔h8 32 ♕xf8+ ♖xf8 33 ♖xf8+ ♔h7 34 ♗e4+ g6 35 ♗f6, mating.

32 ♗e4+ ♔g8 33 ♘d5 ♕d7 34 ♘e7+! 1-0

Black resigned in view of 34...♗xe7 35 ♕f7+ ♔h8 36 ♕g6.

An impressively conducted attack by Ivanchuk, combining accuracy and beauty, don't you agree?

Exercise 34
Sutovsky – J. Polgar
Tilburg 1996

Black's castled position is weakened, and the move that immediately springs to mind is 17 ♕h5, although after 17...♗b6! 18 ♗xb6 ♕xb6+ 19 ♔h1 ♖g8! 20 ♖f4 ♔h8, planning to defend against 21 ♖h4 with 21...♖g7, Black achieves a reasonable position. The typical Sicilian e5-knight is a very strong defensive piece. The position is equally perilous for Black after 21 ♖af1 ♗d7 22 ♖xf7 ♘xf7 23 ♖xf7 ♖g7 24 ♖xg7 ♔xg7 25 ♕h6+ ♔g8 26 e5 (interpolating 26 g6 is less dangerous) 26...♗c6+, but Black appears to hold.

17 ♔h1!! *(D)*

As Sutovsky commented, White aims to exchange off the e5-knight rather than the black bishop.

17...♗b6

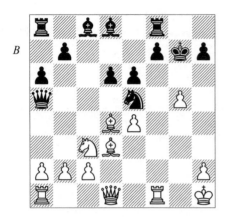

The best practical chance consisted of giving up a piece with 17...♗xg5!? and after 18 ♖g1, not 18...♔h6? 19 ♖xg5! ♔xg5 20 ♕d2+! ♔h5 (if 20...♔f6 21 ♘d5+ the queen drops) 21 ♗e2+ ♘g4 22 ♗xg4+ ♔xg4 23 ♖g1+ mating, but 18...h6 19 h4 f6 20 hxg5 hxg5 21 ♔g2, when White is better but Black has survival chances in practice.

18 ♗xe5+ ♕xe5 19 ♕h5 (D)

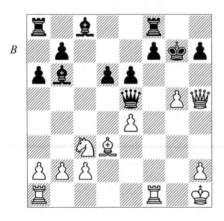

Sutovsky: "It is difficult to believe it, but Black is lost! White plans to play ♖f6, ♖af1, ♕h6(+) and g6; Black can do nothing to prevent this."

19...♗e3?!

Although it does not save Black, a better try was 19...♗d7 20 ♖f6 ♗e3 21 ♖af1 ♗e8 22 ♕h6+ ♔g8 23 ♘d5! exd5 24 exd5 ♕xd5+ 25 ♖1f3 ♕xd3 26 cxd3 ♗c6 27 ♔g2, when White still has technical problems in exploiting his advantage, according to Sutovsky.

20 ♖f3

To double rooks as well as to play ♖h3; there is no defence.

20...♗xg5 21 ♖g1 f6 22 h4 1-0

After 22...h6 23 hxg5 hxg5 24 ♖h3 White invades decisively; for example, 24...♖g8 25 ♕h7+ ♔f8 26 ♕c7 ♕c5 27 ♕d8+ ♔f7 28 ♖h7+ ♔g7 29 ♖h8, mating. The queen on e5 proves a less capable defender than the knight was on that square.

Exercise 35
Svidler – Dreev
Russian Ch, Elista 1997
(Continuation of Exercise 3.)

Black has two pawns for the exchange, which is sufficient in itself, but has a pressing development problem. White's advantage can soon evaporate, so that, as always in these cases, he needs to act with speed.

21 ♗xh6! ♘e5

After 21...gxh6 the attack is tremendous; for example: 22 ♕g4 ♔h7 23 ♖f6! ♕e8 24 ♖xg6! ♘e5 25 ♖e6.

22 ♗f4 (D)

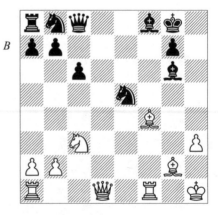

22...♘bd7

Continuing his development. In the event of 22...♘d3 23 ♖f3 ♕d7 (exchanging the knight with 23...♘xf4 24 ♖xf4 leaves White in complete control; for example, after 24...♘d7?! White wins with 25 ♕b3+ ♔h8 26 ♖h4+ ♗h7 27 ♗e4 ♘f6 28 ♗xh7 ♘xh7 29 ♕c2) 24 ♕b3+ ♔h8 (if 24...♗f7 then 25 ♖xd3! ♕xd3 26 ♕xb7 wins) 25 ♖d1 ♘a6 26 ♕c4 ♖d8 (or 26...♘xb2

27 ♖xd7 ♘xc4 28 ♖xb7, with a crushing advantage) 27 ♗g5, and the active d3-knight will perish.

23 ♘e4

Svidler considers that after this move White has a winning position. He has only one pawn for the exchange, but the most important thing is that all the white pieces can quickly join in the attack, while the a8-rook in particular will never be able to come into play.

23...♕e8 24 ♕b3+ ♕f7 25 ♕g3 ♗xe4

This knight was too strong, but now the light squares will have no defender.

26 ♗xe4 ♘f6! (D)

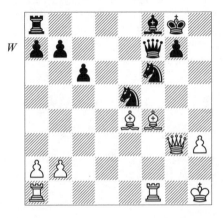

27 ♗g2?!

A clearer continuation is 27 ♗xe5 ♘xe4 28 ♕g2 ♕d5 29 ♖xf8+ ♔xf8 30 ♗xg7+! ♔g8 31 ♗e5+ ♔f7 32 ♖f1+ ♔e6 33 ♕g4+ ♔xe5 (or 33...♔e7 34 ♕g7+ ♔e6 35 ♕f7+ ♔xe5 36 ♖f5+) 34 ♖f5+ ♔d6 35 ♖xd5+ cxd5 with a decisive advantage for White; Black's weak queenside pawns and the strong h-pawn make it an easy win.

27...♘h5?

Black misses the best defence, 27...♘ed7.

28 ♕g5 ♘d3 29 ♗e5! ♕e7 30 ♕xh5 ♕xe5 31 ♕f7+ ♔h8 32 ♖f5 ♘f2+ 33 ♔g1 ♘xh3+ 34 ♔f1 1-0

Exercise 36
Mitkov – Rublevsky
European Clubs Cup, Neum 2000

White has opened the g-file at the cost of giving up the exchange, but this is of little importance since the minor pieces are stronger in this phase of the game. It will be another matter if the attack is beaten off. How can White throw more wood on the fire before it goes out?

18 e5!

First the d3-bishop comes into play, with devastating pressure on h7.

18...dxe5

18...♘e8 fails to 19 ♗g5! f6 20 fxe6 g6 21 ♗xg6 ♕e7 22 exf6 ♘xf6 23 ♗f7!.

19 ♖xg7!! (D)

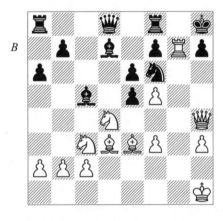

An artistic way to eliminate the best defender, the f6-knight.

19...♖g8

If 19...♔xg7 White wins with 20 ♗h6+ ♔h8 21 ♗g5 ♗e7 22 fxe6.

19...exf5 loses to, among other things, 20 ♘d5! ♖g8 (or 20...♔xg7 21 ♕h6+ ♔h8 22 ♘xf6) 21 ♖xf7 ♖g7 22 ♖xg7 ♔xg7 23 ♗g5.

20 ♖xg8+ ♔xg8

Or 20...♘xg8 21 f6 ♘xf6 22 ♗g5.

21 ♗g5 ♗e7 22 ♘e4 ♘d5 23 f6! ♕b6

If 23...♗f8, 24 ♘d6 wins.

24 ♘c5 ♕xc5 25 ♕xh7+ 1-0

Exercise 37
Vaganian – Shirov
Istanbul Olympiad 2000

To answer the question, it is necessary to analyse and evaluate various continuations, for the attack and the defence. In particular, Black must take into account three main moves: 26 ♕h6, against which it is essential to have the reply 26...♕f8 available, the 26 ♘xg6 sacrifice, and the 26 f5 break.

25...♖e2?, intending 26...♕e3+, does not work, since with the *zwischenzug* 26 ♖f3!, followed by 27 ♘xg6 or 27 ♕h6, depending on Black's reply, White mates.

The correct defence was 25...♗e8! (D), defending g6 against the ♘xg6 sacrifice.

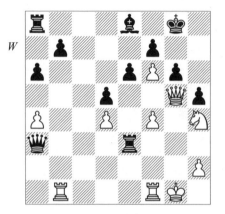

26 f5? is answered with 26...♖e4!, threatening 27...♖g4+ and hitting the h4-knight, and Black wins material. After 26 ♖xb7 ♖e2, 27 f5? is met by 27...♕h3, and once again it is Black who comes out on top; 27 ♖e7? is also bad: 27...♕e3+ 28 ♔h1 ♕h3 29 ♘g2 ♕g4 and Black exchanges queens with a much better ending. The best move is 27 ♕h6! and the game ends in a draw after 27...♕f8 28 ♕g5 (threatening 29 ♘xg6) 28...♕a3 29 ♕h6.

Therefore the correct reply was 'b'.

25...♔h7? (D)

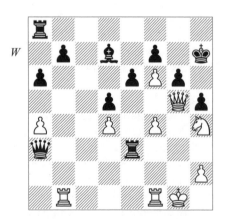

This defends against two of the threats, but neglects f7, and the king is worse placed than on g8, as we shall see.

26 ♖xb7

And there is no defence.

26...♖d8

If 26...♗e8? then 27 ♕xg6+ wins, while 26...♖e2 loses to 27 f5.

27 f5! exf5 28 ♖xd7 ♖xd7 29 ♘xf5 1-0

Exercise 38

Topalov – Bareev

Dortmund Candidates 2002

The black king's defensive cover has been advanced and the pawns themselves are targets. However, 22 a4 is not yet a threat in view of the reply 22...b4, and 22 c4 is not good on account of 22...♖hc8.

22 ♕e2! (D)

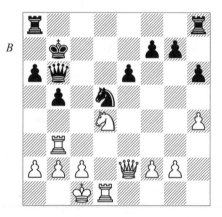

It is a different matter if the most powerful piece comes into play. Now there is a threat of 23 ♘xb5.

22...♔a7

The defence 22...♘c7 allows 23 ♕f3+, followed by 24 ♕xf7, while 22...b4? can be answered by 23 c4!, and now the c4-pawn is already defended.

23 ♘xb5+!

Nevertheless!

23...axb5 24 ♖xb5 ♕c6

If 24...♕a6 then 25 ♖dxd5 exd5 26 ♕e7+ wins. Now there is a similar finish, in which the black king is fatally exposed.

25 ♖dxd5! exd5 26 ♕e7+ ♔a6 27 ♖b3 1-0

Exercise 39
Anand – Rublevsky
Dortmund 2004

Black is two pawns up but is playing a rook down, which helps White create mating threats.

32 ♘g3! *(D)*

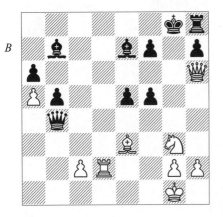

Threatening both 33 ♘xf5 and 33 ♘h5, and winning the game.

32...f4

Surprisingly the natural 32...♕g4 loses to 33 ♘xf5!! ♕xf5 34 ♖d8+! ♗xd8 35 ♗c5 and mate is unavoidable. 32...♕h4 also loses, to 33 ♕xh4 ♗xh4 34 ♘xf5 ♗f6 35 ♖d6.

If the g3-knight now retreats then Black has 33...♕b1+ and 34...fxe3+. So how should White continue?

33 ♘f5!

The incarceration of the black king allows White to give up substantial material and then give mate. This wins more quickly than 33 ♘h5, which does in fact win, for similar reasons. From f5 the knight also ties Black's queen to the defence of e7, which is not the case with 33 ♘h5.

33...♕b1+ 34 ♔f2 fxe3+ 35 ♔e2! 1-0

Exercise 40
Svidler – Leko
FIDE World Ch, San Luis 2005

Black has an uncomfortable position. The a5-knight in particular does not have any useful function in the short term, and might remain out of play. The black queen on b6 and the f2-bishop are also uncomfortably placed; the queen might become stranded a long way from the kingside, while the bishop is short of really safe squares.

If you ask yourself what Black is going to do, there is no clear reply. In contrast, White is planning to play 21 ♕e2, seizing the e-file, followed by ♖f1, and all his pieces will be aiming at the sparsely defended black kingside.

How should Black defend against the positional threat of 21 ♕e2?

Trying to solve the problem of Black's a5-knight by bringing it immediately into play with 20...♘b3? is not the solution, since then White has 21 a5! ♕b5 22 ♖a3 ♘c5 23 ♕e2!, and the f2-bishop has no retreat.

Withdrawing the bishop from the immediate danger with 20...♗g3 is equally unconvincing; after 21 ♖e4! (intending to recapture on e4 with the pawn and gain a strong centre) 21...f5 22 ♖xe8+ ♖xe8 23 ♘d4 g6 24 ♕f3!, all the white pieces are aiming at Black's weakened castled position.

20...d6?

This move leaves the queen and the a5-knight out of play; the knight no longer has the tour ...♘b7-d6 available, and Black's position is becoming critical. Svidler pointed out that the best move is 20...f6! *(D)*:

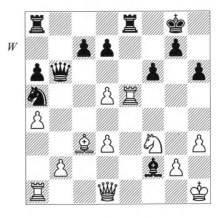

a) The importance of leaving the d6-square free can be seen, for instance, in the line 21 ♖xe8+ ♖xe8 22 b4 ♘b7 23 ♖a2 ♘d6, and the black pieces have achieved a certain harmony.

b) After 21 ♖e4 the main line is 21...♖xe4 22 dxe4 ♘b3 23 ♖b1 d6 24 ♘h2! ♖f8 25 ♘g4

&c5 26 ♕f3 ♘d4 27 ♕d3, when White is just a little better.

c) Svidler did not mention it, but 21 ♖e2!? seems more dangerous, threatening to take on a5 and f2. After 21...♖xe2 22 ♕xe2 ♘b3 23 ♖f1, and then, for instance, 23...♗g3 24 ♘g1, followed by ♕g4, all the white pieces are once again aiming at Black's kingside, with advantage. 21...♘b7!? looks better; even though Black's position is rather suspect after 22 ♘d2 ♖xe2 23 ♕xe2 ♗d4 24 a5 ♕a7 25 ♕g4 ♗xc3 26 bxc3 ♕e3 27 ♘e4, it seems that Black can hold on with 27...♖f8.

21 ♖xe8+ ♖xe8 22 b4!

Not only to misplace the a5-knight even more, but also so that the a1-rook can come into play more quickly.

22...♘b7 23 ♖a2! *(D)*

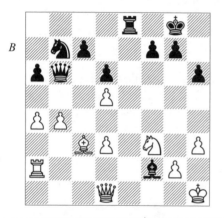

23...♗g3

It is not easy to find anything better. Black wants to bring the bishop into play via e5, but this abandons the g1-a7 diagonal.

If 23...♘d8 Svidler indicates the line 24 a5! ♕a7 25 ♖e2 ♖xe2 26 ♕xe2 ♕e3, and now White gains a winning passed pawn with 27 ♕xe3! ♗xe3 28 b5 axb5 29 ♗d4.

24 ♖e2 ♖d8?!

The rook is exposed to attack by ♘d4-c6. 24...♖f8 is more tenacious, although the position is very difficult to defend after 25 ♖e4 (threatening 26 ♖g4) 25...f6 26 ♖c4 ♘d8 27 ♘d4, as Svidler pointed out. If 24...♖xe2? 25 ♕xe2 ♔f8, White wins by using the abandoned e-file with 26 ♘d4! ♗e5 27 ♘c6 ♗xc3 28

♕e7+ ♔g8 29 ♕e8+ ♔h7 30 ♘e7, mating quickly.

25 ♘d4 *(D)*

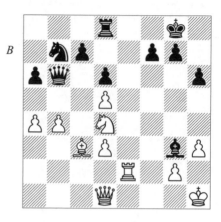

With the threat of 26 ♘f5.

25...a5

This offers alternative paths to White, but there was no longer any defence. If 25...♗e5 then 26 a5 wins material.

26 ♘c6 ♖f8 27 ♗d4 ♕a6 28 b5 ♕a8 29 ♖e7

Absolute domination.

29...♗e5

If 29...♕c8, the possible fork on e7 allows 30 ♖e3 ♗h4 31 ♖g3 g6 32 ♕h5 ♗g5 33 ♖xg5.

30 ♘xe5 dxe5 31 ♗xe5 1-0

Exercise 41

Harikrishna – Vescovi

FIDE World Cup, Khanty-Mansiisk 2005

Black is a pawn up and has a great advantage on the queenside, but his castled position is open and rather unprotected.

White can eliminate a vital defender with 27 ♘xf6+ and after 27...♕xf6 28 ♗c3 ♕f8 29 ♕e4, controlling the e-file and threatening 30 f6, he exerts strong pressure on Black's castled position thanks in part to the strong c3-bishop. But there are some tactical details that allow him to extract even more profit from his accumulation of forces on the kingside.

27 ♗xh6! *(D)*

With the disappearance of the h6-pawn, Black's castled position is left even more unprotected.

27...♕f8

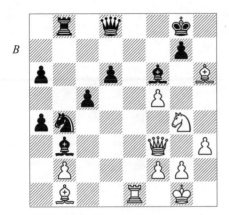

B

After 27...gxh6? 28 ♖e8+ ♕xe8 29 ♘xf6+ ♔f8 30 ♘xe8 ♖xe8 31 f6 the b1-bishop is indirectly protected, for if 31...♖e1+ 32 ♔h2 ♖xb1, then 33 ♕e4 with a double attack.

White's attack is also decisive in the event of 27...♗xb2 28 f6!; for instance, 28...gxh6 29 ♕f5 ♔f8 30 ♕g6 ♖b7 31 ♕xh6+ ♔g8 32 ♕g6+ ♔f8 33 ♕h5!.

28 ♕g3 ♗xb2 *(D)*

If 28...♘c2, White gives up his strong bishop with 29 ♗xc2, since after 29...♗xc2 White has a choice of several winning continuations, such as 30 ♘xf6+ ♕xf6 31 ♖e6 ♕f7 32 ♖g6.

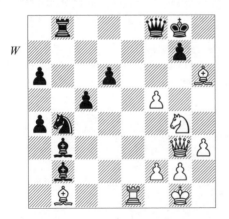

W

29 ♗xg7!

White's moves are like real knockout blows. The f5-pawn is now of decisive importance.

29...♗xg7

If 29...♕xg7 then White wins with 30 f6 ♕f8 (30...♗xf6 is no better: 31 ♘xf6+ ♔f7 32 ♖e7+) 31 ♘e5+ mating.

30 f6 ♘d5

There is another mate after 30...♗xf6 31 ♘xf6++ ♔h8 32 ♕h4+ ♔g7 33 ♕h7+ ♔xf6 34 ♕g6#.

31 f7+!

This is the blow that finally downs the black king. If 31...♔xf7 then 32 ♘h6+ ♔xh6 33 ♕g6#, while if 31...♔h8, mate will not long be delayed after 32 ♕h4+ or 32 ♕d3.

1-0

Exercise 42
L. Dominguez – Yusupov
Turin Olympiad 2006

Black has an extra pawn, which will be very strong if he manages to guard his kingside.

Once again it is essential to act quickly; the a8-rook and the a5-knight are a long way from the kingside, but the knight can get back quickly.

How should White take advantage of the h-file?

26 h6!

This is the right way, weakening the dark squares, especially so that the c1-bishop can invade Black's castled position; in contrast, 26 hxg6? ♕xg6 (hitting c2) is much less promising.

26...♗a4 27 hxg7

Dominguez indicates that this is stronger than 27 ♘f4 ♖e8 28 hxg7 ♕xg7, when Black has managed to regroup.

27...♕xg7 28 ♗g5! *(D)*

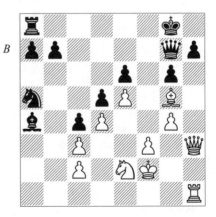

B

Aiming to put the bishop on f6 before bringing the e2-knight into the attack.

28...♗xc2

Black's kingside cannot be defended in the event of 28...♘c6 29 ♘f4 ♖e8 30 ♗f6 ♕d7 31 ♘xg6 ♗xc2 32 ♘f4.

29 ♘f4 ♖e8 30 ♗f6 ♕d7

30...♕f7 is no improvement; White breaks through with 31 ♕h6 ♘c6 32 ♘h3! (not rushing; 32 ♘h5?! fails to 32...gxh5 33 gxh5 ♘e7! 34 ♖g1+ ♘g6) 32...g5 33 ♕xg5+ ♕g6 34 ♕h4 followed by 35 ♘f4.

31 ♕h6 ♘c6 32 ♘h5! *(D)*

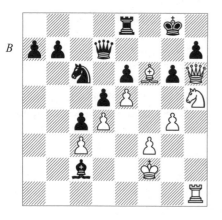

32...♖f8

Now 32...gxh5 33 gxh5 leads to mate with the imminent ♖g1+, since 33...♘e7 is impossible.

33 ♘g7! g5 34 ♘xe6 ♖e8 35 ♕xg5+ ♗g6

Or 35...♔f7 36 ♘c5, winning for White.

36 ♕xg6+! 1-0

The queen sacrifice forces mate: 36...hxg6 37 ♖h8+ ♔f7 38 ♘g5#.

Exercise 43

Adams – Topalov
Wijk aan Zee 2006

At first sight Black's position is solid. He faces no immediate problems on the kingside, while he has pressure on b4 and the possibility of ...♕c4.

It is true that the b5-pawn is weak, and White could consider 22 ♗e2, intending ♖a1, with play on the queenside.

Looking a bit more deeply, we note the latent attack by the g3-bishop upon the black queen on c7 and the b8-rook, the possible sacrifice on

d5 on account of the weakness of f6, and this last idea grabs our attention.

22 f5!! *(D)*

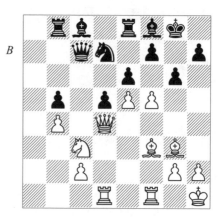

The kingside defences are blown skyward with this brutal initial attacking blow.

22...gxf5

If Black attempts to exchange queens with 22...♕c4, then White wins by using the combination that is present in almost all lines: 23 fxe6 fxe6 24 ♘xd5!! ♕xd4 25 ♖xd4 exd5 26 ♗xd5+ ♔h8 27 ♗f7 (or 27 ♗c6) 27...♖e7 28 e6 ♖a8 29 ♖dd1 (but not immediately 29 exd7? due to 29...♖xf7!) with a winning material advantage. The same occurs after 22...♕b6 23 fxe6 fxe6 24 ♘xd5.

23 ♘xd5! ♕c4 *(D)*

23...exd5? is worse: 24 e6 ♕b6 25 exf7+ ♔xf7 26 ♗h5+.

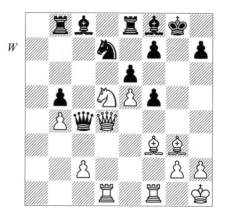

24 ♕d2!

Adams commented that he hesitated between this and 24 ♕e3. Logically, White's first reaction is to keep the queens on, taking into account the weakness of the black king. He decided in favour of the text-move so he could respond to 24...♗b7 with 25 ♘e3.

In the tranquillity of the post-mortem he saw that 24 ♘f6+ ♘xf6 25 exf6 ♕xd4 26 ♖xd4 e5 (or 26...♖b6 27 ♗e5) 27 ♖e1 was also very strong.

24...h6 *(D)*

If 24...exd5 White wins with 25 ♕g5+! ♔h8 26 ♗xd5 ♕g4 27 ♕xg4 fxg4 28 ♗xf7, followed by 29 e6.

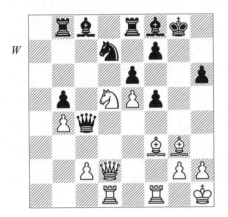

How should White now proceed with the attack? 25 ♕f2 is interesting, since if 25...exd5 26 ♗xd5 ♕g4, defending f5, then 27 ♗c6 is strong, but White continues the offensive in another way.

25 h3!

A multi-purpose move; as well as providing useful *luft*, it controls the g4-square, the importance of which we have already seen, and it asks Black what useful move he has.

25...exd5

And it turns out that there is no good reply to White's question. Black enters complications in which his king will come under a tremendous attack.

If 25...♗g7 White wins with 26 ♘f6+, while 25...♔h8 is met by 26 ♘f6 ♘xf6 27 exf6 e5 28 ♗d5 ♕c7 29 ♕e2! (heading for h5) with a devastating attack, and 29...f4 fails to 30 ♗xf4.

26 ♗xd5 ♕xb4 27 c3 *(D)*

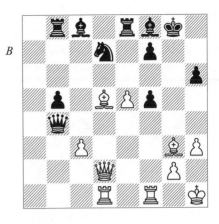

B

27...♕c5?!

27...♕e7! is more tenacious; for example, after 28 ♖xf5 ♘xe5! 29 ♖xe5 ♗e6 Adams commented that a certain accuracy by White is required. Let us see the main line given by him: 30 ♗xe6! (even better than 30 ♖xe6) 30...fxe6 31 ♕e2 ♗g7 32 ♖xb5 ♖xb5 33 ♕xb5 ♖xc3 (it is amazing that with equal material and all the pawns on the same wing, White still succeeds in putting together a winning attack, exploiting Black's lack of a g-pawn and his overloaded queen) 34 ♗h4 ♕f7 35 ♖f1 ♕g6 36 ♖f3 ♗g7 37 ♖g3 ♕f7 38 ♗f6! ♕xf6 39 ♕e8+ ♔h7 40 ♔h2 ♕f5 41 ♕d7 ♕f6 42 ♕d3+, with a winning position.

28 ♖xf5 ♖e6 *(D)*

If 28...♖e7 then White wins by 29 e6, while after 28...♘xe5 29 ♖xe5 ♖xe5 30 ♗xe5 ♖b6, White again wins by direct attack, as in the previous line, moving forward with gain of tempo: 31 ♕f4 ♕e7 32 ♖f1 ♗e6 33 ♗d4 ♖a6 34 ♕e5.

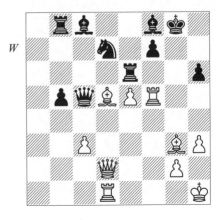

W

29 ♖xf7! *(D)*

A worthy winning blow to crown White's brilliant attack. With the disappearance of the f7-pawn the defence of the black king becomes impossible.

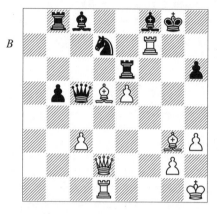

B

29...♘b6

If 29...♔xf7 then 30 ♕f4+ ♔e8 (or 30...♔e7 31 ♗h4+) 31 ♗xe6.

30 ♖df1

Now there are several ways to win. 30 ♕f4! ♗g7 (or 30...♘xd5 31 ♖xd5 ♕a3 32 ♕f5, and White mates soon) 31 ♖f1 ♘xd5 32 ♕g4! is slightly quicker.

30...♘xd5 *(D)*

If 30...♗g7 once again the queen comes to the kingside and decides the struggle with 31 ♕f4 ♘xd5 32 ♕g4.

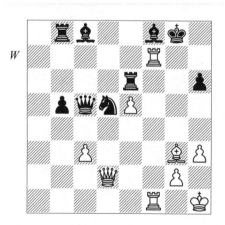

W

31 ♖xf8+ ♕xf8 32 ♖xf8+ ♔xf8 33 ♕xd5 ♔e8

Adams commented that the position is easily won for White because in addition to the material advantage he has a persistent attack against the exposed black king.

34 ♗h4 ♗d7 35 ♗f6 b4 36 ♕e4

36 ♕d3 ♖xf6 37 exf6 bxc3 38 ♕e4+ ♔d8 39 f7 is slightly quicker but there is no cause for alarm, since the position will not change.

36...♗c8 37 cxb4 ♖b7 38 ♕g6+ ♔d7 39 ♕xh6 ♔c7 40 ♕f4 ♔b8 41 h4 ♖c7 42 h5 1-0

Exercise 44

Visser – Speelman

Staunton Memorial, London 2006

White has no advantage. He should have resigned himself to playing 19 ♗xf6, and after 19...♗xf6 20 ♖d3 he has a fully playable position. It is not then possible for Black to open the game for the bishops with 20...b4 21 cxb4 ♕xb4? because of 22 ♖b3, while in the event of 20...♗d5 White can reply 21 ♘d2, maintaining the balance.

19 ♗xh6?

This sacrifice is unsound. White does not have enough attack to compensate for the piece, because Black's forces are no distance away from the main combat zone.

19...gxh6 20 ♕xh6 *(D)*

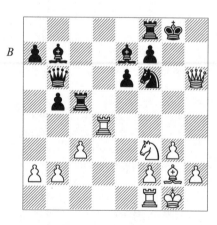

B

20...♗e4!

The b7-bishop comes to the defence of the kingside. It is also good, although not as strong, to play 20...♖h5 21 ♖g4+! ♘xg4 22 ♕xh5 ♗xf3 (22...♘f6? 23 ♕g5+ ♔h8 24 ♕h4+ is a draw) 23 ♗xf3 ♘f6 24 ♕g5+ ♔h7 25 ♖e1 ♖g8.

21 ♘g5

If 21 ♖e1 then Black does indeed continue 21...♖h5. After the text-move, if the e4-bishop retreats then White plays 22 ♖h4. Black has only one defence now, but it is enough to tilt the scales in his favour.

21...♘g4!

Going over to the counter-attack.

22 ♕h4

If 22 ♕h3 the continuation would be similar to the course of the game.

22...♖xg5 23 ♗xe4 f5! 24 ♖d7

And thus we arrive at Exercise 45.

Exercise 45
Visser – Speelman
Staunton Memorial, London 2006

The position is a critical one. Both 24...fxe4? and 24...♖f7? lose to 25 ♖xe7!.

It is advantageous to hang on to the material advantage with 24...♕c5!, although there would still be a struggle after 25 b4 ♖g7 26 bxc5 ♗xh4 27 ♖xg7+ ♔xg7 28 ♗b7, followed by c6. Black has something stronger.

24...♘xf2!

The moment to strike back has arrived.

25 ♗f3 (D)

25 ♖xe7 fails to 25...♘xe4+ 26 ♔h1 ♖g7, and there is no perpetual check thanks to the centralized e4-knight. 25 ♖xf2 loses to 25...fxe4, with a mating attack.

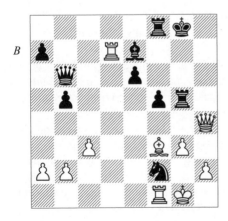

25...♘e4+!

Preparing the decisive combination.

26 ♔h1

If 26 ♔g2 then simply 26...♖xg3+, winning the queen. Now comes a brilliant finish, taking advantage of the strength in attack of the major pieces, helped by the e4-knight.

**26...♖xg3! 27 ♕xe7 ♕g1+! 28 ♖xg1 ♘f2#
(0-1)**

Exercise 46
Timman – Hübner
Wolvega 2006

Black is a pawn up, but is slightly behind in development and White has several pieces threatening Black's castled position.

In Black's favour is the fact that he threatens the g5-bishop, and since the a2-pawn is also hanging, we are in a critical position. If the g5-bishop retreats, for instance with 14 ♗f4, then 14...♗d7 15 ♗e5 ♗c6 can follow, and Black has completed his development, without fearing the latent attack by the e5-bishop upon his queen. The capture ...♕xa2 will be even more attractive once Black has completed his development. White must act quickly.

14 ♗xh6!

Practically forced; it is not a winning sacrifice, but it is definitely the best move.

14...gxh6 15 ♕e5! (D)

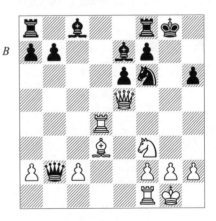

Activating the queen with the threat of 16 ♖g4+ followed by 17 ♕xb2.

15...♕b6?

This logical move that brings the queen to the defence is an error that leads to a very difficult position. The reason is that the queen was still useful on b2, pinning the d4-rook, and

Black could have improved his defence by leaving White with that problem, which would cost him a tempo.

After 15...♔h8!, dealing with the threat, planning ...♖g8 or the defensive ...♘g8, and paralysing the d4-rook, we have a clearer answer to the question, which is that the chances for both sides are equal (thus answer 'c' is correct).

The best line seems to be 16 ♘d2 ♕b6! (not 16...♖g8?! 17 ♘e4 ♗g7 18 c3!, unpinning the d4-rook, with an almost decisive effect) 17 ♖h4 (if 17 ♘e4? then 17...♖d8, while 17 ♖f4? is useless in view of 17...♕d6 {or 17...♕c5} 18 ♕xd6 ♗xd6 19 ♖xf6 ♗g7 20 ♖f3 and now perhaps 20...f5, when Black has the bishop-pair and the better king) 17...♖g8! 18 ♕f4! (worse are 18 ♘e4 ♖g6! and 18 ♖xh6+ ♗g7 19 ♘e4 ♕d8!, but not 19...♔xh6? 20 ♘xf6 with a mating attack) 18...♖g7! 19 ♕xh6+ (not 19 ♖xh6+?! ♔g8 20 ♕h4 ♔f8 21 ♖xf6 ♗xf6 22 ♕xf6 ♗d7) 19...♘h7 20 ♗xh7 (if 20 ♖g4 the 'long' move 20...♕b2! defends adequately) 20...♗xh4 21 ♗d3+ ♔g8 22 ♕xh4, with enough compensation for the exchange.

16 ♖h4! *(D)*

One difference from the 15...♔h8! line is that here the white rook can join in the attack without any loss of time (such as 16 ♘d2).

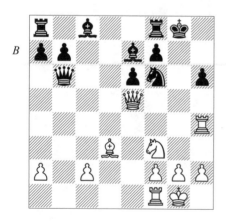

16...♖d8

If 16...♕d6 then 17 ♕e3!, with a winning attack.

17 ♖xh6 ♔f8

As Mikhail Golubev indicates in the digital newspaper *Chess Today*, after 17...♗f8 the

strongest line seems to be 18 ♖xf6 ♗g7 19 ♗h7+! ♔f8 (19...♔xh7 is met by 20 ♕h5+ and 21 ♕xf7+, and 19...♔h8 by 20 ♕h5!) 20 ♖xf7+ ♔xf7 21 ♘g5+ ♔f8 22 ♕f4+ ♔e7 23 ♕f7+ ♔d6 24 ♕xg7 and White wins.

18 ♕g3

Threatening 19 ♖h8+. Now there is no defence for Black.

18...♔e8 19 ♘e5 ♕c7 20 ♗b5+! 1-0

Black has to block with a piece on d7 and then 21 ♕g7 will force mate.

Exercise 47

Suarez Pousa – Salgado Lopez

Liga Gallega, Santiago de Compostela 2007

The black king is in the centre and there are several white pieces attacking. Black will show that in fact it is the white king that stands worse, and that the white 'attacking pieces' are in reality a long way from the defence. The a8-bishop has an important role in this finish by the young Galician IM (now GM) Ivan Salgado, several times Spanish junior champion.

The question was "What is the best defence against 28 ♖xe7+?". I admit that this was a trick question, since here the best defence is attack!

27...♕c1+ 28 ♖e1 ♕xe1+! 29 ♗xe1 ♖xg2! 30 ♖a7 ♗f3 0-1

The whole board is too small for the white queen, which has no escape from the threatened discovery; furthermore there are mating threats.

Exercise 48

Van Wely – Svidler

Wijk aan Zee 2007

It is easy to recognize the Grünfeld structure. Black exchanged bishops on h6, thinking that this would draw the queen from the centre, and from the defence of the d4-pawn.

The lonely white queen, which can do nothing dangerous on its own, now receives some tremendously powerful help, partly taking advantage of the position of the two queens, although at the moment this appears irrelevant.

19 ♖c5! *(D)*

Now we see why the position of the two queens is critical. 19 d5 ♘e5, 19 ♕e3 e5 or 19 ♖fd1 ♗g4 would justify Black's idea of bringing the queen to h6.

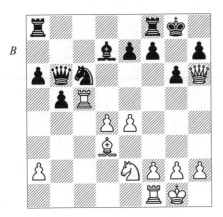

B

19...♗g4?

This allows more pieces to be brought into the attack. Alternatively:

a) 19...♘xd4? is no good either, since White has 20 ♖h5!, winning.

b) If 19...♖fd8 it is not correct to attack with 20 ♘f4? since after 20...♘xd4 21 ♖h5 (not 21 ♘h5? ♘e6 and the attack is over) 21...♕f6 22 ♕xh7+ ♔f8 there does not seem to be any way for White to make progress; in this line Black managed to regroup by bringing the queen to the defence. Nevertheless, Van Wely indicates that White still wins with 20 ♖h5!, opening the diagonal for the d3-bishop, and after 20...gxh5 21 e5 f5 22 exf6 exf6 23 ♕xh7+ ♔f8 24 ♘f4 ♘e7 25 ♖e1! (or 25 ♗g6), there is no defence.

c) The most tenacious move was 19...f6, although after 20 ♖fc1 the centre is well defended and the attacking chances based on h4-h5 or e5 give White a clear advantage.

20 ♘f4!

This is the other piece that joins in; if now 20...♖fd8 then 21 ♖g5!, threatening the bishop, and if it retreats then 22 ♘h5.

White threatens 21 ♘d5 ♕b7 22 ♖xc6 ♕xc6 23 ♘xe7+, winning. There is a defence against it, but this is not the only idea.

20...♘xd4 21 ♖g5!

It is not possible to defend both the bishop and the h5-square.

21...♗f3 22 ♖g3!

With threats of 23 ♖h3 and 23 gxf3, which are unstoppable.

1-0

Exercise 49

Miton – Ivanchuk

Montreal 2007

White's castled position is suspiciously short of defenders. If Black could introduce one of his major pieces into the attack, this would be very strong.

24...♘e7!

Seeking to drive away the c6-rook in order to liberate the e6-rook.

Ivanchuk commented that the immediate 24...♗xh2+? is poor, since after 25 ♔xh2 ♘xe3 26 fxe3 ♕xf1 27 ♖xf1 ♖xc6 28 ♖f4 ♖e8 29 ♖f2, although Black has a rook and two pawns for the two pieces, the position is unclear.

25 ♖6c3? *(D)*

With the benefit of hindsight, it is easy to recommend the exchange sacrifice 25 ♖xc7, when the game remains a fight. Ivanchuk indicated that after 25...♗xc7 26 ♖xc7 ♘d5 27 ♖xa7 ♖c6 28 ♘d2 ♖c3 Black has an advantage.

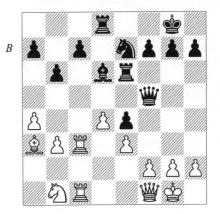

B

25...♗xh2+!!

The lack of kingside defenders makes this typical sacrifice decisive.

26 ♔xh2 ♕h5+ 27 ♔g1 ♖h6 28 f3

28 f4 is more tenacious, although Black has a strong attack after 28...♘f5, which threatens 29...c5, blowing up the centre, as well as the main attacking idea of 29...♕h2+, followed by 30...♖h3 or 30...♕g3+ and 31...♖h2.

28...♘f5 29 ♘d2 ♕h2+ 30 ♔f2 ♕h4+ 31 ♔g1 ♘g3!

The attack is irresistible.

32 ♕d1 exf3 33 ♕xf3

Not 33 ♘xf3? ♕h1+ 34 ♔f2 ♘e4+ 35 ♔e2 ♕xg2+ 36 ♔d3 ♘f2+.

33...♕h2+ 34 ♔f2 ♖f6 *(D)*

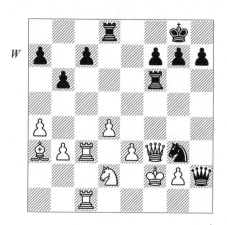

And the attack is transformed into a decisive material advantage.

35 ♕xf6 gxf6 36 e4

If 36 ♖xc7 the quickest way seems to be 36...♘h1+ 37 ♔f1 ♕g3.

36...♘h1+ 37 ♖xh1

Equivalent to resignation, but if 37 ♔f1 then among other things Black can play 37...♕h4, with an attack and a material advantage.

37...♕xh1 38 ♗e7 ♕h6!

This is the clearest refutation of 37 ♖xh1; it defends f6 and attacks the d2-knight.

39 ♖g3+ ♔h8 40 ♘f3

If 40 ♗xd8 then 40...♕xd2+ 41 ♔f3 ♕c3+ 42 ♔f4 ♕xd4.

40...♖e8 0-1

Chapter 5

Exercise 50

Horowitz – Kevitz
New York 1931

There are several white pieces deployed menacingly against Black's castled position, but it is essential to take advantage quickly, because Black is about to retreat with 22...♘f6, defending the kingside and liberating the a8-bishop and the b6-knight, which are out of play at the moment. The weaknesses in Black's back ranks make these defects decisive.

22 ♕g5! *(D)*

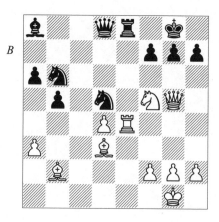

1-0

It is mate in six moves at most: 22...g6 23 ♕h6 gxf5 24 ♖g4+ fxg4 25 ♗xh7+ ♔h8 26 ♗g6+ ♔g8 27 ♕h7+ ♔f8 28 ♕xf7#.

Exercise 51

Vikulov – Dvoretsky
Moscow Ch 1971

The evaluation of this position depends on who is to move. It can be concluded that Black is better after the following strong manoeuvre:

12...♗xe5! 13 dxe5 ♘xd2! 14 ♕xd2 ♘c5

This manoeuvre, based on exchanging on e5 and subsequently occupying the c5-square with the d7-knight, is one of the ideas made possible by the omission of ...c5.

15 ♗c2 dxc4 16 bxc4 ♖fd8 *(D)*

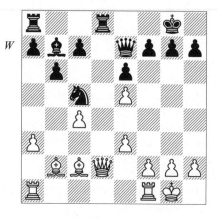

Black occupies the d-file with gain of time. The b2-bishop remains inactive, which often happens in this type of 'Horwitz Bishops'

position after an exchange on e5, leaving a pawn blocking the diagonal. The evaluation of the position depends on whether the remaining pieces are active enough to mask the fact that the b2-bishop is not doing much.

17 &d4

If 17 ♕e2 then Black has 17...♗e4!, which is a very favourable transaction for Black, exchanging the piece that can hurt the black king whilst leaving White with the passive b2-bishop.

17...♘e4! 18 ♗xe4

White relies on the opposite-coloured bishops; it would be difficult to play 18 ♕e1 although this does not seem worse.

18...♗xe4 19 f3 ♗b7 20 ♕c2 (D)

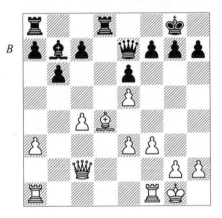

20...c5!

Fixing the weakness on c4, and preventing White from playing 21 c5.

21 ♗c3 ♖d7

The moment has come to occupy the open file.

22 a4

White wants to get rid of the weak pawn. Dvoretsky commented that it was preferable to reduce Black's potential on the d-file by exchanging a rook, although after 22 ♖fd1 ♖ad8 23 ♖xd7 ♕xd7 Black controls the file and has a clear advantage.

22...♖ad8 23 a5 ♕g5! 24 ♖ae1

If 24 f4? then the elegant 24...♖d2! wins. Here we can see why it was appropriate for White to exchange a rook, reducing the power of Black's two rooks.

24...♖d3 25 axb6 axb6 26 ♕b2

The attempt to convert the d3-rook into a tactical weakness with 26 ♗d4 can be met by 26...♖8xd4!? 27 h4 ♕xe5 or 26...♕g6 followed by ...h5.

26...♗a8?!

26...♖8d7 is better, gaining two tempi on the game.

27 h3 h5 28 ♕c2 ♗b7!

Recognizing his error, Black aims to put pressure on the weakness at c4 with ...♗a6.

29 ♖e2 ♖8d7 (D)

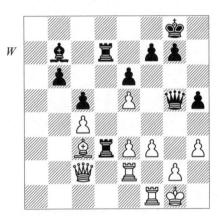

30 ♔h1

If 30 ♕b2 then 30...♗a6.

30...♗a6 31 ♕a4 ♖xc3 32 ♕xa6 ♕d8!

Dvoretsky considers that after this regrouping, Black's position is winning. White cannot protect all his weaknesses: the c4-pawn, the e5-pawn and the weak kingside.

33 ♕a1

The more tenacious 33 ♔h2 is met by 33...h4, planning later to exchange a pair of rooks and invade White's position with ...♖d2 or ...♖d1.

33...♖xc4 34 ♖a2 ♕g5 35 ♖a8+ ♔h7 36 ♕b1+ ♕g6 37 g4 hxg4 38 hxg4 ♖c2 39 ♔g1 ♖dd2 0-1

Exercise 52

Nisman – Dvoretsky
Moscow 1972

The position is similar to that of Exercise 51. The only difference is the position of one rook on each side, and this means that the position is equal.

14...♗xe5?!

In this case this is not the best. Now we shall see that White is not obliged to stay passive, as was the case in the previous exercise.

15 dxe5 ♘xd2 16 ♖xd2 dxc4 17 bxc4

17 ♕xc4? loses to 17...♘xe5!.

17...♘c5 *(D)*

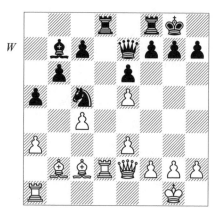

What is the difference between this and the previous example?

18 ♖d4!

The difference is marked by the inclusion of ♖d1 and ...♖d8, thanks to which White has the fourth rank and can manoeuvre to improve his pieces. White now threatens a combination that is well known to us: 19 ♗xh7+ ♔xh7 20 ♕h5+ ♔g8 21 ♖h4.

18...g6 19 ♕g4

White could have eliminated many chances of black counterplay with 19 a4!?.

19...a4!

The c5-knight lacked prospects but now has the b3-square, which distracts the white pieces from a straightforward follow-up. It is essential to do everything possible to prevent White from progressing unhindered.

20 ♖ad1 ♘b3 21 ♗xb3 axb3 22 h4 *(D)*

22...h5

Not 22...c5? 23 ♖d6. Dvoretsky cites Taimanov-Averbakh, Zurich Candidates 1953 as a good example of this type of position.

23 ♕f4

The threats are ♖1d3, capture on b3, play e4, or also eventually g4.

23...♖xd4!? 24 exd4 b5!

The struggle has become very complicated.

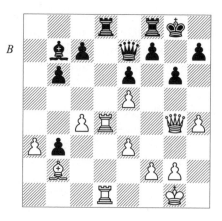

25 d5! ♕c5! 26 ♕f6 ♕xc4 27 ♗c1! ♔h7 28 ♕e7 ♕e2 29 ♖f1 ♖g8?

29...b2! draws, as Black's counterplay against g2 then comes quickly enough.

30 ♗g5! b2 31 ♗f6 ♕xf1+ 32 ♔h2 ♕c1 33 ♕xf7+ ♔h6 34 ♗g5+?

White can win by 34 g3!!, with the idea 35 ♗g5+ ♕xg5 36 hxg5+ ♔xg5 37 ♕f4#.

34...♕xg5 35 hxg5+ ♔xg5 36 ♕f6+ ♔h6 37 ♕f4+ ♔h7 38 ♕b4 ♗xd5 39 ♕xb5 c5 40 ♕xb2 c4 41 ♔g3 ½-½

Exercise 53

Keres – Beliavsky

USSR Ch, Moscow 1973

The missing f7-pawn leaves Black's king exposed, although the strength of the d4-bishop is at least as important; it drills into Black's castled position without opposition. Even so, the exchange of light-squared bishops would reduce his disadvantage. White manages to find another tactical weakness, the a6-bishop.

26 ♕g4! ♖e7 27 ♗xg7! *(D)*

27...♖xg7

Nothing is changed by 27...h5 28 ♕xh5 (or 28 ♕g6) 28...♖xg7 29 ♗xe4.

28 ♕e6+ ♖f7 29 ♗xa6 ♕d2 30 ♗e2

Although Black has a slight initiative, the greater exposure of his king does not allow him to create any serious counterplay.

30...♖d6 31 ♕e5 ♖b6 32 ♖d1 ♕a2 33 ♕xd5 ♕xd5 34 ♖xd5 ♘xf2 35 ♗f3

Slightly quicker was 35 ♖d8+ ♔g7 36 ♖g3+ ♔h6 37 ♗f3 but the text-move, cutting off the knight's retreat, also leads to victory.

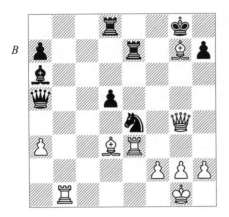

35...罝b2 36 h3 罝c7 37 查h2 罝b1 38 罝d2 罝f1 39 罝ee2 匀h1 40 盒d5+ 查g7 1-0

White wins easily after 41 g4 罝cc1 42 盒g2.

Exercise 54

Petrosian – Browne

Buenos Aires Olympiad 1978

If White could make progress unhindered with 18 匀e5 and a later f5, etc., his initiative would be unstoppable, but with his next move Black manages to draw a lot of the venom out of White's attacking possibilities, so that he can then regroup and put pressure on the hanging pawns.

17...盒e4!

Petrosian considered that Black's chances were slightly better after this exchange.

18 匀d2 盒xd3 19 豐xd3 盒b4! *(D)*

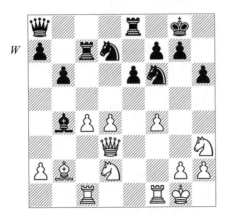

Another strong move, designed to control the e4-square. In principle, in positions where one

side has hanging pawns or an isolated queen's pawn, 'neutral' exchanges, i.e. that make no important concessions, favour the opposing side, who then has fewer worries about his king.

20 匀f3 豐e4 21 豐b3 盒a5 22 盒c3 盒xc3 23 罝xc3 罝ec8 24 g3 *(D)*

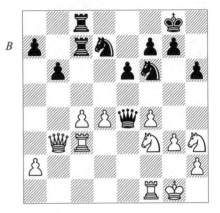

24...匀d5?!

Petrosian commented that Black retains a slight advantage after 24...匀e8!, with the idea of putting pressure on the c4-pawn with a timely ...匀d6.

25 罝cc1 豐g6 26 罝fe1 匀e7 27 匀f2 匀f5 28 豐d3!

The position is approximately equal, but in the following phase White clearly outplays his opponent.

28...匀e7 29 匀e4! 匀d5? 30 豐f1 匀b4 31 a3 匀c6 32 d5 exd5 33 cxd5 匀a5 34 f5 豐h5 35 罝xc7 罝xc7 36 匀d6 匀f6 37 h3 罝c3 38 查g2 匀xd5?? 39 g4 匀f4+ 40 查g3 豐xh3+ 41 豐xh3 1-0

Exercise 55

Miles – Browne

Lucerne Olympiad 1982

White is better; he has all his pieces threatening the kingside, and the a7-bishop is out of play. Even so, the position is not yet ripe for a violent assault on the kingside because the uncastled white king would allow Black to hit back.

17 0-0! *(D)*

It is best to complete development and, as in Game 26, set up a threat.

17 &xh7+? &xh7 18 ₩h5+ &g8 19 &xg7 is premature in view of 19...f6! 20 &xf8 (not 20 ₩h8+? &f7 21 &xf8 ₩e5+ 22 &f1 &xf8) 20...&xf8 21 &c3 ₩e5+ 22 ₩xe5 fxe5 with an unclear position.

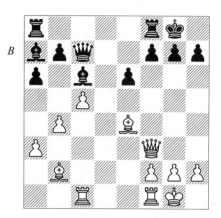

17...&ad8?

Now the a7-bishop is ready to come back into play via b8 but, again as in Game 26, the position now has all the prerequisites for the double bishop sacrifice to work.

17...&fd8 is better, preventing the combination, because the black king can now escape. Even so, White is better after 18 ₩c3 (18 &fd1!? is also interesting) 18...f6 19 ₩h3 f5 20 &xc6 ₩xc6 21 &fd1, when Black's castled position has been weakened.

18 &xh7+! &xh7 19 ₩h5+ &g8 20 &xg7! *(D)*

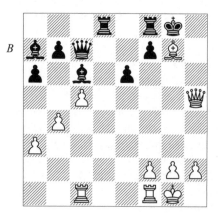

20...&xg7

20...f6 now fails to 21 ₩h8+ &f7 22 &xf8 &xf8 23 ₩h7+ and the undefended position of the black queen is the decisive factor. Were it not for this tactical weakness, the combination would not be sound.

Something similar occurs in Lasker-Bauer (see page 124); Black gains more than sufficient material for the queen, but there is a key move (22 ₩d7!) which wins a piece at the end of the combination, which justifies it.

21 ₩g5+ &h8

Or 21...&h7 22 &c4 mating.

22 ₩f6+!

Better than 22 &c4 f6 23 &h4+ ₩h7 24 &xh7+ &xh7.

22...&g8 23 &c4 1-0

Exercise 56
Portisch – de Firmian
Reggio Emilia 1989/90

Black lacks the defending f6-knight. With 16 d5 White could open the two diagonals leading to Black's king and after 16...exd5 then 17 ₩d3, if there is nothing better, would be a good option.

16 &xc6!

But White finds something even stronger.

16...&xc6 17 &e5 ₩b7 *(D)*

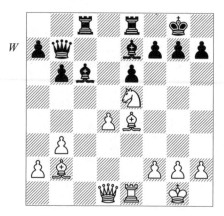

18 &xh7+!

The immediate 18 ₩h5 is also effective: 18...g6 (in the event of 18...&xe4 19 ₩xf7+ &h8 20 d5 &g8 21 d6! White's attack is decisive) 19 ₩f3 &b4!? 20 &xc6! (not 20 &xc6? &xe1 21 ₩f6? &xc6 22 d5 &c3! 23 &xc3 &xc3 and Black wins) 20...&xc6 21 &xc6 &xe1

and once again the b2-bishop comes into play with great force after 22 d5 e5 23 ♕f6 ♕d7 24 ♗xe5 ♖xe5 25 ♕xe5, with a winning endgame.

18...♔f8

18...♔xh7 19 ♕h5+ ♔g8 20 ♕xf7+ ♔h7 (not 20...♔h8 21 ♘xc6! ♖f8 22 ♕xe7 ♕xc6 {22...♕xe7 23 ♘xe7 threatens both the c8-rook and 24 ♘g6+, winning} 23 d5 ♕c7 because 24 ♗xg7+ is now with check) 21 ♕g6+! (better than 21 ♘xc6 ♖f8! 22 ♕xe7 ♕xe7 23 ♘xe7 ♖c2, which is also good, but the struggle would last longer) 21...♔g8 22 d5! ♗xd5 (22...♗f6 23 dxc6) 23 ♘d7! e5 24 ♗xe5 leads to mate.

19 ♕h5 ♗b4 20 ♗d3! (D)

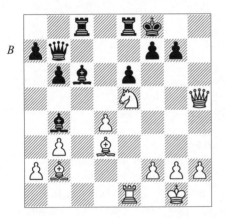

20...g6

If 20...♗xe1? there is a mate after 21 ♗a3+, and 20...♗xg2 is no good either in view of 21 ♗a6! ♕c7 (21...♗f3 22 ♕h8+ ♔e7 23 ♕h4+) 22 ♖c1 winning the queen.

21 ♕h6+ ♔e7

21...♔g8 loses to 22 ♘g4! f5 23 d5.

22 d5! ♗xe1

If 22...♗xd5 then 23 ♕h4+ is decisive.

23 ♗a3+ ♔d8 24 ♕h4+ ♔c7 25 dxc6

White has a decisive attack, and wins elegantly.

25...♕a8 26 ♕f6 b5 27 ♗c5 ♖cd8 28 ♕xf7+ ♔c8 29 ♗xb5 a6 30 ♕d7+! 1-0

Exercise 57

Franco – Verat

Palma de Mallorca 1991

All the white pieces are aiming at Black's castled position, which is very sparsely defended.

The correct course is to open lines, even at the cost of a piece.

21 f5! exf5 22 ♗xf5

Also to be considered was 22 ♘xf5!? gxf5 23 ♗xf5 with a very dangerous attack.

22...gxf5 23 ♘xf5 (D)

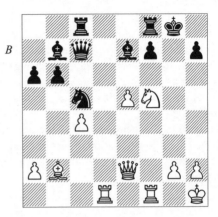

The f5-knight is as strong as the f5-bishop of the previous line, or even stronger.

23...♘e6 24 ♕g4+ ♔h8 25 ♘d6 ♗g5 26 ♖d3

Heading for the weakness at h7.

26...♖cd8 27 ♖h3 (D)

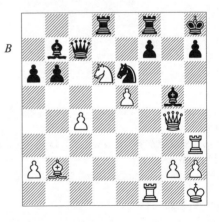

27...♕c6

After 27...♗c6, White wins by 28 ♖h5 ♗d2 29 ♕h4 h6 30 ♗c1!. 27...♖d7 is best met by 28 ♖f5 ♖g8 29 ♖g3.

28 ♖xf7 ♕xg2+?

This loses easily. 28...♔g8!? is better, when although White has the advantage after 29 ♖g3

♖xf7 30 ♕xe6 ♖xd6 31 exd6 ♔f8 32 h4!, there is still a fight.

29 ♕xg2 ♗xg2+ 30 ♔xg2 ♖g8 31 ♖xf8+ ♖xf8 32 ♖g3 ♔h8 33 ♖xg5! ♘xg5 34 e6+ ♔g8 35 e7 1-0

Exercise 58
Franco – Pogorelov
Las Palmas 1994

All the white pieces are aiming at Black's kingside and the position is ready for a strong offensive against the king. It is not even necessary to give up any material as in previous exercises.

20 f5! ♘g5

20...gxf5? 21 ♘xf5 opens the f-file and allows the knight to enter at d6 or else exchange the g7-bishop, followed by an attack on the dark squares.

21 e6! *(D)*

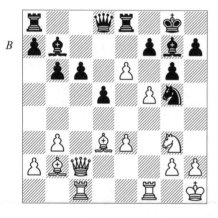

Guaranteeing the opening of Black's castled position.

21...♗xb2 22 ♕xb2 fxe6 23 fxg6 e5 24 ♘h5! hxg6 25 ♗xg6

More ambitious than 25 ♘f6+ ♔g7 26 ♘xe8+ ♕xe8, which is also good.

25...♖e6 26 ♗f5 ♖e7

26...♖h6 is met by 27 ♕xe5, with a very strong attack. For example, 27...♖xh5 28 ♗g6 ♖h6 (28...♖h4 29 ♗f5 ♘e4 30 ♖f7) 29 ♖f6 and the only way not to lose decisive amounts of material is 29...♕b8, although Black's position cannot hold with all his pieces uncoordinated after 30 ♖d6! followed by, among other things, 31 ♖f1.

27 ♕f2

The time has come for the queen to transfer powerfully to the kingside.

27...♕d6 28 ♕h4 ♕h6 *(D)*

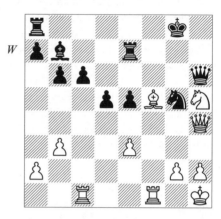

How should White prevent Black from bringing the a8-rook into play?

29 ♗c8! ♖xc8 30 ♖f6 1-0

Exercise 59
Shabalov – Stefansson
Reykjavik 1994

The position cries out for a sacrifice on f5 to open up of the black king's position, and sure enough White gains a winning attack after...

20 ♘xf5! gxf5 21 ♗xf5 ♘g7 22 ♗b1

The threat is 23 ♕d3 or 23 ♕c2.

22...♗c8 23 ♕d3 ♗f5 24 ♖xf5! ♖xf5 25 g4 ♖g5 26 ♕xh7+ ♔f7 *(D)*

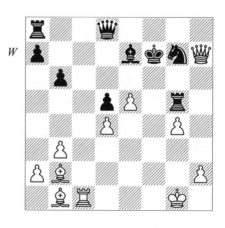

27 ♔h1?

White had two ways to win; the more con-clusive one was 27 ♗g6+!! ♖xg6 28 ♖f1+ ♗f6 29 e6+! ♔xe6 30 ♕xg6 and there is no good de-fence against 31 g5.

27 ♖f1+ ♔e6 28 ♕h6+ ♔d7 29 ♖f7! is also very strong; for example, 29...♘e6 30 ♗a3 ♖xg4+ 31 ♔h1, when 31...♕g8? fails to 32 ♕xe6+! mating.

27...♕h8 28 ♖f1+ ♔e6 29 ♕c2 *(D)*

Now 29 ♗f5+? ♘xf5 30 gxf5+ ♔d7 31 ♕f7? was no longer any good owing to the un-expected counter-blow 31...♕xh2+!, mating.

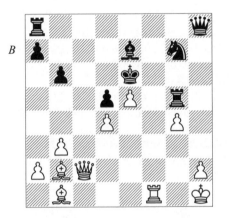

29...♖c8 30 ♕g2 ♖f8 31 ♖c1 ♖c8 32 ♖f1 ♕h4 33 ♖f4?

The final mistake; 33 ♗f5+ ♘xf5 34 gxf5+ ♔f7 35 ♕xd5+, followed by f6, is better. De-spite being a rook down, in view of his very strong trio of centre pawns and Black's weak king, White stands well.

33...♖f8 34 ♗f5+ ♖fxf5! 0-1

After 35 gxf5+ ♘xf5 Black makes his mate-rial advantage count.

Exercise 60
Kurajica – Karpov
Tilburg rapid 1994

The white queen on h6 offers very strong at-tacking possibilities. Since the f6-knight is loose, the offensive can proceed apace.

20 ♘f5! ♕d8

If 20...♘e8 then 21 f4! is powerful: 21...♕d8 (or 21...♘6g7 22 ♘xd6 ♘xd6 23 ♗a3 ♖d8 24 ♕g5 ♘df5 25 ♕f6) 22 ♖f3 and White's attack is tremendous.

21 ♕g7+!! *(D)*

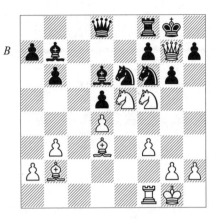

By means of this pretty sacrifice White wins decisive amounts of material, with which he manages to win despite tenacious resistance by Black.

21...♘xg7 22 ♘h6+ ♔h8 23 ♘exf7+ ♖xf7 24 ♘xf7+ ♔g8 25 ♘xd8 ♗c8 26 ♘c6 a5 *(D)*

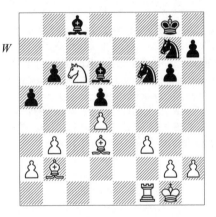

27 ♖e1 ♔f8 28 ♗c1 ♘e6 29 ♗e3 ♗d7 30 ♘e5 ♗e8 31 ♗h6+ ♔e7 32 ♗e3 ♗a3 33 ♖e2 ♘d7 34 ♘xd7 ♗xd7 35 h4 ♗d6 36 a4 ♔d8 37 h5 gxh5 38 ♗xh7 ♘f4 39 ♖c2 b5 40 axb5 ♗xb5 41 ♗xf4 1-0

Exercise 61
Franco – C. Pena
Galicia tt 2003

White's pressure on Black's castled position is enormous, and ought to give conclusive re-sults.

18 ♕f3?!

White could have played the instructive manoeuvre 18 ♘xg7! ♔xg7 19 ♕g4+ ♔h8 20 ♕h4 ♔g8 21 ♕g5+ ♔h8 22 ♕h6 d4 23 ♗xd4 *(D)*.

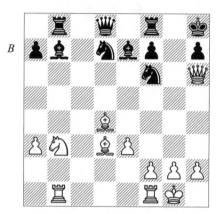

White threatens 24 ♕xh7# and 24 ♗xh7, which cannot be satisfactorily prevented; for instance, 23...♘e5 24 ♗xe5 ♕xd3 25 ♗xf6+ ♗xf6 26 ♕xf6+ ♔g8 27 ♘c5 ♕d5 28 ♘xb7.

18...♔h8 19 ♕g3 ♖g8 20 ♘xe7 ♕xe7 21 ♕h4

White still has a big advantage. The b7-bishop is a useless piece and the pressure on Black's castled position is overwhelming.

21...♖be8 22 ♖fc1 ♘e5 23 ♗xe5 ♕xe5 24 ♘d4 ♖c8 25 ♘f3 ♕h5 26 ♘g5! ♖gf8 27 ♖xc8 ♗xc8 28 ♕xh5 ♘xh5 29 ♖b8 1-0

Exercise 62
Kramnik – Van Wely
Wijk aan Zee 2007

The e3-pawn is attacked, but we already know that material is of secondary importance when there is a mismatch of forces on the wing where the defending king is located.

21 ♕e4!

The threats against the king are too strong, and while the white queen shows all its power, the black queen is a long way away on b8.

21...♘f6 22 ♕g6 *(D)*

22...♔h8

22...♗xe3+ is no better: 23 ♔h1 ♖f8 (if 23...♗g5 then White wins with 24 d5! {24 dxc5 is also strong} 24...e5 25 ♖xf6! ♗xf6 26 d6 and

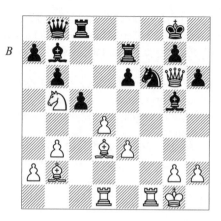

there is no defence) 24 dxc5 ♔h8 25 ♖de1 ♗g5 26 ♘d6 bxc5 27 ♖xe6! and if 27...♖xe6 the final defender of h7 disappears with 28 ♗xf6.

23 dxc5 ♖xc5?!

This allows a pretty finish. 23...♖f8 is more tenacious, although after 24 ♘d6 bxc5 25 ♗e5 Black's position is by far the worse.

24 ♖xf6! gxf6 25 ♗xf6+ ♗xf6 26 ♕xf6+ ♖g7 27 ♕xh6+ ♔g8 28 ♕xe6+ ♔h8 29 ♕h6+ ♔g8 *(D)*

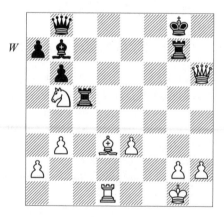

30 e4!

Controlling d5, with the idea of 31 ♗c4+.

30...a6 31 ♘d6 b5 32 ♕e6+ ♔h8 33 ♘f7+ ♔g8 34 ♘g5+ ♔h8 35 ♕h6+ ♔g8 36 ♕e6+ ♔h8 37 ♕h6+ ♔g8 38 ♘e6 ♖h7 39 ♕g6+ ♔h8 40 e5 1-0

There is no defence. The only possible rook retreat is 40...♖d7 and then many moves win, such as 41 ♕h6+ ♔g8 42 ♗h7+ ♖xh7 43 ♕g5+ ♔f7 44 ♘xc5.

Chapter 6

Exercise 63

Smyslov – Panov
Moscow 1943

The f5-knight is not really threatened because the loss of a piece would not be noticed here and also because, as Smyslov points out, 32...gxf5 33 exf5 gives the e4-square to the c3-knight, which is quickly decisive.

So Black can do little and White has a free hand, but White must still find a way to improve his position.

There is one piece that can clearly be improved. Which one?

32 ♔f1! *(D)*

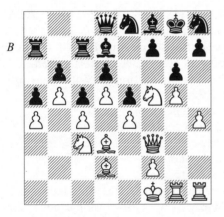

It is the king, which can head for the queenside, where it will be completely safe when the position opens, and only then will White take active measures on the kingside.

32...♗c8

An illustrative example of what can happen if Black captures the knight is 32...gxf5 33 exf5 ♗g7 34 ♘e4 ♗c8 35 h5 ♖ab7 36 ♘f6+ ♔f8 37 ♘xh7+ ♔g8 38 h6.

33 h5 ♖ab7 34 ♖h2 ♖a7 35 ♔e1 ♖ab7 36 ♔d1 ♖a7 37 ♔c2 ♖ab7 38 ♔b3 ♖a7

Once the transfer of the king to the queenside has been completed, it is necessary to look for a way to penetrate the black camp.

The opening of the h-file by itself gives nothing special; Black has placed his rooks so that he can recapture with the f-pawn and adequately defend h7.

What other attacking force can be included in the struggle?

39 ♕g3! *(D)*

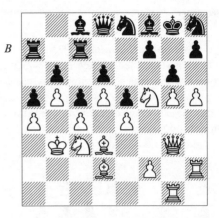

The f2-pawn fits the bill; with the f4 break the attack will gain great force.

39...♖ab7 40 f4 exf4 41 ♗xf4 ♖a7

And thus we arrive at Exercise 64.

Exercise 64

Smyslov – Panov
Moscow 1943

White has opened lines and created new weaknesses, such as the d6-pawn. How can the pressure be increased? By including fresh attacking pieces. Which ones?

42 ♘d1! *(D)*

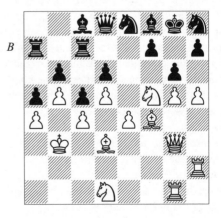

The idea is to execute the manoeuvre ♘e3-g4, and then ♗d2-c3, after which the threat of ♘h6+ will be decisive.

Black decided to accept the sacrifice, but without managing to find a defence.

42...gxf5 43 exf5 ♘g7 44 ♘e3 h6 45 f6 1-0

Exercise 65

Tolush – Keres

Estonian Ch, Tallinn 1945

White has succeeded in playing e4, which is positive, but this does not automatically yield a strong attack. In this case, Black has resources to harass the centre and compensate for White's territorial superiority.

17...dxe4 18 fxe4 ♘ed5! *(D)*

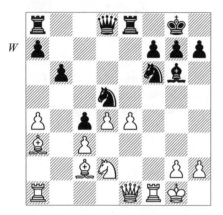

Black takes advantage of the double pin on the e4-pawn to seize the d5-square and attack the c3-pawn.

As Keres pointed out, the positional problem is not complicated. Black will achieve an equal position if he manages to maintain pressure on the pawns, and especially keep the strong knight on d5. On the other hand, if White manages to contain the tactical threats and expel the knight from d5, then the pawn-centre and the bishop-pair will give him the advantage.

19 ♖f3

In response to the defence 19 ♗b2, Black can harass the e4-pawn with 19...♕e7.

19...♖c8

Defending c4, and with the idea of increasing the pressure on e4 with ...♖c6-e6.

20 ♔h1

This rules out combinations based on ...♘xc3 and ...♕xd4+, which would follow, for instance, the unpinning move 20 ♕b1?.

20 ♕h4? is also impossible due to 20...♘xe4.

20...♖c6 *(D)*

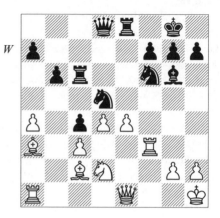

With the idea of ...♘xe4 followed by ...♖ce6.

21 ♕b1?

The decisive error. After Keres's suggestion 21 ♕h4, or even better 21 ♕f1!, which Keres analysed deeply, the struggle continues to rage.

21...♘xc3!

White cannot avoid material loss.

22 ♖xc3 ♕xd4 23 ♗b4

After 23 ♖xc4 ♖xc4 24 ♘xc4 ♕xc4 the e4-pawn also drops.

23...♕xd2 24 a5

When he played 21 ♕b1, Tolush thought he could play 24 ♖xc4 here, overlooking the simple reply 24...♕d7.

24...♗xe4 0-1

If 25 ♗xe4 ♘xe4 26 ♖xc4 then 26...♕e3! 27 ♖xc6 ♘f2+ 28 ♔g1 ♘d1+ and mate.

Exercise 66

Simagin – Bannik

USSR corr. Ch 1963-4

We know that in this structure, the struggle revolves to a great extent around the best moment for White to play e4. Is this a good moment?

25 e4!

Yes it is. The dark-squared bishop will join in the attack, and this will be decisive.

25...dxe4 *(D)*

If 25...cxd4 there follows 26 ♗xh6+! ♔xh6 27 g5+ ♔h7 28 gxf6 ♖e5 29 cxd4 ♖h5 30 e5 with an extra pawn and the better position.

26 ♗xh6+! ♔g8

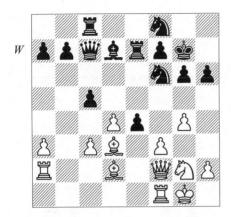

If 26...♔xh6 then 27 g5+ regains the piece with a winning position, since 27...♔xg5? fails to 28 ♕h4+, mating.

27 ♕h4 ♘8h7 28 fxe4

Threatening both 29 ♖xf6 and 29 e5.

28...♖xe4

As bad as any other move. White does not waver from his objective, which is the black king.

29 ♖xf6 ♖xg4 (D)

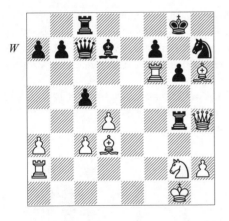

30 ♖xf7! 1-0

Black resigned due to 30...♖xh4 (30...♔xf7 31 ♗c4+ ♔e8 32 ♖e2+ mating) 31 ♖g7+ ♔h8 32 ♘xh4 ♘f8 33 ♖f2!, when there is no defence against 34 ♖xf8+.

Exercise 67
Christiansen – Seirawan
Berkeley 1978

Black has just played 28...g5, to expel the intrusive rook, firm in the belief that the weakness

created in his castled position cannot be exploited by White's scattered forces.

"The combination that follows illustrates the long-range power of the queen." – Christiansen.

29 ♖xh6!! ♔xh6 30 ♖h4+!! (D)

Seirawan had believed that the attack was not going to work, thinking that the best that White had here was 30 ♕c1?, when after 30...f6?! 31 ♖h4+ ♔g7 32 ♖h7+ ♔g8 33 ♕d1 ♗e8! Black might hang on, but 30...♖c4! is a more convincing defence.

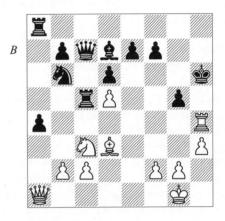

30...♔g7

If 30...gxh4 then 31 ♕c1+ ♔h5 32 ♕d1+ ♔h6 33 ♕d2+ ♔h5 34 ♕e2+ ♔h6 35 ♕e3+ ♔h5 36 ♕f3+ ♔g5 37 ♕xf7 mating.

31 ♖h7+ ♔f6

31...♔f8 is met by 32 ♕d1 with the deadly idea of 33 ♕h5.

32 ♖h6+ ♔g7 33 ♖h7+ ♔f6 (D)

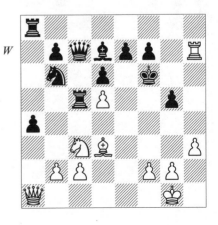

34 ♘e4+ ♔g6

34...♔e5 fails to 35 b4+ ♔xd5 36 bxc5 dxc5 37 ♖xf7 c4, when one way to win is 38 ♖xe7 cxd3 39 ♕a3, as pointed out by Christiansen.

35 ♕d1! g4

There is a typical mate after 35...♔xh7 36 ♕h5+ ♔g7 37 ♕xg5+ ♔f8 38 ♕h6+ ♔g8 39 ♘f6+ exf6 40 ♗h7+ ♔h8 41 ♗g6+.

36 ♕d2! ♖xd5 37 ♕h6+ ♔f5 38 ♖xf7+

The king cannot escape, and now there are various ways to mate, such as 38 ♘xd6++ ♔e5 39 ♘xf7+ ♔d4 40 ♕e3#.

38...♔e5 39 ♕g7+ ♔e6 40 ♖f6+ ♔e5 41 ♖xd6+ ♔f4 42 g3+ 1-0

Exercise 68
Kasparov – Chiburdanidze
Baku 1980

Black has just played 15...g5, which leaves several squares weak, but she considered that White could not exploit them.

16 ♗xc8 ♖xc8 17 ♘e3!!

The g7-bishop will not see the light of day. We already know the strength of a knight on f5, combined with the open g-file. White will only capture the h4-pawn, but this is important because it will allow the use of his own h-pawn as a battering-ram.

Black's idea can be seen in the event of the natural reply 17 ♗g3, when the 'Indian' bishop bursts its bonds in typical fashion, with 17...f5! 18 exf5 e4.

17...gxh4 18 ♘f5 (D)

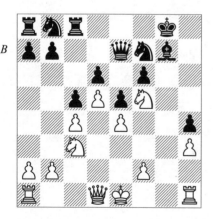

18...♕d8

If 18...♕f8, defending g7, then 19 ♕g4 ♘g5 20 ♘xh4 ♘a6 21 ♘f5 ♘c7 22 h4 ♘h7 and now 23 ♖g1 ♘e8 24 ♔e2, with a clear advantage to White, was Kasparov's original suggestion. Instead, 23 h5 ♘g5 24 h6 is Stohl's improvement for regaining the piece, since 24...♗h8?? fails to 25 h7+ ♔f7 26 ♕h5#.

19 ♕g4 ♘g5 20 ♘xh4! ♘c7 21 ♘f5 a6 22 h4 ♘h7 23 ♖g1 ♕f8 24 ♔e2 (D)

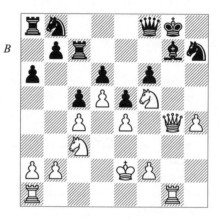

Kasparov commented that the white position is winning, and in fact the rest is simple. Black has no counterplay and White can place all his pieces on their most effective squares unhindered.

24...♖a7 25 a4 b6 26 ♕h5 ♔h8 27 ♖g6 ♖d7 28 ♖ag1 ♖ab7 29 ♕g4 ♖bc7 30 ♖2g2 ♖b7 31 ♔f1 (D)

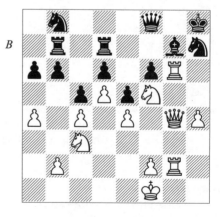

There is a certain similarity with Exercise 63, where Smyslov improved his king before taking any critical measures. Here the king is evading possible problems on the second rank if Black sacrifices material with ...b5.

31...♖a7 32 ♔g1 ♖f7 33 ♘e2 ♛c8 34 f4

Now that g5 is under control, the threat of h5-h6 is renewed.

34 ♘eg3 ♘f8 35 ♛h5+ ♘h7 36 ♘xd6 ♛f8 37 ♘xf7+ ♖xf7 38 ♘f5 was another way to win, according to Kasparov.

34...b5 35 axb5 axb5 36 cxb5 ♖ab7 37 h5 ♘f8 38 ♛h3! ♘xg6 39 hxg6+ ♔g8 40 gxf7+ ♔f8 1-0

Exercise 69
Kasparov – Hübner
Match (game 2), Hamburg 1985

Black's kingside is rather weak on the dark squares, but although the b5-bishop is almost out of play, and the e5-knight is strong, for now the black king is in little danger.

It is essential to introduce new pieces into the attack.

30 ♗g4! *(D)*

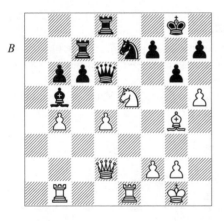

It is not the bishop that is coming into play but the b1-rook, with the threat of 31 hxg6 hxg6 32 ♖b3.

30...♘d5

If 30...♛xd4 then White has 31 ♛g5! with multiple threats, such as 32 ♖ed1 and 32 ♘xf7.

31 hxg6 hxg6 32 ♖b3 f5

To defend the second rank, but of course this weakens Black's kingside even more, now on the light squares as well.

33 ♗d1 ♖g7

White gains a decisive attack after 33...♖h7 34 ♖g3 ♘e7 35 ♗b3+ followed by ♘f7.

34 ♖h3! ♛xb4 35 ♛h6!! *(D)*

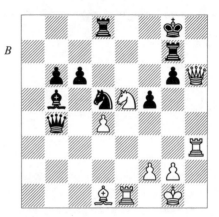

The e5-knight is really powerful.

35...♛xe1+ 36 ♔h2 ♔f8 37 ♘xg6+ ♔g8

Or 37...♔f7 38 ♘e5+ ♔f8 39 ♖g3.

38 ♛h8+ ♔f7 39 ♛xd8 1-0

Exercise 70
L. Dominguez – Morović
Capablanca Memorial, Havana 2004

Black's castled position has been slightly weakened on the dark squares, but even though the black pieces are rather passive, there seems to be nothing immediate, since there are no pieces with quick access to the kingside; the g3-knight seems to have nowhere to go.

23 ♘f5!!

With this elegant leap White gains enough compensation for the piece, which allows him to regain the sacrificed material while leaving the black king very weakened and with a bad structure.

23...gxf5 24 ♛g3+ ♔f8

Dominguez suggested the immediate return of the material with 24...♘g4, although White has the advantage after 25 hxg4 fxe4 26 ♖xe4 ♗f8 27 ♖ae1 ♖xe4 28 ♖xe4 ♛g5 29 ♗e3 ♛d5 30 ♖xb4 ♛xa2 31 ♛f4. This confirms the verdict on 23 ♘f5: Black has four isolated pawns and his castled position is weak.

25 ♛g5 *(D)*
25...♗d8

Other defensive tries:

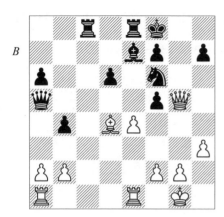

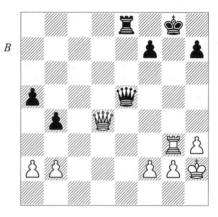

a) 25...♖c4 26 ♗xf6 ♗xf6 27 ♕xf6 ♖cxe4 28 ♕h6+ ♔g8 (if 28...♔e7 then 29 ♖ec1 is strong) 29 ♕g5+ ♔f8 30 ♖xe4 ♖xe4 31 ♖c1, where the general evaluation is similar to what we are seeing.

b) After 25...♕d8 26 exf5 White threatens to double rooks on the e-file and Black can hardly move.

26 ♗xf6 ♗xf6 27 ♕xf6 ♕e5 28 ♕h6+ ♔g8 29 exf5 (D)

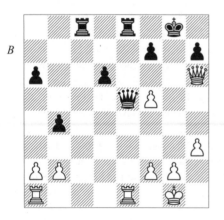

29...♕xf5

29...♕g7 is no better according to Dominguez: 30 ♕xd6 ♕xb2 31 ♖ab1 ♕xa2 32 ♕h6, with the idea of f6.

30 ♕xd6

A pawn down and with a weak king, Black's defensive task is very unpleasant.

30...a5 31 ♖ad1 ♖e6 32 ♖xe6 ♕xe6 33 ♕d4 ♖e8 34 ♖d3 ♕e1+ 35 ♔h2 ♕e5+ 36 ♖g3+ (D)
36...♔h8

If 36...♔f8 Dominguez gave the line 37 ♕h4 h5 38 b3 ♖e6 39 f4 ♕d4 40 ♖g5 with a winning position.

There now follows a short tussle in which White's victory is never in doubt.

37 ♕c4 ♕e6 38 ♕f4 ♖g8 39 ♖xg8+ ♔xg8 40 ♕g4+ 1-0

Exercise 71
Bruzon – Onishchuk
FIDE World Cup, Khanty-Mansiisk 2005

The h5-rook has manoeuvred perilously close to Black's castled position, which has few defenders. Although the c3-bishop is applying pressure, more attacking pieces need to be brought into the attack. Which ones, and how?

24 ♗xg7!! (D)

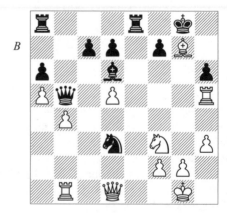

Showing once again the strength of the f5-knight. It helps that the black queen is completely out of play.

24...♔xg7 25 ♘d4 *(D)*

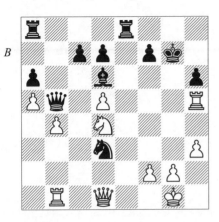

25...♖e1+

If 25...♕c4 then 26 ♕g4+ ♔h7 (or 26...♔f8 27 ♘e6+) 27 ♖xh6+! ♔xh6 28 ♘f5+ ♔h7 29 ♕g7#.

26 ♕xe1 ♘xe1 27 ♘xb5 axb5 28 ♖xe1 ♗xb4 29 ♖b1 ♗xa5 30 ♖xb5 *(D)*

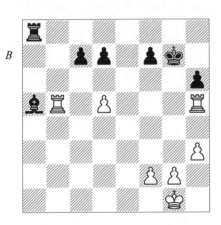

Bruzon now shows good technique to exploit his decisive advantage in the endgame.

30...♗b6 31 g4 ♖a2 32 ♖f5 d6 33 ♖b4 ♖e2 34 ♔g2 ♗a5 35 ♖c4 f6 36 ♖f3 ♖d2 37 ♖cf4 ♖xd5 38 ♖xf6 ♖c5 39 ♖f7+ ♔g8 40 ♖f8+ ♔g7 41 ♖3f7+ ♔g6 42 h4 ♗c3 43 h5+ ♔g5 44 ♔h3 1-0

Exercise 72
Gashimov – Lalić
Cappelle la Grande 2007

If nothing special happens and Black manages to regroup, or play ...c5, his structural

advantage can begin to be an important factor. How should White create an attack?

18 ♖b4!

By means of this 'lift', the rook is transferred to the kingside and links up dangerously with the other three pieces.

18...♕e7 19 ♖f4 *(D)*

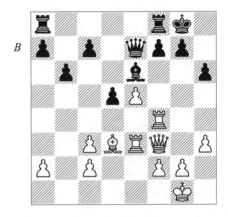

19...c5?

Lalić suggested 19...♖fd8 although White gains the advantage with a manoeuvre similar to the game: 20 ♖f6!! ♔f8 (if 20...gxf6 then White wins with 21 ♕f4! ♔f8 22 ♕xh6+ ♔e8 23 ♗b5+ ♖d7 24 exf6 ♕f8 25 ♕h7! ♔d8 {25...♖ad8 is met by 26 ♖g3 or 26 ♕h5} 26 ♖xe6) 21 ♖g6 ♔g8 22 ♖g3 ♔h8 (if 22...♔f8 then 23 ♕h5) 23 ♕h5 d4 and now 24 ♖xg7! is a clear win: 24...♔xg7 25 ♖g3+ ♕g5 26 ♖xg5+ hxg5 27 cxd4 leaves Black material down and paralysed by White's threats.

20 ♖f6!! *(D)*

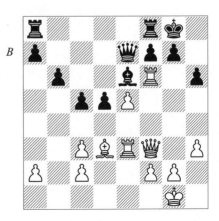

The rook is taboo and provides a screen for the other forces to join in the attack without the black queen being able to prevent them.

20...♖fd8

The attack on the d3-bishop with 20...c4 does not prevent the main threat of 21 ♕h5 cxd3 22 ♖g3, winning. Something similar occurs after 20...♖fe8 21 ♕h5 ♕c7 22 ♖g3 ♔f8 23 ♖xg7!.

21 ♕h5 ♔f8 22 ♖g3 c4 23 ♖xg7! cxd3 24 ♖g8+!

And mate in four moves.

24...♔xg8 25 ♖xh6 1-0

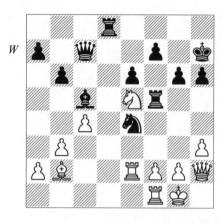

Exercise 73

Leko – Bareev

Candidates match (game 1), Elista 2007

The black pieces are aimed menacingly at the white king, and the bad position of the queen on h2 is a surprise.

28...g5?

Black misses a strong continuation: 28...♘e4! *(D)*.

This increases the pressure on f2, while the knight cannot be captured since 29 ♖xe4 is answered by 29...♖xf2 30 ♗d4 ♖xd4 31 ♖xd4 ♖xf1+ 32 ♔xf1 ♗xd4 33 ♘f3 ♕xh2, when Black has an extra pawn and much the better endgame. If 29 ♘g4 Black wins in spectacular fashion: 29...♘g3! 30 ♖c2 ♗d6 31 fxg3 ♗xg3 32 ♕h1 ♕c5+ 33 ♘f2 ♖xf2 34 ♖cxf2 ♖d1! and wins.

29 ♘g4 ♗d6 30 g3 ♘h5 31 ♘e3 ♗xg3?

An unsound sacrifice which allows White to win quickly.

32 fxg3 ♖xf1+ 33 ♘xf1 ♖d1 34 ♖e3 1-0

Index of Players

Numbers refer to pages. When a player's name appears in **bold**, that player had White. Otherwise the FIRST-NAMED PLAYER had White. An *italic* page number indicates an exercise.

Index of Openings

Numbers refer to pages. Codes are ECO codes.

Other Chess Books from Gambit Publications

Jon Speelman's Chess Puzzle Book
Jon Speelman
This selection of chess puzzles will infuriate, entertain, test and instruct chess-players of all levels. Jon Speelman is one of the most successful British chess-players of all time, and is renowned for the creativity of his play and his remarkable calculating ability.
144 pages, 210 x 145 mm; $19.95 / £10.99

Improve Your Attacking Chess
Simon Williams
250 puzzle positions to train your king-hunting skills. Every position comes from a top tournament encounter, and features a checkmating attack.
160 pages, 210 x 145 mm; $19.95 / £13.99

The Ultimate Chess Strategy Book Volume 1
Alfonso Romero & Amador Gonzalez de la Nava
The opening is reaching its end, and we must make a pivotal decision: what shall our middlegame strategy be? This book features 90 'multi-choice' tests where the reader faces this task. Detailed solutions explain the best plan, and show why other possibilities are less convincing.
208 pages, 248 x 172 mm; $29.95 / £15.99

Secrets of Pawn Endings
Karsten Müller & Frank Lamprecht
This book is the definitive modern work on pawn endgames, from the simple to the highly complex. Many interesting and beautiful positions are included, and there are test positions for the reader to solve.
288 pages, 210 x 145 mm; $29.95 / £15.99

Grandmaster Secrets: Winning Quickly at Chess
John Nunn
For a grandmaster to lose a game in 25 moves or fewer takes something special, and club players can learn a great deal from studying these miniatures. Each of these games is a true battle, with the result often in doubt until near the very end of the struggle.
256 pages, 248 x 172 mm; $29.95 / £15.99

How to Defend in Chess
Colin Crouch
Many books discuss how to attack in chess, but resourceful defensive play is also a vital ingredient in competitive success. This is an area largely neglected in the literature of the game. This book fills the gap admirably.
224 pages, 210 x 145 mm; $24.95 / £13.99

Secrets of Attacking Chess
Mihail Marin
Explains clearly when and how to attack. Topics include: the balance between attack and defence; the premises for starting a successful attack; advantage in development; intuitive sacrifices; typical scenarios. The book features many practical examples from top-level play.
192 pages, 248 x 172 mm; $28.95 / £16.99

How to Beat Your Dad at Chess
Murray Chandler
This popular tactics manual teaches the 50 Deadly Checkmates – basic attacking patterns that occur repeatedly in games between players of all standards. Each mating motif is carefully and simply explained.
128 pages, 230 x 178 mm, hardback $14.95 / £9.99

About the Publisher: Gambit Publications Ltd is a company owned and run exclusively by chess masters. We are passionate about creating innovative and genuinely instructive chess books, suitable for a wide range of skill levels.

www.gambitbooks.com